Lecture Notes
in Business Information Processing 356

More information about this series at http://www.springer.com/series/7911

Boris Shishkov (Ed.)

Business Modeling and Software Design

9th International Symposium, BMSD 2019
Lisbon, Portugal, July 1–3, 2019
Proceedings

 Springer

Editor
Boris Shishkov
Department of Information Systems
and Technologies, Faculty of Information
Sciences
University of Library Studies
and Information Technologies
Sofia, Bulgaria

Institute of Mathematics and Informatics
Bulgarian Academy of Sciences
Sofia, Bulgaria

Interdisciplinary Institute for Collaboration
and Research on Enterprise Systems
and Technology
Sofia, Bulgaria

ISSN 1865-1348   ISSN 1865-1356 (electronic)
Lecture Notes in Business Information Processing
ISBN 978-3-030-24853-6   ISBN 978-3-030-24854-3 (eBook)
https://doi.org/10.1007/978-3-030-24854-3

This Springer imprint is published by the registered company Springer Nature Switzerland AG
The registered company address is: Gewerbestrasse 11, 6330 Cham, Switzerland

Boris Shishkov (Ed.)

Business Modeling and Software Design

9th International Symposium, BMSD 2019
Lisbon, Portugal, July 1–3, 2019
Proceedings

 Springer

Editor
Boris Shishkov
Department of Information Systems
and Technologies, Faculty of Information
Sciences
University of Library Studies
and Information Technologies
Sofia, Bulgaria

Institute of Mathematics and Informatics
Bulgarian Academy of Sciences
Sofia, Bulgaria

Interdisciplinary Institute for Collaboration
and Research on Enterprise Systems
and Technology
Sofia, Bulgaria

ISSN 1865-1348   ISSN 1865-1356   (electronic)
Lecture Notes in Business Information Processing
ISBN 978-3-030-24853-6   ISBN 978-3-030-24854-3   (eBook)
https://doi.org/10.1007/978-3-030-24854-3

This Springer imprint is published by the registered company Springer Nature Switzerland AG
The registered company address is: Gewerbestrasse 11, 6330 Cham, Switzerland

Preface

We light the deepest ocean
Send photographs of Mars
We're so enchanted by
How clever we are
Why should one baby
Feel so hungry she cries
Saltwater wells in my eyes
(*Julian Lennon, 1991*)

What will life be like in 2050? One would say: "Such an easy question – powerful computing, green energy, smart environments, autonomous vehicles." But I would state in turn: "And what?"

Indeed, mankind has witnessed tremendous progress since the 18th century, marking the beginning of industrialization – the steam engine is to be mentioned as one of the key inventions. Then many decades later, the invention of the telegraph and the invention of the telephone; also, electric power was introduced. Later, the first automobile was created. Still later, telecommunications and electronics were "born." All these developments have led to an apogee – the first television coming out in the 1920s. Media has become powerful. Mankind required new developments and the digital era began with the advancement of technology from analog electronic and mechanical devices to digital electronics. Then mainframe computers were introduced and used in enterprises, representing large-scale systems designed for processing and storing huge amounts of data. Nevertheless, it was only possible for larger enterprises to purchase and maintain mainframe machines and it was the appearance of smaller ones in the early 1970s that made computers really popular. During the 1980s, something of crucial importance happened: The Advanced Research Projects Administration (ARPANET) adopted TCP (Transmission Control Protocol)/IP (Internet Protocol) as a suite of communication protocols used to interconnect network devices, and this de facto introduced the Internet and client–server communication, giving way to global telecommunications. Combined with digital multimedia, these advances paved the way to tremendous developments. Further on, Web services and cloud infrastructures have appeared and enterprises facing the challenge of making (some) internal business processes external. And we are now in 2019, enjoying smart mobile devices that give us the impression that *anything* is "one click away." But is it?

In our view, currently we often observe greedy corporations showering customers with services that "they can't refuse." Customers pay a lot for these services but they are rarely capable of precisely understanding what exactly they are paying for. These services are often of low quality but customers have rarely the chance of proving this and receiving compensation. Further, it is rarely realistic to enjoy transparency (with regard to what is going on between persons and big corporations servicing them) as well as accountability (featuring those who "in theory" should be kept accountable if something goes wrong). Finally, we argue that most customers are not at all able to control and protect their privacy (in terms of privacy-sensitive data) and as a result we observe an increasing number of virtual crimes, fake news, and so on. The only thing that is certain is that corporations become more powerful and richer while the average person becomes less happy and poorer. Then what if, for example, this "average person" would be able to let his or her car "park on its own" – what is the "value" of one or more particular technical facilitation if the overall process context is unsatisfactory? Why do administrations become more bureaucratic, more expensive, and less effective, and business processes more and more confusing to customers? Why do we observe more and more errors in service provisioning? Why would everything become more and more complex (instead of becoming less complex)? Why should people suffer from new restrictions with regard to anything they do – technology is supposed to give us more freedom and protect public values but in "doing so" technology imposes severe restrictions on people, making their lives more complex, less happy, more stressful, and more expensive? And if we have this now, how would it be in 2050?

Maybe much of this concerns society and politics. But still, it is worthwhile asking ourselves the question of why science and technology developed so much while the average person is less happy now than in the past (as can be seen from numerous surveys). We argue that this is not only a matter of politics.

A big problem in our view is societal immaturity regarding the utilization of new technology, and this has two essential perspectives:

– How we specify what technology "does for us" (making sure that it really does what we need and not what somebody else claims we should need)
– How we integrate what technology "does" with the "surrounding" enterprise processes.

Unfortunately, 25 years after UML was developed, we are still unable (in our view) to adequately specify software (making absolutely sure that it does what the user needs) and we are still unable to adequately align the software with its corresponding enterprise environment.

Unfortunately, in 2019, we often have to adapt our behavior with regard to the software we are using but it should be the other way around – what the software "does" should be "adapted" to our behavior. We argue that this is what would increase user satisfaction and it is not a matter of yet another technical "fashion" decorated in posh terms. Instead:

– It is a matter of understanding the enterprise construction, the corresponding roles and signs, as well as rules and regulations, in order to reflect them in the specification of software.
– It is a matter of aligning this with coordination and interoperability mechanisms, for the sake of achieving reliable service provisioning.
– It is a matter of harmonizing different enterprise engineering viewpoints (structure, dynamics, data, and so on), achieving overall consistency.

- It is a matter of identifying the domain-imposed requirements and the user-defined requirements, making sure that they will play a role (and not be replaced by what the software developer would "imagine" that the user "should" need).
- It is a matter of possibly providing such solid software solutions in a service-oriented way, rather than showering the user with many different services that would often be in poor synch with each other.
- It is a matter of delivering autonomic and/or context-aware IT services, if needed, but only if this could really be tuned to the behavior of the user – it should not be the case that the user's life gets more complicated by using technological facilitation.
- It is a matter of effectively re-using modeling constructs, software components, etc. featuring "proven solutions," but not mixing up general and specific things that may result in a totally inadequate product in the end.
- It is a matter of considering crosscutting concerns, such as security, logging, and recoverability – they have to be precisely identified and reflected in functional solutions.
- It is a matter of data analytics – the current availability of so much data would allow for the application of advanced approaches based on statistics and machine learning, such that the user behavior is effectively predicted; but if the user behavior is badly predicted, then the software system may even become dangerous for the user.
- It is a matter of incorporating smart contracts and trust mechanisms in the software being developed, but this should not give (as a "side effect") too much power and control to somebody.
- It is a matter of considering IoT, especially currently when there are too many devices and sensors around, but who is responsible if a device "does" something wrong or even harmful to the user?

Is anybody going to claim that currently all the aforementioned issues are effectively taken into account when developing enterprise information systems, in general, and software applications, in particular? We argue that any development covers only some of them but not all of them.

BMSD (http://www.is-bmsd.org) is an annual international symposium that brings together researchers and practitioners who are inspired to dream of better ways of developing (enterprise) information systems and software applications. What is more – the BMSD community is active in proposing innovative ideas, encouraging open discussions, and stimulating community building, driven by the goal of contributing to useful improvements in that direction.

We are proud of our history and for this reason we mention again (as in the 2018 proceedings preface) our editions: Since 2011, we have enjoyed eight successful BMSD editions. The first BMSD edition (2011) took place in Sofia, Bulgaria, and the theme of BMSD 2011 was: "Business Models and Advanced Software Systems." The second BMSD edition (2012) took place in Geneva, Switzerland, with the theme: "From Business Modeling to Service-Oriented Solutions." The third BMSD edition (2013) took place in Noordwijkerhout, The Netherlands, and the theme was: "Enterprise Engineering and Software Generation." The fourth BMSD edition (2014) took place in Luxembourg, Grand Duchy of Luxembourg, and the theme was: "Generic

Business Modeling Patterns and Software Re-Use." The fifth BMSD edition (2015) took place in Milan, Italy, with the theme: "Toward Adaptable Information Systems." The sixth BMSD edition (2016) took place in Rhodes, Greece, and had as theme: "Integrating Data Analytics in Enterprise Modeling and Software Development." The seventh BMSD edition (2017) took place in Barcelona, Spain, and the theme was: "Modeling Viewpoints and Overall Consistency." The eighth BMSD edition (2018) took place in Vienna, Austria, with the theme: "Enterprise Engineering and Software Engineering – Processes and Systems for the Future." The 2019 edition in Lisbon marks the ninth event, with the theme: "Reflecting Human Authority and Responsibility in Enterprise Models and Software Specifications."

We are also proud to have attracted distinguished guests as keynote lecturers, who are renowned experts in their fields: Jan Mendling, WU Vienna, Austria (2018), Roy Oberhauser, Aalen University, Germany (2018), Norbert Gronau, University of Potsdam, Germany (2017), Oscar Pastor, Polytechnic University of Valencia, Spain (2017), Alexander Verbraeck, Delft University of Technology, The Netherlands (2017), Paris Avgeriou, University of Groningen, The Netherlands (2016), Jan Juerjens, University of Koblenz-Landau, Germany (2016), Mathias Kirchmer, BPM-D, USA (2016), Marijn Janssen, Delft University of Technology, The Netherlands (2015), Barbara Pernici, Politecnico di Milano, Italy (2015), Henderik Proper, Public Research Centre Henri Tudor, Grand Duchy of Luxembourg (2014), Roel Wieringa, University of Twente, The Netherlands (2014), Kecheng Liu, University of Reading, UK (2013), Marco Aiello, University of Groningen, The Netherlands (2013), Leszek Maciaszek, Wroclaw University of Economics, Poland (2013), Jan L. G. Dietz, Delft University of Technology, The Netherlands (2012), Ivan Ivanov, SUNY Empire State College, USA (2012), Dimitri Konstantas, University of Geneva, Switzerland (2012), Marten van Sinderen, University of Twente, The Netherlands (2012), Mehmet Aksit, University of Twente, The Netherlands (2011), Dimitar Christozov, American University in Bulgaria – Blagoevgrad, Bulgaria (2011), Bart Nieuwenhuis, University of Twente, The Netherlands (2011), and Hermann Maurer, Graz University of Technology, Austria (2011).

The high quality of the BMSD 2019 program is enhanced by a keynote lecture delivered by an outstanding guest: Jose Tribolet, IST – University of Lisbon, Portugal; the title of his lecture is: "Framing Enterprise Engineering Within General System Theory – Perspectives of a Human-Centered Future." Also, the presence of former BMSD keynote lecturers is much appreciated: Roy Oberhauser (2018), Norbert Gronau (2017), Mathias Kirchmer (2016), Marijn Janssen (2015), and Ivan Ivanov (2012). Most of those outstanding scientists will take part in a panel discussion and also in other discussions stimulating community building and facilitating possible R&D project acquisition initiatives. These special activities will contribute to maintaining the event's high quality and inspiring our steady and motivated community.

We demonstrated for a ninth consecutive year a high quality of papers and we are happy to have succeeded in establishing and maintaining (for many years already) a high scientific quality and a stimulating collaborative atmosphere. Also, our community is inspired to share ideas and experiences.

Essentially considering the modeling of enterprises and business processes as a basis for specifying software, in the broader context of enterprise information systems, BMSD 2019 addresses a large number of research topics:

Business processes and enterprise engineering:

- Enterprise systems
- Enterprise system environments and context
- Construction and function
- Actor roles
- Signs and affordances
- Transactions
- Business processes
- Business process coordination
- Business process optimization
- Business process management and strategy execution
- Production acts and coordination acts
- Regulations and business rules
- Enterprise (re-) engineering
- Enterprise interoperability
- Inter-enterprise coordination
- Enterprise engineering and architectural governance
- Enterprise engineering and software generation
- Enterprise innovation

Business models and requirements:

- Essential business models
- Re-usable business models
- Business value models
- Business process models
- Business goal models
- Integrating data analytics in business modeling
- Semantics and business data modeling
- Pragmatics and business behavior modeling
- Business modeling viewpoints and overall consistency
- Business modeling landscapes
- Requirements elicitation
- Domain-imposed and user-defined requirements
- Requirements specification and modeling
- Requirements analysis and verification
- Requirements evolution
- Requirements traceability
- Usability and requirements elicitation

Business models and services:

- Enterprise engineering and service science
- Service-oriented enterprises
- From business modeling to service-oriented solutions
- Business modeling for software-based services
- Service engineering
- Business-goals-driven service discovery and modeling
- Technology-independent and platform-specific service modeling
- Re-usable service models
- Business-rules-driven service composition
- Web services
- Autonomic service behavior
- Context-aware service behavior
- Service interoperability
- Change impact analysis and service management
- Service monitoring and quality of service
- Services for IoT applications
- Service innovation

Business models and software:

- Enterprise engineering and software development
- Model-driven engineering
- Co-design of business and IT systems
- Business–IT alignment and traceability
- Alignment between IT architecture and business strategy
- Business strategy and technical debt
- Business-modeling-driven software generation
- Normalized systems and combinatorial effects
- Software generation and dependency analysis
- Component-based business-software alignment
- Objects, components, and modeling patterns
- Generic business modeling patterns and software re-use
- Business rules and software specification
- Business goals and software integration
- Business innovation and software evolution
- Software technology maturity models
- Domain-specific models
- Cross-cutting concerns – security, privacy, distribution, recoverability, logging, performance monitoring

Information systems architectures and paradigms:

- Enterprise architectures
- Service-oriented computing
- Software architectures
- Cloud computing

- Autonomic computing (and intelligent software behavior)
- Context-aware computing (and adaptable software systems)
- Affective computing (and user-aware software systems)
- Aspect-oriented computing (and non-functional requirements)
- Architectural styles
- Architectural viewpoints

Data aspects in business modeling and software development:

- Data modeling in business processes
- Data flows and business modeling
- Databases, OLTP, and business processes
- Data warehouses, OLAP, and business analytics
- Data analysis, data semantics, redundancy, and quality of data
- Data mining, knowledge discovery, and knowledge management
- Information security and business process modeling
- Categorization, classification, regression, and clustering
- Cluster analysis and predictive analysis
- Ontologies and decision trees
- Decision tree induction and information gain
- Business processes and entropy
- Machine learning and deep learning – an enterprise perspective
- Uncertainty and context states
- Statistical data analysis and probabilistic business models

Blockchain-based business models and information systems:

- Smart contracts
- Blockchains for business process management
- Blockchain schemes for decentralization
- The blockchain architecture – implications for systems and business processes
- Blockchains and the future of enterprise information systems
- Blockchains and security/privacy/trust issues

IoT and implications for enterprise information systems:

- The IoT paradigm
- IoT data collection and aggregation
- Business models and IoT
- IoT-based software solutions
- IoT and context-awareness
- IoT and public values
- IoT applications: smart cities, e-health, smart manufacturing

BMSD 2019 received 55 paper submissions from which 23 papers were selected for publication in the symposium proceedings. Of these papers, 12 were selected for a 30-minute oral presentation (full papers), leading to a full-paper acceptance ratio of 22% (compared with 19% in 2018) – an indication of our intention to preserve a high-quality forum for the next editions of the symposium. The BMSD 2019 keynote lecturers and authors come from: Bulgaria, Germany, Japan, The Netherlands, Palestine, Portugal, Sweden, Turkey, UK, and USA (listed alphabetically); that makes a total of 10 countries (compared with 15 in 2018, 20 in 2017, 16 in 2016, 21 in 2015, 21 in 2014, 14 in 2013, 11 in 2012, and 10 in 2011) to justify a strong international presence. Four countries have been represented at all nine BMSD editions so far – Bulgaria, Germany, The Netherlands, and the UK – indicating a strong European influence.

BMSD 2019 was organized and sponsored by the Interdisciplinary Institute for Collaboration and Research on Enterprise Systems and Technology (IICREST) and co-organized by Instituto de Engenharia de Sistemas e Computadores (INESC), being technically co-sponsored by BPM-D. Cooperating organizations were Aristotle University of Thessaloniki (AUTH), Delft University of Technology (TU Delft), the UTwente Center for Telematics and Information Technology (CTIT), the Dutch Research School for Information and Knowledge Systems (SIKS), and AMAKOTA Ltd.

Organizing this interesting and successful symposium required the dedicated efforts of many people. First, we thank the authors, whose research and development achievements are recorded here. Next, the Program Committee members each deserve credit for the diligent and rigorous peer reviewing. Further, we would like to mention the excellent organization provided by the IICREST team (supported by its logistics partner, AMAKOTA Ltd.) – the team (words of gratitude to Aglika Bogomilova!) did all the necessary work for delivering a stimulating and productive event, supported by our Portuguese Colleagues - Jose Cordeiro and Colleagues from INESC. We are grateful to Springer for their willingness to publish the current proceedings and we would like to especially mention Ralf Gerstner and Christine Reiss – we tremendously value Ralf's inspiring support and Christine's professionalism and patience (regarding the preparation of the symposium proceedings). Last but not least, we thank our keynote lecturer, Prof. Tribolet, for his invaluable contribution and for his taking the time to synthesize and deliver his talk.

We wish you all enjoyable reading! We look forward to meeting you next year in Berlin, Germany, for the tenth International Symposium on Business Modeling and Software Design (BMSD 2020), details of which will be made available on: http://www.is-bmsd.org.

June 2019   Boris Shishkov

Organization

Chair

Boris Shishkov — ULSIT/IMI-BAS/IICREST, Bulgaria

Program Committee

Hamideh Afsarmanesh	University of Amsterdam, The Netherlands
Marco Aiello	University of Groningen, The Netherlands
Mehmet Aksit	University of Twente, The Netherlands
Paulo Anita	Delft University of Technology, The Netherlands
Paris Avgeriou	University of Groningen, The Netherlands
Jose Borbinha	University of Lisbon, Portugal
Frances Brazier	Delft University of Technology, The Netherlands
Ruth Breu	University of Innsbruck, Austria
Barrett Bryant	University of North Texas, USA
Cinzia Cappiello	Politecnico di Milano, Italy
Kuo-Ming Chao	Coventry University, UK
Samuel Chong	Capgemini, UK
Dimitar Christozov	American University in Bulgaria – Blagoevgrad, Bulgaria
Jose Cordeiro	Polytechnic Institute of Setubal, Portugal
Claudio Di Ciccio	WU Vienna, Austria
Jan L. G. Dietz	Delft University of Technology, The Netherlands
Teduh Dirgahayu	Universitas Islam Indonesia, Indonesia
John Edwards	Aston University, UK
Hans-Georg Fill	University of Vienna, Austria/University of Bamberg, Germany
Chiara Francalanci	Politecnico di Milano, Italy
J. Paul Gibson	T&MSP – Telecom & Management SudParis, France
Rafael Gonzalez	Javeriana University, Colombia
Norbert Gronau	University of Potsdam, Germany
Clever Ricardo Guareis de Farias	University of Sao Paulo, Brazil
Jens Gulden	University of Duisburg-Essen, Germany
Ilian Ilkov	IBM, The Netherlands
Ivan Ivanov	SUNY Empire State College, USA
Marijn Janssen	Delft University of Technology, The Netherlands
Gabriel Juhas	Slovak University of Technology, Slovak Republic
Dmitry Kan	AlphaSense Inc., Finland
Stefan Koch	Johannes Kepler University Linz, Austria
Michal Krcal	Masaryk University, Czech Republic

Han van der Aa	Humboldt University of Berlin, Germany
Marten van Sinderen	University of Twente, The Netherlands
Alexander Verbraeck	Delft University of Technology, The Netherlands
Barbara Weber	Technical University of Denmark, Denmark
Hans Weigand	Tilburg University, The Netherlands
Roel Wieringa	University of Twente, The Netherlands
Dietmar Winkler	Vienna University of Technology, Austria
Shin-Jer Yang	Soochow University, Taiwan
Benjamin Yen	University of Hong Kong, SAR China
Fani Zlatarova	Elizabethtown College, USA

Invited Speaker

Jose Tribolet	IST – University of Lisbon, Portugal

Abstract of Keynote Lecture

Framing Enterprise Engineering Within General System's Theory - Perspectives of a Human Centered Future

José Tribolet

IST - University of Lisbon, Lisbon, Portugal
`jose.tribolet@inesc.pt`

Abstract. The emerging field of Enterprise Engineering is growing in maturity, built on solid scientific grounds. Its principles, methodologies and tools are proving to be valuable in several real life contexts, where complexity and dynamics of change are high and intellectual manageability is essential to make sense the emergent realities and to support consistent visions of the future. An Enterprise is a complex dynamic system and as such, it is subject to the laws of nature, like many other systems. The rich BoK of General Systems Theory and in particular the science of Dynamic Systems Theory and Control are fully applicable to any system, and in particular, to any Enterprise. In this Keynote Lecture, Dr. Tribolet will frame the fundamentals of Enterprise Engineering within the wider framework of General Systems Theory, with emphasis of the use of concepts of Observability and Controllability in Enterprise Design and on the novel concept of ESA - Enterprise Self Awareness, to support viable Enterprise Operations, Control and Governance.

Framing Enterprise Engineering Within General System's Theory – Perspectives of a Human Centered Future

Contents

Full Papers

Rule Style: Patterns of and Extensions to Data System User Interface Specification for Business Rule Violations

Lloyd Rutledge[✉], Erik Bouwer, and Stef Joosten

The Open University of the Netherlands, Heerlen, The Netherlands
Lloyd.Rutledge@ou.nl

Abstract. We propose patterns of the Fresnel semantic browser interface language specifically for business rules violations. Such mapping between rule logic and violation enforcement makes rule system development more flexible, efficient and reliable. We also propose an extension to Fresnel to enable this. Managing business rules independently from presentation using rule styles adds flexibility and efficiency to information system development. We demonstrate our technique by applying it to the EU-Rent case. An existing EU-Rent implementation in the relation algebra-based system Ampersand serves as an example for restriction of input values and display parameters in the interface. Another existing EU-Rent implementation provides Semantic Web inferencing for rule logic. We apply our proposed inference patterns to this implementation. These inferences then apply to our proposed patterns of Fresnel. Finally, we demonstrate the resulting system interface with mock-ups on Semantic MediaWiki.

Keywords: Business rules · Fresnel · Stylesheets · Semantic Web · EU-Rent

1 Introduction

Business rule systems capture laws and agreements as formal logic, which then derive developing system interfaces that consistently and dependably enforce these laws and agreements. They typically either generate a primitive prototype interface by default or allow hard-coding of interface details on one rule system end user interface. Style-based interface generating systems, on the other hand, separate the interface-independent abstraction of what the processes from different ways the interface can convey it to the end user. The best-known example is Cascading Style Sheets (CSS), which maps HTML and XML-encoded document information to styles with which web browsers present them [1]. Such separation of content from style provides efficiency by letting one style apply to many documents, and by letting each document be presented with different styles.

Here, we explore making CSS-like "style sheets" for how a system's user interface enforces business rules for, and with, the end user. This separates the definition of the formal logic determining a violation from the design of how an interface communicates that violation to the user. Style-based approaches generally provide flexibility and

© Springer Nature Switzerland AG 2019
B. Shishkov (Ed.): BMSD 2019, LNBIP 356, pp. 3–16, 2019.
https://doi.org/10.1007/978-3-030-24854-3_1

efficiency by enabling one style sheet to apply to one or more different forms of content to one or more means on conveying them. We seek to enable these and other benefits of style-based approaches to programming rule violations in business data systems.

Fresnel brings CSS-like style sheets closer to rule-based logic by applying them to the Semantic Web data instead of World Wide Web documents [11]. Fresnel code specifies how a semantic browser displays data encoded in the Semantic Web format RDF. Such a display is typically a table showing a given object's properties with their values. Fresnel Forms brings style sheets closer to rule-based systems by extending Fresnel to define form-based interfaces that let users fill in the data these semantic browser tables display [13]. Restrictions on data allowed to be entered in these forms' fields provide some simple business rule enforcement. This work goes a step further with style for conveying the violation of rules.

The rule-based system development tool *Ampersand* defines rule-based logic along with components of an end user system interface for it [6]. This paper uses Ampersand's interface components to model what rule style sheets would map rules to. While Ampersand's use of relation algebra is mainly constraint-based, the *Semantic Web* formats RDFS and OWL provide inference-based reasoning that can also implement logic processing for rule-based systems [2]. RDF encapsulates the data that Fresnel generates user interfaces for. This work's technique defines Fresnel style for rules whose logic RDFS and OWL define.

Fresnel Forms extends Fresnel's data browsing to form-based data input [13]. Fresnel Forms's simple constraints on form field data entry provides some elementary interface components for implementing business rules. *Semantic MediaWiki (SMW)* [8] provides the foundation for the prototype data system interfaces that Fresnel Forms generates.

Much business rule research uses *EU-Rent* case as a standard case for demonstration [10], including using RDFS and OWL [12] and Ampersand [5]. Our work shows how Fresnel can map these RDFS- and OWL-defined EU-Rent rules to this Ampersand-defined interface.

This research focuses on these rule violation scenarios: alethic rules, deontic rules and rule violation lists. Alethic and deontic are two types of logical modalities. *Alethic* rules must never be broken, and thus their interfaces must block them. *Deontic* rules, on the other hand, can be temporarily broken, to be resolved by an end user. In this way, deontic rules guide business processes. Violation rule *lists* show the user temporarily violated deontic rules as a list of suggested next tasks in the overall business process. We implement style for these rule scenarios to illustrate our proposal.

This paper starts by summarizing other work related to this research, such as the Ampersand tool, the Fresnel semantic browser interface language and the EU-Rent business rule example. We then present the methodology we apply here. The three sections thereafter each describe an aspect of business rule style we address. The first of these, Sect. 4, proposes a style approach for deontic violations, which typically appear as warnings. The next section then illustrates how style specifications can generate centralized lists of violations throughout the data system. The final core section explores style for alethic style, which prevents violating data from being entered.

2 Related Work

We consider rule expressions defined in *relation algebra* as a starting point for determining rule styles. We create an ontology for business rules that contains the necessary components to be displayed in the interface. The focus is on how the mapped business rules can be displayed in the interface. The Ampersand tool [6] displays errors directly when detecting business rule violations. The rule modality determines whether the user may or may not proceed *without* resolving the violation. If the user may proceed, a violation message appears in a yellow box as a warning. If the violation may not even be temporary, then the message box is red.

Ampersand classifies rules by the method of enforcement, which can be an axiom, invariant rule, process rule or automated rule [6]. The syntax of a rule in Ampersand contains a purpose, meaning, message, violation text and expression of the rule in relation algebra. The purpose and meaning are used to inform the end user why a rule exists and what it means. The message and violation text contain information to be displayed on screen when the rule is violated. The violation text can contain references to the concepts and relations that cause the violation, whereas the message informs the user without explicitly mentioning the affected instance. We use the message of a rule in our research for displaying rule violations. For process and automated rules, a role is defined that should maintain the business rule.

Another Ampersand feature is limiting input values to a composition of relations. This feature prevents users from selecting values that would trigger a violation. While Ampersand displays violations on screen, it does not change the style of a field when a rule states that this field should be mandatory. The limitation of input values for an input field based on a composition of relations must be configured separately, as the composition is not derived from business rules specified by a business engineer. In earlier work, we use Ampersand to demonstrate how relation algebra implementations of business rules apply to IT alignment [4].

Fresnel displays RDF data in a human readable form on semantic browsers [11]. CSS [1] has a significant influence on Fresnel: CSS does for XML and HTML what Fresnel does for RDF. For example, the CSS concepts of selectors and the formatting model are also important to Fresnel. A CSS selector specifies components of XML and HTML documents so it can apply a given style to them. The formatting model for CSS is the HTML document display, with familiar document structure components such as paragraphs, along with a more abstract box model. A CSS rule has a selector and a style declaration. A CSS declaration can say which type of formatting model component the selected document content appears in. A CSS declaration also defines the more familiar aspects of CSS visual style for selected content, such as font size.

While CSS has its own syntax, Fresnel code consists of RDF triples, which conform to the RDFS-defined ontology for Fresnel. Fresnel has two main concepts: lenses and formats, both of which correspond roughly to the CSS rule. Lenses determine which properties of RDF (Resource Description Format) data to show and in what order. Formats determine how to display, typically using CSS.

The most common type of selector in Fresnel is the name of a class, which is comparable to how CSS selectors are often element names. A lens typically selects a class, specifying that that lens should display all RDF-defined resources in that class. Fresnel's formatting model is its box model, which Fig. 1 shows. It defines the structure of a Wikipedia infobox-like display: a two-column table in which the left column hold property names, and each cell in the right column had one or more values for that property, and this table-like structure as a whole presents all RDF triples for which the displayed resource is the subject.

Fresnel Forms adds active data entry to Fresnel's passive data browsing [13]. It defines an extension to Fresnel, along with how a conforming system converts RDFS-defined (RDFS-Schema) ontologies and conforming Fresnel Form stylesheets for a form-based end user data entry system. The platform Fresnel Forms uses for its end systems is *Semantic MediaWiki (SMW)*, which provides data browsing and data processing [8], and its extension Page Forms, which provides form-based data entry on Semantic MediaWiki [7]. This wiki-based approach facilitates the rapid prototyping that usually accompanies rule-based system development by providing versioning and distributed multi-user editing.

Bos proposes extending Fresnel Forms by using the SMW inline query language to detect rule violations [2]. His study shows this is comparable to how Fresnel uses SPARQL (SPARQL Protocol and RDF Query Language). The resulting user interface shows the results of the query in a deviating style to inform the user of the violations. Bos also demonstrates a role-based factor in trigger rules. This role-based factoring resembles assigning roles to business rules in Ampersand as discussed earlier. His research shows how Fresnel can display different styles for legal right and duty patterns (LRDP) based on roles and rights of the user, by extending the Fresnel specification language. We use a similar method for Fresnel implementation in our research for displaying business rule violations.

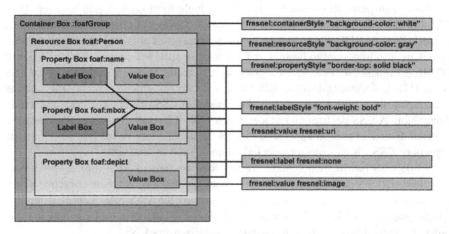

Fig. 1. Fresnel's box model, with some example Fresnel property assignments [11]

Table 1. EU-Rent enforcement levels [8] and our mapping to alethic and deontic rules.

Enforcement level	Explanation in SBVR	Mapping to alethic/deontic
Strict	If the rule is violated, sanctions or other consequences always ensue	Alethic
Deferred	Strict, but enforcement may be delayed	Deontic
Pre-authorized	Enforced, but exceptions are allowed by actors with appropriate authorization	Alethic (role dependent)
Post-justified	If not approved after the fact, the sanction or other consequences will ensue.	Deontic
Override	Override possible with explanation	Alethic (unless explained)
Guideline	Suggested, but not enforced	None

Table 2. Syntax used in Ampersand and Violation ontology for rule properties

Rule property	Ampersand Syntax	Violation ontology property
Name	RULE	owl:Class
Rule expression	RULE (after colon)	owl:equivalentClass, owl:Restriction
Message	MESSAGE, VIOLATION	fresvio:message
Modality	MAINTAINS	rdfs:subClassOf

To contribution to a rule style language, we create a prototype demonstrating the applying rule styles using the *EU-Rent* business rule example [10]. EU-Rent is a fictional car rental company that specifies business rules to support daily operations of a car rental company. The main process is the rental of cars, which are returned either to the same location or a different location from where it has been picked up. EU-Rent includes an explanation of concepts, relations and business rules that apply to the company. Section 4 describes the elements of the case (concepts, relations and business rules) that we use for building a prototype during this research.

As the EU-Rent case is developed to serve as a standard for comparison in research and has been used in several related studies, it increases transparency of our research results. EU-Rent is used in the SBVR (Semantics of Business Vocabulary and Rules) specification as an example for expressing SBVR Structured English [10]. EU-Rent contains different representations of the same types of concepts to illustrate SBVR features and capabilities. The EU-Rent case has also been partially implemented in Ampersand [5] and OWL [12]. While the business rules in the EU-Rent case are not classified as deontic or alethic, they are classified using an enforcement level, as Table 1 shows. The enforcement levels can be mapped to being either deontic or alethic.

3 Methodology

The remaining sections evaluate our proposed model for rule styles by demonstration. We implement business rules retrieved from *EU-Rent* [10]. Our prototype uses and, where needed, extends an OWL-defined ontology for EU-Rent [12] and an Ampersand implementation for EU-Rent [5]. Each demonstration has this structure:

- Explanation of the rule and desired behavior of the rule style
- Demonstration in *Ampersand*
- Encoding in the *Semantic Web*
- Proposed *Fresnel* implementation
- Example of the rule style output in *Semantic MediaWiki.*

Our ontology for alethic and deontic business rules is derived from how Ampersand captures business rules with the rule syntax [6]. We made the rule types in our ontology explicit as OWL restrictions. The ontology can be extended with additional subclasses and properties relevant for each rule type. A business rule is created as subclass of a new general violation class. The rules contain class restrictions modelled as equivalent classes that are asserted by as style in Fresnel with Fresnel Violations. A property for the violation message of the business rules captures the message to be displayed for the violation.

The message annotation is also similar in *Ampersand*. The main difference is that Ampersand can also integrate classes and properties (or concepts and relations) in the message using the keyword VIOLATION, whereas our message is an annotation property that only contains text. A comparison of syntax used in Ampersand and our Violation ontology is listed in Table 2. This paper's code fragments use bold font to emphasis specific aspects in the syntax of the various languages. In Ampersand, bold font indicates where the logic is defined, while the rest is names and strings. The Fresnel code fragments have our own extensions displayed in bold.

This paper's *Semantic Web* definitions of this same type of rule are usually as OWL equivalent classes of OWL restrictions, as the code fragments in the upcoming sections show. Items that violate of the rule get inferred as an instance of the rule's assigned class. The benefit of using this method is that is guides exchange of rule expressions between relation algebra and OWL, provided that the RDFS classes and properties have equivalents in the concepts and relations in Ampersand. In each demonstration, we show Semantic Web code. We use bold font for URLs that we make, either as extensions to existing ontologies, or as our own example triples. The restriction that determines whether an instance will be inferred is listed under the header equivalent class. Constructs that the Violation ontology introduces have the namespace prefix "fresvio:".

We display rule violations using our proposed extension to *Fresnel*, called Fresnel Violations. The extension contains a Fresnel lens that determines whether an instance of a class is also an instance of a violation class using a rule selector class. If so, the message of the violated rule captured as annotation property in the violation ontology will be displayed. We determine the format and position of the message by a Fresnel format linked to the violation lens. The Fresnel format is similar to a CSS class. It

Table 3. Rule styles used in demonstrations. From Annex G EU-Rent [10]

Rule style	Description	Example rule from Annex G EU-Rent
Input validation	Data which violates a business rule may be prohibited	It is prohibited that a rental be open if its authorized driver is barred
Violation overview	A report or list which displays data elements that are missing a mandatory property	It is prohibited that the duration of each rental period is more than 90 rental days
Information about violation	The rule may be violated, but the user is informed	At the actual pick-up date-time of a rental it is obligatory that the fuel level of the rented car of the rental is full

contains display properties for data to be displayed and can be reused by multiple lenses [11]. A lens can also combine multiple formats, with deviating styles for different situations. Each of the following sections demonstrates an implementation of a rule style type. We show which rules are implemented and demonstrate a method for creating the desired rule style. Table 3 lists the topics of the subsections.

4 Business Process Style for Deontic Violations

Our implementation of deontic violations shows their messages as warnings but still allows users to enter them in the system. Such messages effectively serve as instructions guiding the user to execute business processes, whose completion then resolves the violation. Our example of deontic violations is a rule from EU-Rent that states that if a car is returned without a full tank then the renter will be charged a fine. EU-Rent classifies this rule as post-justified, which we map to deontic rules. Note that the property that states whether or not the fuel level is sufficient gets modelled on the car movement with relation algebra as well as RDFS and OWL, as we do not want to evaluate the fuel level of the car, but the fuel level when the car was returned.

The rule is created as a process rule in *Ampersand*, as the violation does not need to be solved immediately and can thus guide a business process when unresolved. A user action is required to solve the violation, which might be from another user or role than the user who triggered the violation. This demonstration shows the violation and allows the user to correct it later. When a car is returned with insufficient fuel, a warning shows as displayed in Fig. 2. However, the interface does not block entry of this data. Instead, it lets it though, and then instructs the user to address the violation later, as this example shows. The Ampersand code is:

```
RULE fuelLevelFullWhenReturned :
  I[Carmovement]/\is_returned/\-fuel_penalty
  |- fuel_level_ok
MESSAGE "There are cars returned with insufficient fuel,
a penalty needs to be charged"
```

Our *Semantic Web* encoding includes a class in our extension ontology `fresvio:`**`Violation`**. Fresnel Violation systems treat each member of this class as some kind of business rule violation. Since RDFS- and OWL-defined logic predominantly uses inferencing, we implement business rules here by inferring membership in the class `fresvio:Violation`. For this scenario in EU-Rent, we define the class **`vio-FeeFuel`** with RDFS as a subclass of violations. Additionally, an OWL restriction implements the rule as by inferring membership in the class `vioFeeFuel` for all car movements with true `isReturned` properties and false `fuelLevelOk` and `penaltyCharged` values as false. The violation message is stored in our extension property `fresvio:`**`message`** for display to the user. The RDF code for this is:

```
vioRent:vioFeeFuel owl:equivalentClass
  rdfs:subClassOf fresvio:Violation ;
  [ owl:intersectionOf ( EURent:Car_Movement
  [ owl:onProperty EURent:fuelLevelOk ;
    owl:hasValue  "false"^^xsd:Boolean ]
  [ owl:onProperty EURent:isReturned ;
    owl:hasValue  "true"^^xsd:Boolean  ]
  [ owl:onProperty EURent:penaltyCharged ;
    owl:hasValue  "false"^^xsd:Boolean ] ) ] ;
fresvio:message "A driver must pay a fee if returning a
car without a full tank" .
```

In *Fresnel*, Fresnel Forms [13] can generate the desired fields for a rental request. Deontic style in Fresnel puts the message at the top of the lens display and gives the row of each property involved in the violation a yellow background (See Fig. 2). Our Fresnel implementation triggers the `vioFeeFuelDeoLns` lens when the browser displays a member of the class `vioFeeFuel`. We use a format lens to configure how the violation message is displayed to the user. The Fresnel code is:

```
vioRent:vioFeeFuelDeoLns rdf:type fresnel:Lens ;
  fresnel:classLensDomain vioRent:vioFeeFuel      ;
  fresnel:use             vioRent:vioFeeFuelMsgFmt ;
  fresnel:showProperties ( EURent:movement_ID
  [ fresnel:property EURent:fuelLevelOK         ;
    fresnel:use     vioRent: vioFeeFuelPrpFmt  .]
  [ fresnel:property EURent:isReturned          ;
    fresnel:use     vioRent: vioFeeFuelPrpFmt  .]
```

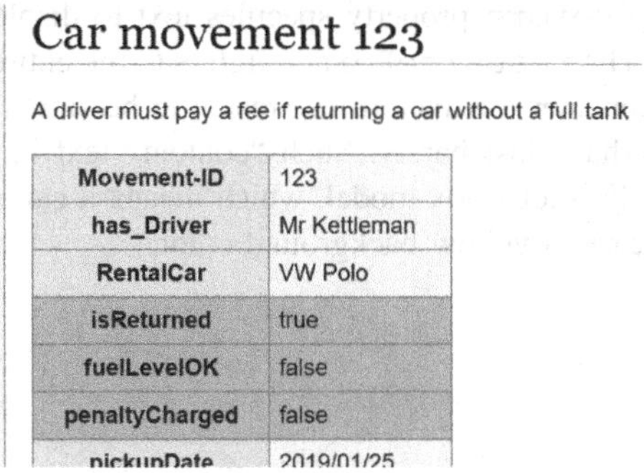

Car movement 123

A driver must pay a fee if returning a car without a full tank

Movement-ID	123
has_Driver	Mr Kettleman
RentalCar	VW Polo
isReturned	true
fuelLevelOK	false
penaltyCharged	false
pickupDate	2019/01/25

Fig. 2. Portion of SMW display of a deontic violation message

```
[ fresnel:property EURent:penaltyCharged      ;
    fresnel:use        vioRent: vioFeeFuelPrpFmt  .]).
vioRent:vioFeeFuelMsgFmt rdf:type fresnel:Format ;
 fresnel:classFormatDomain vioRent:vioFeeFuel ;
 fresnel:resourceFormat [ fresnel:contentBefore
  "A driver must pay a fee if returning a car without a
full tank"^^xsd:string ].
vioRent:vioFeeFuelPrpFmt rdf:type fresnel:Format ;
 fresnel:propertyFormatDomain EURent:fuelLevelOK,
  EURent:isReturned, EURent:penaltyCharged ;
 fresnel:valueStyle
  "deonticViolation"^^fresnel:styleClass .
```

This code uses Fresnel styling hooks to assign a CSS class named "deonticViolation" to components of a lens's Fresnel box model for which special deontic styling applies. The CSS style sheet for the semantic browser then applies the style instructions to that CSS class to give a yellow background. In our SMW implementation of Fresnel, that code is in a MediaWiki CSS page MediaWiki: Common.css. This relevant segment of CSS code is:

```
.deonticViolation { background-color: yellow !important }
```

This puts the CSS styling for all deontic violation displays for this Fresnel browser in one place. This example uses the background color yellow, which is typical for the permissive warning nature of such deontic violations that trigger user processes. Our implementation requires the code "!important" to have this override other styles.

One challenge here is determining where to display the violation, because a rule violation can occur due to a combination of properties that is not allowed. Therefore, we create a format lens to display the violation message above the entire Fresnel display, rather than with any particular property. The display indicates which properties are involved in the message's violation with the yellow background.

Fresnel's `contentBefore` property specifies text to display before the current part of the box model. The `resourceFormat` refers to the entire Fresnel lens display for the resource. We consider this pattern in Fresnel to be suited for display violation messages, although perhaps just barely. Such "content" text in Fresnel style has no devoted component in Fresnel's box model, which means it cannot have its own CSS style, such as, in this case, a yellow background color.

Fig. 3. Warning message in Ampersand for process rule violations on the home screen

5   User Task Lists

This section's implementation shows a list of violations of the *EU-Rent* rule that prohibits a rental period from exceeding 90 days. While an alethic rule would prevent any initial car rental reservation from lasting more than 90 days, one can extend reservations during rental, and renters can return cars late. Therefore, an open car rental can become overdue and thus trigger a rule violation. Process lists inform the user of this kind of rule violation. Since neither relation algebra nor the Semantic Web perform math, we simply add a data property to the RDFS ontology code, and a relation in relation algebra representation, each of which indicate overextended rentals. For Ampersand, an example for computing the maximum rental days is made [5].

This rule is post-justified, and thus deontic, and similar to the process rule in *Ampersand*. The Ampersand tool displays existing process rule violations as a list (see Fig. 3). Clicking on the warning message shows the elements causing the violation. Clicking on one presents a form to amend information about the element. This can be viewed as a process list. The rule in *Ampersand* is expressed as follows:

```
RULE max90Days : I[Carmovement] |- -longerthan90days
MESSAGE
    "There are car rentals open for more than 90 days"
```

As before, we define this on the *Semantic Web* as an OWL restriction. A data property states whether the car movement exceeds the 90-day maximum. We verify the rule with an example with a Car Movement individual whose property `isOverdue` is true, which then infers it as a `CarMovementOpenOverdue`.

Our goal is to show all instances of class `CarMovementOpenOverdue` in a table overview, similar to how Ampersand displays a process list. Our *Fresnel* code defines a

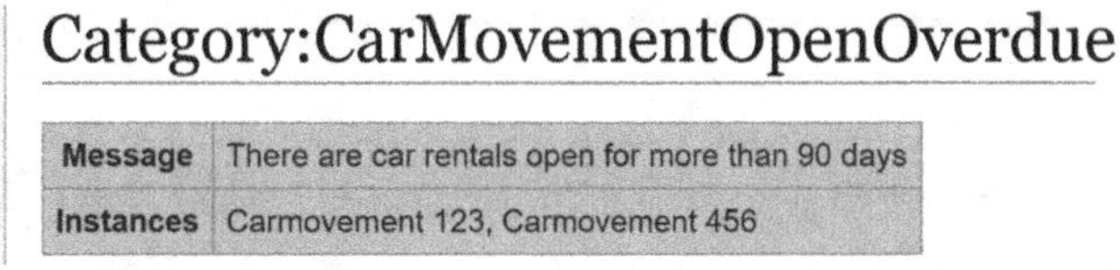

Category:CarMovementOpenOverdue

Message	There are car rentals open for more than 90 days
Instances	Carmovement 123, Carmovement 456

Fig. 4. List of overdue rentals in Semantic MediaWiki

lens that selects the URL for the class. This lens displays the message and then all objects linked by the inverse property for `rdf:type`, which thus infers all movements violating this rule. The Fresnel lens code is:

```
vioRent:CarMovementOpenOverdueLns a fresnel:Lens ;
 fresnel:instanceLensDomain
 VioRent:CarMovementOpenOverdue ;
 fresnel:purpose fresnel:defaultLens;
 fresnel:showProperties
 ( fresvio:message fresvio:hasInstance ) .
```

when the user browses to the page for the violation itself as a concept, the lens shows the violation message, followed by all the instances of the violation. Figure 4 shows an example display on *SMW*. Fresnel Violations infers instances with the following code:

```
fresvio:hasInstance owl:inverseOf rdf:type .
```

While this lens selects the message and instances for display, the following Fresnel format code assigns the display of this violation as having the same CSS class for deontic violation as before, with a yellow background:

```
vioRent:CarMovementOpenOverdueFmt fresnel:Format ;
 fresnel:instanceFormatDomain
 VioRent:CarMovementOpenOverdue ;
 fresnel:resourceStyle
 "deonticViolation"^^fresnel:styleClass .
```

6 Blocking Style with Alethic Violations

The interface supports rules styled as alethic by prohibiting user entry of any data that violates them. Our alethic example from *EU-Rent* is the rule prohibiting a rental from being open if a driver who is authorized for it is barred [10]. The violation gets displayed when a barred driver is entered on a rental request. The rule is classified as pre-authorized in EU-Rent, which makes it alethic in our mapping from Table 1.

Fig. 5. Violation message for a barred person in Ampersand

This corresponds to invariant rules in *Ampersand*. Ampersand requires immediate resolution of invariant rules. Selecting a barred person triggers a violation message display (see Fig. 5). The corresponding Ampersand code is:

```
RULE noBarredDriver :
  has_driver~;has_driver /\ I[Person] |- -is_barred
MESSAGE "A barred person cannot have a car reservation"
```

Our *Semantic Web* class for barred persons in our EU-Rent extension code as a subclass of class `fresvio:Violation` called `vioBarred`. An OWL restriction infers a `vioBarred` for open rentals with `has_driver` properties linking into the `BarredPerson` class. We can validate the rule by creating an individual as a subclass of `BarredPerson` and an individual as a subclass of class `Car_Movement`. When we create a property `has_driver` for the movement individual to the barred person individual, the movement individual is inferred as an instance of class `vioBarred`, a subclass of `fresvio:Violation`. By changing the individual to class `Person`, the individual is no longer in the violation class. The code is:

```
:vioBarred owl:equivalentClass
  rdfs:subClassOf fresvio:Violation ;
  [ owl:intersectionOf ( EURent:Car_Movement
   [ rdf:type          owl:Restriction ;
     owl:onProperty    EURent:has_driver ;
     owl:allValuesFrom EURent:BarredPerson ] ) ] ;
  :message "A barred person cannot reserve a car" .
```

Our *Fresnel* code for this is:

```
vioRent:vioBarredAlethLens rdf:type fresnel:Lens  ;
fresnel:classLensDomain vioRent:vioBarred            ;
fresnel:use                    vioRent:barredMsgFmt ;
fresnel:showProperties ( EURent:movement_ID
  [ rdf:type           fresnel:PropertyDescription ;
    fresnel:property EURent:has_Driver             ;
    fresnel:use        vioRent:barredPrpFmt          .]).
vioRent:barredMsgFmt rdf:type fresnel:Format  ;
fresnel:classFormatDomain vioRent:vioBarred ;;
fresnel:resourceFormat [ fresnel:contentBefore
  "A barred person cannot reserve a car"^^xsd:string ] .
vioRent:barredPrpFmt rdf:type fresnel:Format  ;
fresnel:propertyFormatDomain EURent:has_driver ;
fresnel:valueStyle
  "alethicViolation"^^fresnel:styleClass             .
```

The corresponding CSS code that gives alethic violations a red background is:

```
.alethicViolation { background-color: red !important } .
```

The fresnel:valueStyle property here assigns the CSS class "alethicViolation" for reference from a central CSS style sheet. The style sheet gives that class a red background color, instead of yellow.

In *Semantic MediaWiki*, we display the violation message, saying what the user must change to resolve the conflict (see Fig. 6). OWL-defined reasoning infers membership of the class vioBarred, which is a subclass of CarMovement. A challenge with forms in SMW is that as long as data is not submitted, triples are not created as data in the endpoint and thus cannot be asserted for detecting violations. A solution could be to pass the entered values as parameters to the template for the rule.

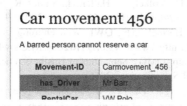

Fig. 6. SMW display portion for violation when selecting a barred person

7 Conclusion

This work shows how Fresnel, with our Fresnel Violations extension, can encode style for business rule violations in end user interfaces. End user scenarios demonstrate style code for are alethic rules, deontic rules and violation lists. Our evaluation treats the Ampersand implementation of EU-Rent as a demonstration target. A Semantic Web implementation of EU-Rent puts the demo in a technical context Fresnel can process and, with some extension, provides the required semantics and logic. Finally, we present Fresnel code for the three types of rule scenarios in EU-Rent. The results show how Fresnel's style for browsing data, and its extension Fresnel Forms for styling simple form-based entry, can apply, with some further extensions, to defining interface style for business rule violations. This work is from the master's thesis of Erik Bouwer [3]. The source code presented here is online at http://is.cs.ou.nl/OWF/index.php5/ Rule_Style_2019.

References

1. Bos, B., Lie, H.W., Lilley, C., Jacobs, I.: Cascading style sheets, level 2 CSS2 specification. W3C Recommendation (2011). https://www.w3.org/TR/CSS2/
2. Bos, J.: Specification of a user interface template for semantic web-implemented Hohfeldian right and duty legal rules using the Fresnel data interface language (Master's thesis). Open University of the Netherlands (2018)
3. Bouwer, E.: Patterns of and extensions to semantic browser style specification for business rule violations (Master's thesis). Open University of the Netherlands (2019)
4. Grave, F., van de Wetering, R., Rutledge, L.: Strategy-IT alignment. In: Shishkov, B. (ed.) BMSD 2018. LNBIP, vol. 319, pp. 352–361. Springer, Cham (2018). https://doi.org/10. 1007/978-3-319-94214-8_26
5. Joosten, R.: AmpersandTarski/ampersand-models. https://github.com/AmpersandTarski/ ampersand-models/tree/master/EURent/. Accessed 08 Apr 2019
6. Joosten, S.: Software development in relation algebra with ampersand. In: Höfner, P., Pous, D., Struth, G. (eds.) RAMICS 2017. LNCS, vol. 10226, pp. 177–192. Springer, Cham (2017). https://doi.org/10.1007/978-3-319-57418-9_11
7. Koren, Y.: Page Forms. https://www.mediawiki.org/wiki/Extension:Page_Forms. Accessed 08 Apr 2019
8. Krötzch, M., Vrandecic, D., Völkel, M., Haller, H., Studer, R.: Semantic Wikipedia. J. Web Semant. 5(4) (2007). https://doi.org/10.1016/j.websem.2007.09.001
9. McGuinness, D.L., van Harmelen, F.: OWL Web Ontology Language Overview - W3C Recommendation (2004). http://www.w3.org/TR/2004/REC-owl-features-20040210/
10. Object Management Group (OMG): Semantics of Business Vocabulary and Business Rules (SBVR), v1.4. Technical Specification (2016)
11. Pietriga, E., Bizer, C., Karger, D., Lee, R.: Fresnel: a browser-independent presentation vocabulary for RDF. In: Cruz, I., et al. (eds.) ISWC 2006. LNCS, vol. 4273, pp. 158–171. Springer, Heidelberg (2006). https://doi.org/10.1007/11926078_12
12. Reynares, E., Caliusco, L., Galli, R.: SBVR to OWL 2 mappings: an automatable and structural-rooted approach. CLEI Electron. J. 17(3), 3 (2014)
13. Rutledge, L., et al.: From ontology to semantic wiki – designing annotation and browse interfaces for given ontologies. In: Molli, P., Breslin, John G., Vidal, M.-E. (eds.) SWCS 2013-2014. LNCS, vol. 9507, pp. 53–72. Springer, Cham (2016). https://doi.org/10.1007/ 978-3-319-32667-2_4

Business, Business Processes and Formal Models

Coen Suurmond[(✉)]

Cesuur B.V, Velp, The Netherlands
coen@cesuur.info

Abstract. Business processes as seen from the business point of view are often not only highly structured linear processes but less structured control processes with feedback and mutual adjustments are also important. In case of conflicting rules decision making in business processes is sometimes automatically by predefined decision rules, and sometimes by human assessment of context and interests. There seems to be an inclination in more formalised approaches to business process modelling to adhere to the machine metaphor for analysing organisations and its processes, with a lack of concepts to deal with more complicated process structures. In this paper I will look into the implicit background notions such as the machine metaphor for organisations, the assumption that the organisational world can be represented as a set of clear-cut facts, and the market metaphor for the internal workings for an organisation. A practical example will be presented to analyse different kinds of business processes, and to show where the machine metaphor is too narrow to be of much practical interest for the wider concept of business processes as used in business.

Keywords: Business process · Metaphor ·
Business process model and notation (BPMN)

1 Introduction

An Enterprise Information System (EIS) is by nature a heterogeneous information system. Doing business is ultimately based on agreements between business partners in natural language (partly formalised in contracts), while operationally business information in a company and between companies is processed by a combination of human interpretation and communication and a number of IT systems. This generates questions of how such an information system, heterogeneous in multiple dimensions, should be designed to serve business, and which general rules must be obeyed.

Business process modelling is an important aspect in designing an EIS. This is often approached by analysing business processes as sequences of transactions and decisions governed by business rules. However, the problem with such models seems to be that they are not well understood and often not used by actual business people. This casts doubt both on the validity and on the usefulness of such an approach.

An alternative way of looking at business processes and Enterprise Information Systems would be to start by looking at higher level business processes as encompassing "business process loops", such as the lifecycle of a sales order or a purchase

© Springer Nature Switzerland AG 2019
B. Shishkov (Ed.): BMSD 2019, LNBIP 356, pp. 17–30, 2019.
https://doi.org/10.1007/978-3-030-24854-3_2

order (ordering/delivering/invoicing); production planning, monitoring and accounting; or the lifecycle of production orders. Sequences of primary processes are mostly concrete, order-based and transactional; second order loops of processes for coordinating, controlling and facilitating the sequences of primary processes are mostly non-transactional and often have nested variants dealing with different time spans and different abstraction levels. Being competitive means having efficient primary processes as well as being smart with the critical second order processes.

Let us make first a few observations. The first is that for a company doing business means creating value for the customers as well as creating value for the company. Both are required for the continuity of the company. Without customer value a company would not have no sales, without a positive margin between revenue and cost the financial health of a company would be endangered. The second observation is that doing business is essentially a social process. Business contracts are subject to interpretation based on social conventions and backed up by laws as interpreted by courts. The third observation is that the products and services for the customers are directly or indirectly created by business processes. The fourth observation is that in order to discuss business processes they must be described in some form or other. The fifth observation is that such business process descriptions can have many forms, from totally free use of natural language in combination with ad hoc diagrams to comprehensive methodologies with standardised notation. The sixth observation is that in practice such methodologies often seem to reveal an engineering approach, based on a combination of a view of an organisation as a machine in combination with a form of logical atomism.

In this paper I want look first into a few aspects of business processes in relation to the business, followed by a discussion of some background notions of the more formalised methods of business modelling. A practical example of business processes is presented with a combination of different kinds of business processes, followed by a short analysis and conclusions.

2   Business Processes

2.1   What Are Business Processes?

According to the OED [1], a process is "A continuous and regular action or succession of actions, taking place or carried on in a definite manner, and leading to the accomplishment of some result; a continuous operation or series of operations. (The chief current sense.)". Accordingly, business processes would be about getting business results for customers or about getting internal intermediate results that contribute to the end results, in an effective and efficient way. That is the bottom line. Both effectiveness (getting the right results) and efficiency (consumptions of resources for getting the results) are important issues in the executing of the business processes. The final result of the primary processes would deliver a product or service for the customer outside the company. The internal intermediate results would yield either intermediate semi-finished products or provide information or material for executing and controlling processes.

2.2   Doing Business on Markets

John Kay wrote about the foundations of neo-classical economics as "The Arrow-Debreu results are the culmination of a long tradition in economics which emphasises supply and demand, perfectly competitive markets and the search for market equilibrium, conducted by independent, self-regarding agents. This framework is today known as 'neo-classical economics'" [2] and "there is no escaping the fundamental theorems of welfare economics if we are to examine the claim that competitive markets necessarily lead to efficient outcomes". This idealised view on doing business on markets is still dominant today. Economic exchanges are in this view considered to be fully specified, instantaneous events on markets. The essential assumptions of this dominant views are criticised since many years. Ronald Coase asked in 1937 the fundamental question "why a firm emerges at all in a specialised exchange economy" [3]. If the market would provide the best mechanism for coordination and optimisation of economic exchanges, then each human individual would be best off by being an autonomous independent actor on the market. By what right would a firm exist? His analysis was that classical economics neglected transaction costs, resources that are consumed in order (1) to find the best transaction, (2) to do the transaction, and (3) to enforce the transaction. Therefore, his answer was that the rationale for a firm was the reduction of transaction costs by organising economic activities in a hierarchical organisation.

As a scholar of law Ian MacNeil analysed classical contract law and its assumptions about business exchanges [4]. He found that classical contract law assumes atomic and fully specified exchanges, and by examining the objective facts a court is to decide if the terms of the contractual exchange were fulfilled, or not. However, by studying business contracts in practice he found that business practices are mostly relational by nature. A written business contract is secondary to a business agreement. The agreement between business parties is about promising future performance under circumstances that might not be fully known at the time of the agreement, and a business contract is an imperfect written representation of the agreement. The business parties will expect the agreement to be fulfilled, when one of the partners is disappointed in the other's behaviour this will hamper or preclude future business. MacNeil identified five basic elements of contract: (1) co-operation; (2) economic exchange; (3) planning for the future; (4) potential external sanctions; and (5) social control and manipulation. Co-operation is about trust, sanctions and/or social control are about enforcement of the agreement. Legal sanctions based on the written contract are mostly a means of last resort. Even in such cases the court will have to look not only at the letter of the contract but will also consider the context and conventions in business. From an economical point of view, this social practice of business agreements based on promises, expectations, trust and a mix of social and legal sanctions is efficient. Relying only on fully specified and legally watertight contracts (if possible) would force up transaction costs hugely, and this would imply a huge competitive disadvantage.

The concept of the relational contracts is one of the pillars of the John Kay's book "Foundations of Corporate Success" [5]. Kay argues that the success of a company is founded in the distinctive capabilities of the company: "The firm is defined by its contracts and relationships. Added value is created by its success in putting these contracts and relationships together, so it is the quality and distinctiveness of these contracts that promote added value. The distinctiveness is at least as important as the goodness. The reason is that in an efficient market there are few opportunities to make good contracts" (p63). Economic success cannot be explained by contracts and specifications only (the component that will be written down in texts), but is dependent on the relationship of the firm with its business partners. And, to avoid misunderstanding, this has nothing to do with being nice for your customer and solving all his problems. With some budget airline companies it is known that they behave consistently nasty and rather unfriendly to their consumers. Not the behaviour by itself, but the consistency of behaviour defines the reliability and reputation of the company. In combination with price and network such a company may offer attractive opportunities and be successful.

To summarise: contrary to the assumptions of neo-classical economics real markets are based on longer term business agreements represented in imperfect specifications in written business contracts. Trust reduces transactions costs, and the business success of a company is therefore for a major part dependent on its reputation of reliability in the market.

2.3   Triggers to Business Processes

A business process can be triggered by some event (a customer calls the service desk), or by the clock (start of the working day), or by the ending of the previous process (start of a new batch in the blender), or without a trigger (homeostatic processes for maintaining a stable environment). Highest level processes such as "sales" or "order fulfilment" could also be considered continuous processes. Most lower processes are either triggered by an external event, or cyclic (started by the clock or the end of the previous cycle).

If a business process is directly triggered by a demand for the output, the process is pulled. If not, the process is pushed. However, the rationale of any business process should be making products (either material of informational) available as input for a next business process, or for the external customer. In that sense all processes ought to be pulled by the demand for better value. That demand could be the immediate primary customer product (a car, electricity supply), or an immediate secondary customer service (providing a replacement car when your car is broken), or an internal project that should benefit future service levels for the customer or better margins for the organisation itself. On a lower level, many processes are pushed. Production planning is pulled by actual or expected customer demand, but in production itself a subsequent process may be pushed by the output of the preceding process. That is, push and pull are not clear-cut absolute concepts, but are dependent on context and viewpoint. A concrete process can be considered as pushed because it is caused by the supply of input material that must be processed. The same process can be considered pulled because the work on the input material is determined by demand. Suppose a packaging line can produce three different finished products out of one kind of semi-finished product. When an intermediate stock of about 1000 units of semi-finished products must be processed, the production order might be: package 200 units into product A, 350 products into product B, and the rest into product C. The resulting amounts of A and B could be considered as pulled, and C as pushed.

2.4   Process Flow

When we look at the work of Shigeo Shingo about improvement of production processes, he is not talking about processes as such, but rather at process delays. Essentially, he is discussing lossless transitions between (sub)processes and reduction of avoidable waste in transformation (sub)processes [6]. Any storage that is not required for stabilisation of the product is considered a process delay, and as such a loss to be avoided. However, when the period between order and delivery is shorter than the actual time it takes to manufacture a product, stocks are necessary. Therefore, reduction of process delay is key to Shingo's thinking. Faster production throughput implies less need for stocks, and shifts production from push to pull.

Process improvement is fundamentally about time and timing. Underutilisation of production capacity is allowed when it reduces significantly throughput time. As an example, imagine a production company where the packaging is the bottleneck. The company has to find a balance between order lead time, customer service levels, idle time of expensive packaging equipment, and scrapped stock waiting for orders that did not materialise. Considerations of production cost would argue against investments in equipment, market considerations would argue against higher lead times. Taiichi Ohno writes "In production, 'waste' refers to all elements of production that only increase cost without adding value – for example, excess people, inventory, and equipment" [7]. The company will have to balance excess equipment against excess stocks. "Idle equipment" cannot always be equated to "excess equipment".

To summarise, this kind of process thinking is primarily about pull, flow and avoidance of delays. This requires balancing on both the design level (production capacities) and the operational level (mechanisms for mutual adjustment/modification of production capacities). Processes can be recognised on different aggregation levels. They can be continuous or discrete. To realise flow through processes mechanisms must be in place that prevent unwanted intermediate stocks and unnecessary waiting between (sub)processes.

The relation of a business process to preceding and subsequent processes is another thing. The classic waterfall approach of IT projects is a prototypical example where each subsequent process is triggered by its preceding process and the chain of processes is carried out linearly, without going back to previous processes, until the end result. A second kind of process structure is linear with feedback, either directly feeding information back to a preceding process, or indirectly via some monitoring process. This process structure is found in conventional production companies. A third kind of process structure is with mutual adjustment between preceding and subsequent processes. Here a kind of reciprocity is to be found between preceding and subsequent processes, and this process structure is more likely to be found in production organisations that are based on the lean ideas.

2.5   Coping with Variability

In order to create constant outputs that are useful for customers or internal subsequent processes, business processes must be able to absorb variability. Irregularities in inputs or in the processing that are not absorbed will be passed on as irregularities in outputs.

Often, there will be a trade-off between extra costs caused by eliminating variability in the processes (creating extra consumption of resources. extra waste, and/or late delivery) and the extra costs of not fulfilling specifications and expectations for customers or for subsequent processes. Dealing with such trade-offs might be subject to coordination processes within the company or between the company and its customers.

In the design and execution of business processes there are different dimensions of variability, and different ways for coping with variability. One dimension is quality and deals with specifications and tolerances. Elimination of output variability can be achieved by elimination of variability of input in combination with standardisation of processes (Mintzberg: standardisation of work) [8]. A second way of elimination of output variability is to allow variability of input and have processes in place that eliminate variability in the processes (Mintzberg: standardisation of output). The third option is to allow variability at the output of the process, and then the question is how much the customer or the next internal process can and will tolerate.

Another dimension of variability is quantity and timing. This dimension is about getting the right amount of output at the right time available out of the process, and this requires the right amounts of resources at the right time available for consumption in the process. Some variability will be absorbed in the process. Variability in quantity and time between processes must be resolved by mutual adjustments of the processes, or by rescheduling. Major readjustments will be made dependent on a broad range of competing values. Will a delivery be on time but incomplete, or late and complete? Will an internal process be on time but generate extra costs, or late without extra production costs? This kind of decision making might also depend on the creativity of experienced people. Sometimes people can find smart ways to lessen the negative effects of product or production variability, by balancing requirements and possibilities of efficiency, specifications, timing, and allowable tolerances. Decision making in this kind of adjustment processes requires that a broad range of experience and competence is represented, because (1) heterogeneous values must be weighed against each other and (2) detailed knowledge about processes is needed to evaluate what is really possible in the given situation. And, where the output for customers is affected, both the specific agreement with the customer and the general conventions are important factors in balancing obligations and costs.

3   Background Notions in Literature About Business Processes

3.1   Machine Metaphor

Gareth Morgan wrote about the mechanical view on organisations "When we talk about an organisation, we usually have in mind a state of orderly relations between clearly defined parts that have some determinate order. Although the image may not be explicit, we are talking about a set of mechanical relations. We talk about organisations as if they were machines, and as a consequence we tend to expect them to operate as machines: in a routinized, efficient, reliable, and predictable way" [9]. Peter Senge wrote about the machine metaphor something similar: "A machine exists for a purpose conceived of by its builders" and "To be effective, a machine must be controllable by its operators. This, of course, is the raison d'être of management – to control the enterprise" [10]. Such a view on organisations is reflected in the usage of the concept of enterprise engineering, which suggests that a company can be engineered like a machine. The Complete Business Process Handbook defines a business process "as a collection of tasks and activities (business operations and actions) consisting of employees, materials, machines, systems and methods that are being structured in such a way as to design, create, and deliver a product or service to the customer" [11] In the formal BPMN specification of the OMG a business process is defined as "A defined set of business activities that represent the steps required to achieve a business objective. It includes the flow and use of information and resources." [12] These definitions match pretty good with the OED entry for a machine "An apparatus for applying mechanical power, consisting of a number of interrelated parts, each having a definite function" [1], apart from the application of mechanical power.

Of course, Morgan has offered not only the machine metaphor, but also the metaphors for the organisation as an organism, as a brain, as a culture, as political system, as psychic prison, as flux and transformation, and as domination. Each metaphor helps to see certain aspects of an organisation by comparing typical organisational features with features of the concept of the machine, organism, brain, et cetera. In this sense each metaphor is "true" in the sense that the organisation can be considered to have similar features as a machine. At the same time, the concepts brought together in the metaphor differ in many other respects. Morgan has described this paradox of the metaphor as the phenomenon that the statement "A is B" can be both very useful and patently false at the same time. Taken metaphorically, the statement "the organisation is a machine" or "the organisation is an organism" can generate insights in the workings of an organisation as a consequence of the similarities between machine and organisation or between an organism and an organisation.

3.2   Logical Atomism

This philosophical stance is perhaps best represented by the famous first propositions of Wittgenstein's Tractatus Logico Philosophicus: "1. The world is everything that is the case. 1.1. The world is the totality of facts, not of things. 1.1.1. The world is determined by the facts, and by their being *all* the facts" and "1.2. The world divides into facts" [13]. This worldview is mirrored in a definition such as from Dietz "The ontological model of a world consists of the specification of its state space and its transition space" [14]. The modelled world as it exists for the business analyst is composed of states and transitions. Please note that while the classical philosophical notion of ontology is about the study of being as such, an ontology (or ontological model) in information systems research is a specification of a model of some universe of discourse. This is clearly another meaning of ontology.

The Complete Business Process Handbook is less strict than Dietz in the requirements for an ontology, and defines "ontology engineering as a discipline that can support corporate knowledge creation through the definition of fundamental concepts, as well as semantic relations and correlations between these concepts" [11]. Relationships should preferably be described as class hierarchies, and it should have fully integrated and standardised relationship attributes. In other words: an ontology should preferably be defined as a formal structure of concepts and relationships.

This view on language and the world can be contrasted with the philosophical stance of the later Wittgenstein of the Philosophical Investigations, where he described the relation between language and world as something that is learned by experiencing practical situations, and not by giving definitions [15]. Our social world is constituted by the use of our language, and they evolve together in continuous adaptation to practical challenges. Natural language is fundamentally different from formal language, and representing social constructs (like business) into a formal language is not possible without loss. The discussions about imperfect specifications in contract law are another illustration of the limits of the use of formalised specifications in our social world. In the latter view language is based in a set of habits in a social community, meaning are the more or less stable patterns that have emerged in such habits, and syntactical rules are structural conventions. Meaning and syntax are abstractions of linguistic habits that are changing over time.

3.3 Internal Customer

The third background notion that must be mentioned is the notion of the internal customer. In the Fundamentals of Business Process Management the outcome of a business process is defined as something "of value to at least one customer" [16], the Complete Business Process Handbook as "a product or a service to the customer" [11], and Kirchmer as "value for an internal or external customer" [17]. This concept of "customer" within the same company and subject to the organisational structure of the company is fundamentally flawed. Coase made the fundamental distinction between coordination by markets and prices mechanism on the one hand, and coordination within an organisational structure on the other hand. The concept of the internal customer is in denial of this distinction. Exchanges between internal processes are governed by specifications, mutual adjustments, and subject to the hierarchy in the organisation. Exchanges with customers are based on business agreements, relational contracts and subject to market sanctions (always) and legal sanctions (sometimes).

3.4 Influence of Background Notions on the Approach to Business Processes

The combination of the background notions discussed very briefly in the preceding sections – machine metaphor, logical atomism and internal customer – can lead to a rather reductive approach to business process modelling. The world of business process modelling seems to represent an idealised world of events and transactions, like the world of neo-classical economics is defined by idealised perfect markets of individual agents and atomic transactions. Of course, time and again in the literature about business process modelling, business process management (BPM) and business process model and notation (BPMN) it is emphasized that the model is not equal to the modelled reality, that models are not true or false but more or less useful, and that there is a certain degree of arbitrariness in the model chosen to represent reality. At the same time, however, metaphors are guides to thinking. The gap between IT systems and the messy social world could be approached from two sides. One way is by looking at the organisation and its processes through the lens of the machine metaphor, by taking fully specified classical contracts for internal and external customers as norm and by trying to 'discipline' the social world. The other way is to take for granted that business and its processes are about agreements and trust, that some processes need a machine-like approach in order to achieve efficiency, and that other processes are better approached with the metaphors of the organism and the brain. The latter processes are about adapting to circumstances, and are as important for business as efficiency.

Another point is the validation of the models of business process. The formal specification of BPMN of the Object Management Group states explicitly that "The primary goal of BPMN is to provide a notation that is readily understandable by all business users, from the business analysts that create the initial drafts of the processes, to the technical developers responsible for implementing the technology that will perform those processes, and finally, to the business people who will manage and monitor those processes" [12]. However, Thomas Allweyer has taken one of the examples of the OMG document "BPMN 2.0 by Example" as an exercise to verify the readability of the resulting model. His conclusion about the resulting model in the example case of a few simple business processes was "This picture is not worth a thousand words, but it requires a thousand words of explanation in order to understand it" [18]. Next, he has reformed the model in a readable form by relaxing some rules and representing parts of the process in free form. His analysis indicates a trade-off between more readable free form representation with annotations and less readable formalised representation, at the same level of precision of specification.

4 Example: Pre-packaged Meat for Retail Chain Stores

This line of business is characterised by short lead times and extremely high service levels (99.7% and higher). Demand for part of the product range is rather stable, promotions and specific products are much more volatile ("barbecue weather"). Typically, about 150 different finished products are produced out of a range of about 40 different types of meat. In the production process the main variables are the cut of the meat, different recipes and spices for minced meats, and different portion sizes. The primary processes are: distribution to the stores ← order picking ← packaging/price labelling ← production ← purchasing and buffering fresh and frozen meat. Production, packaging, order picking and truck loading occur in a time span of about 16 h in total. Production volumes per production day are planned two weeks before the production week (to roughly calculate the quantities of meat to be purchased), adjusted one week before, and made final in the afternoon before the production day. In the morning of the production day the orders are reviewed and might lead to a readjustment of the production plan. Outbound logistics is organised in waves, and stores are each assigned to one wave. In each wave its moments of ordering, picking, truck loading and delivery at the store are organised in a strict time schedule. Promotions are planned 6 weeks in advance, because of the much bigger demand for specific meat at the suppliers, and the need to buy from other suppliers than the regular ones. Promotions "cannibalise" the

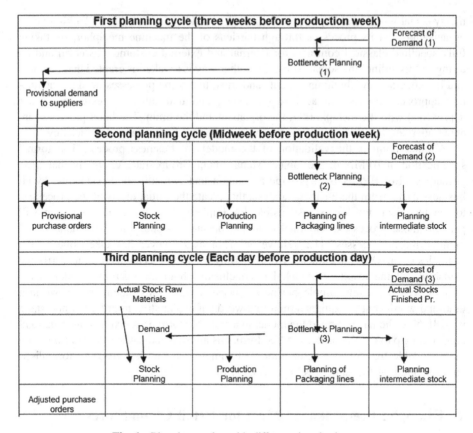

Fig. 1. Planning cycles with different time horizons.

demand for other products, making demand forecasting even more difficult. Typical lead times are 8–12 h between ordering and order picking.

The planning processes in Fig. 1 are represented as hierarchical and unidirectional. In organisational literature this is often the preferred view of processes, and the reality of longer term planning processes mostly meets these two conditions. In normal situations demand of finished products generates demands of resources and raw materials, and each demand is to be fulfilled by a dedicated business process. However, in short term planning, in shop floor control, and in the primary processes this is not always the case. Fluctuations in demand, irregularities in production and shortages in raw materials or production capacity may require mutual adjustments of processes. Conflicts of demand and supply lead to a negotiated planning solution, and in shop floor processes reciprocal fine-tuning of processes is certainly not unusual. Examples of such reciprocal fine-tuning are:

1. Finished products: balancing expected (possible) demand, short-time buffer stocks, production capacity, availability of raw materials

Receipt of raw materials	Raw Materials	Production	Semi-finished Product	Packaging & Price-labelling	Finished Product	Orderpick & Loading
Receipt ──▶	Stock 1					
	──▶	Transform 1				
			──▶ Stock 2			
				──▶ Transform 2		
					──▶ Stock 3	
						──▶ Picking & Loading

Fig. 2. Physical flow of goods. The individual stocks are the combined result of the preceding processes and the actual consumption by the subsequent processes.

2. Packaging lines: balancing efficiency (minimising changes in set-up), demand for finished products, availability of semi-finished products, minimising waiting times of semi-finished products (this is the point where the product is most vulnerable, between production and packaging)
3. Production: balancing production capacity, demand for semi-finished products, availability of raw materials, optimising consumption of lots of raw materials
4. Raw material: balancing buffer sizes needed to cope with fluctuations in demand, while minimising storage time, respecting limits of storage life and limits of storage capacity.

Depending (1) on the stability/volatility of the various processes, and (2) on the capabilities of individuals on key positions in planning and production, detailed planning and scheduling decisions can be made before production in the planning process, or during production in shop floor control. Minor fluctuations are mostly resolved on the shop floor, major disruptions such as break-down of equipment or rejects of raw materials require re-planning.

This implies that monitoring, control and adaptation during the production day, when the planned receipt and production is realised and when actual orders from the stores are placed, is a crucial part of the process landscape.

Another reason why monitoring, control and adaptation processes are important is because of the fact that physical production is not quite an exact science. Quantities are not precise. Production yields are variable, dependent on properties such as fat-content and size of the raw material. For some products trace information such as country where the animal was born, raised, slaughtered, cut must be printed on the consumer label, which is why lots with different trace-information must be separated in production. In order to avoid production losses caused by lot separation, production has some leeway to consume somewhat less or more raw materials than planned.

In the process landscape pictured in Fig. 3 we can distinguish the following overlapping and interacting business processes:

1. Planning processes before the production day
   a. Assessing demand for finished products
   b. Planning for production and demand of raw materials
   c. Securing the supply of raw materials

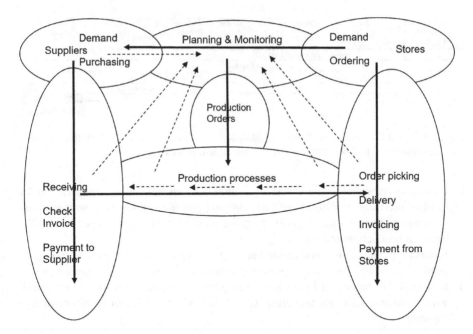

Fig. 3. Process landscape for a production unit of pre-packaged meat

2. Just before and during the production day
   a. Purchasing – receiving/inspecting – checking invoices – payment
   b. Ordering – order picking – delivering – invoicing – payment
   c. Production from raw materials to finished products, controlled by production orders, mutual adjustments, and monitoring.

In stark contrast to the previous schema of longer term planning processes, Fig. 3 shows a lot of non-hierarchy and non-linearity. Feedback and mutual adjustment are essential parts of the primary processes.

5   Analysis of the Example

The example in the preceding section represents a situation with overlapping groups of processes. If we apply the criterion used by the Delft Systems Approach for identifying borders of subsystems (a discontinuity that represents a change of technology, position and/or time) [19] then the subsystems are marked by stocks or datasets. In physical processes the stocks are physical (raw material, semi-finished product, finished product, packaging materials), in control processes the datasets represent demand (mix of forecast and sales orders) for finished products, semi-finished products and raw materials. We can distinguish two types of processes. The first type is the 'simple' linear transformation of inputs to outputs. This type is used in the physical processes (executing receipt, production and shipment orders) and in the demand calculations in planning (given the required outputs in dataset X, determine the required inputs in dataset Y). The second type of process is the adjustment of the amounts in the datasets mentioned above. Here, the sales person, planner, or purchaser will look at the numbers, use his experience, ask for further information, and consult his colleagues. In this kind of process the two most important criteria are value for customer (in this case: a delivery reliability of at least 99,7%) and value for the company (risk of excessive stocks leading to waste). This second kind of process is a combination of standardised calculations and decisions with context-dependent assessment of problems and solutions. People are sometimes able to find creative solutions that allow to obey the business agreements while not obeying the business rules as formally defined. To allow such solutions, and to have organisational mechanisms in place to assess such solutions before and after execution defines the difference between a bureaucratic organisation and a business.

Minor variability in the primary processes (both in quality and quantity) is absorbed in the execution of the primary processes, decisions made by production employees are partly based on written norms and procedures, and partly based on emerged working patterns. Major production deviations are decided by production managers and planners. Deviations in demand, production and purchasing that exceed the planned safety margins are preferably resolved by the production planner and purchaser, imminent shortages that are due to a lack of resources (availability of production capacity and raw materials) will be discussed on a higher level (with input of the specialists).

Process flows are based on habitual or standardised base patterns. This rhythm of production is repeated every day, with variations for products that are in much higher demand in that week. This way of organising production processes is described by Peter King and Jennifer King in "The Product Wheel Handbook – Creating Balanced Flow in High-Mix Process Operations" [20]. As the subtitle indicates, this approach is meant for production processes that produce each day a broad range of products. Because of the repetition of the same pattern each day, people are used to the rhythm, and patterns create flow. Processes are triggered by a combination of the cyclic character of the pattern plus information about actual starting times and actual quantities from production planning, and production employees will anticipate on processes that are about to start because they know what is coming. It is an interesting example of information that is provided by background knowledge of daily patterns.

6 Conclusions

Doing business, fulfilling agreements and creating a healthy profit for the company asks for a combination of efficiency and flexibility in business processes. Approaches based on the machine metaphor in combination with the worldview of logical atomism can be very useful for achieving efficiency, and such processes might be represented adequately in a notation such as BPMN. Still, validation of such models by people from the business can be problematic because of the readability, see the analysis of Allweyer. Business processes involving flexibility and adaptation to circumstances, especially in those processes that matter directly for the fulfilment of business agreements and customer's expectations are much less suited for such a formalised approach. Such processes are probably better analysed by less formalised methods. Probably the development and application of notations like BPMN will be best served when they do not try to cover all business processes, but formulate under what conditions and for which kinds of processes this is a useful tool.

References

1. OED: The Oxford English Dictionary. Oxford University Press, Oxford (1989)
2. Kay, J.: The Truth About Markets. Allan Lane, London (2003)
3. Coase, R.H.: The nature of the firm. In: Williamson, O.E., Winter, S.G. (eds.) The Nature of the Firm: Origins, Evolution, and Development, pp. 18–33. Oxford University Press, Oxford (1993)
4. Campbell, D. (ed.): The Relational Theory of Contract: Selected Works of Ian MacNeil. Sweet & Maxwell, London (2001)
5. Kay, J.: Foundations of Corporate Success. Oxford University Press, Oxford (1993)
6. Shingo, S.: A Study of the Toyota Production System. CRC Press, Boca Raton (2005)
7. Ohno, T.: Toyota Production System. CRC Press, Boca Raton (1988)
8. Mintzberg, H.: The Structuring of Organizations. Prentice-Hall, Englewood Cliffs (1979)
9. Morgan, G.: Images of Organization, 2nd edn. Sage Publications, Thousand Oaks (1997)
10. Senge, P.M.: Foreword. In: De Geus, A. (ed.) The Living Company, pp. 1–6. Nicholas Brealy, London (1997)
11. Von Rosing, M., Scheer, A.W., Von Scheel, H.: The Complete Business Process Handbook, vol. 1. Morgan Kaufman, Waltham (2015)
12. OMG. https://www.omg.org/spec/BPMN/2.0#documents. OMG document number formal/2011-01-03. Accessed 03 May 2019
13. Wittgenstein, L.: Tractatus Logico-Philosophicus. Routledge, Oxon (2005). Translated from the German by Ogden, C.K. Original edition by Routledge (1922)
14. Dietz, J.L.G.: Enterprise Ontology. Springer, Berlin (2006). https://doi.org/10.1007/3-540-33149-2
15. Wittgenstein, L.: Philosophical Investigations, Revised 4th edn. Wiley-Blackwell, Chichester (2009). Translated from the German by Anscombe, G.E.M., Hacker, P.M.S., Schulte, J. Original edition by Basil Blackwell (1953)
16. Dumas, M., La Rosa, M., Mendling, J., Reijers, H.A.: Business Process Management, 2nd edn. Springer, Berlin (2018). https://doi.org/10.1007/978-3-642-28616-2
17. Kirchmer, M.: High Performance Through Business Process Management, 3rd edn. Springer, Berlin (2017). https://doi.org/10.1007/978-3-319-51259-4
18. Allweyer, T.: Human-readable BPMN diagrams. In: Fischer, L. (ed.) BPMN 2.0 Handbook, 2nd edn., pp. 217–232, Future Strategies, Lighthouse Point (2014)
19. Veeke, H.P.M., Ottjes, J.A., Lodewijks, G.: The Delft Systems Approach. Springer, Berlin (2008). https://doi.org/10.1007/978-1-84800-177-0
20. King, P.L., King, J.S.: The Product Wheel Handbook. CRC Press, Boca Raton (2013)

Value-Driven Robotic Process Automation (RPA)

A Process-Led Approach to Fast Results at Minimal Risk

Mathias Kirchmer[1,2][✉] and Peter Franz[3]

[1] BPM-D, West Chester, USA
Mathias.Kirchmer@bpm-d.com
[2] University of Pennsylvania, Philadelphia, USA
[3] BPM-D, Kingston upon Thames, Surrey, UK
Peter.Franz@bpm-d.com

Abstract. Digitalization has transformed the way organizations operate. New digital tools are available with increasing regularity – and many of them have the potential for a major impact. They enable the transformation of business processes to become more efficient, agile, meet compliance requirements, enhance customer experience or improve the general quality of deliverables. They may help achieve a level of process performance not previously envisaged. Robotic Process Automation (RPA) is one of those digital enablers which has been applied, or at least discussed in many organizations as practice reports and conference presentations show. This process technology is becoming a mainstream trend, relevant for many businesses. However, many organizations struggle to realize the full potential of RPA. According to newer statistics even 30–50% of RPA initiatives fail completely. The paper discusses opportunities and challenges of applying RPA as process improvement approach. The approach of Value-driven Robotic Process Automation addresses the challenges and realized the identified opportunities. It proposes an approach that helps to focus on the right sub-processes to automate, improve those business processes considering the end-to-end process context and sustain the results through appropriate governance and hybrid workforce management. Agile principles are combined with the required focus and direction. Value-driven RPA is a part of a discipline of process-led digital transformation management, leveraging the capabilities of business process management (BPM) to realize the full value of digital initiatives, fast and at minimal risk.

Keywords: BPM · Business process management · Digitalization · Digital transformation · Intelligent automation · Process design · Process governance · Process improvement · Process modelling · Robotic Process Automation · RPA · Value realization

© Springer Nature Switzerland AG 2019
B. Shishkov (Ed.): BMSD 2019, LNBIP 356, pp. 31–46, 2019.
https://doi.org/10.1007/978-3-030-24854-3_3

1   Introduction

Most organizations have started digital transformation initiatives or at least plan for them (Kirchmer et al. 2016). New digital tools are available with increasing regularity – and many of them have the potential for a major business impact. They enable the transformation of business processes to become more efficient, agile, meet compliance requirements, enhance customer experience or improve the general quality of deliverables. They may help achieve a level of process performance not seen before. Robotic Process Automation (RPA) is one of those digital enablers which has been applied or at least discussed in many organizations as practice reports and conference presentations show (Scheer 2018) (Accenture 2017) (McKinsey 2017). This process technology is about to become a mainstream trend relevant for many businesses.

However, many organizations don't realize the full potential of RPA. According to newer statistics as many as 30–50% of RPA initiatives fail completely (Cantara 2015) (Kirchmer 2017a). The approach of Value-driven Robotic Process Automation addresses this challenge. It proposes an approach that helps to focus on the right subprocesses to automate through RPA, improve those business processes considering the end-to-end process context and sustain the results through appropriate governance and hybrid workforce management (Kirchmer 2017b). Value-driven RPA is a part of a discipline of process-led digital transformation management, leveraging the capabilities of business process management (BPM) to realize the full value of digital initiatives, fast and at minimal risk (Franz and Kirchmer 2012).

The article defines RPA and explains it significance. Then it introduces an approach for Value-driven RPA, combining academic findings and practical project experience. The conclusion shows a possible way forward and highlights related research opportunities.

2   Definition and Significance of Robotic Process Automation (RPA)

Based on a definition and some background on Robotic Process Automation (RPA), its current use and expected value is discussed. This leads to the identification of key challenges of current approaches to implementation and roll-out of RPA.

2.1   Definition of RPA

Robots have been used in manufacturing environments for a long time (Scheer 2018). Whole manufacturing lines have been automated using robots to execute manufacturing steps, handle parts or transport them to then next production unit. RPA transfers this automation approach into the administrative and management work of an organization.

RPA tools, so called "Bots", are software programs that operate on the user interface of other computer systems in the way a human would do (Wikipedia 2018). They basically recognize and read fields on a screen of an application software, modify the content if necessary and enter it into other fields of the same or different software.

All of that happens based on predefined rules (Harmon 2017). This means the Bots execute business process steps using the appropriate application software. In addition, they influence the business process directly by driving a specific process flow, for example, a business process that enables the automated handling of standard situations and the work on exceptions through humans. The definition of RPA is summarized in Fig. 1.

The integration of artificial intelligence (AI) and Cognitive Automation components into the RPA tools makes them even more powerful since RPA starts handling unplanned situations and deals with unstructured data. Also the handling of verbal information is possible using "Chatbots" in an RPA environment (Scheer 2018). The combination of the RPA with AI is often referred to as Intelligent RPA (iRPA) or Smart RPA (sRPA), as part of intelligent automation in general.

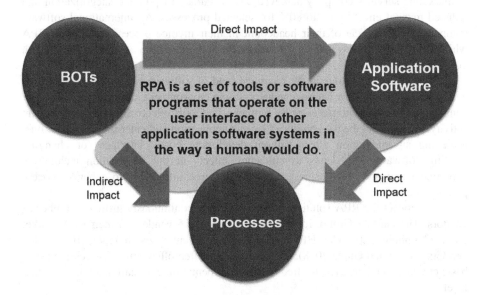

Fig. 1. Definition of Robotic Process Automation (RPA)

Just like industry robots automate manufacturing and assembly steps, RPA robots automate the human work with data and information. This is the extension of the first automation phase of business activities through traditional software, such as Enterprise Resource Planning (ERP) systems and the following automation of the workflow through integrated business process management systems (BPMS). It is estimated that over 50% of current human interaction with those systems can be automated through RPA resulting in significant performance increases (Scheer 2018) (Modi et al. 2017). All this can be achieved with relatively moderate investments which makes RPA even more attractive for organizations. It has become a core component of many digital business transformation initiatives.

2.2   Current Status of RPA Utilization and Value

RPA offers significant opportunities to improve business process performance. This has been proven in various business process areas in thousands of organizations (see, for example, Davison et al. 2018). The check of vendor invoices, handling of routine insurance claims, or the processing of loan applications are just a few examples where RPA has been used successfully. In general non value-added working steps, such as entering data from one application into another or extracting and re-entering spreadsheets, are automated, freeing up related human workforce for higher qualified activities, leading to cost reductions and shorter cycle times. These effects are combined with other benefits like the reduction or even elimination of errors entering data, enforcing of compliance rules, or easily scaling data processing capacity "on demand".

A bank, for example, reduced the onboarding time from 16 days to 9 min. A marketing services company achieved 97% accuracy of product categorization and reduced manual effort by up to 80% for selected processes. An international software company reduced 67% of their headcount in their invoice processing through RPA while achieving 20% less help desk inquiries through more accurate results (Modi et al. 2017).

RPA can also add value in the technical field of software integration. Without the availability of RPA, in a heterogeneous systems environment, applications are either connected by system interfaces or by humans. The tools effectively mirror the human activity and can read the data produced by one application and enter it into another one, achieving an integration effect without developing costly interfaces or changing existing software. This leads to efficiency effects in the information technology department and provides business users the required integration to enhance process performance.

In the meantime RPA solutions are offered by a continuously growing number of vendors. The Gartner Group, for example, mentions 15 vendors in their RPA market guide (Tornbohm 2016) or HFS examines in a recent research report 10 selected vendors (Fersht and Gupta 2018). RPA software is often offered at an aggressive price, basic entrance versions even for free. Also implementation cost start at a relatively low level.

All this makes RPA look like a pragmatic and powerful solution, a big business opportunity. Value-driven RPA has to realize those opportunities systematically.

2.3   Key RPA Related Challenges

However, the use of RPA can also have downsides. RPA creates risks, like basically every automation technology does (Kirchmer 2017b). RPA helps to do routine work faster and at a higher quality but it also can make mistakes faster and with certainty. There is no human check before executing an action. Humans apply intuition and experience even to routine tasks. Poor data quality or the insufficient definition of business rules can lead, for example, to the ordering of the wrong parts – fast and in big quantities. Or missed claim types can lead to significant rework in the claims handling, overcompensating the automation benefits. RPA requires detailed knowledge about the business process it is used in – otherwise expected performance improvements will not be realized.

The CIO of a major financial firm described at the Process Excellence Conference 2018 in Orlando, for example, how they stopped the use of over 1000 bots due to significant issues. Processes had changed faster than expected so that related bots did not operate properly, creating huge amounts of exceptions that people had to handle. This significantly negated the initial workforce reduction. In other processes the elimination of individual bottlenecks created issues in downstream processes, resulting again in additional work efforts.

The use of RPA may also just cover symptoms without correcting the real reasons for issues. RPA was, for example, used for the automated reconciliation of account differences in an investment bank. However, in the mid and long-term it would be much more beneficial to correct the up-stream issues leading to those differences. In this situation, RPA has become an obstacle to real progress. It is a transformation that brings change but not the full possible improvement.

While one of the benefits of RPA is lauded as being efficiency, the reduction of time for specific working steps does not automatically lead to a workforce headcount reduction. Saving a few hours for different roles may lead to more time for the related people, however, they are still required to do the remaining work. In an insurance company this led to a situation that RPA was perceived as not creating any benefits at all. Real cost reduction, should this be the objective, requires a systematic re-structuring of roles and appropriate workforce management, including human and digital workforce.

RPA vendors stress that their tools are easy to implement and use – also for a business person. This may be right for simple straight-forward applications. However, to achieve full potential of sophisticated larger RPA environments some expert know how is required for implementation and ongoing adjustment (Harmon 2017). For a robot to be reliable in an enterprise context, it can be necessary to provide for antic-ipated exception conditions. This exception processing is often developed using coding and is difficult to do by the average business user. This should be part of the process management capabilities of the organization or RPA expectations may not be met at all or at least not be met fully. A basic business process management discipline should be in place or established to support RPA operations.

An RPA implementation, just driven through various business demands, without a proper automation strategy, also leads to significant issues since up and down stream process effects are not, or not sufficiently considered. The lack of appropriate priori-tization and roll-out planning limits the business results significantly as some of the above examples show.

Combining RPA with artificial intelligence capabilities can also lead to challenges. For example, if machine learning (ML) is used to handle more complex process instances, such as the handling of specific claims, the results depend heavily on the available data AI learns from. If the historical data, inputted into the ML algorithms, is of a low quality, resulting bad decisions and actions will be only executed faster. Artificial intelligence turns into artificial stupidity.

These potential challenges can make RPA a dangerous illusion. All these effects are mainly due to a functional technology focused approach to RPA. Value-driven RPA minimizes those risks.

3   Focus RPA on the Right Processes

A company only competes through 15–20% of its business processes (Franz and Kirchmer 2012). If some of those high impact processes have a low maturity level these are excellent targets for improvement initiatives, including RPA. Here RPA can achieve the highest business impact. However, before deciding on an RPA implementation it has to be verified if this is indeed the right solution to address the weak points of those processes.

3.1   Identify the High Impact Business Processes

The impact of a business process depends on the strategy of an organization. In order to identify high impact processes we need to operationalize the strategy. This can be done through a value-driver tree, breaking down the strategic direction into goals and those are linked to value-drivers. Value-drivers describe what an organization has to get right to deliver on its strategy. Experience in has shown that 8–10 value-drivers can describe what it takes to make a strategy happen (Franz and Kirchmer 2012). Figure 2 shows an example of such a value-driver tree, captured in an appropriate tool, here the BPM-D Application (Kirchmer et al. 2018).

The value-drivers can then be linked to different processes of an organization by defining the impact of each process on each value-driver. The weighted total impact of a process is basis for the identification of the high impact processes of an organization. For those high impact processes the maturity level is identified by comparing its performance to an industry average or other benchmarks. Result of this process segmentation is the identification of high impact low maturity processes (Kirchmer 2017a, 2017b). An example of such a process impact assessment matrix is shown in Fig. 3, again using the BPM-D Application. The process Early Market Research has, for example, a high impact on the value-driver Optimize Prices, but in total only a low

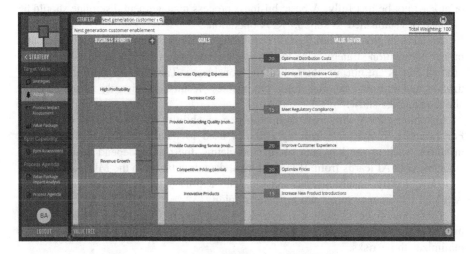

Fig. 2. Value-driver Tree in the BPM-D application

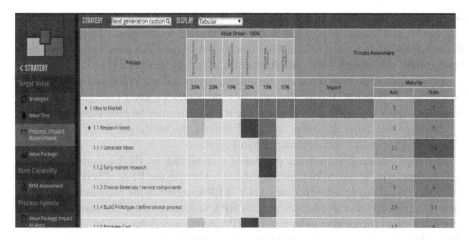

Fig. 3. Process impact assessment matrix in the BPM-D application (excerpt)

impact on all value-drivers and with that on the strategy. Hence, this would not be a good candidate to launch an impactful improvement initiative.

At least in a first phase, only high impact low maturity processes are examined to verify where RPA fits to improve the maturity level and with that the performance of the process in regards to the strategy. The focus on this process segment enables RPA initiatives to deliver best value. If RPA is not the right improvement solution, alternatives are identified.

3.2 Verify the RPA Technology Fit

RPA is best fit for repetitive transactional processes with a high transaction volume. This enables a simple straight forward use of RPA with little risk and high economy of scale. Automating exceptions, for example the handling of special high risk claims, do in general not pay off since they may only happen a few times per year and may in each case require adjustments to the RPA bot.

A process benefitting from RPA requires digital input and output of data, for example the creation of a spreadsheets with customer data from one system that needs to be entered into another application. A business process with lots of manual analogue working steps benefits less from RPA. It is also helpful if the data to be handled is straight forward text or numeric data. Complex images are more difficult to deal with – although the continuous improvement of Optical Character Recognition (OCR) technologies can help here.

If several application systems that support a process are not integrated through APIs, this could be another opportunity for creating value through the use of RPA. RPA can provide the required integration. In this situation it is helpful if the technical system access is easy, for example it simplifies the RPA application if there is no need to address security software of cloud-based applications. In general, the change rate of the systems RPA has to access should be low to avoid frequent RPA configuration adjustments.

The decisions in RPA-enabled processes should be based on clearly defined rules that can be automated. Judgement-based decisions are much more difficult to handle through RPA. However, Artificial Intelligence (AI) capabilities can increasingly help here. Hence, this option has to be checked on a case by case basis.

In general RPA is a good fit for stable, well defined processes with as few exceptions as possible. Frequently adjusting processes or even emerging processes normally require significant RPA management effort that may be prohibitive for its use.

Some of the most important technical criteria, to verify the fit of RPA as an improvement approach, are summarized in Fig. 4.

If a high impact low maturity process is a candidate for RPA according to these technical criteria, it has to be determined now whether the RPA effects support the value-drivers related to this processes. Only if RPA improves the process in regards to these value-drivers it is worth launching an RPA implementation. The result is a set of processes suited for improvement through RPA deployments that can be used to define appropriate projects and project portfolios (Kirchmer et al. 2018).

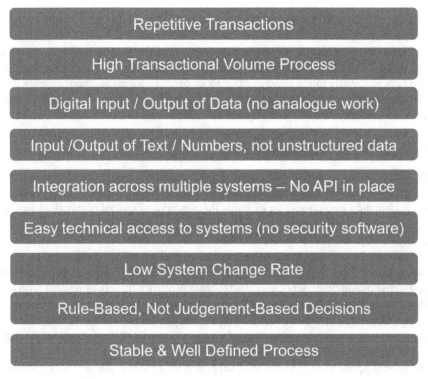

Fig. 4. Selected criteria to verify the fit of RPA as improvement approach

4 Improve Processes in the Appropriate Context Using RPA

In order to realize the full potential of RPA, and avoid the discussed issues, it is necessary to understand the process context in which RPA is used in detail and plan the implementation and roll out systematically. An agile approach to the RPA-based process design and system configuration enables fast value realization and helps to minimize risk.

4.1 Analyze As-Is Processes

Many RPA technology vendors and promoters suggest that the Bots can be used without much analysis upfront. However, this reduces the business impact and can create many of the up and downstream challenges, as discussed before. As in any improvement initiative it is important to understand the current business process context to identify improvement opportunities and create a baseline for the expected value and the business cased based thereon. To avoid key challenges of RPA it is important to understand the end-to-end process and the expected effects of RPA. Since RPA touches all dimensions of a process, they all need to be included in the analysis, using methods like BPMN 2.0 (Fisher 2012): organization (roles, departments, etc.), data, functions, process control flow, process deliverables and underlying technology (Scheer 1998) (Kirchmer 2017a) (Kale 2018). To realize the full potential of RPA, the analysis has to answer specifically questions like the following:

- Which roles can be eliminated or re-directed? This allows the calculation of efficiency effects, especially cost reduction but also potential quality improvements by avoiding mistakes.
- Which functions of remaining roles can be eliminated (automated? This supports value identification in the same way discussed above.
- How is the cycle time effected? This provides information about increased agility, leading, for example, to better customer or supplier experience.
- Can the use of existing software systems be discontinued or the development of complex system interfaces be avoided? This helps to evaluate technology cost reductions and increased systems performance.

The RPA related process analysis requires in a second step a deeper examination of the process components that will be automated. A move of the specification from pure business aspects to high level systems related activities is required: the documentation and analysis of every field that is read and entered by current users that may be replaced by a bot (Scheer 2018). This creates the foundation for the evaluation of the detailed requirements for the use of RPA.

The analysis can be automated itself, at least partly, through process mining approaches (Scheer 2018) (Kirchmer 2017a). Since most of the processes, that are good candidates for RPA, are already supported through conventional application software, process mining systems can examine the systems log files to deliver process analytics or even models of specific process instances. Process mining tools are excellent complements to RPA tools in analysis but also during the later governance and continuous improvement of those processes.

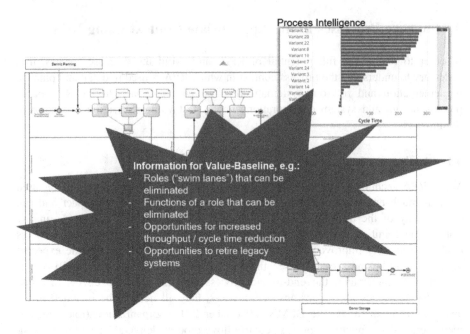

Fig. 5. Value-baseline through As-Is Process Analysis

A focused process simulation is often helpful to properly understand the current execution effort, cycle times and major bottlenecks. This simulation can then be used to demonstrate the impact of using RPA to automate certain steps in the process, highlighting the overall impact on the process performance. The characteristics of processes suited for RPA, especially the degree of automation, simplify the data collection to enable a process simulation.

The as-is process analysis is illustrated in Fig. 5. The analysis allows a simplification of the processes before transforming it using RPA as enabler. This simplifies RPA deployment and change management as well as the following value realization.

4.2   Agile Process Design and RPA Development

The end-to-end vision of the to-be process is defined and guides the following detailed design and RPA realization activities. The detailed design of the RPA-based to-be processes and the RPA development or configuration are executed in an agile way, realizing the final to-be of a process in stages (Sutherland 2014). This enables a fast value realization and minimizes risk since stop-go decisions can be included systematically in the design and deployment approach.

In most cases a first use of RPA automates the standard situations handled through a process, leaving the handling of exceptions to the human workforces. An example is the onboarding of mortgage applicants where only candidates with questionable financial background may have to be handled through an exception process. These manually handled processes components can then be automated in following stages – depending on the additional value expected. This "build" approach is explained in Fig. 6.

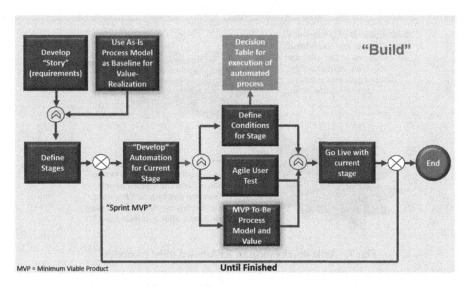

Fig. 6. Agile approach to build an RPA enabled process

The development of the RPA solution often requires a combination of different components, including other automation approaches such as Business Process Management Systems (BPMS), Artificial Intelligence (AI), Optical Character Recognition (OCR), Analytics and more. Hence, an appropriate solution architecture, supporting the process improvement objectives, is crucial for a successful RPA deployment.

It is important not to reduce the agile approach of building Minimum Viable Products (MVP) only to the RPA technology but to define for each MVP also the appropriate intermediate to-be process. This provides for the value to be defined per stage, sets the right expectations and enables an appropriate change management. Business and Information Technology (IT) departments get aligned. It can, for example, be identified, which roles can be eliminated in a specific stage and when existing legacy systems or APIs can be retired. The development of MVP process stages to manage the value-realization is illustrated in Fig. 7.

This approach enables a rapid value-realization while still working within the end-to-end process context, avoiding typical RPA challenges. The agile realization of different stages is aligned through the overall end-to-end process vision, defined for overall guidance.

4.3 Process-Led RPA Deployment

The deployment and roll-out follows the same agile principles as the development. Each MVP process scenario is deployed while the existing processes are left to handle the excluded cases. For example, specific insurance claims or purchase requisitions of a manufacturing company, in place. The kind of process execution (using RPA or using the former as-is process) is defined based on a decision table reflecting the current development status of the RPA solution and the enabled processes.

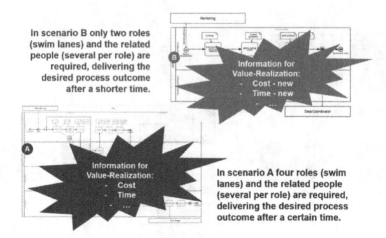

In scenario B only two roles (swim lanes) and the related people (several per role) are required, delivering the desired process outcome after a shorter time.

Information for Value-Realization:
- Cost - new
- Time - new

Information for Value-Realization:
- Cost
- Time
- ...

In scenario A four roles (swim lanes) and the related people (several per role) are required, delivering the desired process outcome after a certain time.

Fig. 7. Agile development of RPA-based to-be processes

Formal testing, as with any application, is still often a critical necessity to minimize business risk. However, in more and more RPA initiatives, this risk is at least partly mitigated through the immediate execution of the process through users. If issues occur, users can still switch back to the traditional process until the RPA configuration is adjusted. Innovation becomes part of the day-to-day business. This approach is explained in Fig. 8.

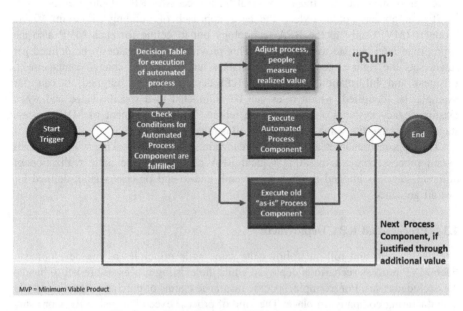

Fig. 8. Agile deployment of RPA-based processes

An important component is the appropriate workforce management, enabling the value realization and ensuring the appropriate processing of exceptions. The handling of a hybrid workforce, including human and digital members, requires appropriate preparation: people need to have clear new roles and expectations and Bots need to be updated and adjusted systematically based on experiences in the ongoing business. The creation of appropriate roles is often a pre-condition to free up people for other activities.

People change management, including information, communication and training, plays a key role (Kirchmer 2017a). This aspect is often underestimated in RPA initiatives since the changing role of humans for exception handling, which in most cases leads to more demanding work, is not considered sufficiently.

5 Sustain RPA Benefits and Results

Once an RPA enabled process is executed in the daily business, it is important to keep on managing the value realization and adjust the process as well as the enabling automation components. This management discipline is crucial for the overall success of the new process and the delivery of related benefits. Hence, an appropriate process governance is required. Figure 9 shows a high level example of a process governance organization.

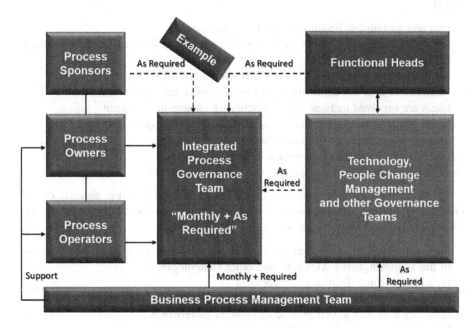

Fig. 9. Agile deployment of RPA-based processes

This process governance plays a key role for digitally enabled processes. RPA, as well as other automation approaches, impact different departments and functional organizations. Hence, the decision on changes of the processes and underlying technology requires well defined governance processes and appropriate roles to realize the expected agility, sustainable cost reductions and other benefits (Kirchmer 2018a).

Process governance is part of a larger business process management discipline (BPM-Discipline) that manages the digital transformation of an organization towards value creation and aligns the different improvement initiatives (Kirchmer 2015). This BPM-Discipline, executed through the process of process management, can be set up or expanded during RPA or other automation and improvement initiatives. It should be functional once the first business processes go live using new digital technologies and business practices.

Value-driven RPA is about adding a new process improvement and transformation option to the toolset of the BPM-Discipline. This integrated approach and thinking makes RPA at the end successful.

6   Conclusion

The approach of Value-driven Robotic Process Automation (RPA), embedded in a larger BPM-Discipline and leveraging agile principles, brings significant advantages compared to an ad-hoc use of this automation technology as often promoted in the market:

– Fast and sustainable benefits from RPA initiatives
– Integrated incremental value-realization and management of return-on-investment (ROI)
– Realistic expectations regarding benefits from automation stages
– Minimize risk of not achieving return on a process automation initiative
– Users are involved incrementally, simplifying change management
– Saves formal testing time while keeping the automation quality up
– Innovation becomes part of daily business
– Drives alignment between business and IT
– Flexible application of the approach to ongoing initiatives.

However, the presented approach for Value-driven RPA is still in an early development and roll-out phase. Hence, it also creates a basis for further research and development opportunities, such as:

– Integration of RPA into larger automation architectures and appropriate extension of the approach, using AI, OCR, and other technologies
– Hybrid workforce definition management
– Process governance for digital processes and alignment with other governance areas, such as data governance or technology governance
– Use of RPA based process reference models.

First practice experiences, at a number of organizations engaged by the authors, with Value-driven RPA and its integration into a larger BPM-Discipline showed positive encouraging results. This clear view of the end-to-end business process combining attention to people and technology aspects, e.g. an integrated Center of Excellence including Automation (RPA and other approaches), people change management, classical process improvement, etc. avoids RPA silo solutions and delivers real performance improvement. Value-driven RPA is another way the BPM-Discipline makes a difference and advances digital transformation to deliver real business outcomes (Kirchmer 2018b). This process-led approach delivers fast results at minimal risk. It helps organizations to master another step of their digital transformation journey.

References

Accenture: The emergence of robotic process automation software (2017). https://www.accenture.com/gb-en/robotic-process-automation-software

Cantara: 'Start up your Business Process Competency Center'. In: Documentation of The Gartner Business Process Management Summit, National Harbour (2015)

Davison, Magana, Holbrook: How is your RPA Journey going? Where is it going? In: ISG presentation at IA World Series, September 2018

Fersht, P., Gupta, S.: HFS top 10 RPA products 2018. In: Presentation of HFS Research Report, August 2019 (2018)

Fisher, L.: BPMN 2.0 Handbook – Methods, Concepts, Case Studies and Standards in Business Process Modelling Notation (BPMN). Lighthouse Point (2012)

Franz, P., Kirchmer, M.: Value-Driven Business Process Management: The Value-Switch for Lasting Competitive Advantage, 1st edn. McGraw-Hill, New York (2012)

Harmon, P.: Robotic process automation comes of age. In: BPTrends.com, June 2017 (2017)

Kirchmer, M.: Enterprise architecture enabling process governance for agility, compliance and more. In: CIO Review, Enterprise Architecture Special, 5 April 2018 (2018a)

Kirchmer, M.: Enabling high performance in the digital age – from Europe to Australia, Industry 4.0 requires the discipline of business process management 4.0. ISE Mag. **50**(11) (2018b)

Kirchmer, M., Franz, P., Gusain, R.: From strategy to process improvement project portfolios and value-realization - a digital approach to the discipline of business process management. In: Proceedings of the Eighth International Symposium on Business Modelling and Software Design, Vienna, 03–05 July 2–4 2018 (2018)

Kirchmer, M.: Robotic Process Automation (RPA) – pragmatic solution or dangerous illusion 10/17 (2017a). http://insights.btoes.com/risks-robotic-process-automation-pragmatic-solution-or-dangerous-illusion

Kirchmer, M.: High Performance through Business Process Management –Strategy Execution in a Digital World, 3rd edn. Springer, New York (2017b). https://doi.org/10.1007/978-3-319-51259-4

Kirchmer, M., Franz, P., Lotterer, A., Antonucci, Y., Laengle, S.: The value-switch for digitalisation initiatives: business process management. BPM-D Whitepaper, Philadelphia – London (2016)

Kirchmer, M.: The process of process management – mastering the new normal in a digital world. In: BMSD Proceedings, July 2015 (2015, in publication)

McKinsey: Harnessing automation for a future that works (2017). http://www.mckinsey.com/global-themes/digital-disruption/harnessing-automation-for-a-future-that-works

Modi, A., Jayapriya, K., Burnett, S.: Creating business value through next generation smart digital workforce – from task automation to digital capability creation. In: An Everest Group View Point, distributed by WorkFusion 2017 (2017)

Scheer, A.-W.: Unternehmung 4.0 – Von disruptiven Geschaeftsmodell zur Automatisierung von Geschaeftsprozessen, 1st edn. AWSi Publishing, Saarbrucken (2018)

Scheer, A.-W.: ARIS – Business Process Frameworks, 2nd edn. Springer, Berlin (1998). https://doi.org/10.1007/978-3-642-58529-6

Sutherland, J.: SCRUM – The Art of doing Twice the Work in Half the Time. Penguin Random House, New York (2014)

Tornbohm, C.: Market guide for robotic process automation software. In: Research Report of The Gartner Group, 07 November 2016 (2016)

Kale, V.: Enterprise Process Management Systems Engineering Process-Centric Enterprise Systems using BPMN 2.0. CRC Press, Boca Rotan (2018)

Wikipedia: Robotic Process Automation. In: Wikipedia.org (2018)

Failure and Change Impact Analysis for Safety-Critical Systems
Applied on a Medical Use Case

Philipp Lohmüller[(✉)], Julia Rauscher, and Bernhard Bauer

Department of Computer Science, University of Augsburg, Augsburg, Germany
{philipp.lohmueller,julia.rauscher,bauer}@informatik.uni-augsburg.de

Abstract. Nowadays, safety-critical systems are used in various domains including Internet of Things of medical devices. However, such systems are usually very complex and fault-prone. This means, safety, security and real-time aspects are often only insufficiently considered. To mitigate or avoid safety-critical failures, it is mandatory to analyze effects by means of a failure and change impact analysis. In this paper, we propose an approach to analyze a hierarchical structured model to determine critical goals. Afterwards, the effects and impacts of failures are calculated and determined to identify components which have a need of counter measures. Furthermore, it is analyzed which kind of effects these counter measures will have within the hierarchical model. Finally, the developed approach is evaluated by means of a realistic medical use case.

Keywords: Impact analysis · Risk assessment · Safety-critical system

1 Introduction

The level of complexity in IT systems is rising constantly. Therefore, these systems are also getting more complicated and hardly manageable. However, if there is a safety-critical system, like in automotive or medical field, e.g., to guarantee the airbag triggering or the correct administration of drugs, humans or assets, like data, can be endangered if the systems was not controlled. As 50% of flaws happen in the design phase [18] an identification and elimination of safety and security vulnerabilities at an early stage is essential. However, it is not enough to identify potential failures as weak points can be complex and have impacts on other components or relations too. To remove or mitigate the weak points components with a need of counter measures (CMs) have to be identified as well. As existing approaches do not combine the identification of weak points, the impacts of failures and the subsequent determination of CMs, we developed a holistic process to increase the safety of safety-critical systems. To address the aforementioned issues our approach identifies critical elements in an architecture model by the usage and adaptation of architecture analysis approaches which enable not only to identify flaws, but also their impacts and needs of CMs.

© Springer Nature Switzerland AG 2019
B. Shishkov (Ed.): BMSD 2019, LNBIP 356, pp. 47–63, 2019.
https://doi.org/10.1007/978-3-030-24854-3_4

Therefore, we developed an approach which uses a safety goal hierarchy (SGH) combined with FMEA to identify weak points and conduct a failure impact analysis (FIA) to determine failure effects. Following, architectural changes will be recognized through a change impact analysis (CIA). The paper is structured as follows: Sect. 2 contains related work for failure and change impacts as well as safety-critical systems. Afterwards needed basics of Failure Mode and Effects Analysis (FMEA), Bayesian Belief Networks (BBN) and dependencies between safety and security are presented. Section 4 describes the approach in 4 detailed steps, which are evaluated in Sect. 5 with aid of a medical smart home use case. A conclusion and outlook are given in Sect. 6.

2   Related Work

There are numerous projects and scientific publications with respect to FIA and CIA as well as safety-critical systems, which are presented hereinafter.

2.1   Failure and Change Impacts

The work of Langermeier et al. [10] provides a CIA approach based on Enterprise Architecture Models. By means of their approach, which is based on a data-flow analysis technique, it is analyzed which model elements are affected. The algorithm of the authors aims to apply a CIA in context of Enterprise Architecture Models. However, our paper proposes an approach how to apply FIA and CIA taken safety-critical concerns like, e.g., safety and security into account. [16] propose an Eclipse based tool named Chianti and analyzes change impacts of regression or unit tests. By means of the execution behavior a set of affected changes is determined for each affected test. Chianti does not analyze change impacts on models but on Java code. Such as [10], Ren et al. [16] don't consider safety-critical aspects in their approach in order to enable a maximum degree of safety and security by means of the CIA. The paper of Hanemann et al. [5] dealing with resource failures, which might endanger service level agreements by influencing services. Therefore, [5] presents an approach, which identifies the effect of resource failures with respect to the corresponding services and service level agreements. In addition to those effects, a technique is proposed in order to improve services and to provide them. Such as [10] and [16], Hanemann et al. [5] also do not take safety-critical issues into account. In summary, each of the presented scientific publications provide either a FIA or a CIA but there is no combination of them. Furthermore, all publications do not consider the topic of safety-critical systems.

2.2   Safety-Critical Systems

For instance, there is a project, which is called SESAMO (**Se**curity and **Sa**fety **Mo**delling) and focuses on safety and security requirements, aiming "to develop a component-oriented design methodology based upon model-driven technology, jointly addressing safety and security aspects and their interrelation for net-worked embedded systems in multiple domains" [1]. This project focuses on identifying safety and security hazards in order to calculate a trade-off between contradicting safety and security issues. Furthermore, another project concerning safety is called SafeCer (**Safe**ty **Cer**tification of Software-Intensive Systems with Reusable Components). The purpose of this project is to increase "[...] efficiency and reduce(d) time-to-market by composable safety certification of safety-relevant embedded systems." [9] The main focus of this project is to provide a procedure of composing safety arguments for a system by reusing of already certificated arguments of subsystems. In this way, it enhances efficient safety assurance and certification. Furthermore, there is the work of Lohmüller et al. [12], which proposes an approach for calculating trade-offs between contradicting safety-critical concerns. These include safety, security and timing. However, it aims to guarantee an optimal solution, which is as safe as possible. When comparing these works, one will realize that all of them cover safety and security. The work of [1] and [12] even combines safety with security or security and timing. In contrast to this paper, no scientific work integrates a FIA or CIA in their approaches.

So far, it has not been scientifically evaluated how to combine the results of a FIA with a CIA in context of safety-critical systems. Therefore, the approach, which will be presented in this paper, is innovative.

3   Basics

Following, essential basics for the concept of this paper will be presented. These include the FMEA, BBN and the interplay between safety and security.

3.1   Failure Mode and Effects Analysis

Nowadays, the software development process in context of safety-critical systems requires risk assessment. The FMEA is a widely used and established technique and is applied in different domains like, e.g., medical information science, automotive, avionics and railway industry. It is purpose of the FMEA to mitigate risks as much as possible. This is done by detecting and preventing failures. For the failure prevention, it is essential to indicate and to prevent failures in early stages of product cycle. The later a failure will be indicated the more expensive the development costs. Accordingly, the costs will increase about 10 times for each posterior stage [2]. The failure detection has four essential goals:

1. Detection of possible fault sources, which can cause failures
2. All causes and consequences must be identified, mitigated or avoided
3. Faultless organization of process during the development cycle
4. Vulnerabilities of the system, products or processes must be identified in order that a constructive revision can be performed.

To prevent and detect failures it is necessary to determine potential risks by means of the FMEA. whereas occurrence complies with the probability whether a hazard occurs. Severity corresponds to the severity of hazard. The detection complies with the probability that a hazard will be detected. Each of the three factors can range between 1 and 10, i.e., the RPN can range between 1 and 1000. In general, the lower the RPN the better the potential risk. Depending on the value of the RPN, the degree of risk and the necessity of CMs can be identified by means of Table 1 [2].

Table 1. Interpretation of the RPN [3]

RPN	Risk of error	Counter measure
RPN = 1	None	No CMs required
$2 \leq RPN \leq 50$	Acceptable	Additional warning required
$50 < RPN \leq 250$	Medium	Additional protective CMs required
$250 < RPN \leq 1000$	High	Constructive CMs absolutely required

3.2 Bayesian Belief Networks

BBN are highly complex networks which represent the probabilities of conditional dependencies of variables. Many research approaches of plenty research fields used or described BBN, e.g., [8], [17] or [4]. As a detailed description is out of scope in this paper, the most important parts are described afterwards. The formulas and theorems are abstracted from [14]. BBN are probabilistic, graphical models which are used to represent and calculate the conditional probabilities of model elements. Important characteristics are directed and acyclic relations, random variables with discrete states and dependencies to ancestor and descendant nodes. These networks are not restricted to a specific field. The majority of use cases for BBN are networks with questions about dependent probabilities of nodes with different possible states, e.g., the determination of correctness of a disease test. To determine the corresponding conditional probability distribution of every node in the graph a Conditional Probability Table (CPT) has to be defined. This table contains all possible combinations of the diverse states of ancestor nodes to determine the probability of these combinations. Depending on the leading question a model can be analyzed with different approaches and formulas. However, these are the required formulas of our approach:

Bayesian Theorem: $P(B|A) = P(A|B) * P(B)/P(A)$
Conditional Independencies: $P(AB) = P(A) * P(B)$

Markov Assumption/Joint Probability: $P(X) = \prod_{i=1}^{n} P(X_i|ancestor(X_i))$.

3.3 Influences of Security on Safety

Nowadays, it is possible that security violates safety aspects. The following example from the past demonstrates this scenario in more detail. Due to the terrorist attacks of September 11th, 2001 on the World Trade Center in New York City it has been decided to perform stricter security measures. Given the fact that the airplanes from the terrorist attacks has been hijacked a security measure has been introduced that the access to the cockpit is denied during the flight. This security precaution became an obstacle for the Germanwings flight 4U9525 on March 24th, 2015, which crashed in the French Alps. The captain within the cockpit has full control over the door and can even inhibit emergency access. Based on voice records, the co-pilot is suspected of deliberately destroying the plane while preventing the captain from reentering the cockpit. This means, increasing security against hijackers intensified reliance on the pilot being left on his one and carrying full responsibility for flying the airplane [19]. As demonstrated by this example, security has decisive impacts on safety.

4 Concept

After presenting related work and required basics we introduce our impact approach. The concept is based on diverse architecture analysis approaches, which are mighty tools in the design phase of system development. These kinds of analyses can check different aspects depending on the application field and the leading question of analysis. One field is Enterprise Architecture Management (EAM), which uses the analyses to outline and check coherences of business components, relations and processes. [15] provides an overview and classification of these analysis types with their several aims and techniques.

The concept of this paper is subdivided into four essential steps, which are presented in Fig. 1. First, it is necessary to define a SGH in order to model safety-critical matters and to take trade-offs into account. On the basis of this SGH, potential failures will be identified by applying the FMEA. Step 3 conducts a FIA to determine impacts and effects of these potential failures and aims in identifying components which requires CMs. However, applying new CMs involve modifying other goals within the SGH. These goals will be identified and the effect types are determined. The following subsections will cover the aforementioned steps in more detail.

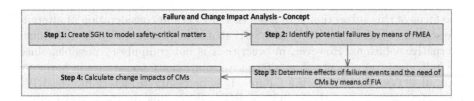

Fig. 1. Concept picture of the approach

4.1 Modeling SGH

The SGH (cf. Fig. 2) is a hierarchical structure, i.e., there must be a root goal, which represents a safety aspect like, e.g., a system or a part of is acceptably safe. The root goal is refined by further safety-critical concerns, which influence the safety of this goal. These include, e.g., security or timing. Goals, which cannot be refined anymore are called Point of Vulnerabilities (POVs) and thus represent vulnerabilities of a system. Goals and POVs must accomplish quality attributes, i.e., they are annotated with attributes including a valid range of values. For instance, the goal *Airbag triggers in time* should be annotated with attribute `triggerTime` and range of values $0 <$ `triggerTime` ≤ 100 ms. In safety-critical systems there is a number of hardware components or software components installed, which have different safety requirements than other components, i.e., an individual component set must be defined for which the SGH should be applied. In this context, we speak about alternative solutions. Each of the alternative solutions accords with the aforementioned POV to a different extent.

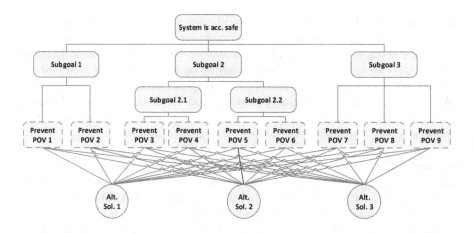

Fig. 2. Basic structure of a SGH supporting three alternative solutions

4.2 Identifying Failures

The focus of this subsection is to asses risk of POVs in consideration of alternative solutions. Ideally, all POVs of a SGH should be prevented by the individual alternative solutions. However, in practice it is not compulsory possible, since the individual components of an alternative solution are not always in harmony with all POVs. To identify the failures, it is necessary to determine the RPN values (cf. Sect. 3.1) of the individual POVs depending on the corresponding alternative solutions. This means in particular that we first need the probabilities of occurrence, severity and detection in order to finally determine the RPN assessments of them (cf. Sect. 3.1). Subsequently, it is necessary to classify the resulting RPN according to Table 1. If there is a risk of error classified with *medium* or *high*, i.e., $50 \leq RPN \leq 1000$ it is mandatory to identify the related elements with a need of corresponding CMs, which will be described in Sect. 4.3.

4.3 Failure Impact Analysis

After the identification of a potential failure we have to analyze the impacts on other elements. Since we already know the theoretical causal relation of a failure we do not have to analyze our system top-down. Therefore, we have to apply a bottom-up approach to monitor effects on elements which are logical dependent on the faulty element. Components which are highly negative affected by the failure have to be adapted by CMs. Architecture analyses are a possibility to identify these elements. As described above, EAM already uses these analyses successfully what yields us to conduct a concept transfer of a FIA approach by [6]. However, a few important aspects have to be changed to make the approach suitable for safety-critical systems. The most important change is the type of leading question for analysis as [6] analyzing their system top-down. Therefore, we need to shift metrics, variables, tools and use other BBN formulas.

Our FIA approach is divided in 5 (**A–E**) steps to clarify the execution of the analysis:

(**A**) A graphical representation of the whole system or of a specific process/service is required. To model our system we adapted on ArchiMate version 3.0.1 since it is an updated version with elements for Internet of Things (IoT) systems, which are kinds of safety-critical systems. Therefore, we distinguish between active/passive structure elements and behavioral elements for the representation of nodes. In addition, there are 11 relation types categorized in 4 classes which address diverse connections concerning structure, dependency and other aspects. Depending on the use case different layered approaches can be used. Exemplary, a layered architecture approach for IoT is presented in Fig. 3. This approach differs strongly from EAM layers as IoT systems have other features like openness, flexibility, connection of autonomous devices with each other to measure and send data, etc. The presented layered approach is based on [13] and [7] and consists of 8 layers.

(**B**) Before mapping the model into a BBN model an analysis attribute, e.g., availability, has to be chosen. Depending on this attribute the BBN relations respectively dependencies can be determined.

(**C**) Translation of the model into a BBN structure to enable the modeling of probabilistic dependencies and the prediction capabilities. To transform the system model we conduct two sub-steps. First, we map every system element into a BBN node, i.e., variable. Thereby, all different kinds of element types transform and remain in the same layer. However, if an element is not involved into the dependency structure it will be excluded. Secondly, the relation transformation has to be conducted depending on the attribute defined in (B). Every system relation is mapped to a causal BBN relation. Attention should be paid to the

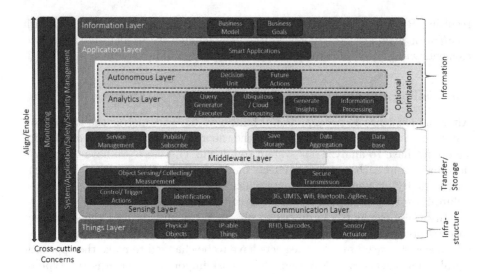

Fig. 3. Layered architecture for IoT systems

BBN characteristics presented in Sect. 3.2. Therefore, all acyclic or undirected relations of the system model have to be deleted or modified.

(D) Discretization of variables and determination of CPTs. As every BBN node represents a variable the variables' attributes get discretized and the corresponding probabilities are determined, e.g., a node *Weather* has the discrete attribute states with probabilities "Sunny = 95%" and "Rainy = 5%". Afterwards, the CPTs of every variable have to be defined including all possible combinations of the node's parents. This can be conducted by expert interviews, estimations or historical data analysis. To identify the impact of a failure we have to determine the nodes' probabilities before the occurrence of the failure. If causes of a failure have to be identified the Bayesian Theorem is used. However, if impacts of a failure are the focus of the analysis the Joint Probability formula is used with CPT values to identify the conditional probability of effects spreading out to the node.

(E) Calculation of impacts and determination of point for CM application. After the determination of the BBN model including probability states the failure is simulated and the probability of the faulty node is set accordingly. Consequently, the CPTs and probabilities of the BBN model have to be updated. The update can be conducted through new interviews or statistical calculations. Following this, a delta of probabilities of the nodes, before and after the failure, emerges which represents the impacts. This delta has to be evaluated by experts or a predefined scale, which divides the impacts into categories. Elements in a category of highly negative impact triggered by failures need CMs. As a last step the most affected layer can be identified.

4.4   Change Impact Analysis

Assuming that experts have realized CMs in the last step, a CIA is needed to analyze which kind of effects necessary CMs will have. As a CM can require new nodes or the elimination of nodes, i.e., the SGH requires an update. Only an updated SGH can be used to evaluate the new safety-as-is status of an model in the future. First, it must be clarified which node types of the SGH are affected by the CIA and in which direction (top-down ↓ or bottom-up ↑) the impacts will be propagandized:

1. Goal → Goal: ↓↑
2. Goal → POV: ↓
3. POV → Goal: ↑
4. POV → Alternative Solution: ↓.

This means, that an amendment of a goal can have both impacts on goals with higher abstraction level and goals with lower abstraction level. Moreover, POVs are involved as well. Modifications regarding POVs will affect goals on the next overlying layer. Furthermore, amendments of the POVs directly influence the alternative solutions. To perform the CIA step by step we need impact rules [10] with the following syntax:

$$\texttt{A.X} \to \texttt{B.Y}$$

In general, this statement expresses if source element $\texttt{A}$ has the characteristic $\texttt{X}$, it follows that target element $\texttt{B}$ has the characteristic $\texttt{Y}$. Concretely, this implies $\texttt{A} \in \{Goal, POV\}$ and $\texttt{B} \in \texttt{A} \cup \{AlternativeSolution\}$. The operations or effects, which are represented by $\texttt{X}$ and $\texttt{Y}$ are defined as follows: $\texttt{X,Y} \in \{noEffect, extend, modify, delete\}$. Extending a SGH element means to refine an element, e.g., by adding new elements. If an element is modified, the necessary information will be updated. Deleting a SGH element implies to remove it from the SGH. For instance, if the impact rule $\texttt{G1.modify} \to \texttt{G2.extend}$ is applied, it means that $G1$ will be modified and, in this regard $G2$ must be extended as an impact. In this paper, we distinguish between Best-Case (BC) and Worst-Case (WC) CIA. The first one requires a minimum number of change impacts or lightweight change impacts and vice versa for the WC analysis. In the following, we define the change impact rules for the SGH, split into BC and WC (cf. Table 2). Hereinafter, the WC rules are explained in more detail. In case of deleting, modifying or extending a goal, the underlying goal or POV must deleted, modified or extended as well. Furthermore, if a goal or POV is deleted, modified or extended the overlying goal must be modified in each case since information of the child nodes must be transmitted onto the corresponding parent node. The consequence of amendments on POVs is modifying all concerned alternative solutions. This can be justified by the fact that solutions directly and only depend on the POVs.

So far, it was not specified to what extent the rules must be applied. Therefore, an algorithm (cf. Algorithm 1) is needed to consider this. The CIA is started initially by means of an impact rule according to Table 2. Subsequently, it is performed recursively until no more rules can be applied. Since the effects of some

Table 2. Change impact rules

	BC	WC
Goal → Goal ↓ Goal → POV ↓	A.delete → B.extend A.modify → B.noEffect A.extend → B.modify	A.delete → B.delete A.modify → B.modify A.extend → B.extend
Goal → Goal ↑ POV → Goal ↑	A.delete → B.extend A.modify → B.noEffect A.extend → B.modify	A.delete→ B.modify A.modify → B.modify A.extend → B.modify
POV → Alternative Solution ↓	A.delete → B.noEffect A.modify → B.noEffect A.extend → B.noEffect	A.delete → B.modify A.modify → B.modify A.extend → B.modify

---

Algorithm 1. Change Impact Analysis

1: **procedure** CHANGEIMPACTANALYSIS(node, operation)
2:    **if** node **isTypeOf** *Goal* **then**
3:        **if** *checkPrefAndApplyRule(node, getParentGoal(node), operation)* **then**
4:            *changeImpactAnalysis(g, getEffectType(node, operation))*
5:        **end if**
6:        **for all** *cg* ∈ *childGoals* **do**
7:            **if** *checkPrefAndApplyRule(node, cg, operation)* **then**
8:                *changeImpactAnalysis(g, getEffectType(node, operation))*
9:            **end if**
10:      **end for**
11:      **for all** *pov* ∈ *POVs* **do**
12:          **if** *checkPrefAndApplyRule(node, pov, operation)* **then**
13:              *changeImpactAnalysis(pov, getEffectType(node, operation))*
14:          **end if**
15:      **end for**
16: **else**
17:      **if** *checkPrefAndApplyRule(node, getParentGoal(node), operation)* **then**
18:          *changeImpactAnalysis(g, getEffectType(node, operation))*
19:      **end if**
20:      **for all** *s* ∈ *solutions* **do**
21:          *ApplyRule(node, s, operation)*
22:      **end for**
23: **end if**
24: **end procedure**

---

goals, POVs or solutions would be set multiple it is mandatory to define preferences of the effects types depending on BC or WC calculation. In case of BC the preferences are defined as *delete* $\succ_P$ *modify* $\succ_P$ *extend* whereas for WC the preferences are defined as follows: *extend* $\succ_P$ *modify* $\succ_P$ *delete*. This is due to the fact that it is more complex to extend a node more as to delete it. The resulting set of nodes including effect types, which must be enhanced by applying Algorithm 1 is defined as A_{CI}. So far, A_{CI} only consider the hierarchical structure of the SGH, but not any semantics within the SGH. Therefore, we also need the attributation within the SGH as proposed in Sect. 4.1. If the constraints of an attribute are violated because of invalid values, the SGH must be browsed for nodes with the same attributes and range of values. The set of all matches within the SGH is defined as B_{CI}. The final result of the CIA C_{CI}, i.e., the set of nodes which are affected by the violation of any constraints is defined as follows: $C_{CI} = A_{CI} \cap B_{CI}$.

5   Evaluation

After presenting the steps of our approach we conduct the evaluation with aid of a medical use case. As mentioned before IoT is a kind of safety-critical system if devices with safety goals are included, like IoT of medical devices or medical smart homes. Therefore, we use a system for Ambient Assisted Living (AAL) to evaluate our approach. Figure 4 depicts an exemplary AAL system with 4 medical or wellbeing devices delivering health support. As it exceeds the scope of our evaluation, just a small cutout of the system is shown and only 5 layers of the presented layered architecture in Sect. 4.3 are visible. The devices include sensors, actuators or RFID tags to measure and to trigger actions. For instance, the insulin pump measures data which are sent to the IoT-Hub which reviews the data and to trigger the SOS call if necessary.

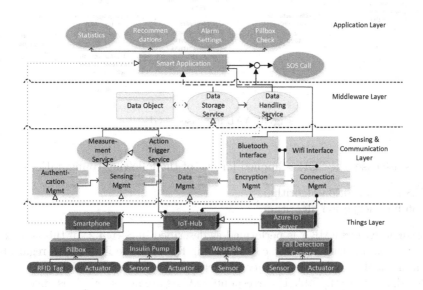

Fig. 4. AAL use case - medical smart home

Step 1 and 2: First, we need to create a SGH (cf. Fig. 5) representing an AAL, which is acceptably safe. For this purpose, the root node *AAL is acceptably safe* representing a safety goal is mandatory. The AAL SGH is further refined in consideration of the following context: For the success of an AAL system correctly functioning of the AAL sensors is a prerequisite, e.g., insulin pump sensors. Furthermore, AAL actuators must work correctly, e.g., activating pillbox. Moreover, the software running on an AAL system must work correctly. To ensure this, results of calculations must be correct and be performed in time without any delay. In addition, software must be acceptably secure against third party hacking attacks. The fourth aspect, which has been taken into account is the reliability of the AAL communication. For this purpose, the system must be secured against data theft and manipulation. Moreover, messages must be correctly transferred in time. As mentioned in Sect. 4.1 all nodes within the SGH must be annotated with an attribute. These attributes will be described in detail in step 4. The SGH of the AAL use case is extended by two alternative solutions.

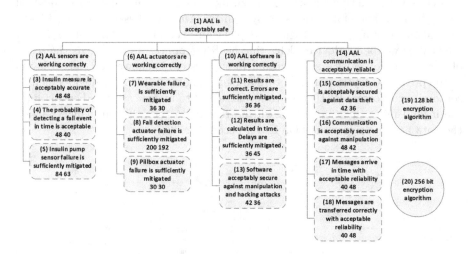

Fig. 5. AAL use case - SGH

In this use case, the SGH is applied for one of the following configurations:

1. 128 bit encryption algorithm
2. 256 bit encryption algorithm.

Subsequently, the FMEA is performed as described in Sect. 4.2. In this context, it is essential to determine the corresponding RPNs of the POVs with regard to the individual alternative solutions. If there is a RPN classified with medium or high risk of error (cf. Table 1) corresponding CMs are necessary. This affects two of the POVs: *Insulin pump sensor failure is sufficiently mitigated*, rated with a RPN of 84 or 63 and *Fall detection actuator failure is sufficiently mitigated*, which is rated with 200 or 192. An insulin pump sensor failure means that blood glucose level cannot be measured correctly. If the fall detection actuator fails, the SOS call cannot be performed.

Step 3: As the FMEA results yield potential failures in two nodes we have to check these nodes for impacts in case of a failure to be able to identify elements with a need of CMs. In the following case we merely inspect the failure event of node *Sensor* of the insulin pump. The FIA is conducted with the steps described in Sect. 4.3.

(A) The graphical representation of our use case is already shown in Fig. 4 including different kinds of element and relation types of an AAL.

(B) As described, we need to choose an analysis attribute to be able to map the system into the BBN model accurately. As the diverse nodes can have multiple attributes we have to elect an attribute which is most suitable for the predictive leading analysis question. As we want to spot the impact of a failure of a data measuring node we decide to choose data quality as the analysis attribute. We define data quality as a combination of reliability, accurate amount of data measure sets and data intervals. To simplify the next step and the whole analysis we constrain data quality to correct data intervals as a irregular measurement can lead to faulty results.

(C) After having chosen the attribute we conduct the BBN mapping. At first, we map the system nodes into BBN nodes. In this use case we are able to transfer every element to a BBN node except the *Data Object*. This element has no dependencies for data intervals. Afterwards, we map the system relations into BBN relations. Hereby, we have to keep in mind the chosen analysis attribute as the conditional BBN relations can vary depending on the attribute. As this use case is highly dependent on data measurement we are able to transfer every directed relation. However, only some undirected relations could be modified and mapped. Figure 6 presents, i.a., the results of the mapping step.

(D) To determine the probabilities we have to discretize our analysis attribute data quality. As we consider the timing aspect of data quality we discretize the variables with the states "Up" for accomplishing the data interval and "Down" for contravening the interval. Afterwards, every node, i.e. variable, is assigned its own probability for both states. Once, the probabilities are set the CPTs are determined for every node depending on the combinations of their ancestor states. For instance, the probabilities of the *insulin pump* are "Up = 60%" and "Down = 40%" as well as "Up = 45%" and "Down = 55%" for the *wearable*. Table 3 shows a exemplary CPT of the IoT Hub. To be able to simulate the model random numbers were chosen for this use case. The scope of Fig. 6 impeded the illustration of all probabilities and CPTs on the according nodes.

(E) As a last step we want to identify the impacts of the insulin pump sensor failure. As the probabilities before the failure event are already determined we can simulate the failure now by setting the probability of the sensor on "Down = 100%". Accordingly, all nodes which depend on the sensor have to update their probability and CPTs. Therefor, the Joint Probability formula by multiplying the CPTs is used. Afterwards, the delta of probabilities before and after the failure event can be identified. We present an exemplary impact

Table 3. CPT example

Insulin pump	Wearable	U	D
U	U	0.9	0.1
D	D	0,01	0,99
U	D	0,4	0,6
D	U	0,3	0,7

identification on the nodes *Measurement Service* and *Connection Management*. For instance, Fig. 6 displays the faulty sensor and the probabilities of both nodes for the attribute data quality before and after the failure. Since both nodes are negatively affected which leads to deterioration of more than 40%, both nodes need CMs to be prepared in case of a failure.

After the identification of effected nodes we have to transfer the knowledge to find the matching POV.

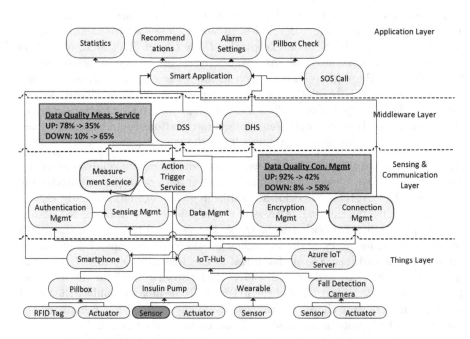

Fig. 6. BBN after Model Mapping with conducted analysis results

Step 4: Deductive to step 3, there is a CM necessary for the POV *Messages arrive in time with acceptable reliability*. However, it must be checked if there are further nodes within the SGH, which must be amended as well. Therefore, we need to apply the change impact rules according to Table 2. First, we have to check for the nodes' attributes which were annotated in step 1 and 2. Since we examine within this evaluation data quality, we annotated the corresponding nodes within the SGH with a suitable attribute. To match the analysis attribute data quality we use the node attribute `timeLimit` for the POVs *Results are calculated in time. Delays are sufficiently mitigated.* and *Messages arrive in time with acceptable reliability* as well as for the solutions *128 bit encryption algorithm* and *256 bit encryption algorithm.* Each of them are tagged with `timeLimit` = 200, i.e., there is a maximum time limit of 200 ms in order to achieve the goals.

In this use case, we consider the WC scenario, i.e., $A_{CI} = \{1, ..., 20\}$ and $B_{CI} = \{12, 17, 19, 20\}$. The entire sequence of change impact rules (necessary for A_{CI}) for this use case is listed in Table 4. According to Sect. 4.4 $C_{CI} = A_{CI} \cap B_{CI}$, i.e., $C_{CI} = \{12, 17, 19, 20\}$ since these nodes are also annotated with the corresponding `timeLimit` attribute. In summary, POV #17 from which the CIA has been started must be either deleted, modified or extended depending on CM action of #17. In addition, goal #12 and the solutions #19 and #20 must be modified. The CIA of this use case explicitly considers the specified time limit. When amending timing-critical goals or POVs, reliability is also fulfilled since messages arrive in time or calculations are performed in time. In this way, the desired number of messages or calculations can be done within a specified time limit.

Table 4. AAL use case - sequence of change impact rules (WC)

delete	modify	extend
{17}.delete → {14}.modify	{17}.modify → {14}.modify	{17}.extend → {14}.modify
	{14}.modify → {1}.modify	
	{1}.modify → {2,6,10,14}.modify	
	{2}.modify → {3,4,5}.modify	
	{6}.modify → {7,8,9}.modify	
	{10}.modify → {11,12,13}.modify	
	{14}.modify → {15,16,17,18}.modify	
	{3-5,7-9,11-13,15-18}.mod → {19,20}.modify	

In summary, we analyzed a medical AAL system for potential failures, their impacts and effects of realized CMs.

6   Conclusion and Outlook

In this paper, an approach has been presented in order to perform a FIA and a CIA in context of safety-critical systems, which has been demonstrated for a medical use case. For this purpose some prerequisites must be met: An attributed SGH is required with subsequent FMEA analysis to identify potential failures. Afterwards, the impact of a failure event have been identified including the need of CMs by the usage of a FIA. Finally, we examine the effects of CMs through applying the change impact rules of the CIA. Due to the complexity of safety-critical systems, the utilization of impact analyses during design phase is becoming increasingly important. For future work, it might be useful to automatize some processes of this approach in order to renounce expert knowledge. These include, e.g., automation of CPT or a semantical analysis within the SGH. Furthermore, it might be useful to extend the approach of this paper by software product lines as used in [11].

Acknowledgment. This work has been partially supported by the German Federal Ministry of Economics and Technology (BMWi) in the framework of the Central Innovation Program SME (Zentrales Innovationsprogramm Mittelstand) within the project CBMD (https://www.informatik.uni-augsburg.de/en/chairs/swt/ds/projects/mde/cbmd/).

References

1. SESAMO Project (2015). http://sesamo-project.eu/. Accessed 31 Jan
2. Bertsche, B., Göhner, P., Jensen, U., Schinköthe, W., Wunderlich, H.J.: Zuverlässigkeit mechatronischer Systeme, Grundlagen und Bewertungen in frühen Entwicklungsphasen. Springer, Heidelberg (2009)
3. Bundesverwaltungsamt: Fehlermöglichkeits- und einflussanalyse (FMEA). Organisationshandbuch (2017)
4. Cai, B., Huang, L., Xie, M.: Bayesian networks in fault diagnosis. IEEE Trans. Ind. Inform. **13**(5), 2227–2240 (2017). https://doi.org/10.1109/TII.2017.2695583
5. Hanemann, A., Schmitz, D., Sailer, M.: A framework for failure impact analysis and recovery with respect to service level agreements. In: 2005 IEEE International Conference on Services Computing (SCC 2005), vol. 1 (2005)
6. Holschke, O., Närman, P., Flores, W.R., Eriksson, E., Schönherr, M.: Using enterprise architecture models and Bayesian belief networks for failure impact analysis. In: Feuerlicht, G., Lamersdorf, W. (eds.) ICSOC 2008. LNCS, vol. 5472, pp. 339–350. Springer, Heidelberg (2009). https://doi.org/10.1007/978-3-642-01247-1_35
7. Khan, R., Khan, S.U., Zaheer, R., Khan, S.: Future internet: the internet of things architecture, possible applications and key challenges. In: 2012 10th International Conference on Frontiers of Information Technology. IEEE (2012)
8. Koski, T., Noble, J.: Bayesian Networks: An Introduction, vol. 924. Wiley, Hoboken (2011)
9. Kristen, E., Althammer, E.: FlexRay robustness testing contributing to automated safety certification. In: Koornneef, F., van Gulijk, C. (eds.) SAFECOMP 2015. LNCS, vol. 9338, pp. 201–211. Springer, Cham (2015). https://doi.org/10.1007/978-3-319-24249-1_18
10. Langermeier, M., Saad, C., Bauer, B.: Adaptive approach for impact analysis in enterprise architectures. In: Shishkov, B. (ed.) BMSD 2014. LNBIP, vol. 220, pp. 22–42. Springer, Cham (2015). https://doi.org/10.1007/978-3-319-20052-1_2
11. Lohmüller, P., Bauer, B.: Software product line engineering for safety-critical systems. In: Proceedings of the 7th International Conference on Model-Driven Engineering and Software Development - Volume 1: MODELSWARD, Prague, Czech Republic (2019). https://doi.org/10.5220/0007246102110218

12. Lohmüller, P., Fendt, A., Bauer, B.: Multi-concerns engineering for safety-critical systems. In: Proceedings of the 6th International Conference on Model-Driven Engineering and Software Development - Volume 1: MODELSWARD, Funchal, Portugal (2018). https://doi.org/10.5220/0006631705040510
13. Microsoft: Azure IoT reference architecture - version 2.0. Download Center (2018)
14. Neapolitan, R.E., et al.: Learning Bayesian Networks, vol. 38. Pearson Prentice Hall, Upper Saddle River (2004)
15. Rauscher, J., Langermeier, M., Bauer, B.: Classification and definition of an enterprise architecture analyses language. In: Shishkov, B. (ed.) BMSD 2016. LNBIP, vol. 275, pp. 119–139. Springer, Cham (2017). https://doi.org/10.1007/978-3-319-57222-2_6
16. Ren, X., Shah, F., Tip, F., Ryder, B.G., Chesley, O.: Chianti: a tool for change impact analysis of java programs. In: Proceedings of the 19th Annual ACM SIGPLAN Conference on Object-oriented Programming, Systems, Languages, and Applications, pp. 432–448 (2004)
17. Shin, J., Son, H., Heo, G., et al.: Development of a cyber security risk model using bayesian networks. Reliability Eng. Syst. Safety **134**, 208–217 (2015)
18. Viega, J., McGraw, G.R.: Building Secure Software: How to Avoid Security Problems the Right Way, Portable Documents. Pearson Education, Essex (2001)
19. Yu, Y.: Germanwings flight 4u9525: a victim of the deadlock between safety and security demands (2015). http://theconversation.com/germanwings-flight-4u9525-a-victim-of-the-deadlock-between-safety-and-security-demands-39386. Accessed 3 May 2019

Chasing the Crowd: Digital Transformations and the Digital Driven System Design Paradigm

Ivan I. Ivanov[(✉)]

Empire State College of the State University of New York,
Hauppauge, NY 11788, USA
ivan.ivanov@esc.edu

Abstract. These days business successes and economic opportunities steadily depend on IT-capabilities and digital driven business transformations. Digitalization continues to advance with new business models and growing prospects in various dimensions from higher margins and greater public sector funding to new customers, markets and more diverse suppliers' networks. The key digital transformation drivers of change –fundamental redesign of business activities, processes, and models– are each significantly facilitated by integrated mix of digital technologies that includes, but not limited to, social, mobile, analytics and cloud (SMAC) and sometimes SMACIT when counting the Internet of Things. Increasingly the actual digital transformation has much more to do with information, data, analytics, workflow, culture, and management than traditional IT/IS. In the last decades IT/IS has been essential driver of organizational changes, the recent developments in digitalization and innovations shifted the emphasis on the *information* rather than the *technology* in "IT" abbreviation. To understand the prospects and challenges associate with the digital driven business strategy and operational transformations, a modified model of the socio-technical system is created and presented. It depicts at macro level how digital technologies and utility type computing platforms act as drivers for supporting digital business strategies and advancing with the customers. While it simplifies the relations of the internal organization socio-technical model with the external world, the *enhanced socio-technical (EST) model* indicates the interactions of the four organization's forces: structure, people, technology and processes with the platform technologies such as O2O and SMACIT and further with the crowds. The paper confers the impact of digital driven transformations to the system design and development process and specifically emphasizes on agile transformational practices aligning better with business agility, asset utilization, and greater customers' satisfaction.

Keywords: Enhanced Socio-Technical (EST) model · Digital transformation · Digital technologies · SMAC · SMACIT · Systemic effect · Agile transformational approach · Crowd business models · Utility type digital platforms

© Springer Nature Switzerland AG 2019
B. Shishkov (Ed.): BMSD 2019, LNBIP 356, pp. 64–80, 2019.
https://doi.org/10.1007/978-3-030-24854-3_5

1 Digital Transformation and the Crowd

These days business successes and economic opportunities steadily depend on IT-capabilities and digital driven transformations. Digitalization continues to advance with new digital driven business models and growing prospects in various dimensions from higher margins and greater public sector funding to new markets and customers and more diverse supplier networks. We have witnessed radically changes in companies' digital capabilities, services, collecting and exploring data and all focusing on enabling business agility and driving greater revenue.

Large number of current studies indicates that in the recent economic reality where many industries are disrupted, *data* and *information* have become critical enablers and core business assets, fostering a data-driven business strategy. Most of the advancing businesses embrace digital transformation strategies to create value through reshaping of critical customer touching business processes and operations. The key digital transformation drivers of change –fundamental redesign of business activities, processes, and models– are each significantly facilitated by integrating a mix of digital technologies that includes, but not limited to *social, mobile, analytics* and *cloud* (SMAC) and sometimes SMACIT when counting the *Internet of Things*. Even though the actual digital transformation may have much more to do with information, data, analytics, workflow, culture, and management than traditional IT/IS, the latter is often seen as a miraculous remedy which can magically transform an organization into a lean, trim version of its former self with a least possible effort. While in the last decades IT/IS has been essential driver of organizational changes, the recent developments in digitalization and innovations shifted the emphasis on *the information* rather than the *technology* in the "IT" acronym. As it will be discussed later in the paper, this new development directly triggers "systemic effect" affecting the four key components of the Socio-Technical system -structure, people, technology, and processes- and amplifies the power of the new digital platforms to exploit data, extend the reach and driving profits.

The 2018 Gartner CIO Agenda Report [1] reveals the rationales of transforming the CIO's role from "delivery executive to business executive" and the importance of this change in the "structure" component to promote and support digital business operations. Among the most substantial challenges of the new role are leading the digital transformations, fostering a data-driven business strategy, building a culture of innovation leadership, and utilizing security analytics. McKinsey analysis "Why CIOs should be business-strategy partners" argues that IT performance and capabilities increase significantly when CIOs are involved in shaping the business strategy. In addition, there is a very high correlation between IT ability to innovate and the level of overall satisfaction with IT [2]. Carry on data and innovation is a force driving not only IT ecosystem forward, but delivering new methods to collaborate, adapting new approaches for designing and developing systems, and do business over-all. It is time for the CIOs to use data-driven methods, to take advantage of and adapt new platform technologies, to prioritize and manage performance metrics when take direction from business objectives and strategy and align with them [3].

This paper is structured as follows. Section 2 discusses a possible Framework of Digital Transformation strategy and more specifically the driving digital strategy core components and the concept of *enhanced socio-technical* EST system. It also highlights the necessities of digital technologies bridges to closing the gaps between current state and desired long-term strategy. Section 3 determines the key alterations of the traditional SDLC vs. Driving Digital Paradigm in terms of directing digital business objectives. Section 4 précises and analyzes key findings in driving digital transformations. Section 5 summarizes and concludes the paper.

2   A Background of Digital Transformation Strategy

To better understand the evolution to digital transformation strategy, it is important to know the basic business mindset when doing so, which ultimately begins with a discussion on *strategy*. Some authors state that strategy cannot be planned, since doing so would suggest a controlled environment. These theorists state that strategy happens in an uncontrolled environment, thus it is more useful to consider it to be an art or tool over a plan [4].

According to the online business dictionary "…the objective of strategic management is to achieve better alignment of corporate policies and strategic priorities." "A brilliant strategy or breakthrough technology can put any company on the competitive map, but only solid execution can keep it there" [5]. Essentially, three major phases formulate this process: *Strategic Thinking*, *Strategic Planning*, and *Strategic Momentum* [6]. Strategic Thinking is a phase when the organization should grasp both the detailed view of itself: what it does well & what seems to be lacking; and the systematic picture of the external environment. Strategic Plannins is the next phase when a situational examination, such as SWOT -Strengths, Weaknesses, Opportunities, Threats- analysis should be performed based on the previous stage findings. The final stage of Strategic Momentum includes formulating the strategy and the plan for its implementation. The essence of **Strategy** according to Harvard Business School professor and one of the world's most advanced thinkers on strategy - Michael Porter is *"about being different."* Which means a company to choose for their core business different and unique set of activities or to perform already known activities in a different way. With a set of activities, different from those of the other competitors in an industry, a company winning strategy means creation of "unique and valuable position" on the market [7].

2.1   Industry Analysis and the Role of Digital Technologies

Speak of Michael Porter theory on strategy again, the structure of an industry is embodied in five forces that collectively determine profitability and should be considered in strategic formulation: Rivalry among Existing Competitors, Bargaining Power of Buyers, Threat of Substitute Products or Services; Bargaining Power of Suppliers; Threat of New Entrants. The shared power of the five forces varies for different industries as does the profitability [7]. The model exposes comprehensive outer view of the organization with its traditional direct competitors and the correlation with four other forces within its market environment.

The first force, Rivalry among Existing Competitors, represents the magnitude to which fierce battling for position and aggressive competition occur in the industry. The term *hyper-competition* refers to industries characterized by fierce rivalry among existing firms and very rapid pace of innovations leading to fast obsolescence of any competitive advantage and a consequent need for a fast cycle of innovations. The consumer electronic industry –mobile and smart devices in particular- is the most current example as *hyper-competition*. The second force Bargaining Power of Buyers, signifies the extent to which customers of those organizations in the industry have the ability to put downward pressure on prices, highly concentrated buyers (such as Amazon, Wal-Mart, Home Depot, Costco) and low switching costs typically conspire to increase the bargaining power of buyers. The Threat of Substitute Products or Services force denotes the extent to which the products or services marketed by the company are subject to potential substitution by different products or services that fulfill the same customer needs and expectations. The fourth force, Bargaining Power of Suppliers, represents the magnitude to which the firms or individuals who sell fabrication input to other organizations in the industry have the ability to maintain high prices. The Threat of New Entrants force represents the extent to which the industry is open to entry by new competitors, or whether significant barriers to entry make it creates comfortable shelter, so the existing firms need not to worry about competition from outside.

The industry analysis framework suggests that industry differences can be analyzed a priori by managers using the Porter's analytical framework, and based upon the results of this analysis, executives can decide whether to enter an industry or forgo investment. Scholars and experts who have embraced industry analysis to search and identify technology-dependent strategic initiatives and opportunities advise to consider information systems effects on one or more of the industry forces, thereby tipping it to the company's advantage or preventing foreseeable losses. Investment in and the use of emerging technologies could raise or increase barriers to entry in the industry. In so doing the existing firms would reduce the threat of new entrants. This particular option is most likely applicable in information technology intense and highly regulated industries such as Healthcare, Banking, and Finance [4].

Essentially advances in the digital technologies are transforming many industries as structure, services and operating models and alter each of the discussed above five competitive forces, creating the need and opportunity for changes and thriving industries' products as well. The far and wide adoption of SMACIT technologies, and more specifically data analytics products, searches and online transactions, contribute immensely to shifting power away from suppliers, so toward buyers. As much as digital technologies help firms to unlock the value in the vast amounts of data they collect and strengthen their bargaining position toward either suppliers or buyers, the similar process of monetizing data also could reduce their bargaining power just before either one. While Porter's five competitive forces model is truly important when strategic planning and managerial decisions are taken, the impact of key internal forces clearly associated with the digital transformations are particularly critical to the operational effectiveness and to find new ways to shape the organizational business strategy and benefits.

2.2   The Evolution of Socio-Technical System

To explore the complexity of the problems inside organizations, and to avoid unrealistic expectations when aligning technologies and processes to the business strategy, a formal methodology of examining and evaluating technology capabilities in the organizational context should be applied. According McKeen, Smith and Singh [8], "capability is the ability to marshal resources to affect a predetermined outcome." The core digital technology capabilities are discussed later in the paper and they are critical to meet the enduring challenges of digital driven business strategy, designing and delivering digital services.

The contemporary Information Systems approaches incorporate multidisciplinary theories and perspectives with no dominance of a single discipline or model. Gabriele Picolli in his Information Systems for Managers text features IT as a critical component of a formal, sociotechnical information system designed to collect, process, store, and distribute information [9]. Kenneth and Jane Laudon in Managing Information Systems define Information Systems as Sociotechnical Systems incorporating two approaches: *Technical* and *Behavioural*, with several major disciplines that contribute knowledge and competency in the study of Information systems [10].

The notion of above definitions is based on the Sociotechnical theory work developed by Tavistock Institute in London in late fifties of the last century. The IS Sociotechnical approach not only visualizes the concept, but reveals the impact of new technologies and processes –the technical subsystem- on the entire organization system, and the dependencies and interactions between all other facets and components of the sociotechnical system. According to Picolli any organization Information System can be represented as a Sociotechnical system which comprises four primary components that must be balanced and work together to deliver the information processing and functionalities required by the organization to fulfill its information needs. The IS Sociotechnical model validates the most important components, and at the same time illustrates primary driving forces, within organizations: structure, people, process, and technology. The first two – *people* and *structure* – shape the *social subsystem*, and represent the human element of the IS. The latter two – *process* and *technology* – contour the *technical subsystem* of the IS and they relate to a wide range of technical resources and services intertwined with a series of steps to complete required business activities [4].

The sociotechnical system approach is instrumental in helping policy and decision makers to strategize and manage organizational change particularly when introducing and implementing new technologies. This approach not only validates the four critical components of the system's interdependency, but proves that none of them works in isolation. They all interact, are mutually dependent, and consequently are subject to *"systemic effects"* - defined as any change in one component affecting all other components of the system. The process of changes and reciprocal adjustment of both technical and social subsystems should continue to interplay and growing closer until a mutually satisfying results are reached. However, the model in reality could not be with equal subsystems' changes. It should grow from micro to macro level to reflect crucial influences of the external environment, including regulatory requirements, social and customers' expectations, business trends, competitive pressures, and to some extend - interoperability of the platforms and systems within associated institutions.

To understand the prospects and challenges associate with the digital driven business strategy and operational transformations, a modified model of the socio-technical system is created and presented at Fig. 1. The figure depicts at macro level how digital technologies and utility type computing platforms act as drivers for supporting digital business strategies and advancing with the customers. While it simplifies the relations of the internal organization socio-technical model with the external world, the enchanced socio-technical model indicates the interactions of the four organization's forces: structure, people, technology and processes with the platform technologies such as SMACIT and further with the crowds.

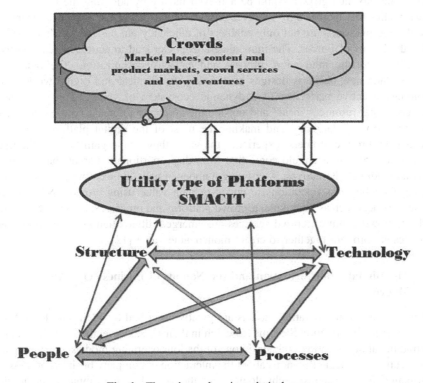

Fig. 1. The enhanced socio-technical system

The enchanced socio-technical (EST) model is holistic and instrumental in helping policy and decision makers to strategize digital transformations and to devise systemic organizational changes towards digital disruptions. Its concept is supported by recent surveys and analyses conducted from Gartner, Forrester, MIT's CISR and other leading consulting companies specifically with regards to *executive* (structure) and *human* (people) changes leading to build a new organizational ecosystem to support digital transformation strategy. The Gartner 2018 CIO survey report put forward "the CIO's role is transforming from delivery executive to business executive" with a broader set of business expectations for growth and profit improvement from economies of scale and scope, new sources of revenue, transformative innovations and sharpened customer focus [1]. The ample of structure change is necessary to build bridges between leaders and "their people," to empower them with knowledge, skills and intelligence provided and supported by single or group of platform technologies. As defined by techopedia, "a platform is a group of technologies or systems that are used as a base upon which other applications, processes or technologies are developed." At present, most of the platform technologies such as SMACIT are available as utility based services or contracted by providers.

While in-house technologies and infrastructure are still important handling the internal systems and external integration, the critical differentiation and advantage in creation and revenue growth could be achieved mostly by adopting the new techno-logical reality that increasingly revolves around digital platforms. The core technolo-gies of these platforms are not only enablers of efficiency but has led to what Gartner called the Nexus of Forces. The immediate effects can lead to actionable/campatitive intelligence, holistic innovation, process and capacity optimization. The outcomes would include new business designs by blurring the physical and digital worlds and becoming an active performer of a dynamic ecosystem of values. This ecosystem connects digital resources inside and outside the company to create new services and value to customers targeting and making the most of the digital platforms and the crowds [11]. From customers' experience the value they would gain through the new channels and platforms should come first from disproportionate market shares versus direct and indirect alternatives. A growing number of new and existing companies are shaping their business operations to create or gain value using crowds. New crowd business models such as marketplace, crowd platform and processes, content & product markets, crowd ventures, crowd services are emerged differentiating themselves how resources are brought together to create monetizable value [12].

2.3   The Digital Transformation and the Notions of Business Operating Models

The well-known four operating models are greatly described by Weill and Ross from MIT Center for Information Systems Research in their IT Savvy textbook [13]. Overall, any traditional organization operates in one of the four operating models, depending on the executives' strategic decisions about the interaction of company business processes, information flow, systems, technologies and the way they contribute value to the organization:

- *diversification model* - organizations operate in a decentralized mode with inde-pendent transactions, unique units with few data standards, most technological decisions are made within the units;
- *coordination model* - is used by organizations that deliver customized services and solutions by unique business units, while accumulating and providing access to integrated data across divisions. The decisions are made in consensus for designing the integrated services, while IT applications are deal with within units;

- *replication model* - typically provides high operational autonomy to business units while requiring highly structured and standardized business processes. All decisions related to IT infrastructure, applications and services are centrally mandated;
- *the unification model* – the organization is centralized and managed with highly integrated and standardized technology and business processes.

In the digital driven transformations, when the business decisions and success depend on accurate and quickly delivered information, digital technologies unquestionably needs to serve as a platform for the business operations. The author of Driving Digital, Issac Sacolick defined precisely "Digital Transformation is not just about technology and its implementation. It's about looking at the business strategy through the lens of technical capabilities and how that changes how you are operating and generating revenues [14]. In the "IT Savvy" book, Weill and Ross describe the concept of Digitized Platform (DP) as an "integrated set of electronic business processes and the technologies, applications and data supporting the processes." Therefore the DP becomes a prerequisite to compete in the digital economy and it should be used for achieving growth and profitability [4].

The Digitized Platform, the Operating Model and Digital Transformation are multi facets interrelated. First, a company needs to have a vision what they want to do (business strategy), and then to think over how technology can help to create a platform to accomplish their vision and later to execute digital transformation for achieving progress and profit. Weill and Ross exemplify the IT role in this process as "... IT can do *two things* very well – *integration* and *standardization*." The integration – delivers data access across the business, while the standardization – reduces variation in business processes and increases quality, efficiency, and predictability in the operations [15]. By identifying what the company wants to integrate and standardize, actually defines its Operating Model. In fact, the Operating Model establishes the objectives and the requirements for the company's specific Digitized Platform. Ultimately, digital transformation is a product of strategy, technology, culture and leadership and it is a journey that iterates towards organization's digital future. For new and existing businesses it requires automating more of operations, generating revenue-leveraging digital capabilities, enabling new product offerings, providing new convenience and value to customers.

Let makes the above narrative real by illustrating with three examples how different companies, some with well-defined operating models, others – newly established, bring together specific requirements to their company's digital driven strategy to achieve remarkable success. In order to support its business strategies to innovate and remain on leading position in the industry, Procter & Gamble (P&G) not only spends 3.4% of revenue on innovation, more than twice the industry average, but has created the most efficient and effective IT architecture by employing a "Diversification" operating model. To accomplish that feat, P&G created Global Business Services (GBS) as internal shared services organization, to provide a base of over seventy common, repetitive, non-unique services for the company's 250 world-wide units. GBS delivers shared services ranging from core IT systems to advanced collaborative tools that allow researchers, marketers, and managers to gather, store, and share knowledge and information, such as: Web 2.0 based social networking and collaborative tools;

integrated services that include unified communications, instant messaging, live video meetings, web conferencing, and content management. The listed above collaborative systems illustrate how well-planned advanced technologies stimulate sharing knowledge, ideas, innovations and support teamwork across company's world-wide spread autonomous businesses. All these systems help P&G to accelerate the decision making and increase the speed of new products to the market, while reducing the operational costs and increase resource utilization. Clearly P&G business success is derived from its efforts in product innovation and collaboration, developed and supported by company's constantly evolving digitized platform [4].

The second example is about the unconventional creative project for developing a new product: Opal ice maker by General Electric (GE). GE -a well-known american multinational corporation with several major business lines of services and products with a typical *coordination* operating model and revenue for 2017 was over $122 billions- does not need money for preorders to creates new products. However, the company experimented a new way to tap into the market intelligence as well as to test the market demand for its new ice maker. In July 2015 GE launched in the crowd-funding site *Indiegogo* a campaign for its new ice maker named Opal. Indiegogo was initially created to serve people and small businesses without or limited access to finances to invest in their business ideas, but in mid-2015 large companies were using the site to test the demand for potential products. With the crowdfunding Opal ice maker campaign, GE asked individuals to contribute $399 (later increased to $499) and set a goal of raising $150000. Within a few hours the campaign raised more than twice that, and within a week it attracted in excess of $1.3K. By the end of it closed in late August of 2015, the Opal ice maker compaign had attracted more than $2.7 million on Indiegogo. Making it one of the site's ten most popular compaigns. The finished Opal ice maker product was shipped to more than 5000 preordered customers by the end of 2016 before going to sale to the general public [16]. The epitomized GE crowd venture demonstrates the importance of the *crowd,* the startlingly large amount of human knowledge, expertise, and enthusiasm distributed all over the world and now available to be chased online through digital platforms.

The last case exemplifies the creativity of newly established companies by implementing digital driven strategy and using utility type digital platforms some of them better-known as *online to offline* (O2O) to create new customer focus products. These platforms represent the richest combination of the economics of scale, they handle huge volumes of information about members and their choices and activities, the availability of pricing of goods and services, payments and problems, and all this information approaches the ideas of free, perfect and instant. Initially Uber transportation platform was suggested in 2009 on a simple idea of app-based limo service. Three years later the company vision transformed significantly to: changing the transportation industry by tapping into the power of the two sided network effects that the company had created –more cars on Uber's platform meant more riders, and more riders meant more cars. Since 2012, when Uber has launched its websites and mobile apps allowing standard cars and their drivers to join the platform and to provide peer-to-peer ridesharing and taxi cab hailing, the company expanded the services combining rides at a lower price, food delivery, and bicycle-sharing system. The digital O2O platform and the worldwide network effects created one of the fastest growing companies in the history. In 2018 the company reported revenue of $11.3 billions and net income of $1.8 billions with 16000 employees and over 100 million users worldwide and a 69% market share in the USA. Uber is a prominent leader in the so-called "sharing economy" and the term *Uberisation* became common for many startups to describe their platforms and services as "Uber for X." Airbnb and Breather are other examples of transformational companies utilizing a crowd-based O2O platform and creating a similar distructive effect to the hotels' workspace businesses. Both companies are innovators in the sharing economy and operate online via websites and mobile apps offering lodging or office spaces while neither company owns any of the real estate listings, nor does it host events but as brokers they receive commissions from every booking. The most common of the last three companies is the extraordinary disruptive power of the utility type online platform of the kind that significantly reduces technology and systems implementation costs, provides enormous crowd market place grasp and increases business efficiency and gainful outcomes.

3 Systems Development and Digital Driven Paradigm

As many options exist for developing new information systems and applications and yet the most often used are structured analysis, which is based on the traditional waterfall method, object-oriented (O-O) analysis, which is the most recent approach that many analysts and developers prefer, and agile methods, also called adaptive methods, which include the latest trends in software development. Over time, many companies discovered that systems are created by teams composed by IT professionals, users, and managers and they complete their work more efficiently and produce better results by adopting one of the two methodologies: joint application development (JAD) or rapid application development (RAD). The difference is that JAD is focused on team-based fact-finding, which is only one phase of the development process, whereas RAD is more like a compressed version of the entire traditional process. Regardless of the development model, to complete and implement any developed system it will be necessary to manage people, tasks, technologies, schedules, and expenses using various tools and techniques [17].

The Structured analysis is a traditional system development methodology which utilizes a series of phases called systems development life cycle (SDLC) to plan, analyze, design, implement, and support an information system. As the structured analysis is focused on processes that transform data into useful information, it is called also a process-centered technique. In addition, it uses the SDLC methodology which describes all activities, functions and the deliverables within the phases and their continuing logical flow from where comes the other name of it: a waterfall method – see Fig. 2.

Whereas structured analysis treats processes and data as separate components, object-oriented analysis combines data and processes that correlate into objects. Object-oriented methods usually follow series of analysis and design phases that are similar to SDLC, although there is less agreement on the number of the phases and their names.

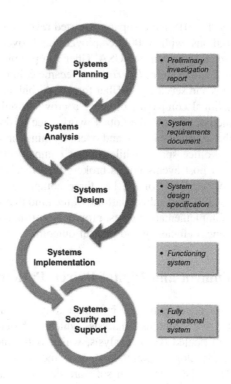

Fig. 2. The Waterfall SDLC Model – the circular symbols indicate interaction among the phases [17]

In the O-O model the phases are more interactive, and the results are better aligned to the current business processes. Substantial element of this method is creating and running Prototypes for testing specific processes or operations and for achieving better aligned to the users' expectations solutions. O-O methodology provides easy transition to and utilization of object-oriented programming languages – see Fig. 3.

The notion of interactive development process can be tracked back to Japanese automaker that were able to boost productivity by using a flexible manufacturing system where team-based efforts and short-term milestones help the company to improve the quality and keep costs down. Agile methods have attracted a wide-range of followers especially in the software development field and in general includes planning and developing the system incrementally. They typically use a spiral model, which represent a series of interactions or revisions, based on the user feedback. An agile approach requires intense interactivity between developers and individual users. It does not begin with a clear scope; instead the agile process determines the end result. Although agile methods are recently quite popular and allow developers to be more flexible and responsive, they are riskier that the traditional approaches, normally produce weak documentation, blurred lines of accountability and too little emphasis on the larger business picture [17].

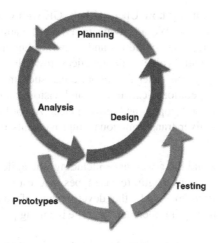

Fig. 3. Object-Oriented Model – Planning, Analysis and Design interact to create Prototypes to be Tested [17]

While many businesses still are using one of the three above described methods or a flavor of them not only to stay with traditions, company culture and existing infrastructure and resources, but because of lacking stamina and good understanding of the transforming power of digital technologies and how they should be selected and implemented. With escalating IT operational costs and the inability to get adequate value from the IT investments, firms are striving to convert their IT from a strategic liability to strategic asset. According recent surveys from Gardner, Forrester, and CISR most of the IT budgets are spent for keeping the existing applications and infrastructure running. Many firms typically spend over 80% of their IT budget for supporting existing systems, and the budget for renovation or new systems, if exists, is below 20%. The widely adopted piecemeal approach results in set of isolated systems wired together to meet the next immediate need. And while there are some valuable IT-based products and services in every company IS environment, the organizations find that it takes longer and longer to test and integrate the new patches with the existing systems, this increases vulnerability to systems outages, and makes more difficult to respond to changing business conditions. Reversing such IT fortunes requires different thinking from the type that "helped" the organization to create its messy legacy [4]. The challenges are for all executives and for people involve in the process as there is no clear framework applicable universally for any businesses. While working with traditions as Peter High in his World Class IT Strategy book illustrates the seven facets in cascading logic from strategy to technology: strategic intentions, business context, business value, business process, data architecture, application architecture, systems (IT) architecture [18], the companies should innovate and should pursuit for set of technologies and customers they can better serve or satisfied with new developing products.

The most appropriate approach in such fuzzy adventure would be applying a modified agile tactic to gain the most of creative and transformative strategy for new business products – very similar how Uber, Airbnb, GE with Opal ice maker did in a disruptive and innovative way. We are living in a very dynamic world where many markets and business forces are colliding and transforming in parallel. The transforming organization should evolve agile practices towards a disciplined scalable process, a venture that connects other functional areas such marketing and products, business processes and operations, capabilities and vision, and perform changes to enable an agile culture, philosophy and governance. According Isaac Sacolick, a possible framework to deliver transformational improvements through agile methodology should include [14]:

- define *agile planning* and the governance including: the agile team structure, roles, responsibilities, tools, sprint length, release types, and estimation guidelines
- leverage *agile planning* to enable the development of roadmaps. Apply agile practices to execute in a sprint, then use the agile planning practices to get visibility into future sprints
- ensure *agile development* through evolving technical and testing practices in parallel in as much as agile execution helps only to the extend that there is an underlying strong technical practice
- formalize *release delivery* plans to align agile teams with customers and business stakeholders
- oversee *completion and monitoring* after the first deployment by checking the customers behavior through metrics captured from the application of feedback collected directly from the users for any issues – see Fig. 4.

Fig. 4. Agile transformational practice

In the agile transformational approach the following feasible practices should be considered: version integration control, quality assurance and verification, managing technical debts. The version integration control is critical for aligning the internal systems and applications with the external set of digital platform technologies and customer tools and apps. This will eliminate any holdups in the system implementation and communications with the crowds. With increasing complexity of the multitier applications, crossing multiple APIs transactions, and performed computing operations on multisites clouds, the quality assurance and testing must be fundamentally embedded in the agile practices. The range of QA tests in every spring should include but not limited to: functional testing, automation, user experience, data integrity, security, performance and load testing. The other important consideration is the technical debt of the final system, or everything related to some short cuts in the agile process: bad design, bad code, technical areas for improvements. Dealing with the technical debts should be embedded into the agile transformational process as culture, incentives, rules and priorities on fixing technical debts problems to stakeholders satisfaction. The digital driven transformations and enhancements are embedded into agile practices because the process flexibility for selecting and funneling into the set of technologies used for the developing system and the direct communications with the crowd/end users for instant feedback and improvements.

4   Insights on Digital Driven Transformations

For the benefit of any business it is vital to consider the needs reimaging their organization's operations, products and services to be digitally driven towards smarter, faster and more profitable results. In the evolving digital transformations three key areas for imperative changes should be considered: customer experience, operational processes and business models. The following findings emerged from the previous sections: *correlating system forces* depicted at the Enhanced Social-Technical model, *harmonizing digital technologies* to bridge with the crowds, *orchestrating culture, processes, the platform technologies* to sharpen the customer focus and positive experience.

The first finding reflects **the strong correlation between the internal organizational system** forces -structure, people, technology, processes- with the utility type *digital platforms and crowds*. The following thoughts should be considered echoing the alignment of the internal company structure and its market channels:

- Transformation of activities, services or new products through SMACIT to reap economies of scale and scope;
- Product, services and operation transformations through innovation for broader and stronger customer focus;
- Profit improvement flowing from new sources of revenue;
- Gain advantage from business agility and utility type of digital platforms while chasing the crowds.

The second finding emphasizes **harmonization of the selected set of digital platform technologies to bridge with the crowds.** Based on the EST model and the presented above cases it is critical customer service technology ecosystem to be easy, effective, and instill positive experience. According to the Gartner research from 2016, the digital business technology platform is "… a symbiotic collection of technology capabilities and components that form a platform…" [19]. Even though the set of digital technologies collection and SMACIT applications are different for Uber, Airbnb, and other "shared services" type of companies, the most important for all of them is their customer apps to be easy to use and compatible, intuitive and transferable, prompt, reliable and to guarantee the customer satisfaction.

The third finding is about **orchestrating organizational culture, business processes, and the platform technologies** to sharpen the customer focus and bond with the crowd to achieve positive experience. Businesses are capitalizing on the customization and proliferation of developing applications targeting increasing productivity and profitability, broadening market shares and customer satisfaction through:

- New agile transformational practices when design, develop and implement new customer-focused systems;
- New business operating models with consolidated customer service technologies and embedded features customers to control their time, selections, and exploring emerging channels to reduce frictions;
- Strengthen the customer bond with feedback about their products, services, processes;
- Insights from connected devices by triggering preemptive services with built-in prescriptive power for offers, decisions, and connections.

In the recent Capgemini Digital Transformation Institute publication "Understanding digital mastery today" the research team conclusions actually confirm the three expressed above findings and support them with some of the results of their world-wide digital mastery survey.

Aligning customer experience and the internal operations is critical for "*digital masters*" companies as they realize the importance of organizing their operations to meet customer demands. As Fig. 5 shows, 73% of digital masters incorporate both customer experience and operations priorities into their vision and 71% use digital technologies to link customer-facing and operational processes in new ways. For example, the LEGO Group links customers directly to their product design process through its Lego Ideas website. The company stimulates users to design their products and then the company builds an actual Lego product based on the most popular design [20].

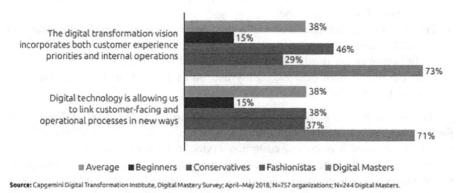

■ Average ■ Beginners ■ Conservatives ■ Fashionistas ■ Digital Masters

Source: Capgemini Digital Transformation Institute, Digital Mastery Survey; April–May 2018, N=757 organizations; N=244 Digital Masters.

Fig. 5. Digital transformation and aligning customer experience with internal operations [20]

5   Conclusion

There are many other considerations and challenging implications in digital driven transformations - speed of innovations, speed to the crowds/customers and new markets, speed of business operating models' evolution. All these challenges require yet more efforts and analyses on how to select the set of technologies and to boost the strategic business objectives to excel on digital platforms capabilities. The proposed concept of enhanced socio-technical model, the simplified framework of new agile developing practices, and the outlined three findings for digital driven transformations considerations, should to provide a consistent, predictable, and positive experience when dealing digital business conversions. By taking advantage of the attained kno-whow, the work presented at this paper can serve as a foundation to explore deeper into the internal companies' structures, utility digital platforms and their market crowds/channels.

Further work is planned in two main directions: examining the new extra layer of new digital technologies (SMACIT) and analysing from a business point of view the effects of SMACIT on doing business and transforming strategies. The first direction is oriented towards technologies and will focus more on detailed analysis on customers' security and risk associated with the digital platform technologies; how sustainable and proper the data quality management based on the newly created products and services of the crowd platforms is. The second track will be focused on the changes of com-panies as consequence of the extra SMACIT layer and how the business must/will adapt to both the availability of new possibilities and the erosion of the "old" market channels, along with the impact of the Web 3.0 technologies on the digital driven business operating models.

References

1. Insight From the 2018 Gartner Agenda Report: Time to "remix": Digitalization and technological innovation are changing the nature of the CIO's job, Gartner Stamford, USA (2019). http://gartner.com/cioagenda
2. Khan, N., Sikes, J.: IT Under Pressure: McKinsey Global Survey Results. McKinsey & Company (2014). http://www.mckinsey.com/business-functions/business-technology/our-insights/it-under-pressure-mckinsey-global-survey-results
3. Info-Tech Research Group: Info-Tech's 2016 CIO Trend Report (2015). http://www.infotech.com/research/2016-cio-trend-report-executive-brief
4. Ivanov, I.I.: Exploring business - IT nexus: make the most of IT-enabled capabilities. In: Shishkov, B. (ed.) BMSD 2015. LNBIP, vol. 257, pp. 152–170. Springer, Cham (2016). https://doi.org/10.1007/978-3-319-40512-4_9
5. Neilson, G., Martin, K., Powers, E.: The Secrets to Successful Strategy Implementation, HBR's 10 Must Reads On Strategy. Harvard Business School Publishing, Boston (2010)
6. Swayne, L., Duncan, W., Ginter, P.: Strategic Management of Health Care Organizations. Blackwell Publishing, Malden (2006)
7. Porter, M.: On Competition. Harvard Business School Publishing, Boston (2008)
8. McKeen, J., Smith, H., Singh, S.: A framework for enhancing IT capabilities. Commun. Assoc. Inf. Syst. **15**, Article 36 (2005)
9. Picolli, G.: Information Systems for Managers: Text and Cases. Wiley, Hoboken (2012)
10. Laudon, K., Laudon, J.: Management Information Systems: Managing the Digital Firm. Pearson Education, Upper Saddle River (2016)
11. Bartlam, M., Day, A.: Digital Transformation in Financial Services, DLA Piper Global (2019). https://www.dlapiper.com/fsdigitaltransformation/
12. Dawson, R., Bynghall, S.: Getting Results from Crowds. Advanced Human Technologies Incl., San Francisco (2012)

13. Weill, P., Ross, J.: IT Savvy: What Top Executives Must Know to Go from Pain to Gain. Harvard Business School Publishing, Boston (2009)
14. Sacolick, I.: Driving Digital – The Leader's Guide to Business Transformation through Technology. AMACOM, American Management Association, New York (2018)
15. Ross, J., Beath, C.: Maturity Still Matters: Why a Digitized Platform is Essential to Business Success, CISR, Sloan School of Management, MIT, Research Briefing, vol. XI, no. II, Boston (2011)
16. McAfee, A., Brynjolfsson, E.: Machine Platforms Crowd Harnessing Our Digital Future. W. W. Norton & Company, New York (2017)
17. Tilley, S., Rosenblatt, H.: Systems Analysis and Design. Cengage Learning, Boston (2017)
18. High, P.: Implementing World Class IT Strategy. Jossey-Bass A Wiley Brand, San Francisco (2014)
19. LeHong, H., Howard, C., Gaughan, D., Logan, D.: Building a Digital Business Technology Platform. Gartner, 8 June 2016
20. Buvat, J., Puttur, R., Bonnet, D., Slatter, M., Westerman, G., Crummenerl, G.: Understanding digital mastery today, Capgemini Digital Transformation Institute (2018)

Supporting the Use of Decision Aiding Methods by Non-specialists

Ana Sara Costa[1,2]([✉]), Rúben Rodrigues[2], André Xiang[2], José Rui Figueira[1], and José Borbinha[2]

[1] CEG-IST, Instituto Superior Técnico, Universidade de Lisboa, Lisbon, Portugal
{anasaracosta,figueira}@tecnico.ulisboa.pt
[2] INESC-ID, Instituto Superior Técnico, Universidade de Lisboa, Lisbon, Portugal
{ruben.andre.rodrigues,andre.xiang,jlb}@tecnico.ulisboa.pt

Abstract. Multiple Criteria Decision Aiding (MCDA) is a domain focused on the development of methods to help decision makers. DEC-SPACE is an online Decision Support System (DSS) intended to be a workbench for the use of MCDA methods. DECSPACE supports projects as persistent spaces where users can explore different solutions for the same problem, and share those solutions in other projects. It is made available as an online service, and it can use methods implemented in a local server, as part of the local application, or methods available from remote web services. This paper describes DECSPACE as a DSS suited for use in teaching, researching, or for professional use in engineering and management.

Keywords: Multiple Criteria Decision Aiding · Decision Support Systems · Online service · User experience

1 Introduction

Multiple Criteria Decision Aiding (MCDA) is a domain of Operations Research and Management Science mainly devoted to the development and implementation of methods and tools with the aim of supporting decision makers handling decision situations that involve multiple criteria [17–19,23]. The main purpose is to take the decision makers' preferences into account during the decision-making process. This is usually the case in, for example, risk management, supply chain management, or even in industrial processes, where having to deal with multiple criteria for either ranking or grouping entities can be a complex challenge [9]. An MCDA approach allows a structured and transparent understanding of the decision process, even when involving multiple stakeholders.

The number of MCDA methods and publications has been increased, and consequently, several software solutions have been developed [11,21]. Thus, the use of this kind of methods by both researchers and professionals has increased too [13]. Using tools with MCDA methods can provide a feasible way of modeling the problem, and visualize the data, processes, and results. However, MCDA tools can be challenging to use for those not familiarized with the domain.

DECSPACE is a web-based Decision Support System (DSS) of MCDA methods, it was developed with the clear objective of facilitating the usage of those methods not only by experts in MCDA but also by non-specialists. Unlike many existing MCDA related tools which offer limited methods or often provide an interface with a steep learning curve that is too complex for the average user, DECSPACE offers a modern interface and several features that make it possible for users of any level of expertise to take advantage of MCDA methods.

One of the main goals DECSPACE accomplished was the ability to either easily add MCDA methods newly developed to the system or reuse existing open reference implementations of those that already exist (which is the case for many of them), and have those methods available to all users from diverse backgrounds [4]. Another important aspect that differentiates DECSPACE from the most MCDA tools is that it does not require the user to download any software or to install anything on their own computer. Developing DECSPACE as a web-based workbench with support for all popular browsers makes it simple and easy for anyone to experience and use the available MCDA methods without needing any prior setup, going as far as providing an anonymous mode, despite offering registered user features.

The aim of this paper is to present the current version of DECSPACE, describing its features and highlighting the advantages that it can offer to the potential users, with or without a background in MCDA, both for academic and professional purposes.

This paper is organized as follows. Section 2 briefly introduces the MCDA domain, which serves as the background. Section 3 analyses a set of tools relevant to this work. Section 4 presents DECSPACE, the web-based DSS workbench, explaining its contributions and features. Section 5 provides the proof of concept, demonstrating the use of this DSS and highlighting some of its features. Section 6 provides the main conclusions, as well as lines of research and future developments.

2 Background

Decision situations can involve multiple criteria and multiple stakeholders. That can turn complex due to the number and heterogeneity of the criteria to consider. MCDA approaches can offer methods and techniques to handle different types of decision problems (e.g., ranking and choice), allowing to provide recommendations that take into account the preferences of the decision makers [17–19,23].

The main objective of MCDA is, therefore, to provide aid to decision makers, including the support in complex and ill-structured problems. For that, it offers methods that can be adapted according to the decision makers' preferential system and judgments. MCDA intervenes in all phases of the decision process, beginning from the problem structuring, followed by the formulation of criteria, up to the implementation of the recommended solution [5].

MCDA methods are suitable for problems that can be categorized in one of the following four groups [18]:

- **Choice problems** when the purpose is to select the group of the most favorable actions (objects of the decision, alternatives or entities) from an initial set of actions, to then choose the single best possible action (e.g., choosing a house);
- **Sorting problems** when the aim is to assign each action to a predefined category (e.g., classifying business companies);
- **Ranking problems** when it is required to order all actions (e.g., ranking the schools in the country);
- **Description problems** when the objective is to describe the actions and their corresponding consequences, identifying their main distinctive features (these kinds of challenges are usually posed in the early steps of the decision problem when one is still struggling to understand the main characteristics of the problem).

MCDA methods can be classified into three main groups, according to the type of approach [18]:

- **Multi-Attribute Utility and Value Theory** is the classic approach: to each action is assigned a utility value (it indicates the overall utility/preference of the action), which results from a combination of many different criteria, weighted accordingly to scaling factors representing trade-offs between criteria (usually called weights). Examples of methods are Analytic Hierarchy Process (AHP), which structures a decision problem into a hierarchy with a goal, and Analytic Network Process (ANP), which structures it as a network.
- **Outranking methods** are based on the pairwise comparison of actions to build outranking relations according to the preferences of the decision maker. It considers that an action, a, outranks another action, b, if there are enough arguments in favor of a to conclude that "a is at least as good as b" (outranking relation). Examples are all methods belonging to ELECTRE (ELimination Et Choix Traduisant la REalité) family and to PROMETHEE (Preference Ranking Organization METHod for Enrichment of Evaluations) family.
- **Non-Classical MCDA Approaches** include all other proposed methods that do not fit into the previous categories. Examples are decision rules, fuzzy set approach, fuzzy measures, integral approach, and verbal decision analysis.

In any case, most MCDA methods may require calculations unreliable to do manually, so they need to be supported by software tools. Indeed, they can be useful to all stakeholders of the decision situation at hand, not only making the calculations but also facilitating to model the problem with computational support, as well as to visualize input and output data, and analyze the results [12].

3   Related Work

Research on MCDA has been increasing, with a notably dissemination work done by EWG-MCDA, short for European Working Group on Multiple Criteria

Decision Aiding[1], which is a working group with the objective of promoting original research in the field of MCDA at the European level, as well as facilitating contacts and collaborations, stimulating the emergence and exchange of new ideas. As one of the working groups of EURO, the Association of European Operational Research Societies, EWG-MCDA today has approximately 350 members from 38 countries. By providing a platform for members to submit their research, while also organizing meetings and conferences, this EURO Working Group facilitates its members to easily exchange ideas and create collaborations.

A notable project that started within the EWG-MCDA is the Decision Deck project[2]. Its main objective is to develop open source software tools implementing MCDA techniques to support complex decision-making situations [6]. Decision Deck includes many initiatives related to MCDA, namely the development of *diviz* [14], a workbench that uses MCDA methods to build workflows with these methods and call their execution, as a desktop application. *diviz* also defined the XMCDA format to represent data and MCDA objects, as well as a web services interface.

While many users, especially researchers in the MCDA domain, still choose *diviz* as their tool of choice, it is mainly due to the wide variety of available MCDA methods, the application interface still suffers from an outdated design,

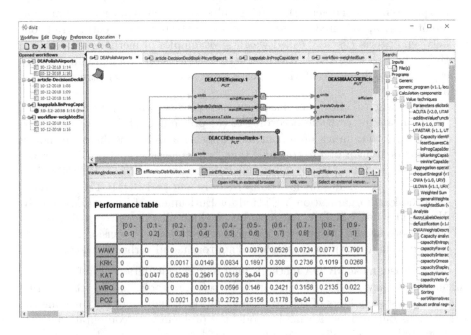

Fig. 1. Example of interface in *diviz* with visible toolbars, workbench, and output

---

[1] https://www.euro-online.org/web/ewg/1/ewg-mcda-euro-working-group-on-multiple-criteria-decision-aiding.

[2] https://www.decision-deck.org/project/.

as can be seen in Fig. 1. DECSPACE follows a similar architecture, but as a web-based online alternative with different features and a more simplistic interface.

Most of the available software tools mainly meet the requirements of the people familiar with MCDA or researchers in this area. In addition, those tools generally provide a single method or restricted methods (see, for example, [21] and [15], for surveys on MCDA software). Besides *diviz*, there are few tools offering a large number of methods.

Examples of tools with a significant number of methods are 1000minds[3], a web application making available for use conjoint analysis and prioritization tools, but lacking some popular model constructions (e.g, hierarchical model and visual scoring), and Analytica[4], a general-purpose visual software application where the user can implement practically any method, but lacking some group decision support features. Both are commercial products of MCDA methods. 1000minds is a web-based application with a wide range of visualization options, whereas Analytica presents a very dated interface, mainly due to being a desktop application. 1000minds is more extensive and it is also prepared for scenarios of group decision-making. Still, *diviz* seems to be the most complete solution among free and commercially available tools, presenting a platform with flexibility for using several methods and a solid user experience. However, it presents the disadvantage of being a desktop standalone application.

Table 1 presents a general comparison of some relevant features of the analysed MCDA tools.

Table 1. Features comparison of the selected MCDA tools

Feature	diviz	1000minds	Analytica
Web-based		✓	
Open-source	✓		
Cross-platform		✓	
Modern user interface	✓	✓	
Large number of methods	✓		
Develop new methods	✓		✓
Data import and export	✓	✓	✓
Data visualization	✓	✓	✓

4   DecSpace Overview

DECSPACE is a DSS that is offered as a web-based service available in most browsers, it aims to have a user-friendly interface, providing a simple and straight

---

[3] https://www.1000minds.com/.
[4] https://www.lumina.com/why-analytica/.

forward way to create, modify and share multiple projects in the form of work-flows (see Fig. 2) [3,4,16,22]. DECSPACE differentiates itself from other MCDA tools in how it does not require the user to be an expert in the domain. Thus, the user is able to start exploring DECSPACE and create basic workflows using the available methods. DECSPACE provides similar features to the ones of other MCDA solutions that already exist, but it offers those features together into a standalone web-based service available for anyone, aiming at include group support and ways to facilitate the sharing of projects.

With DECSPACE being offered as an online service, it supports a system of registered actors with different roles and permissions:

– **Anonymous non-registered users** can create temporary projects to test MCDA workflows, but they cannot save them. They also have access to public projects made available to everyone by other users, as shown in Fig. 3;
– **Registered users** are able to save and edit projects anytime;
– **Developers** implement additional MCDA methods, can add them as either local implementations or as remote services;
– **Administrators** support the back-end of the system. They can manage projects, users, and available existing and new methods.

To facilitate the use of decision aiding methods, DECSPACE offers an easy sharing of work and ideas among users, such as export and import workflows (see Fig. 4) and public projects, an intuitive interface with features that makes it easy-to-use for any user (e.g., drag-and-drop to move or connect modules in the workspace), while requiring no installation of any software from its users to make it work. It is due to these available features in the system and the

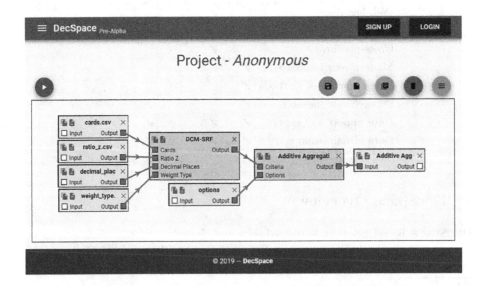

Fig. 2. Example of a typical DECSPACE workflow

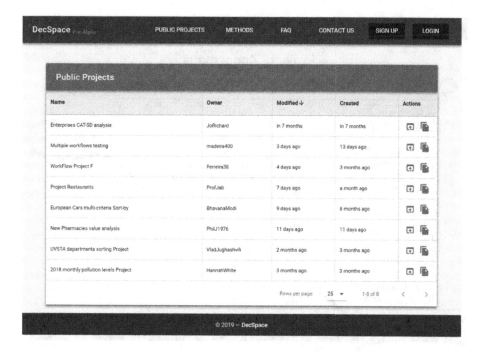

Fig. 3. Public projects interface in DECSPACE

straightforward workbench design, where the users create workflows of MCDA methods, that DECSPACE is suitable to both beginners that are just starting to learn MCDA methods, and professionals looking to create elaborate MCDA projects with complex workflows.

DECSPACE follows a three-tier client-server software architecture, which structures the logical system into three main components:

- **Presentation tier** is the user interface with the main function of exposing the service in a user-friendly way;
- **Application tier** is the business logic where the main computations are made. It handles multiple clients through HTTP requests received from the presentation tier, and responds to the user with the corresponding visual feedback;
- **Data tier** receives from the application tier the data that must be persistent and gives it back when requested.

In the next subsections, we provide a more detailed functional (use cases) and structural (domain model) overview of DECSPACE.

4.1 DecSpace Use Cases

The UML use case diagram in Fig. 5 models the DECSPACE uses cases.

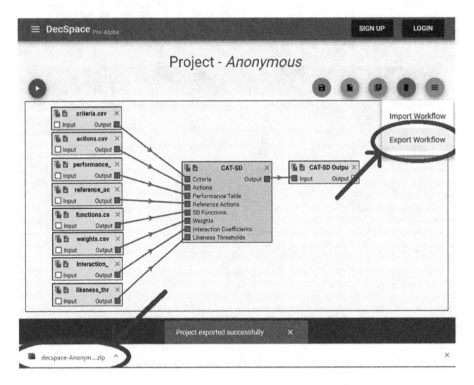

Fig. 4. Exporting a temporary workflow that was created anonymously

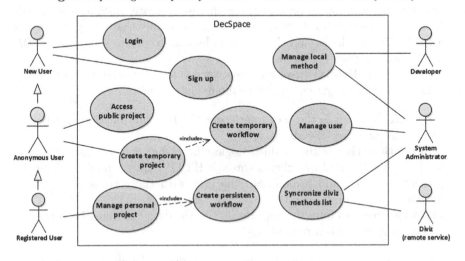

Fig. 5. Use case diagram of the DecSpace service

A New User is anyone that has just accessed the service. A user can log in if already registered, otherwise, the user can sign up a new account or stay anonymous.

An Anonymous User is able to browse and explore public projects, but can only work on temporary and non-persistent workspaces.

A Registered User has access to all features of the Anonymous User, and can also save work persistently, as private or public projects.

A Developer can add newly-developed local MCDA methods (a feature made easy if the new method can be developed in JavaScript).

The System Administrator can manage all the users and all the public or private projects, as well as all methods, local or remote (including the remote methods made available by the Decision Deck initiative).

Each use case is briefly described in Table 2.

Table 2. Description of the use cases

Use case	Description
Login	The registered user introduces the email and password to log into his/her account
Sign up	The new user provides an email and a password to create a new user account
Access public project	The anonymous user consults the public projects
Create temporary project	The anonymous user creates, edits, removes or publishes his/her temporary projects
Create temporary workflow	The anonymous user initiates the workspace and creates temporary workflows with methods connected to the respective input and output data
Manage personal project	The registered user consults, creates, edits, removes or publishes his/her own projects as private or public projects
Create persistent workflow	The registered user initiates the workspace and creates and edit workflows with methods connected to the respective input and output data
Manage local method	Both the developer and the system administrator can manage the availability of the local methods for the user, by adding or removing MCDA methods from the catalog
Manage user	The system administrator manages a user in the system, having access to all users' information with the possibility to delete users accounts
Syncronize *diviz* methods list	The system administrator fetches the XMCDA methods available on the *diviz* framework

4.2 DecSpace Domain Model

The domain model is illustrated in Fig. 6.

A User can own multiple projects, and consult all public projects.

A Project has a user as the owner and can comprise one or more Workflows.

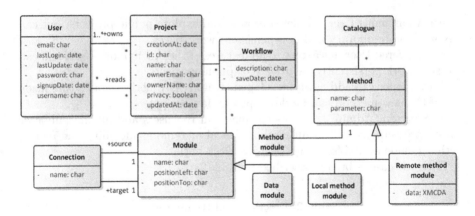

Fig. 6. UML domain model diagram of the DECSPACE service

A Workflow is a set of Modules that can be linked by Connection.

A Module can be either a Method Module or a Data Module, which can be either data imported by the user or data generated by a Method Module.

A Method Module contains one, and only one method.

The Catalogue lists all the available methods.

Each Method entity has a name and parameters, which are specific for each implementation of each method. A Method Module is in fact, either a Local Method Module, which contains its own implementation and algorithms of execution, or a Remote Method Module, which contains a link to an XMCDA method from a remote server (in the case of as Decision Deck, these must be Simple Object Access Protocol requests).

5 Demonstration

To exhibit the capabilities of DECSPACE and what a typical use scenario for a regular user would be, an example is provided in this section. In our example, we suppose that a decision maker (a user) wants to choose a restaurant to go among a set of potential restaurants. As input data, we have a list of criteria for evaluating restaurants and the respective criteria weights (i.e., values that represent their relative importance) that should be taken into account when deciding (see Table 3). Additionally, there is a list of options containing several restaurants and their score for each criterion, as displayed in Table 3.

A simple MCDA algorithm is Additive Aggregation, which is essentially a weighted sum. For very basic decision-making and taking into account the fact that the user already has defined the weights of the criteria, Additive Aggregation is enough to judge the restaurants in a very primitive way. A user can either already have his/her own data files prepared in advance or take advantage of the interface provided by DECSPACE to fill in the data manually. For large data sets the best option is to use data files and upload them to DECSPACE.

Table 3. Restaurants example data set

(a) Criteria

Criterion	Weight
Price	50
Location	25
Schedule	10
Parking	10
Menu	2.5
Variety	

(b) Options

Name	Price	Location	Schedule	Parking	Menu	Variety
Maria	7.8	2.0	12.5	30	15
Roma	9	0.2	5	55	30
Frutalmeidas	6.5	0.34	11	13	6
Sakura	13	1.3	7.9	29	24
Ni Hao	8.5	0.61	20	46	40
Nipal	10.75	0.9	7.5	38	36
HappyPizza	8	1.5	15	89	21

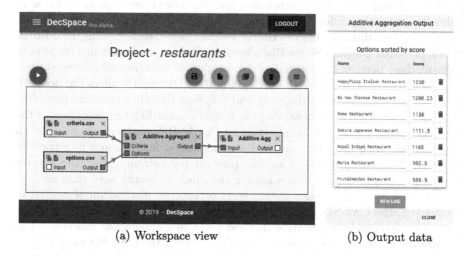

(a) Workspace view   (b) Output data

Fig. 7. The restaurants' example in DECSPACE

Firstly, the user creates a new project and uploads two data files, which create in the service two data modules. Secondly, from the method catalogue, the user then selects the Additive Aggregation method and connects the data modules to the generated method module. DECSPACE will warn the user if there is anything missing or if the data is not in the correct format, otherwise, the input endpoints will be colored green. Finally, the user can execute the workflow by clicking the Execute button, which will result in a scenario similar to that shown in Fig. 7a. A new data module is generated, containing the output of the executed Additive Aggregation (i.e., the expected results). The output data can be seen in Fig. 7b - it displays the aggregated score of the options, sorted in descendant order. *HappyPizza* restaurant has the highest score (1530) based on the provided criteria and their weights. Therefore, the "best" restaurant, given the available data, is *HappyPizza* restaurant by a considerably large margin (with a score approximately 27% higher than the second highest). The user is then able to save the project, which can also be made public for anyone else, with the possibility of seeing it and making copies. If the user needs the data on a local computer file, the workflow can be exported in the form of a `.zip` file containing `.csv` files with the data modules' content. These files can be imported into, for example, a spreadsheet, for further processing.

The methods currently available in DecSpace have been applied to real-world decision-making scenarios. For instance, in [8] it is addressed a classification problem related to the adaptive reuse (it refers to the redevelopment or use of old sites or abandoned buildings for a different purpose of the one for which were originally built). The case study presented in [8] aimed at analyzing the adequacy of each building from a set of underused buildings located in the city of Turin, Italy, to host cultural and art events. To this end, a family of criteria was constructed and five nominal categories (i.e., no order exists among them) were defined representing different kinds of cultural and art events. Then, the decision maker assigned distinct sets of criteria weights per category, using DCM-SRF (Deck of Cards Method-Simos-Roy-Figueira) [10] implemented in DecSpace. This method permits to determine the weights of criteria mainly based on a rank of cards constructed by the decision maker. DecSpace offers the possibility of placing the "cards" by dragging and dropping them in a rank and providing the parameters needed for obtaining the weights, according to preferences of the decision maker. Indeed, the application of DCM-SRF can be done online in an intuitive way with this DSS, due to its visualization features and user-friendly interface. The obtained sets of weights (one set per category, since the relative importance of the criteria differs among the kinds of event) were then used as one of the inputs (preference parameters) of another method implemented in DecSpace, the CAT-SD (CATegorization by Similarity-Dissimilarity), a multiple criteria nominal classification method [7]. Thus, a workflow was created in the workspace (as the one illustrated in Fig. 4) using the CAT-SD module with the proper connections of all inputs of the decision model constructed in the case study. The respective output provided by DecSpace was the classification of each underused buildings analyzed in the study into the categories of events.

Currently, we have been implemented new MCDA methods, namely Electre Tri-C [2] and Electre Tri-nC [1], which were also designed to handle classification problems with multiple criteria, but using categories with a preference order among them (usually designated sorting problems). The main difference, in practice, is that Electre Tri-C was conceived to consider a single reference action to define a category and Electre Tri-nC allows to provide more than one reference action per category, offering advantages for the decision maker.

6   Conclusion

In this paper, we presented an innovative DSS service that is currently in development, DecSpace. This new tool takes advantage of cutting-edge web technologies to deliver a maintainable, user-friendly system to easily create, execute and share projects. Developing a solution that targets not only the experts in

MCDA but also inexperienced users can be very beneficial, and it can contribute to the growth of the MCDA field. Designing DECSPACE to have a user-friendly interface and is easy-to-use can reduce the entry barrier for non-specialist people exploring decision aiding methods.

To demonstrate and prove the value of DECSPACE's features, an example of a simplified case and a real-world case study that already used this DSS were presented.

As this tool is still in development, it also has limitations, namely the system still lacks some of the most known MCDA methods in its catalogue, which can be attributed to the complexity of these methods that are not yet easily supported by the back-end code of the system due to missing components (e.g., data transformation and visualization modules) that deal with data. In general, there are smaller user interface limitations attributed to the system being web-based and therefore being potentially limited by JavaScript.

Future research work includes an iterative improvement of this DSS online service, by adding more MCDA methods and missing features (e.g., more user feedback notifications, alternative data visualization, a filter to select methods as described in [20] for helping non-specialists to choose adequate methods for their decision problems), as well as setting new integrations with other available tools. Currently, there is planned the integration of DECSPACE with the open-source technology used by the *diviz* desktop application, this would help to add a much wider variety of available methods. This includes frameworks related to XMCDA, such as the XMCDA data standard to store MCDA data objects and information, and XMCDA web services integrated as remote methods.

Acknowledgments. This work was supported by national funds through Fundação para a Ciência e a Tecnologia (FCT) with reference UID/CEC/50021/2019. Ana Sara Costa acknowledges the financial support from Universidade de Lisboa, Instituto Superior Técnico and CEG-IST (PhD Scholarship). José Rui Figueira acknowledges the support from the FCT grant SFRH/BSAB/139892/2018 under POCH Program and European Union's Horizon 2020 research and innovation program under Grant Agreement No. 691895 SHAR-LLM ("Sharing Cities").

References

1. Almeida-Dias, J., Figueira, J.R., Roy, B.: A multiple criteria sorting method where each category is characterized by several reference actions: The ELECTRE TRI-NC method. Eur. J. Oper. Res. **217**, 567–579 (2012)
2. Almeida-Dias, J., Figueira, J.R., Roy, B.: ELECTRE TRI-C: A multiple criteria sorting method based on characteristic reference actions. Eur. J. Oper. Res. **204**, 565–580 (2010)
3. Amador, J.: DecSpace: User Interface Challenges in an MCDA Framework. Instituto Superior Técnico (2018)
4. Barbosa, A.: DecSpace: A Multi-Criteria Decision Analysis Framework. Instituto Superior Técnico (2017)
5. Bouyssou, D., Marchant, T., Pirlot, M., Tsoukiás, A., Vincke, P.: Evaluation and Decision Models with Multiple Criteria: Stepping Stones for the Analyst. Springer, New York (2006)

6. Cailloux, O., Tervonen, T., Verhaegen, B., Picalausa, F.: A data model for algorithmic multiple criteria decision analysis. Ann. Oper. Res. **217**, 77–94 (2012)
7. Costa, A.S., Figueira, J.R., Borbinha, J.: A multiple criteria nominal classification method based on the concepts of similarity and dissimilarity. Eur. J. Oper. Res. **271**, 193–209 (2018)
8. Costa, A.S., Lami, I.M., Greco, S., Figueira, J.R., Borbinha, J.: A multiple criteria approach for defining cultural adaptive reuse of abandoned buildings. In: Huber, S., Geiger, M.J., de Almeida, A.T. (eds.) Multiple Criteria Decision Making and Aiding – Cases on Decision Making Methods and Models with Computer Implementations, International Series in Operations Research & Management Science, vol. 274, pp. 193–218. Springer, Cham (2019). https://doi.org/10.1007/978-3-319-99304-1_6
9. Costa, A.S., Vieira, R., Verdasca, C., Figueira, J.R.: The Applicability of Multi-Criteria Decision Aiding Methods to Risk Management. In: Zúquete, A., Preguiça, N. (eds.) INForum 2016 - Atas do Oitavo Simpósio de Informática, pp. 37–48. Dep. de Eng. Informática e Computadores do Instituto Superior Técnico, Universidade de Lisboa, Lisbon (2016)
10. Figueira, J.R., Roy, B.: Determining the weights of criteria in the ELECTRE type methods with a revised Simos' procedure. Eur. J. Oper. Res. **139**, 317–326 (2002)
11. Ishizaka, A., Nemery, P.: Multi-criteria Decision Analysis: Methods and Software. Wiley, Chichester (2013)
12. Liu, D., Stewart, T.J.: Integrated object-oriented framework for MCDM and DSS modelling. Dec. Support Syst. **38**, 421–434 (2004)
13. Mardani, A., Jusoh, A., MD Nor, K., Khalifah, Z., Zakwan, N., Valipour, A.: Multiple criteria decision-making techniques and their applications – A review of the literature from 2000 to 2014. Economic Research-Ekonomska Istraživanja **28**, 516–571 (2015)
14. Meyer, P., Bigaret, S.: diviz: A software for modeling, processing and sharing algorithmic workflows in MCDA. Intell. Decis. Technol. **6**, 283–296 (2012)
15. Mustajoki, J., Marttunen, M.: Comparison of multi-criteria decision analytical software for supporting environmental planning processes. Environ. Model. Software **93**, 78–91 (2017)
16. Rodrigues, R.: DecSpace: front-end migration and user experience improvements in an MCDA framework - Master Project in information and software engineering. Instituto Superior Técnico (2018)
17. Roy, B.: Méthodologie Multicritére d' Aide à la Décision. Economica, Paris (1985)
18. Roy, B.: Multicriteria Methodology for Decision Aiding. The Kluwer Academic Publishers, Dordrecht (1996)
19. Roy, B., Bouyssou, D.: Aide Multicritàre à la Décision: Méthodes et Cas. Economica, Paris (1993)
20. Wątrobski, J., Jankowski, J., Ziemba, P., Karczmarczyk, A., Ziolo, M.: Generalised framework for multi-criteria method selection. Omega Int. J. Manage. Sci. **86**, 107–124 (2019)
21. Weistroffer, H.R., Smith, C.H., Narula, S.C.: Multiple criteria decision support software. In: Greco, S., Ehrgott, M., Figueira, J.R. (eds.) Multiple Criteria Decision Analysis: State of the Art Surveys, 2nd edn, pp. 989–1009. Springer, New York (2016)
22. Xiang, A.: Integrating MCDA tools: DecSpace with diviz - Master Project in Computer and Information Systems Engineering. Instituto Superior Técnico (2019)
23. Zopounidis, C., Pardalos, P.M.: Handbook of Multicriteria Analysis. Springer, Heidelberg (2010)

Accelerating Knowledge

The Speed Optimization of Knowledge Transfers

Marcus Grum[1(✉)], Simon Rapp[2], Norbert Gronau[1], and Albert Albers[2]

[1] University of Potsdam, 14482 Potsdam, Germany
mgrum@lswi.de
[2] Karlsruhe Institute of Technology, 76131 Karlsruhe, Germany

Abstract. As knowledge-intensive processes are often carried out in teams and demand for knowledge transfers among various knowledge carriers, any optimization in regard to the acceleration of knowledge transfers obtains a great economic potential. Exemplified with product development projects, knowledge transfers focus on knowledge acquired in former situations and product generations. An adjustment in the manifestation of knowledge transfers in its concrete situation, here called intervention, therefore can directly be connected to the adequate speed optimization of knowledge-intensive process steps. This contribution presents the specification of seven concrete interventions following an intervention template. Further, it describes the design and results of a workshop with experts as a descriptive study. The workshop was used to assess the practical relevance of interventions designed as well as the identification of practical success factors and barriers of their implementation.

Keywords: Knowledge transfers · Business process optimization · Interventions · Product development · Product generation engineering · Empirical evaluation

1 Introduction

Knowledge-intensive business processes are characterized by the exchange of knowledge and information among process participants [10,12,16,23,24] as well as the knowledge application within concrete situations [1]. While many aspects of knowledge-intensive processes have been examined in-depth, e.g. modeling methods, the use of information systems (IS) in business processes and the potential of knowledge management systems (KMS) for knowledge transfers, findings on the speed of knowledge transfer are quite rare and just have been quantified by empirical findings once [11]. Grounding on statistically proven models, which quantify the influence of the velocity and quality of knowledge transfers, the knowledge transfer itself as well as its situation can be controlled and used in IS in order to effectively transfer knowledge among organizational units. Regrettably, neither a situation-specific collection of concrete measures optimizing the speed of knowledge transfers, nor a framework for the validation of corresponding

© Springer Nature Switzerland AG 2019
B. Shishkov (Ed.): BMSD 2019, LNBIP 356, pp. 95–113, 2019.
https://doi.org/10.1007/978-3-030-24854-3_7

measures is not available in literature, yet. This particularly refers to measures building on statistically proven, quantitative knowledge transfer models.

Following the motivation to optimize knowledge transfer speed by concrete adjustments of the manifestation of knowledge transfers in their concrete situation, here called intervention, the modification of statistically proven influence factors on the speed of knowledge transfer can directly be connected to the adequate speed optimization of knowledge-intensive process steps. If it were possible to adjust this speed by interventions, the design of IS, their integration with business processes, the use of KMS and technical as well as organizational strategies are enabled. The original contribution of this paper therefore refers to the design of an intervention standard leading to concrete interventions, which fit to statistical proven, quantitative findings on knowledge transfer velocity available in literature. Based on them, for the first time, the model-driven and quantitative effect of knowledge transfers as method of process optimization can be determined. Further, the original contribution of this pater refers to the demonstration of the standard defined (here called *intervention template*) by seven example cases and their empirical validation by experts on behalf of a workshop designed. All together, this forms an *intervention validation framework*, which enables the practicable and effective optimization of knowledge transfers.

The following research will focus on the optimization of knowledge transfers with the intention to answer the following research question: "How can the speed of knowledge transfers in knowledge-intensive processes be optimized?" As the development of new products can be interpreted to be always based on existing products, knowledge is transferred among product development situations via persons and media. Hence, the product generation engineering context is very suited for the observation of knowledge transfers [4]. This paper intends not to draw an all-embracing description of concrete, technical realizations of those novel process optimization techniques. It intends to set a first step to a speed-optimized business process design. Before the examination of concrete interventions in laboratory studies, their selection and validation by practitioners was carried out described here. Hence, sub research questions addressed here are:

1. "How can time-dependent knowledge-transfer models be used in order to derive interventions, which optimize speed of knowledge-intensive business processes?"
2. "How can process interventions be best realized by practitioners?"

The research approach is intended to be design-oriented as Peffers proposes [19,20], such that the remaining paper is structured as follows: The second section presents a foundation and underlying concepts, the third section derives objectives and presents a methodology for the specification and validation of knowledge transfer speed optimizations in knowledge-intensive processes. Those are separated from the design of required artefacts, which will be presented in the fourth section, because of their function as quality gates. Their demonstration presented in the fifth section shows the application of designed artefacts. This is evaluated in the sixth section. The final section concludes the paper.

2 Theoretical Foundation and Underlying Concepts

Concepts underlying the research presented here refer to the domain of process optimization and knowledge transfers. As interventions designed in this contribution are considered in the context of product development, relevant concepts are presented thereafter.

2.1 Business Process Optimization

Activities and decisions leading to a desired optimization of business processes, are designated as *business process optimization* [13]. Considering processes as they are (as-is processes) to be a reference, any adjustment carried out in order to optimize these processes in regard to a certain objective are called process optimization. Since those adjustments implement changes of the as-is process, we call them *intervention*.

Focusing on the optimization of knowledge-intensive business processes, all activities and decisions that lead to the improvement of a certain knowledge transfer in its concrete situation and application context, are therefore designated as *knowledge transfer intervention* [4]. The success of any intervention then can be measured by key performance indicators (KPIs), such as assembly times, failure rates and success rates, the number of produced components, etc. There can be found two basic approaches for business process optimizations that are reflected in various methods and variations:

First, a management concept called *Kaizen*. Originally, it was inspired by a Japanese living and working philosophy. Realizing an iterative never ending improvement of processes and products in small steps, they are optimized continuously. Therefore, these kinds of optimization approaches are referred to as *continuous improvement process* (CIP) cycles [15].

Second, the redesign of as-is processes from the scratch refers to an optimization concept called *business process reengineering* (BPR) [14]. Since this is mostly connected with far reaching changes or a completely redesign of products and processes, experiences and knowledge of the former design are reused but only considered implicitly in new process designs.

As both kinds of optimizations realize adjustments of a process, the implementation of interventions can be considered in both. So, the dealing with interventions intends to realize a common process optimization character and interventions designed in this contribution intend to be implementable in both, cyclic process optimization approaches and BPR approaches.

2.2 Knowledge-Intensive Processes and Knowledge Transfer Models

Based on the definition of *knowledge* to be the unity of skills, cognition and capabilities, which are used by individuals for the solution of given problems [9, 21, 25], the processual consideration of a problem solution refers to knowledge-intensive processes. These demand for knowledge to be transferred from a knowledge carrier to a knowledge receiver and the definition of knowledge transfer has to consider the transfer process itself as well as its content to be transferred. Following the conceptual model of Minbaeva et al. [17], the knowledge transfer further includes the application of knowledge, so that the knowledge transfer can be observed. This research therefore defines a *knowledge transfer* as the identification of knowledge, its transfer from knowledge carrier to knowledge receiver, and its application by the knowledge receiver. Hence, a successful knowledge transfer intervention is intended to be implemented in knowledge-intensive processes, and the effect of a successful knowledge transfer can be measured by KPIs at the correct knowledge application.

Following the definition of the *knowledge transfer velocity* of Gronau and Grum, who define it to be the relation of a clearly distinguishable amount of knowledge, which is required for the successful solution of a certain task and transferred from a knowledge carrier to a knowledge receiver within a certain amount of time [11], the knowledge transfer velocity can be made concrete, as the time for the realization of a knowledge-intensive process is measured and the successful transfer of knowledge is conducted. Therefore, interventions designed in this contribution have to consider this operationalization and implement adjustments here.

The only empirical model available about a knowledge transfer velocity is given by Gronau and Grum [11]. It sets focus on the following variables to influence the knowledge transfer velocity:

- As the *competence* of process participants is raised, the knowledge transfer velocity can be increased.
- As the *stickiness* of knowledge to be transferred is raised, the knowledge transfer velocity can be increased.
- As the *complexity* of the task to be solved is lowered, the knowledge transfer velocity can be increased.
- As the *mother tongue* is used for the knowledge transfer, the knowledge transfer velocity can be increased.
- As the *educational background* is close to the knowledge transfer, knowledge transfer velocity can be increased.

Statistical models are even established for the four *conversions* of the SECI model [18]:

- The *socialization* considers knowledge transfers of tacit knowledge into tacit knowledge.
- The *externalization* considers knowledge transfers of tacit knowledge into explicit knowledge.
- The *combination* considers knowledge transfers of explicit knowledge into tacit knowledge.
- The *internalization* considers knowledge transfers of explicit knowledge into explicit knowledge.

For the implementation of interventions focused here, this means a consideration of the only available empirical model inclusive its influence variables. Following the research overview of Gronau and Grum, the application of an empirical knowledge transfer velocity model has not be realized, yet. Hence, the implementation knowledge transfer interventions focused here is missing and a research gap becomes visible.

2.3   Product Generation Engineering

The approach of Product Generation Engineering (PGE) describes fundamental aspects of product development as such with two main hypotheses [3]. Both are provided in the following:

First, existing technical systems are the basis for every development of new technical products. The development of a new product is therefore perceived as the development of a new product generation. Those already existing technical systems, which serve as a basis or starting point for the development of a new product generation, are *reference products*. Reference products can be preceding product generations from the same company, but also from competitor's products, products from other branches or systems from research projects, which are not even present in the market, yet. A basic distinction is the one between "internal" reference products of a company and "external" reference products [5].

Second, with reference products as a basis and starting point for the structure and subsystems of a new product generation, the development of the new product generation consists of three types of variation. *Carryover variation* (CV) refers to the direct carryover of a subsystem from a reference product with changes occurring only at system boundaries due to system integration. *Embodiment variation* (EV) and *principle variation* (PV) include changes in the embodiment of a subsystem or its working principle, respectively, using the corresponding subsystem from a reference product as starting point for development activities. All subsystems developed by embodiment or principle variation together form the share of new development in the development of the new product generation.

Both elements, reference products and variations, especially the share of new development, contribute to development risks and costs and connect to knowledge transfer as well [7]. On the one hand, the organizational origin of a reference product is important. External reference products imply an increased development risk compared to internal reference products because a product documentation is usually not available and it is impossible to gather the same amount of information just by analyzing an external reference product. Furthermore, looking at reference products from other branches rather than at reference products from its own branch, a company tends to lack more knowledge, which is necessary to analyze a reference product successfully. Because of the described lacks of competence and knowledge, building up and transferring knowledge is crucial for successful product development. This applies as well when using internal reference products, if the developer of the reference product is another person than the developer of the new product generation as there is always a certain amount of knowledge, which is not explicated in the product documentation. On the other hand, challenges and costs come along with the share of new development. This is due to the degree of technical novelty [2]. The successful realization of new technical solutions demands the creation and transfer of new knowledge. For today's products, this usually includes knowledge transfer within interdisciplinary development teams.

All together, this makes product generation engineering environments very attractive for interventions optimizing the knowledge transfer velocity. Although aiming to create interventions optimizing the common knowledge transfer, the focus of this contribution will be on this kind of environment as a first step.

2.4 Product Profiles and Knowledge Transfer Interventions

Product profiles are a tool, usually at an early stage in a product development process [6]. They aim at specifying the need for a certain product without limiting the search for potential technical solutions by making too precise technical specifications. Product profiles consist of a product profile claim, an initial product description and information about the benefit for the provider, customers and users. Furthermore, information about the competitive context, use cases, intended reference products, demands, validation approaches and boundary conditions is included, as far as available. A possible way for the evaluation of product profiles is the use of short videos, which depict especially the identified demand situation that is to be covered with the planned product [22].

Albers et al. have analyzed important influence factors on the speed of knowledge transfer and provided a prioritization taking into account the time span in which those factors could be influenced [4]. They also collected and characterized some typical settings in product development where successful knowledge transfer is important according to practitioners. Building up on the set of influence factors, they propose a *framework for the analysis of knowledge transfer situations* based on the idea that a low speed of knowledge transfer is caused by the use of inappropriate transfer methods. The selection of interventions here is derived by the match of concrete knowledge transfer situations and interventions, both being characterized by profiles using influence factors identified similar to the tool of product profiles.

Using the framework for the analysis of knowledge transfer situations and the concepts of interventions presented by Albers et al. [4], this contribution designs a first collection of concrete interventions, which are going to optimize the knowledge transfer in product development environments.

3   Objectives and Methodology

In accordance to the DSRM of Peffers [19, 20], before the realization of required artefacts was carried out, requirements were defined that serve as design maxims for the definition and validation of interventions for knowledge transfer optimizations. The separation of requirement definition and artifact creation guarantees that artefacts are finalized, only when all requirements are fulfilled. Hence, they work as quality gates for artefacts presented here and facilitate to connect subsequent research with research presented here.

3.1 Objectives

As one assumes to have a given process model and one aims to implement interventions within a concrete situation of that process model inclusive its manifestation of knowledge transfers, the following generic objectives have to be considered about the creation of interventions:

1. Interventions must consider empirically proven factors that influence the speed of knowledge transfers.
2. Interventions must consider all kinds of knowledge transfers, which is up to now the socialization, externalization, internalization and combination.
3. Interventions must be able to be implemented in any company or university.
4. Interventions must be controllable, which demands for their measurability and changeability.
5. Interventions must show effects in short-term horizons.

As interventions created are intended to be validated by practitioners and experts are faced with novel concepts, a workshop design was chosen. It considers the following objectives:

6. Since the practicability focuses on both, universities and companies, the workshop must include experts form both kinds of institutions.
7. The workshop must include experts form the domain of knowledge management and the specific knowledge application context, which is here product development.
8. The workshop must enable experts with concepts required for knowledge transfer speed optimizations.
9. The workshop must ensure that experts consider interventions within their individual situation.

Each objective identified is relevant for the validation of interventions for the optimization of knowledge-intensive business processes and serves as input for the following sections.

3.2 Methodology

In order to answer the question regarding the specification and validation of interventions optimizing knowledge transfer situations and corresponding manifestations in knowledge-intensive business processes as well as the characterization of best implementation strategies from perspective of practitioners, a workshop with experts was realized as descriptive study in compliance with Blessing and Chakrabarti [8]. This includes four *main stages* as follows:

First, literature is analyzed in a *research clarification*. This helps to clarify goals for a research, which here refers to the design and validation of interventions.

Second, empirical data available is analyzed in a *descriptive study I*. Typically, influence factors are identified here, which serve as initial description of the excising situation. In the context presented here, this refers to the identification of empirical proven influence factors, that can be used for the characterization of the knowledge transfer situation as well as for the intervention characterization. Hence, this stage helps to create an understanding for the intended research. Further, it becomes clear, which factors a workshop should address for validation by practitioners.

Third, a *prescriptive study* is realized, which builds on the increased understanding of researchers. Here, artefacts are designed, such as the concrete interventions presented in Sect. 4.1 and the workshop design presented in Sect. 4.2.

Fourth, empirical data is analyzed in a *descriptive study II*. Here, the support of artefacts designed is investigated, so that an evaluation is established. This refers to the support of practitioners from the area of knowledge management as well as from product development of universities and companies.

Since those stages are designed to be cyclic, insights of consecutive stages can be used in iterative stage realizations. Artefacts and insights presented here therefore refer to the final iteration of stages.

4   Design of an Intervention Validation Framework

The following conceptualizes knowledge transfer interventions in a first sub section and designs a workshop-based way to validate interventions (second sub section). All together, this forms an *intervention validation framework*, which can be used in order to expand and systematically collect validated interventions for knowledge transfer speed optimizations, which go beyond the context and examples presented here.

4.1   Knowledge Transfer Interventions

Figure 2(a) presents the template to characterize interventions for the optimization of knowledge-intensive business processes. While an *intervention title* helps refer to concrete interventions, a *short description* characterizes the situation of knowledge transfers. Each is accompanied by a *schematic*, which summarizes the current situation, supports a medial processing and guarantees a fast access and recognition of the intervention. The separation in *before* and *after* helps to characterize as-is situations and make the effect of interventions visible in to-be situations.

The transfer from as-is situation to to-be situation is realized by the implementation of a concrete *intervention*. It is characterized in a further text block and makes the best realization subject of discussion.

The connection of the concrete intervention to theory and grounding, empirical models is provided in a *background* section. Here, the meaning of the concrete intervention in regard to empirically proven influence factors, such as *competence, stickiness, complexity, mother tongue, educational background, internalization, externalization, socialization* and *combination,* is reflected (see Sect. 2.2).

The following *intervention categories* are designed to be applied in concrete contexts. Since categories can be carried out by various communication channels and manners, concrete interventions can be connected to all: socialization, externalization, internalization and combination.

- **Animation:** Knowledge to be transferred can not only be presented in a static manner. By the presentation of images or objects that show how they evolves over time, dynamic aspects of knowledge transfers can be visualized.
- **Instructions:** Knowledge to be transferred can be involved in a guided process. Various kinds of instructions (orally, visually, haptic, etc.) draw attention to a specific aspect, which is required for consecutive steps and therefore simplify knowledge transfers by providing structure.
- **Labellings:** Knowledge to be transferred can be augmented by labels over the whole object of investigation. The use of the same technical terms simplify knowledge transfers since conflicts in the use of terms are avoided and improve the stickiness.
- **Repetitive layouts:** Knowledge to be transferred can be provided by the same layouts. The use of the same layout simplifies knowledge transfers since mappings among different layouts can be avoided. This improves the stickiness.
- **Entropic visualizations:** Knowledge to be transferred can not only be presented by various visualizations. Several visualizations of the same type can be combined so that the entropy of the resulting visualization can be raised. This simplifies the knowledge transfers since mappings among visualizations can be avoided.
- **Functional integrations:** Knowledge to be transferred can not only be presented by various visualizations. Several visualizations of different types can be combined so that the entropy of the resulting visualization can be raised. This simplifies the knowledge transfers since mappings among visualizations can be avoided.
- **Realizations:** Knowledge to be transferred can be provided as realization. By dealing with the realized object of interest, relations are made clear easily, which have not been considered before. This simplifies the knowledge transfers.

4.2 Workshop Design

The workshop is designed to be carried out with knowledge management experts and context-specific experts. The teaming is a crucial element since both kinds of experts have the assignment to consider their individual background, their personal experience made in concrete projects and to reflect in regard to concrete relevant knowledge situations of the intended context. Only then, fruitful discussions will evolve and a validation considers multiple perspectives. The workshop was structured by the following steps:

1. **Individual context identification:** The workshop is started by an introduction to the general idea of knowledge transfer speed optimization. Then, participants are introduced and objectives for the workshop are clarified. A first brainstorming about the meaning of knowledge transfer optimizations in individual knowledge transfer situations intends to activate participants.
2. **Relationship establishment:** Workshop participants are enabled by the provision of basic knowledge. In concrete, this refers to concepts of knowledge transfers, empirical experiments about knowledge transfers and statistical models of the knowledge transfer velocity. Further, this includes context-specific knowledge, such as product generation engineering for the product development context. A second brainstorming about *intervention categories* in regard to the individual context prepares the dealing with interventions and establishes the relationship of theory and the individual's knowledge transfer situations.
3. **Selection of interventions:** Concrete examples of interventions for the intended context are provided by posters. Each participant has the chance to study the interventions carefully and create an opinion about their application in the individual situation. As questions occur, they are clarified for all participants. Workshop participants are asked to create further examples using clean template sheets following the design of Fig. 2 (a). Those are presented and discussed by all. The group consensus selects interventions to be considered in consecutive workshop steps.
4. **Identification of success factors and barriers:** Selected interventions are collected and each participant is asked to identify one main success factor and one main barrier for each intervention. Those are written on separate cards, which were pinned next to intervention posters. Identified factors are then presented and discussed. The group consensus selects success factors and barriers to be considered in consecutive workshop steps.
5 **Assessment of interventions:** Each participant is equipped with a print-out following the design of Fig. 1. Here, only by the consensus selected interventions, selected success factors and selected barriers can be found. Each participant then is asked to assess elements in regard to individual knowledge transfer situations. A consensus is found thereafter.

While the applicability of a certain success factor or barrier on an intervention is indicated by a checkmark put to the corresponding cell, its practicability is categorized by three kinds of interventions. A first kind refers to interventions, that can be implemented in any company and university. A second kind focuses on interventions, that can only be implemented when they are modified so that they fit to the specific need of an organization. A third kind issues the intervention's impractically high modification effort because of a high specification. Here, the participants is asked to denominate the corresponding cell. Further,

Interventions	Factors	Success Factors							Barriers							Assessment	
		Main Factor Intervention 1	Main Factor Intervention 2	Main Factor Intervention 3	Main Factor Intervention 4	Main Factor Intervention 5	Main Factor Intervention ...	Main Factor Intervention n	Main Factor Intervention 1	Main Factor Intervention 2	Main Factor Intervention 3	Main Factor Intervention 4	Main Factor Intervention 5	Main Factor Intervention ...	Main Factor Intervention n	Practicability (A/B/C)	Short-term Controllability
Intervention 1		✓							✓								
Intervention 2			✓							✓							
Intervention 3				✓							✓						
Intervention 4					✓							✓					
Intervention 5						✓							✓				
Intervention ...							✓							✓			
Intervention n								✓							✓		

Legend:
A - Interventions, that can be implemented in any company and university.
B - Interventions, that can only be implemented when they are modificated in regard to the specific need of an organization.
C - Interventions, that are highly specific and can only be implemented in organizations under very high modification efforts..
✓ - Interventions are controllable and show results in short-term horizonts.

Fig. 1. Intervention assessment design.

the short-term controllability is indicated by a checkmark, that is put by the participant if the intervention is controllable and shows results in short-term horizons.

5   Demonstration of Interventions in PGE

Following the DSRM of Peffers [19], the *intervention validation framework* designed in Sect. 4 is demonstrated by the realization of the workshop designed (Sect. 4.2) and the application of the intervention design in the PGE context. The *workshop design* was carried out with 2 knowledge management experts (1 from university, 1 from a company) and 3 product development experts (1 from university, 2 from companies). Applying the seven *intervention categories* of Sect. 4.1 to the PGE context with help of the template design (see Fig. 2a), seven PGE-specific interventions have been prepared as they can be found in Fig. 2(b)–(d) and Fig. 3(a)–(d). They have been presented in the third phase of the workshop. Assuming to have universities or companies, which show as-is situations presented here, those interventions optimize the speed of knowledge transfers observed in the individual's situations if relevant influence factors are adjusted.

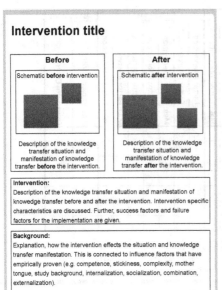

(a) Intervention Template

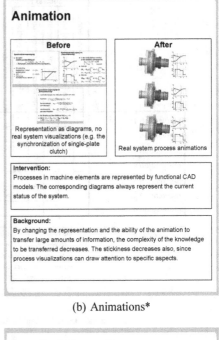

(b) Animations*

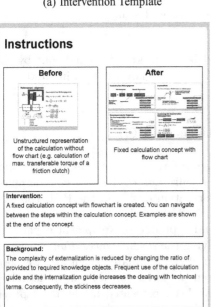

(c) Instructions*

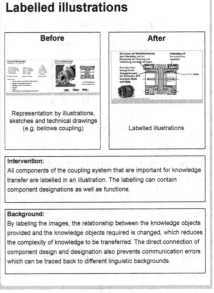

(d) Labellings*

Fig. 2. Intervention examples (*exemplified with product development context).

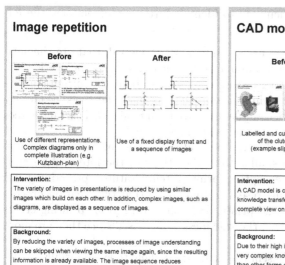

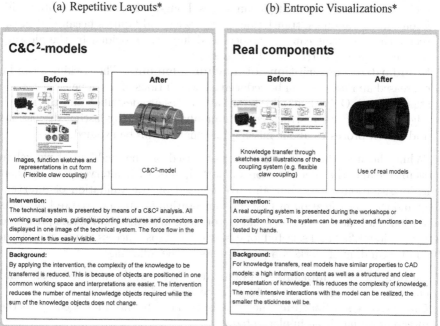

(a) Repetitive Layouts*

(b) Entropic Visualizations*

(c) Functional Integrations*

(d) Realizations*

Fig. 3. Intervention examples (*exemplified with product development context) continued.

As it was task of the participants to identify further interventions, the following have been identified:

- **Fantasy denominations:** If new products are developed, that are thematically positioned between several domains, technical terms can be overloaded. Experiences showed, that long-lasting discussions about the current understanding of engineers about technical components can be shortened as fantasy denominations are used until components have been finalized. This guarantees a small stickiness because terms are used impartially.
- **3D prints:** 3D printouts fasten the realization process of real components. Hence, this intervention is similar to explanations of the intervention *realizations* with the following exception: printing temperatures, procedures and materials still are an evolving research domain, so that the creation process itself can be more complex and prints might show typical 3D printing errors or are bad compromises. Then, the stickiness is increased since they are more complicated to interpret.
- **Expert presentations:** Presentations of experts help to avoid pitfalls, structure unknown terrain, mention relevant vocabulary and therefore decrease stickiness. Particularly educational concepts support the raise in competences.
- **Language glossary:** A collection of technical terms supports the use of correct technical terms in multiple languages. Long-lasting discussions about different understandings, translation inaccuracies and failures because of incorrect technical terms can be avoided as definitions provided by the glossary have high quality entries in all languages.
- **Standardized descriptions of machine elements:** The stickiness can be decreased and failures can be reduced as descriptions of machine elements are standardized. Only then, all relevant attributes are described and the knowledge transfer can be structured commonly. Hence, long-lasting discussions and search processes about missing information can be avoided.

While the first three workshop steps focused on the enabling of workshop participants and the identification of participants with interventions in their concrete situation, phase four and five focused on the validation of interventions and the identification of best implementation strategies. Figure 4 presents validation-relevant interventions and factors forming a matrix. Factors presented here, were identified and selected for consecutive steps. Success factors refer from the understanding of workshop participants to the following:

- **Simplicity of adaption:** Relevant knowledge can be adapted easily and efficiently to the form required by the corresponding intervention.
- **Clarity of visualization:** The visualization can be interpreted easily, as the intervention has been implemented.
- **Conclusiveness:** Relevant knowledge is understandable after the intervention has been implemented.
- **Function-based mapping:** Knowledge can be mapped function-wise by the intervention.
- **Need for action:** The knowledge to be transferred is essential and as-is knowledge transfers are bad so that the need for action exceeds inactivity.

- **Simplification:** The intervention simplifies relevant knowledge.
- **Scope of internalization:** The scope of knowledge to be transferred is clearly characterized and interventions focus on exactly this scope.

Barriers identified and selected for consecutive steps are from the understanding of workshop participants the following:

- **Intellectual property protection:** Relevant knowledge is intellectual property and it is infringed by the intervention.
- **Linguistic expression:** The intervention does not consider linguistic nuances, so that knowledge transfers can be hampered.
- **Update effort:** The effort to keep knowledge uptodate is to big so that outdated knowledge objects hamper knowledge transfers.
- **Creation effort:** The effort to modify knowledge in regard to the intervention is to big so that the intervention is rejected by process designers.
- **Standard operating procedure problem:** The transfer of relevant knowledge is simplified by the optimization, but regrettably then is not supporting the act of thinking any more. It enables only the processing of standard procedures.
- **Prerequisites:** Competences required to interpret knowledge after the intervention are high and knowledge carriers are not able to receive knowledge.
- **Limitations:** Relevant knowledge is hindered because of intervention-specific limitations, e.g. space limitations, color limitations or decoding limitations.

6   Evaluation

An evaluation of interventions by the workshop is built on the following: First, only relevant interventions have been selected by workshop participants. Second, interventions have been assessed in regard to their practicability by individuals. Third, interventions have been applied in imaginary projects in order to assess their short-term controllability.

The evaluation of best realization strategies is built on the following: First, the identification of relevant success factors as well as barriers of each intervention by individuals and the discussion by all. Second, the verification of their influence on several interventions. Third, the act of consensus identification.

So, interventions have been validated and attractive interventions can be identified for subsequent research.

Success Factors: While only the main success factor of a certain intervention has been colored in Fig. 4, their effect on further interventions has been highlighted on a consensus base by checkmarks. There is not any success factor, that is only relevant for its original intervention. Further, main factors are not redundant. This underlines the specific consideration of each intervention and draws attention to some factors, that are very meaningful. The factor showing the most influences is the *simplification*, which is relevant for six interventions. The factor showing the fewest influences is the *need for action*, which is relevant

Interventions	Factors	Success Factors							Barriers							Assessment			
		Simplicity of adaption	Clarity of visualization	Conclusiveness	Function-based mapping	Need for action	Simplification	Scope of internalization	Intellectual property protection	Linguistic expression	Update effort	Creation effort	SOP problem	Prerequisites	Limitations	Practicability (A/B/C) A	B	C	Short-term Controllability
CAD model		✓	✓	✓			✓	✓	✓		✓	✓			✓	0,4	0,6	0	0,6
Labeled illustrations			✓	✓			✓			✓	✓					0,8	0,2	0	0,8
Image repetition		✓	✓	✓			✓	✓			✓					1	0	0	0,8
Animation		✓	✓		✓		✓	✓			✓	✓			✓	0,4	0,4	0,2	0,6
Instructions		✓		✓	✓	✓	✓			✓			✓			0,4	0,4	0,2	0,8
Real components				✓		✓		✓			✓		✓	✓		0,2	0,4	0,4	0,6
C&C² models		✓	✓	✓	✓	✓		✓		✓				✓	✓	0,2	0	0,8	0,2

Legend:		
	A	- Interventions, that can be implemented in any company and university.
	B	- Interventions, that can only be implemented when they are modified in regard to the specific need of an organization.
	C	- Interventions, that are highly specific and can only be implemented in organizations under very high modification efforts..
	✓	- Factors are relevant for indicated interventions.
	✓	- Main factor of a certain intervention in consens of participants.
	▓	- Main category of practicability
	▓	- Interventions are controllable and show results in short-term horizonts.

Fig. 4. Intervention assessment (consensus of participants).

for two interventions. The intervention demanding for the most success factors is the $C\&C^2 models$. The intervention demanding for the fewest success factors is the *real components*.

Barriers: On a consensus base, the effect of barriers has been highlighted with checkmarks and the main factor is colored in Fig. 4. There is not any barrier, that is only relevant for its original intervention. Further, main factors are not redundant. This underlines the specific consideration of each intervention and draws attention to some factors, that are very meaningful. The factor showing the most influences is the *update effort*, which is relevant for four interventions. The factor showing the fewest influences is the *SOP problem*, which is relevant for one intervention. The intervention demanding for the most success factors is the *CAD model*. The intervention demanding for the fewest success factors is the *instructions*.

Practicability: Considering the assessment of all participants, the average assessment is visualized by values element-wise in Fig. 4. The maximum highlighted in purple is interpreted as the main category of an intervention. Interventions clearly showing the ability to be implemented in universities and companies are *labeled instructions* and *image repetitions*. The interventions *CAD model* and *real components* can be identified without doubts as interventions requiring modifications before their implementation. Only the $C\&C^2 models$ have been characterized as highly specific and to be able to be implemented only under high modification efforts. The interventions *animation* and *instructions* can be both: either, they can be implemented immediately or they require modifications. Discussions showed that this is connected to the specific animation object and instruction example. The intervention *real components* can be either categorized as practicability type B or C. Discussions showed that this is again connected to the specific component example: Highly specific components, such as complex molecule models, demand for high modification efforts and the realization of simple components, e.g. printable by 3D printers, just demands for simple modification efforts.

Short-Term Controllability: Considering the assessment of all participants, the average assessment is visualized by values element-wise in Fig. 4. Elements above the threshold of 0.5 are highlighted in green and can be interpreted as an intervention, which is controllable in short-term horizons. Nearly all interventions can be identified to be controllable and show short-term effects. Hence, they are very suited for an implementation in universities and companies. Only $C\&C^2 models$ are not evaluated to be an intervention, which can be implemented quickly, is controllable and shows short-term effects.

7   Conclusion

The first research question (How can time-dependent knowledge-transfer models be used in order to derive interventions, which optimize speed of knowledge-intensive business processes?) can be answered by interventions, that consider a modification of empirically proven influence factors. While generic intervention categories have been defined, twelve concrete interventions have been characterized. The concrete situation is considered similar to product profiles, so that a best intervention can be selected.

The second research question (How can process interventions be best realized by practitioners?) can be answered by the consideration of success factors and barriers, which support or hamper the implementation of intervention in concrete situations or process instances. The assessment of interventions by practitioners identified representatives, which are very suited for both, universities and companies. This was realized on base of the practicability and the short-term controllability.

Faced with workshop results, interventions have been validated by practitioners on a quality-based level. With exception of the $C\&C^2 models$, all interventions have been identified to be very attractive for the observation in project settings. Only the $CAD\ model$ and *real components* intervention are attractive for this, when required modifications are manageable. Hence, the validation of their functioning will be evaluated on base of product development projects in labor studies, which allow the observation of projects under realistic circumstances. Here, best implementation strategies can be proven and success factors and barriers can be relativized.

References

1. Alavi, M., Leidner, D.: Review: knowledge management and knowledge management systems: conceptual foundations and research issues. MIS Q. **25**(1), 107–136 (2001). https://doi.org/10.2307/3250961
2. Albers, A., Bursac, N. and Rapp, S.: PGE-product generation engineering-case study of the dual mass flywheel. In: Marjanović, D. (ed.) DS 84: Proceedings of the DESIGN 2016 14th International Design Conference: Engineering Design Practice, Cavtat-Dubrovnik, Croatia, pp. 791–800 (2016)
3. Albers, A., Bursac, N., Wintergerst, E.: Product generation development-importance and challenges from a design research perspective. New Developments in Mechanics and Mechanical Engineering, pp. 16–21 (2015)
4. Albers, A., Gronau, N, Rapp, S., Grum, M., Zaiser, A., Bursac, N., Weber, E.: Influencing factors and methods for knowledge transfer situations in Product Generation Engineering based on the SECI model. Nord Design (2018)
5. Albers, A., Haug, F., Heitger, N., Arslan, M., Rapp, S., Bursac, N.: Produktgenerationsentwicklung-Praxisbedarf und Fallbeispiel in der automobilen Produktentwicklung. In: Proceedings 12. Symposium für Vorausschau und Technologieplanung (2016)
6. Albers, A., Heimicke, J., Walter, B., Basedow, G.N., Reiß, N., Heitger, N., Ott, S., Bursac, N.: Product profiles: modelling customer benefits as a foundation to bring inventions to innovations. Procedia CIRP Elsevier **70**(1), 253–258 (2018)
7. Albers, A., Rapp, S., Birk, C. and Bursac, N.: Die Frühe Phase der PGE-Produktgenerationsentwicklung. Stuttgarter Symposium für Produktentwicklung (2017)
8. Blessing, L.T., Chakrabarti, A.: DRM: A Design Research Methodology. Springer, London (2009)
9. Davenport, T.H., Prusak, L.: Working Knowledge: How Organizations Manage What They Know. Ubiquity, ACM (2000). http://doi.acm.org/10.1145/347634. 348775
10. Gronau, N.: Modeling and Analyzing Knowledge Intensive Business Processes with KMDL: Comprehensive Insights Into Theory and Practice, vol. 7. GITOmbh, Berlin (2012)
11. Gronau, N. and Grum, M.: The creation of a time-dependent knowledge transfer model. Work report, University of Potsdam, WI-2018-01 (2018)
12. Gronau, N., Weber, E.: Management of knowledge intensive business processes. In: Desel, J., Pernici, B., Weske, M. (eds.) BPM 2004. LNCS, vol. 3080, pp. 163–178. Springer, Heidelberg (2004). https://doi.org/10.1007/978-3-540-25970-1_11
13. Grum, M., Gronau, N.: A visionary way to novel process optimizations. In: Shishkov, B. (ed.) BMSD 2017. LNBIP, vol. 309, pp. 1–24. Springer, Cham (2018). https://doi.org/10.1007/978-3-319-78428-1_1
14. Hammer, M., Champy, J.: Reengineering the Corporation: A Manifesto for Business Revolution (1993)
15. Masaaki, I.: Kaizen: The Key to Japan's Competitive Success. McGraw-Hill Education Ltd., New York (1986)
16. Marjanovic, O. and Freeze, R.: Knowledge intensive business processes: theoretical foundations and research challenges. In: Proceedings of the 44th Hawaii International Conference on System Sciences, pp. 1530–1605 (2011)
17. Minbaeva, D., Pedersen, T., Björkman, I., Fey, C.F., Park, H.J.: MNC knowledge transfer, subsidiary absorptive capacity, and HRM. J. Int. Bus. Stud. **34**(6), 586–599 (2003). https://EconPapers.repec.org/RePEc:pal:jintbs:v:34:y:

18. Nonaka, I., Takeuchi, H.: The Knowledge-Creating Company: How Japanese Companies Create the Dynamics of Innovation. Oxford University Press, Oxford (1995)
19. Peffers, K., Tuunanen, T., Gengler, C.E., Rossi, M., Hui, W., Virtanen, V., Bragge, J.: The design science research process: a model for producing and presenting information systems research. In: 1st International Conference on Design Science in Information Systems and Technology (DESRIST), vol. 24(3), pp. 83–106 (2006)
20. Peffers, K., Tuunanen, T., Rothenberger, M.A., Chatterjee, S.: A design science research methodology for information systems research. Manag. Inf. Syst.D **24**(3), 45–78 (2007)
21. Polanyi, M., Sen, A.: The Tacit Dimension. University of Chicago Press, London (2009)
22. Richter, T., Heimicke, J., Reiß, N., Albers, A., Gutzeit, M., Bursac, N.: Pitch 2.0-Concept of early evaluation of product profiles in product generation engineering. In: Proceedings of TMCE 2018, Las Palmas de Gran Canaria, Gran Canaria, Spain (2018)
23. Sigmanek, C., Lantow, B.: A survey on modelling knowledge-intensive business processes from the perspective of knowledge management. In: Proceedings of the 7th International Joint Conference on Knowledge Discovery, Knowledge Engineering and Knowledge Management, vol. 3, pp. 325–332 (2015). https://doi.org/10.5220/0005597903250332
24. Strambach, S.: Knowledge-Intensive Business Services (KIBS) as drivers of multilevel knowledge dynamics. Int. J. Serv. Technol. Manag. **10**(2/3/4), 152–174 (2008). https://doi.org/10.1504/IJSTM.2008.022117
25. von Krogh, G., Ichijo, K., Nonaka, I.: Enabling Knowledge Creation: How to Unlock the Mystery of Tacit Knowledge and Release the Power of Innovation. Oxford University Press, New York (2000)

Declarative Modelling of Transactions for IS Development

Bert de Brock[(✉)] [iD]

Faculty of Economics and Business, University of Groningen,
PO Box 800, 9700 AV Groningen, The Netherlands
E.O.de.Brock@rug.nl

Abstract. In the development life cycle of an information system (IS) - from initial user wishes up to a running IS - an intermediate mathematical model is very useful, both as a clear and unambiguous capture of the user wishes regarding the functional requirements as well as a formal model of the system to be built. Based on decades of experience, we tackle the problem to develop a suitable, practical modelling method for formal, declarative, and implementation-independent specifications of information systems that can serve as a clear, unambiguous capture of the user wishes regarding the functional requirements. The theory should integrate data and transactions in a uniform way, because data and transactions are closely related. The theory should also be suitable for *incremental* and *agile development*, where we must quickly determine where, what, and how to change when necessary.

The notion of an *information machine* turns out to be very suitable for this goal. Several related notions will be defined. We introduce a general structure of transactions which includes a *generic rollback*, taking consistency into account. Several notions are generalizations of notions from database theory, such as *transaction, query,* and *view*.

We also explore some common practical structures for *states* and *transactions* in an information machine because they can become rather subtle in practice. In particular, transactions can be very subtle and complicated, also because they can be 'rolled back' and/or can be 'compound'. Our formal, declarative specifications of transactions must (and do) account for that. Fortunately, many of the transactions in practice have more or less the same form. We study and formally define several of such common *transaction patterns* in a declarative way.

We first sketch a development path for functional requirements which is straightforward. In order to handle the inherent complexity of development, the path enables 'stepwise clarification', 'stepwise specification', and traceability. It gradually goes from the informal natural language and way of thinking of users to a formal model (with inputs, outputs, procedures, parameters, etc.).

Keywords: Functional requirement · User wish · Use case ·
System sequence diagram · Information machine · Data model ·
(Compound) transaction · Query · View · (Database) state ·
Input & output sequences · Rollback · Transaction pattern · Create ·
Update · (Cascading) delete · Counter · 'Next' number

© Springer Nature Switzerland AG 2019
B. Shishkov (Ed.): BMSD 2019, LNBIP 356, pp. 114–133, 2019.
https://doi.org/10.1007/978-3-030-24854-3_8

1   Introduction

In the development life cycle of an information system - from initial user wishes up to a running information system - an intermediate mathematical model can be very useful, both as a clear, unambiguous capture of the user wishes regarding the functional requirements, as well as a formal specification of the system to be built (where it can aid implementation). Such a semantic model should include *data* as well as *transactions*, in an *integrated* way, because data and transactions are closely related to each other. Ideally, it should provide a *declarative* semantics. However, the problem is that there is currently no suitable, practical theory about formal, implementation-independent specifications of information systems that can serve as a clear, unambiguous capture of the user wishes regarding the functional requirements, a theory that also integrates data and transactions in a uniform way. During (and beyond) development it should also be easy to make changes in the design (i.e., ease of *design change*). In this paper we tackle that problem by developing such a formal, integrated, declarative, implementation-independent semantic model, one that is usable in practice as well. We gradually developed our theory based on many and quite diverse field cases over decades of interaction between theory development and practical experience.

Comparison with Related Approaches
We compare our work with some related approaches, i.e., to *approaches*, not so much to each and every *paper* within such an approach.

Much work has been done on the <u>implementation</u> of transactions (transaction processing, algorithms, concurrency control, recovery, coordination of distributed transactions, ACID-properties, etc.); see the comprehensive [1] for instance. This is indeed a difficult topic. However, our paper is about (declarative) <u>specifications</u> of transactions, i.e., specifying the transactions the user would need. It also takes care of the consistency of transactions w.r.t. constraints and it is more general than only in case of databases.

One approach to the specification of transactions is by <u>operational semantics</u>, see [2] for example. Operational semantics is already looking forward to implementations, e.g., looking at execution models, order of execution, intermediate states, parallelization, etc. However, this is not a user concern. E.g., for a user there are only two relevant states in case of a transaction: the state *before* the transaction and the state *after* the transaction. That is exactly what our specification approach is doing.

Another approach is to introduce an intermediate logical language for the specification of transactions, as in [3] for instance. We don't want (nor need) to do that, because we quite directly go from the natural language of the user, say English or Dutch, to a mathematical model (as an intermediate stage towards implementation): The initial user wishes can be elaborated in *use cases* [4, 5] and then reflected in *system sequence diagrams* [6], from where we can go directly to the mathematical model.

There are several approaches to bridge the gap between business processes and software specifications, e.g. [22], but they hardly treat data and transactions in an integrated and detailed way. However, the devil is usually in those details…

What still lacks is a formal, purely declarative, and implementation-independent model for transactions with a clear semantics, treating data and transactions in an integrated and detailed way, one which is also applicable and useful in practice.

Our contribution consists of a mathematical model for transactions which is formal, declarative, and implementation-independent. Moreover, we introduce and formally define several common *transaction patterns*. The model is an intermediary which decouples user aspects from implementation aspects and facilitates design changes. The model bridges/reduces the gap between user requirements and software specifications.

Overview of the Paper

Section 2 sketches how the just mentioned development path for functional requirements can work, also in an incremental or agile development environment.

The notion of **information machine** (IM) turns out to be very suitable for implementation-independent, declarative formal specifications of information systems which also integrate data and transactions [7]. This central notion will be introduced in Sect. 3. Essentially, an IM determines a set of possible *inputs* and a set of possible *states*, and for each input-state combination it determines the corresponding *output* and *next state*. It provides a formal, implementation-independent representation of the user wishes and the system (to be) developed. So, it includes the possible inputs and outputs and the relation between them, as well as the possible states and possible state transitions. An IM is developed from a usage/user point of view, not from an implementation point of view.

On the other hand, the IM forms a solid basis for a correct implementation. For an implementation in an imperative system, it mentions the procedures/methods with their parameters (and their types), it indicates the desirable data structures and additional constraints (to be guarded by the system to be developed), and specifies the postconditions per transaction (for the state and for the output). For an implementation in a declarative (e.g., relational) system, it mentions the (stored) procedures with their parameters (and their types), indicates the desirable data structures and additional (database) constraints, and contains the specifications for the declarative statements needed (e.g., within SQL-procedures).

Several IM-related notions will be introduced in the subsequent sections. They are often generalizations of notions from database theory, as presented in [8–10] for example. Section 4 extends the database notions **transaction**, **query**, and **view** to IMs.

The definition of an information machine determines the output and the next state upon an input in a given state. This also implicitly determines the *sequence* of outputs and the *sequence* of state changes upon a **sequence of inputs**, as made explicit in Sect. 5.

In a few cases, a state can be very simple, for instance an integer (e.g., indicating a temperature) or even a Boolean (e.g., for a light switch). However, in practical situations a state must represent the values of many components. In that case, a state could be a *function* that assigns to each component the corresponding value. Such a component value, in its turn, could be a set for instance. In Sect. 6 we explore some common structures for **states** in an information machine, including **database states**.

Sections 7 and 8 introduce a general structure of transactions, including generic rollbacks, taking consistency into account. Section 7 first introduces some useful auxiliary notions.

Many of the common transactions in practice have more or less the same form. Section 9 defines several such common **transaction patterns**, also for the well-known functions **C**reate, **U**pdate, and **D**elete, transactions that are generally applicable to data in a system. Section 9 also treats transaction patterns in (simple and complex) cases of 'counters' and 'next' numbers.

Finally, everything will be illustrated in Sect. 10, that presents an example of an information machine. Although the example is relatively small, it illustrates many subtle and/or complex points, e.g., system-generated (and system-managed) numbers, integrity checking to be done by the system, cascading and non-cascading deletes, compound transactions, and also differentiated output messages. Section 10 also demonstrates how a design change could work in our approach, from initial user request down to the information machine (and even the software). Section 10 illustrates the traceability, extendibility, and scalability of the approach as well.

2 Some Preliminary Notions

We will sketch a development path for individual functional requirements. It is an adapted version of the one in [7, 11], where its use in the complete development life cycle is explained in more detail. The origin of a functional requirement does not matter (e.g., whether domain-imposed or user-defined).

The development path for functional requirements is straightforward and starts with the notion of *simple user wishes* and then goes from *parameterized* (or *full*) *user wishes* via *use cases* and their *system sequence diagrams* to an *information machine* (model synthesis) and finally to a realization, an *information system*.

We explain the notions of user wish, use case, and system sequence diagram in the current section and the notion of information machine in the next section. The realization in an *information system* is beyond the scope of the current paper, but we refer to Chapter 9 of [8] for a transformation to SQL-based systems.

Informally, a **simple user wish** is a (short) expression in natural language, expressing a 'wish' of a (future) user which the system should be able to fulfil. E.g., for a student registration system a wish could simply be to '*Register a student*'. So, a simple user wish is not yet very specific. Simple user wishes might originate from requirements elicitation, business process modelling, and/or enterprise modelling, for instance.

A **parameterized user wish**, the next 'clarification' step, is a simple user wish extended with the relevant parameters, e.g., the wish to '*Register a student with a given name, gender, and phone number*'. So, a parameterized user wish (UW) is a more detailed 'specification':

$$\text{Parameterized UW } = \text{ SimpleUW } + \text{ relevant parameters}$$

In practice, determining the set of relevant parameters of a user wish might not be simple. For instance, what to register about a student? Several stakeholders might have a say in it. Moreover, in an incremental or agile development approach, the parameter set might gradually grow. Apart from that, the set of necessary parameters might change over time.

A **use case** (UC) is a sequence of sentences in natural language describing the sequence of steps in a typical usage of the system [4, 5], say to realize a parameterized UW. A use case roughly corresponds to an *elementary business process*, a building block in business process engineering [12].

User wishes and use cases are all expressed in the natural language of the user (say English or Dutch). So, it is feasible for users (and/or domain experts) themselves to write the user wishes and use cases and/or at least validate them, maybe with the help of some (business) analyst.

A **system sequence diagram** (SSD) of a UC is a schematic representation emphasizing the interaction between the primary actor (user), the system (as a black box), and other actors (if any), including the messages (with their parameters) between them [12]. An SSD (a kind of stylised UC) makes the prospective inputs, state changes, and outputs of the system more explicit. An SSD clarifies the work still to be done by the developer. In principle, there should be a correspondence between the steps in the SSD and those in the UC. Given the desirable correspondence between the SSD and the underlying UC, an SSD can be checked against that UC together with the users. SSDs are often drawn as UML - diagrams [12]. We simply denote a basic step in an SSD as:

<Actor1> → <Actor2> : <Message>

meaning: <Actor1> sends <Message> to <Actor2>

Suppose that in our example the system also has to provide the student number for the new student, then the SSD for our sample parameterized UW could look as follows:

1. User → System: RegisterStudent(<name>, <gender>, <phone number>);
2. System → System: use the next unused student number as the new student number;
3. System → System: register the name, gender, phone number, and student number;
4. System → User: "Assigned student number is" <student number>;
5. System → System: increase the next unused student number by 1

So, the SSD makes the prospective inputs, state changes, and outputs of the system explicit.

A simple user wish often has the form: <u><(action) verb></u> **a** <u><noun (phrase)></u>, as pointed out in [11]. For example: '*Register a student*'. A parameterized UW often has the form: <u><(action) verb></u> **a** <u><noun (phrase)></u> **with a given** <parameter list>. For example: '*Register a student with a given <u>name</u>, <u>gender</u>, and <u>phone number</u>*'.

If α denotes the action verb and β the noun phrase in the user wish, the first step in the SSD can be chosen as: **User → System:** $\alpha\beta$(<parameter list>), as in our SSD-example. Hence, the first step of the SSD follows directly from the parameterized user wish.

3   Information Machines

An **information machine** (IM) is a 5-tuple (I, O, S, G, T) consisting of:

- a set I (of *inputs*), called its *input space*
- a set O (of *outputs*), called its *output space*
- a set S (of *states*), called its *state space*
- an *output function* G: I × S → O,

  mapping pairs of an input and a state to the corresponding output

- a *transition function* T: I × S → S,

  mapping pairs of an input and a state to the corresponding next state

The above notation 'f: X → Y' means that f is a function with domain X and its range being a subset of Y. The working of an IM, shown as a 'black box' (with $i \in I$ and $s \in S$):

$$i \to \boxed{s \mapsto T(i,s)} \to G(i,s)$$

In words: Upon input i, the IM produces output G(i,s) and its internal state s changes into T(i,s). Both the output and the new state depend on the input as well as on the internal state.

We could have chosen for other (but equivalent) forms for G and T, e.g.:

$$T : I \to (S \to S) \text{ and } G : I \to (S \to O) \tag{A1}$$

If F is a function then we sometimes write F_x instead of F(x), especially if F(x) itself is a function again. In case of (A1), each input $i \in I$ leads to a function T_i (called a transaction) that assigns a 'new' state to an 'old' state, and to a function G_i that assigns an output to an 'old' state (in some cases G_i is called a query, see Sect. 4).

The state space of an IM reflects the static aspects. It shows structure of (the data about) the entities and how they are related to each other. The transactions of an IM (together with the use cases) reflect the dynamic aspects. The transactions describe the possible state changes. Transactions often follow from the use cases. Rules and regulations are (partly) reflected in the UCs and in the *constraints* expressed in the state space of the IM (via keys, foreign keys, data formats, check digits, etc.). See Sect. 10 for an illustrative example.

The SSD-steps of the form **User → System:**<Message> indicate that <Message> will become an input for the IM. The input space of the IM contains all those potential messages.

Our notion of *information machine* is equivalent to the notion of *data machine* in [13]. An IM can also be considered as a – not necessarily finite – Mealy machine without a special start state; cf. [14, 15]. (For a quick lookup we added a Wikipedia link too.)

4   Extending Database Terminology

When we use the above form (A1) for G and T of an information machine M then:

G_i is called a **query within** M $\Leftrightarrow$ for i the state always stays the same,

i.e., $T_i(s) = s$ for each $s \in S$

(i; G_i) is called a **view within** M $\Leftrightarrow$ G_i is a query within M

T_i is called a **transaction within** M

So, a view is a 'named query', where i is the view name and G_i is the view definition.

Strictly speaking, a concrete input i can (and often will) include parameter values, in which case we are inclined to call the part without parameters the name of the view: For example, 'RegisterStudent(J. Brown, M, 0612345678)' would officially be the view name whereas we are inclined to call 'RegisterStudent' the view name.

5   Sequences of Inputs and Corresponding Outputs

If an information machine receives a *sequence* of inputs then the information machine goes through a *sequence* of states and produces a *sequence* of outputs.

In general, each next state is the result of applying the transition function to the pair of the previous state and the received input, and each next output is the result of applying the output function to that same combination of the previous state and the received input.

Formally: If an information machine (I, O, S, G, T) receives a sequence $<i_1; i_2; \ldots; i_n>$ of inputs and initially is in state s_0, then the IM goes through the sequence $<s_1; s_2; \ldots; s_n>$ of states and produces the sequence $<o_1; o_2; \ldots; o_n>$ of outputs where, for all k from 1 up to n, state s_k is defined as $T(i_k, s_{k-1})$ and output o_k is defined as $G(i_k, s_{k-1})$.

6   On the Structure of *States* in an Information Machine

(a) Sometimes a state can be very simple, for example an integer, e.g., when it only has to represent the current temperature (say, in Celsius). The state space could then simply be $[-273 \ldots)$, say. Or the state could only be a Boolean (e.g., for a light switch).

(b) Usually, however, a state has to represent the values of many components. Then a state could be modelled as a *function* that assigns to each component the corresponding value. For instance, if each state has to represent two temperatures, say one for inside and one for outside, then a state could be a function over the set of components {Inside, Outside}, assigning a temperature to each of the 2 components.

In general, if L is a set (of 'component labels') then S is called a **state space over** L iff S is a set of functions over L (i.e., each state is a function over L). In that case, an element of L is called a **component of** S (and of each s ∈ S).

(c) A state often represents several sets, e.g., a set representing students, a set representing lecturers, a set representing courses, etc. Then we might model a state as a function that assigns such sets to certain components; e.g., s(STUD) might represent the set of students in state s. An element of such a set, e.g., t ∈ s(STUD) representing an individual student, often is modelled as a function as well, a function that assigns to each relevant property its value for that element, e.g., t(NUMBER) representing the student number.

(d) This brings us to explain *database universes*, which are special kinds of state spaces.

If A is a set (of 'attribute names') then T is called a **table over** A iff T is a set of functions each with domain A. We call A **the heading of** T. The elements of T are usually called *tuples* and the elements of A are usually called *attributes*.

If F is a set-valued function (assigning to each 'table name' a set of corresponding 'attribute names') then s is called a **database state over** F iff s is a function over dom(F) and s(E) is a table over F(E), for each E ∈ dom(F).

S is called a **database universe over** F iff S is a set of database states over F. We then call F the **database skeleton of** S. In other words, the database skeleton is the function that assigns to each relevant 'table name' the set of corresponding 'attribute names'.

Often the state space of an IM is a database universe, with the 'table names' as the components. All the notions under (d) are explained in detail in [8], for instance.

7 The General Structure of Singular Transactions

Before we treat the structure of transactions in more detail, we need some auxiliary notions.

State changes usually concern only one or a few components at a time, leaving all the other parts of a state s unchanged. Therefore, we introduce $s \, \theta \, g$, the *modification* of a function s by a function g. If s and g are functions, then we define the function $s \, \theta \, g$ over $\text{dom}(s) \cup \text{dom}(g)$ for each $x \in \text{dom}(s) \cup \text{dom}(g)$ as follows:

$$\underline{s \, \theta \, g} \, (x) \; = \; \begin{array}{l} / \; s(x) \text{ for } x \in \text{dom}(s) - \text{dom}(g) \\ \backslash \; g(x) \text{ for } x \in \text{dom}(g) \end{array}$$

We call $s \, \theta \, g$ **the modification of** s **by** g (or, looking the other way around, **the extension of** g **with** s). Note that the 'modifying' function g 'overrules' s in $s \, \theta \, g$.

Singular changes (and rollback)

If an intended state change concerns only <u>one</u> component, we call it a *singular* transaction. In that case we have to specify *which* component it is and, for each state, what *the new value* for that component has to be. Therefore, for a state space S over a component set L, an individual component $E \in L$, and a function h over S (with h(s) representing the new E-value for each $s \in S$), we define the function **Main1(S, E, h)**, called the *maintenance of* E *according to* h *over* S, for each $s \in S$ as:

$$\textbf{Main1(S, E, h) (s)} = \begin{array}{l} / \text{ s } \theta \text{ \{(E; h(s))\}} \quad \text{if it is in S} \\ \backslash \text{ s} \qquad\qquad\qquad \text{otherwise} \end{array}$$

In other words, the function **Main1(S, E, h)** assigns to each $s \in S$ the new state in which h(s) is the (new) value for the component E and where the value for every other component stays the same, provided that $s \theta \{(E; h(s))\}$, the new state, is 'allowed', i.e., is in S; otherwise, the state stays the same. (This is related to the notion of *rollback*; see [9, 10, 16].)

Note that <u>Main1(S, E, h): S $\rightarrow$ S</u>, i.e., Main1(S, E, h) is a function from S *into* S again. Hence, Main1(S, E, h) always specifies an allowed state! This is related to the notion of *Consistency*, one of the so-called *ACID properties* [9, 10, 17, 18]. Many of the well-known standard transaction classes are of this form, as we will show in Sect. 9.

8 The General Structure of Compound Transactions

We note that in the above case, i.e., where the state change concerns only one component, $g_s = \{(E; h(s))\}$ is the modifying function, assigning h(s) to E.

We can generalize this to a state change that concerns <u>several</u> components: Let S be a state space over a component set L, $L' \subseteq L$, and g be a function over S such that for each $s \in S$, g_s is a function over L' (where $g_s(E)$ is the new E-value for each $E \in L'$ and each $s \in S$). Then we define the function **Main(S, g)**, the *(compound) transaction* (or *compound maintenance*) *according to* g, over S for each $s \in S$ as follows:

$$\textbf{Main(S, g) (s)} = \begin{array}{l} / \text{ s } \theta \, g_s \quad \text{if s } \theta \, g_s \in \text{ S} \\ \backslash \text{ s} \qquad\quad \text{otherwise} \end{array}$$

In other words, the function **Main(S, g)** assigns to each $s \in S$ the new state $s \theta g_s$, in which $g_s(E)$ is the (new) value for component E for each $E \in dom(g_s)$ and the value for every other component stays the same, provided that this new state is 'allowed', i.e., is in S; otherwise, the state stays the same, i.e., stays s. This is related to the notion of *rollback* [9, 10, 16].

Note that $\underline{\text{Main}(S, g)}: S \rightarrow S$, i.e., Main(S, g) is a $\underline{\text{transaction}}$ from S *into* S again. Hence, Main($\overline{S}$, g) always specifies an allowed state! Again, this is related to the *ACID*-notion of *Consistency* [9, 10, 17, 18]. Section 10 contains examples of compound transactions.

We note that Main is a generalization of the special case Main1:

Main1(S, E, h) = Main(S, g), where $g_s = \{(E; h(s))\}$ for each $s \in S$

9   Common Patterns for Singular Transactions in an IM

Now we are ready to concretely define several common 'transaction patterns', which all have the form Main1(S, E, h). In those cases we only have to specify the part h(s).

We start with the well-known and ubiquitous basic functions that generally apply to data in a system, known as **CRUD** (Create, Read, Update, and Delete); see [19, 20]: One can *add* data to the system (Create), only 'look at' data in the system (Read), *change* data in the system (Update), or *remove* data from the system (Delete). Read indicates a *query* (where the state always stays the same) while Create, Update, and Delete indicate state *changes*.

For each of these three kinds of maintenance operations (Create, Update, and Delete) we will distinguish 4 situations, i.e., whether the operation applies to: (1) an individual element, (2) a cohesive set of elements ('*all-or-nothing*'), (3) several elements in arbitrary order, and (4) several elements in a specific order. See Sect. 9.1 for Create, Sect. 9.2 for Delete, Sect. 9.3 for Update. Sections 9.1–9.3 consider a component E of S for which s(E) is a set (for each state $s \in S$).

9.1   Create

9.1.1   Create Element
A Create (e.g., *Create Course*) might indicate a situation where an element t has to be added to the set s(E). In that case, $\underline{h(s) = s(E) \cup \{t\}}$. Section 10 contains two such examples, '*Create Course*' and '*Create Course Registration*'.

In some cases, the system itself must generate one or more parts of t, e.g., an order number and/or an order date. Those system-generated values should probably also be part of the output given back to the user, because otherwise the user wouldn't know that generated value. Section 10 contains an example with a system-generated value (*Create Student*).

We note that t might depend on s (e.g., because of a state-dependent 'next' order number).

9.1.2   Create a Cohesive Set of Elements
A Create might also indicate a situation where *a set of* elements has to be added *as a whole* to the set s(E), e.g., *Create the set of order lines* belonging to a certain order. If V represents that set then $\underline{h(s) = s(E) \cup V}$. We note that this is an '*all-or-nothing*' addition, as follows from the definition of Main1(S, E, h). This is related to *Atomicity*, one of the *ACID properties*; see [9, 10, 17, 18]. We note that V might depend on state s.

9.1.3 Create Several Elements Individually

A Create might also be used when several elements have to be added to s(E) *indi-vidually* (and *independently* from each other), e.g., *Create the new students of last week*. This can be treated as a sequence of individual applications of Sect. 9.1.1 (Create element). See Sect. 5 for *sequences* of inputs. We note that an individual element can either be added, if that particular element is allowed (at that moment), or that it can be refused. So, in general a *subset* of the original set will be added. The end result might depend on the order in which the elements are added; for instance, when a 'next unused (student) number' has to be assigned to each individual element or when there is a maximum for the size of s(E).

The added elements might depend on state s (e.g., their generated student numbers).

9.1.4 Create Elements in a Specific Order

A Create might also be used in a situation where several elements have to be added to s(E) but *in a specific order*, for instance, '*Add (and process) the recent ticket requests, in order of request time*'. Here, the order in which the elements have to be added is given (and relevant), in contrast to Sect. 9.1.3. This is again a sequence of individual applications of Sect. 9.1.1 (Create element). See Sect. 5 for *sequences* of inputs. We note that an individual element can either be added, if that element is allowed (at that moment), or that it can be refused. So, in general a *subset* of the original set will be added. We note that the added elements might depend on state s (e.g., those generated (next) ticket numbers).

9.2 Delete

9.2.1 Delete Element

A Delete (e.g., *Delete Student*) might indicate a situation where one element t has to be deleted from the set s(E). In that case, $h(s) = s(E) - \{t\}$. The user wish '*Delete Course Registration*' in Sect. 10 is a clear example.

We note that t might depend on s (e.g., when the 'most recent' element has to be deleted).

9.2.2 Delete a Cohesive Set of Elements

A Delete might also indicate a situation where *a set of* elements has to be deleted *as a whole* from the set s(E), for instance *Delete the set of order lines* belonging to a certain order. If V represents that set then $h(s) = s(E) - V$. In the case of the order lines, the set V might be something of the form *{t | t is an order line belonging to order x}*. We note that this is an '*all-or-nothing*' deletion, which simply follows from the definition of Main1(S, E, h). For example, the user wish '*Delete Student*' in Sect. 10 not only leads to the deletion of a single student but also to the deletion of *a set of* elements (i.e., course registrations).

Like in Sect. 9.1.2, this is related to the ACID-notion of *Atomicity* [9, 10, 17, 18]. V might depend on state s (for instance, if V must be the set of order lines of the 'latest' order of a certain client).

Formally speaking, Sect. 9.2.1 is a special case of Sect. 9.2.2, namely where $V = \{t\}$.

9.2.3 Delete Several Elements Individually

A Delete might also be used when several elements have to be deleted from s(E) *individually* (and *independently* from each other), e.g., *Delete the members who notified that they want to cancel their membership*. This can be treated as a sequence of individual applications of Sect. 9.2.1 (Delete element). See Sect. 5 for *sequences* of inputs. We note that an individual element can either be deleted, if that is allowed (at that moment), or that it can be refused (e.g., because that member didn't pay all his debts yet). So, in general a *subset* of the original set will be deleted. The end result might depend on the order in which the elements are deleted, for instance, when there is a minimum for the size of s(E).

We note that the deletions might depend on the original state s (e.g., *Delete the 3 lowest study results of student 1234*).

9.2.4 Delete Elements in a Specific Order

A Delete might also be used in a situation where several elements have to be deleted from s(E) *in a specific order*, e.g., '*Handle and then delete all recent ticket requests, in order of request time*'. Here the order in which the elements have to be deleted is given (and relevant), in contrast to Sect. 9.2.3. This is again a sequence of individual applications of Sect. 9.2.1 (Delete element). See Sect. 5 for *sequences* of inputs. We note that an individual element can either be deleted, if that is applicable (at that moment), or not. So, in general a *subset* of the original set will be deleted.

We note that the end result might depend on the original state s (e.g., *Delete the lowest result, 10 times in a row*).

9.3 Update

The CRUD-function Update is about modifications of (parts of) some existing elements within a set. This CRUD-function is much subtler than the functions Create and Delete.

9.3.1 Update Element

This is a special case of the next one, Sect. 9.3.2, namely if it concerns only 1 element (e.g., only *Student with student number 1234*). The two updates in Sect. 10 are of this form.

We note that the end result might depend on state s.

9.3.2 Update a Cohesive Set of Elements

If s(E) is a set of which some elements have to be updated and all its elements are functions over an argument set (or attribute set) A, then we need to indicate for *which elements* in s(E) *which arguments* in A must be changed in *what way*. E.g., we might want to update for each master course the number of expected students (indicated by the argument NES) and the work load (indicated by the argument WL), say by +10% and by +5% respectively.

This can be modelled by a function f over a *subset* of s(E), i.e., the set of elements to be changed, where for each $t \in dom(f)$, f_t represents the altered fragment of t. In our example, if E = Courses then f might be a function over $\{t \mid t \in s(Courses)$ and $t(Level) =$ 'Master'$\}$, the set of elements to be changed, and f_t, representing the altered fragment of t, can be the function over {NES, WL} defined by $f_t(NES) = 1.1 * t(NES)$ and $f_t(WL) = 1.05 * t(WL)$.

In other words, dom(f) indicates *which elements* must be changed; and for each $t \in$ dom(f) the function f_t indicates *which arguments* of t have to be changed in *what way*. The last part rephrased again: to each argument b to be changed, f_t assigns its new value $f_t(b)$. So, t will be replaced by $t \theta f_t$ (yes indeed, the modification of t by f_t).

For h(s) this means: $\underline{h(s) = (s(E) - dom(f)) \cup \{t \theta f_t \mid t \in dom(f)\}}$, or, maybe clearer:

$h(s) = \{t \mid t \in s(E) \text{ and } t \notin dom(f)\} \cup$ $\{t \theta f_t \mid t \in dom(f)\}$	the set of unchanged elements of s(E) $\cup$ the set of changed elements of s(E)

For our example this results in:

$h(s) = \{t \mid t \in s(Courses) \text{ and } t(Level) \neq \text{'Master'}\} \cup$ $\{t \theta f_t \mid t \in s(Courses) \text{ and } t(Level) = \text{'Master'}\}$	the unchanged elements of s(Courses) $\cup$ the changed elements of s(Courses)

where f_t is defined over {NES, WL} by: $f_t(NES) = 1.1 * t(NES)$ and $f_t(WL) = 1.05 * t(WL)$.

We note that this pattern is an '*all-or-nothing update*', similar to the '*all-or-nothing addition*' in Sect. 9.1.2 and the '*all-or-nothing deletion*' in Sect. 9.2.2. Like in Sect. 9.1.2 and Sect. 9.2.2, this is related to the ACID-notion of *Atomicity*, see [9, 10, 17, 18].

We note that the end result might depend on the original state s.

9.3.3   Update Several Elements Individually

This can be treated as a <u>sequence</u> of individual applications of Sect. 9.3.1 (Update element). See Sect. 5 for *sequences* of inputs. We note that an individual element can either be updated, if that is allowed (at that moment), or that the update can be refused. So, in general a *subset* of the original set will be updated. The end result might depend on the order in which the elements are updated. The end result might also depend on the original state s.

9.3.4   Update Elements in a Specific Order

This one is similar to Sect. 9.3.3 but here the order in which the elements have to be updated is given (and relevant), in contrast to Sect. 9.3.3. This is again a <u>sequence</u> of individual applications of Sect. 9.3.1 (Update element). See Sect. 5 for *sequences* of inputs. We note that an individual element can either be updated, if that is allowed (at that moment), or that it can be refused. So, in general a *subset* of the original set will be updated.

We note that the end result might depend on the original state s.

9.4   Increase, Decrease, and 'Next' Number

This section treats the operations *Increase* and *Decrease* in case of a (simple or complex) 'counter'. Here, s(E) is a number (for each state s ∈ S). Also, the notion of 'next' number will be discussed in this section.

An Increase (e.g., *Increase next order number*) might indicate a situation where, for a certain component E of S (a 'counter' component), s(E) is an integer in each state s ∈ S, and where s(E) has to be increased by 1. Then h(s) could simply be s(E) +1.

If the value always has to be divisible by 11 for instance (as a rudimentary validation check) then, upon an Increase, h(s) could be s(E) +11, which is the next number divisible by 11 (assuming that s(E) was already divisible by 11). Section 10 gives such an example.

For a simple Decrease, h(s) could simply be s(E) – 1. More general, when there is a reason to be able to decrease by a number other than 1 (e.g., *Decrease the number of open requests by n*), then h(s) could be s(E) – n.

In several applications the 'next' number is not simply 1 higher (or 11 higher, as in the just mentioned example) but that 'next' number has to be computed in a special way, because it has to satisfy some complicated validation check (e.g., an 11-test). Examples are bank account numbers (such as the IBAN), credit card numbers, International Standard Book Numbers (ISBN), Universal Product Codes (UPC), European Article Numbers (EAN), bar codes, maybe patient identification numbers, fiscal identification numbers, etc. In such cases, h(s) can have the form OurNextNumber(s(E)), where OurNextNumber(s(E)) will be the 'next' number after s(E) that satisfies that complicated validation check.

10   An Illustrative Example of an Information Machine

We want to specify an information machine representing students and courses. Students have a *name*, an *address*, a *gender*, and a system-generated *student number*. Student numbers consist of (at least) 6 digits and are divisible by 11 (as a simple validation check). The system should manage those generated numbers. Courses have a unique *Course ID* (of at most 7 characters) and also a unique *Course name*. Students and courses can be created, updated, and deleted. Moreover, (known) students can be registered – and de-registered – for (known) courses. Upon deletion of a student, all his/her course registrations must be deleted as well (*cascading delete*). The system must be initialized to an 'empty' state, with suitable start values. We ignore the many possible Reads (i.e., queries) one could think of. For any possible Read, where the state always stays the same, we simply have T(i,s) = s.

On the next pages we will specify a suitable information machine in the form of a 'quick reference guide' consisting of 4 tables:

Table 1 specifies the **input space**, derived from a set of 9 user wishes that implicitly follow from the first paragraph in this section. The input space is the union of 9 subsets. In the specification, ℕ indicates the set of natural numbers, Str the set of character strings (over a certain alphabet), and Str(7) the set of character strings of at most 7 characters.

Table 2 specifies the **state space**. Using the terminology from Sect. 6(b), it is a state space over {NUSN, STUD, CRS, REG}, where NUSN stands for Next Unused Student Number, STUD represents the set of students, CRS the set of courses, and REG the set of course registrations. Table 2 also specifies the attributes, their sets of possible values, and their additional constraints. We chose Str as the value set ('type') for Address, just to keep the model simple here. In a practical model, Address could (and should) have a substructure (say with street + house number, postal code + city, and country), with further constraints on the possible values (e.g., format constraints for the postal code). Something similar might hold for the types of some other attributes (e.g., only particular letter-digit formats for Course IDs).

The table also mentions some provable properties (though there is no space here to give the formal proofs). These properties ('invariants') hold in each state of our IM, after correct initialization. They are consequences of how the specified machine works.

Table 3 specifies the **transition function**, using the constructions from Sects. 7, 8, and 9 for the specification of the transactions. CS(x,a,e), DS(n), and Initialize are compound transactions and, DS(n) is also a *cascading delete* [9, 10, 21].

Table 4 specifies the **output function**. Some inputs might encounter constraints that were formulated in the state space, e.g., (foreign) key constraints (see the CC-, CR-, DC-, and UC-inputs). In those cases, we distinguished different kinds of output. (We note that we could have differentiated the outputs for CC and CR further by a refined case analysis.)

Ease of Design Change

During development it should be easy to make changes in the design. With the 'quick reference guide' on the next two pages we can quickly find where, what, and how we have to change things when needed. E.g., let's consider the proposed change:

> In the case of an attempt to delete a course for which there are still registrations, we would also like to know how many students, or even which students are still registered.

Hence, we have to look up the user wish Delete Course (in Table 1). So the input is DC(c). Then look at the output function (in Table 4), under DC(c), in particular the case 'otherwise'. That output should change into, e.g.:

> "There are still " N " registrations for this course; the state stayed the same" or even
> "The state stayed the same: There are still " N " registrations for this course, notably: "
> {t | t ∈ s(REG)s ⋈ (STUD) and t(CID) = c}

with $N = |\{t \mid t \in s(REG) \text{ and } t(CID) = c\}|$, i.e., the number of registrations for course c, and with '⋈' representing the natural join.

Thanks to the demonstrated traceability, the necessary change (and the appropriate place) in the software follows directly from this.

In the next 4 tables we subsequently specify the **input space** (derived from the parameterized UWs mentioned there), the **state space**, the **transition function**, and the **output function** of the IM. To save space we use abbreviations like CS, CC, etc. for CreateStudent, etc. There are 9 kinds of input: 1 for initialization, 3 sets of Creates, 3 sets of Deletes, and 2 sets of Updates. All this is clearly traceable, extendable, and scalable: Each newly introduced input leads to one new row in 3 of the 4 the tables. (The effect on the state space table might be different.) As explained earlier, the specifications form a solid basis for a correct implementation.

Table 1. From User wishes to the Input space

Parameterized user wish	Input space	
Initialize the state	{Initialize}	
Create Student with name x, address a, and gender e	∪ {CS(x,a,e)}	x ∈ Str and a ∈ Str and e ∈ {M, F} }
Create Course with course ID c and name x	∪ {CC(c,x)}	c ∈ Str(7) and x ∈ Str }
Create Course Registration with course ID c and student number n	∪ {CR(c,n)}	c ∈ Str(7) and n ∈ N }
Delete Student with number n including all his/her course registrations	∪ {DS(n)}	n ∈ N }
Delete Course with course ID c	∪ {DC(c)}	c ∈ Str(7) }
Delete Course Registration with course ID c and student number n	∪ {DR(c,n)}	c ∈ Str(7) and n ∈ N }
Update, for Student with number n, the address into a	∪ {US(n,a)}	n ∈ N and a ∈ Str }
Update, for Course with course ID c, the name into x	∪ {UC(c,x)}	c ∈ Str(7) and x ∈ Str }

Table 2. State space

State space: Description of the components and their properties	Component labels & Property labels	Set of values	Additional constraints	Provable properties
Next Unused Student Number	NUSN	N		Will be divisible by 11
Students	STUD			
Student number	SNR	N		Will be unique within STUD, smaller than NUSN, divisible by 11, and at least 100,000
Student name	NAME	Str		
Address	ADDR	Str		
Gender	SEX	{M, F}		
Courses	CRS			
Course ID	CID	Str(7)	Must be unique within CRS	
Course name	CNAME	Str	Must be unique within CRS	
Course Registrations	REG			
Course ID	CID	Str(7)	Must refer to CID in CRS	
Student number	SNR	N	Must refer to SNR in STUD	Same four SNR-properties

Table 3. Transition function

Input i	State T(i,s)	Modifying function g_s	Added element t
CS(x,a,e)	Main(S,g) (s)	$g_s(\text{STUD}) = s(\text{STUD}) \cup \{t\}$ and $g_s(\text{NUSN}) = s(\text{NUSN}) + 11$	{(SNR; s(NUSN)), (NAME; x),(ADDR; a), (SEX; e)}
CC(c,x)	Main(S,g) (s)	$g_s(\text{CRS}) = s(\text{CRS}) \cup \{t\}$	{(CID; c), (CNAME; x)}
CR(c,n)	Main(S,g) (s)	$g_s(\text{REG}) = s(\text{REG}) \cup \{t\}$	{(CID; c), (SNR; n)}
DS(n)	Main(S,g) (s)	$g_s(\text{STUD}) = \{ t \mid t \in s(\text{STUD}) \text{ and } t(\text{SNR}) \neq n\}$ and $g_s(\text{REG}) = \{ t \mid t \in s(\text{REG}) \text{ and } t(\text{SNR}) \neq n\}$	
DC(c)	Main(S,g) (s)	$g_s(\text{CRS}) = \{ t \mid t \in s(\text{CRS}) \text{ and } t(\text{CID}) \neq c\}$	
DR(c,n)	Main(S,g) (s)	$g_s(\text{REG}) = s(\text{REG}) - \{(\text{CID};c), (\text{SNR};n)\}$	
US(n,a)	Main(S,g) (s)	$g_s(\text{STUD}) = \{ t \mid t \in s(\text{STUD}) \text{ and } t(\text{SNR}) \neq n \} \cup \{ t \,\theta\, \{(\text{ADDR}; a)\} \mid t \in s(\text{STUD}) \text{ and } t(\text{SNR}) = n \}$	
UC(c,x)	Main(S,g) (s)	$g_s(\text{CRS}) = \{ t \mid t \in s(\text{CRS}) \text{ and } t(\text{CID}) \neq c \} \cup \{ t \,\theta\, \{(\text{CNAME}; x)\} \mid t \in s(\text{CRS}) \text{ and } t(\text{CID}) = c\}$	
Initialize		{ (NUSN; 100,001), (STUD;∅), (CRS;∅), (REG; ∅) }	

Table 4. Output function

Input i	Cases	Output G(i,s)	Which output when
Initialize		"Done: The start value for the Next Unused Student Number is 100,001 and all sets are empty (i.e., the set of students, of courses, and of course registrations)"	
CS(x,a,e)		"Done. The student number will be " s(NUSN)	
CC(c,x)	(a)	"Done"	if $c \notin \{ t(\text{CID}) \mid t \in s(\text{CRS}) \}$ and $x \notin \{ t(\text{CNAME}) \mid t \in s(\text{CRS}) \}$
	(b)	"Course ID " c " and/or course name " x " already existed; the state stayed the same"	otherwise
CR(c,n)	(a)	"Done"	if $c \in \{ t(\text{CID}) \mid t \in s(\text{CRS}) \}$ and $n \in \{ t(\text{SNR}) \mid t \in s(\text{STUD}) \}$
	(b)	"Unknown course and/or student; the state stayed the same"	otherwise
DS(n)		"Done"	
DC(c)	(a)	"Done"	if $c \notin \{ t(\text{CID}) \mid t \in s(\text{REG}) \}$
	(b)	"There are still registrations for this course; the state stayed the same"	otherwise
DR(c,n)		"Done"	
US(n,a)		"Done"	
UC(c,x)	(a)	"Done"	if $x \notin \{ t(\text{CNAME}) \mid t \in s(\text{CRS}) \}$
	(b)	"Course name " x " already existed; the state stayed the same"	otherwise

11 Results and Conclusions

To be able to proceed from initial user wishes to a running information system in a direct and straightforward way, we developed a practical theory on formal, implementation-independent specifications of information systems triggered by such initial user wishes. Our theory also integrates data and transactions in a uniform way.

First we sketched a straightforward development path for functional requirements. In order to handle the complexity, the development path enables 'stepwise clarification' and 'stepwise specification' as well as traceability. Subsequently we introduced an intermediate mathematical model that can constitute a clear, unambiguous capture of the user wishes regarding the functional requirements on the one hand, and a formal model of the system (to be) built on the other hand. It constitutes an intermediate stage between the natural language of the user (say English or Dutch) and the language of the system (say Java or SQL). The notion of an *information machine*, together with its related notions, turned out to be very useful for that purpose.

A significant contribution of the paper is the introduction and definition of a general structure of transactions which has a clear semantics and which includes a generic rollback, taking consistency into account (Sects. 7 and 8).

Another contribution is the introduction and formal (declarative) specification of several common *transaction patterns*. These include the well-known functions *Create*, *Update*, and *Delete*, transactions that are generally applicable to data in a system. We also treated transaction patterns for (simple and complex) 'counters' and 'next' numbers (Sect. 9).

Section 10 illustrated the practical applicability with an example of an IM that contains several subtle and/or complicated points, e.g., compound transactions, cascading and non-cascading deletes, system-generated (and system-managed) numbers, specifications of the integrity checks to be executed by the system, and differentiated output messages. Section 10 also illustrated the traceability, extendibility and scalability of the approach. Recently we also successfully used the approach in the development of a system meant to support participatory budgeting (30–40 user wishes, with a lot of external interaction), and in the past we even developed a data-dictionary system (meta-database) along these lines.

The theory can be considered as a generalization of the more familiar *database theory*. Thanks to its extendibility and scalability, the approach is well applicable in *incremental* and *agile* development environments as well, where (quickly changing) specifications of the (growing) information machine might result from newly introduced user wishes.

12 Future Work

Until now we only worked out patterns of *singular transactions* (in Sect. 9), but we also want to develop a general theory on patterns of *compound transactions* (although Sect. 10 already contained a few examples of compound transactions).

In Sect. 10 we also gave an example of a so-called *cascading delete* or *cascading rollback* [9], but we want to develop a more general theory on cascading deletes (e.g., along the lines of [21]). In general, cascading deletes are compound transactions too.

Until now we supposed that the output of a system (as reaction on an input) will always (and only) be sent to the user triggering that input. However, in practice such a one-to-one interaction between user and system is not always the case. For instance, as reaction on an input (e.g., from a human user or a sensor) the system might send messages (e.g., e-mails) to several other recipients or send a command to another system (*interacting systems*). We will extend our theory to include these kinds of interactions too.

We did not yet consider *dynamic constraints*, i.e., constraints on state *transitions* (when moving from one state to another) but we want to extend our theory to include dynamic constraints as well. In the future we also want to study the relationship with work flows.

Acknowledgements. We thank the reviewers for their suggestions to strengthen the paper.

References

1. Weikum, G., Vossen, G.: Transactional Information Systems, Morgan Kaufmann, San Francisco (2002). https://www.elsevier.com/books/transactional-information-systems/weikum/978-1-55860-508-4. Accessed 17 June 2019
2. Prinz, A., Thalheim, B.: Operational semantics of transactions. In: Schewe, K.-D., Zhou, X., (eds.) Proceedings of 14th Australasian Database Conference, CRPIT, vol. 17, pp. 169–179. ACS, Adelaide, Australia (2003). http://crpit.scem.westernsydney.edu.au/confpapers/CRPITV17Prinz.pdf. Accessed 17 June 2019
3. Bonner, J.A., Kifer, M.: An overview of transaction logic. Theoret. Comput. Sci. **133**, 205–265 (1994). https://ac.els-cdn.com/0304397594901902/1-s2.0-0304397594901902-main.pdf?_tid=3aa6ea0f-6383-4d79-94f9-9b41c55f87be&acdnat=1526056319_b741a4dffca23f08156e420a777e109b. Accessed 17 June 2019
4. Jacobson, I., et al: Use Case 2.0: The Guide to Succeeding with Use Cases. Ivar Jacobson International (2011). https://www.ivarjacobson.com/publications/white-papers/use-case-ebook. Accessed 17 June 2019
5. Cockburn, A.: Writing Effective Use Cases. Addison Wesley, Boston (2001). https://www.infor.uva.es/~mlaguna/is1/materiales/BookDraft1.pdf. Accessed 17 June 2019
6. https://en.wikipedia.org/wiki/System_sequence_diagram. Accessed 17 June 2019
7. De Brock, E.O.: Towards a theory about continuous requirements engineering for information systems. In: 4th CRE-Workshop, REFSQ (2018). http://ceur-ws.org/Vol-2075/CRE18_paper4.pdf. Accessed 17 June 2019
8. De Brock, E.O.: Foundations of Semantic Databases. Prentice Hall, London (1995). https://dl.acm.org/citation.cfm?id=556146. Accessed 17 June 2019
9. Ullman, J.D., et al.: Database Systems: The Complete Book. Pearson, Upper Saddle River (2009). https://pdfstores.files.wordpress.com/2016/04/ullman_the_complete_book.pdf. Accessed 17 June 2019

10. Elmasri, R., Navathe, S.B.: Fundamentals of Database Systems. Pearson, Upper Saddle River (2016). http://www.pearson.com.au/products/D-G-Elmasri-Navathe/D-G-Elmasri-Ramez-Navathe-Shamkant-B/Fundamentals-of-Database-Systems-Global-Edition/97812920 97619?R=9781292097619. Accessed 17 June 2019

11. De Brock, E.O.: An NL-based foundation for increased traceability, transparency, and speed in continuous development of ISs. In: 2th NLP4RE-Workshop, REFSQ (2019). http://ksuweb.kennesaw.edu/∼pspoleti/REFSQJP19/NLP4RE19_paper18.pdf. Accessed 17 June 2019

12. Larman, C.: Applying UML and Patterns. Pearson Education, Upper Saddle River (2005). https://aanimesh.files.wordpress.com/2013/09/applying-uml-and-patterns-3rd.pdf. Accessed 17 June 2019

13. Pieper, F.T.A.M.: Data machines and interfaces. Ph.D. thesis, TU Eindhoven (1989). https://pure.tue.nl/ws/files/2488162/305250.pdf. Accessed 17 June 2019

14. Mealy, G.H.: A method for synthesizing sequential circuits. Bell Syst. Tech. J. **34**, 1045–1079 (1955). https://ia802705.us.archive.org/12/items/bstj34-5-1045/bstj34-5-1045.pdf. Accessed 17 June 2019

15. https://en.wikipedia.org/wiki/Mealy_machine. Accessed 17 June 2019

16. https://en.wikipedia.org/wiki/Rollback_(data_management). Accessed 17 June 2019

17. Härder, T., Reuter, A.: Principles of transaction-oriented database recovery. ACM Comput. Surv. **15**(4), 287–317 (1983). https://web.stanford.edu/class/cs340v/papers/recovery.pdf. Accessed 17 June 2019

18. https://en.wikipedia.org/wiki/ACID. Accessed 17 June 2019

19. Martin, J.: Managing the Data-Base Environment. Prentice Hall, Upper Saddle River (1983). https://books.google.nl/books?id=ymy4AAAAIAAJ&pg=PA381&redir_esc=y. Accessed 17 June 2019

20. https://en.wikipedia.org/wiki/Create,_read,_update_and_delete. Accessed 17 June 2019

21. Brock, Bert: Declarative specifications of complex transactions. In: Saake, Gunter, Schwarz, Kerstin, Türker, Can (eds.) FoMLaDO 1999. LNCS, vol. 1773, pp. 150–166. Springer, Heidelberg (2000). https://doi.org/10.1007/3-540-46466-2_8

22. Shishkov, B., Dietz, J.L.G.: Design of software applications using generic business components. In: Proceedings of the 37th Hawaii International Conference on System Sciences (2004). https://ieeexplore.ieee.org/document/1265644. Accessed 17 June 2019

Tuning the Behavior of Context-Aware Applications

Using Semiotic Norms and Bayesian Modeling to Establish the User Situation

Boris Shishkov[1,2,3](✉)

[1] Faculty of Information Sciences, University of Library Studies and Information
Technologies, Sofia, Bulgaria
b.b.shishkov@iicrest.org
[2] Institute of Mathematics and Informatics, Bulgarian Academy of Sciences,
Sofia, Bulgaria
[3] Institute IICREST, Sofia, Bulgaria

Abstract. Context-aware applications are to adapt their "behavior" to the surrounding context. In this paper, we analyze different ways to achieve adequate application behavior adjustment (based on context data) and we stress upon: (i) Bayesian modeling that is not only considered useful in this regard but is also not enough explored as it concerns context-aware applications; (ii) semiotic norms that have specific relevant strengths. Even though there is much experience as it concerns the challenge of capturing context data, more knowledge is still needed about how to use context data in order to effectively make the right judgement about the "current" user situation (context state). We consider this paper's contribution as relevant to the above-mentioned challenge.

Keywords: Context-awareness · Context data · Semiotic norm ·
Bayesian model

1 Introduction

A person would often need to adapt his or her behavior to the "current" situation, for example: if the nearby supermarket is open, then Samuel may purchase products and then cook dinner at home but if it is too late and all nearby shops are closed, then he would opt for getting back home and calling a 24/7 delivery company to order a pizza. In a similar way, an organization would "behave" differently in different situations, for example: if there are indications for an impending recession, then the organization managers would go for firing employees and cutting spending also in other ways while if the prospects are good, then the managers would be more relaxed as it concerns costs. Alferez and Pelechano claim that it is desirable to translate the ideas of adaptation in the natural world to software, assuming that such adaptations are carried out in response to changing conditions in the supporting computing infrastructure and/or in the surrounding physical environment; this is referred to as "context-awareness", especially as far as (enterprise) information systems are concerned - there should be

© Springer Nature Switzerland AG 2019
B. Shishkov (Ed.): BMSD 2019, LNBIP 356, pp. 134–152, 2019.
https://doi.org/10.1007/978-3-030-24854-3_9

"automatic" adaptation mechanisms to reconfigure them according to contextual changes because assigning manual reconfiguration tasks would be impractical [1, 2]. This is in line with the views of Dey et al., expressed still in 2001, suggesting that context-aware applications use context that is relevant to the interaction with users – by "application" is meant "ICT (Information and Communication Technology) application"; by "context" they mean information that concerns the state of people, places, and objects [3]. In further studies, Dey and Newberger argue that context is typically gathered in an automated fashion [4]. This claim (as it concerns context-aware applications) is in concert with the views of Alferez and Pelechano (see above) and is inspired by the observation that currently many users have to deal with diverse devices (including small (wearable) devices with sensing and computing capabilities) accessed through diverse interfaces and used in diverse environments. Hence, it is not surprising that in 2009, Papadimitrious stated that: Context-awareness, ubiquity (device independence, mobility, wireless support), quality of service provisioning, seamless discovery of services and content, and enhanced user control and effective delivery are important requirements of the future Internet [5].

This is the focus of the current paper, in general, and in particular - we address the specification of context-aware applications. The paper builds on the research presented in [6–8]. As it concerns such applications, we call "behavior" what the application delivers as functionality and we assume that different behavior variants are to be triggered corresponding to different (surrounding) situations. Further, we have identified three behavior perspectives (in this regard), namely: context-driven optimization of system-internal processes, context-driven maximization of the user-perceived effectiveness, and context-driven value-sensitivity. Nevertheless, we stay challenged by the adaptation issue itself: HOW the application "knows" which is the right behavior change to implement upon changing conditions? It is for sure that much data is available - we are showered by sensor data, reports, inferred data, and so on. Still, it would rarely be trivial reflecting such data into MEANINGFUL INFORMATION, as a basis for the application to adequately "establish" the "current" situation and hence "know" which behavior variant to trigger. We address this problem in the current paper.

The '16 claim of Alegre et al. that "the challenges of context-aware systems development are diverse and complex, provoking development techniques (and methods) to be commonly disconnected from each other, and focused on solving specific issues" [9] indirectly justifies the validity of the identified problem as well as the claim of Bosems and Van Sinderen that "designers cannot always anticipate the dynamics of context and associated user requirements" [10]. Actually, we elaborate the adaptation challenge as follows: (i) if a situation occurs that has been "foreseen" during the design, then a corresponding behavior variant (specified at design time) is triggered; (ii) otherwise, there is no other option but relying on an intelligent run-time adaptation. In the current paper, we focus on (i) and abstract from (ii).

Further, we make the following assumptions: • There are several possible situations in which the context-aware application ("application", for short) of consideration can be, featured as: Hypothesis 1, Hypothesis 2, Hypothesis 3, and so on. • It is possible to know in advance each of the hypotheses. • For each of the hypotheses, there is a corresponding desired application behavior variant and this corresponds to the adequate functioning of the application.

Hence, we pose the following research question: HOW CAN CONTEXT DATA BE USED TO EFFECTIVELY ADJUST THE APPLICATION BEHAVIOR FOR ACHIEVING ADEQUATE PERFORMANCE?

We consider this research question as relevant to the identified problem (see above) and we therefore claim the following contribution (of the current paper) that is two-fold: • We explicitly consider the way context data is used to adjust application behavior and in our view, even though this has been covered by related work (some related work was already discussed in this section), this has not been done explicitly. • We analyze different ways to achieve adequate application behavior adjustment (based on context data) and we stress upon Bayesian modeling [16] that is not only considered useful in this regard but is also not enough explored as it concerns context-aware applications. We also consider semiotic norms [13] in this regard.

The remaining of the current paper is structured as follows: A problem elaboration follows in Sect. 2 and a related work analysis – in Sect. 3. Section 4 is featuring the paper's conceptual background. Further, Sect. 5 is providing an analysis-driven proposal (complemented by a partial exemplification) featuring the use of semiotic norms and Bayesian modeling for the sake of establishing the user situation. Finally, Sect. 6 concludes the paper.

2 Problem Elaboration

As mentioned in the introduction, we do problem elaboration in the current section, considering as a starting point the aim of effectively using context data for the sake of adequately adjusting application behavior. As also mentioned in the introduction, we are particularly challenged in general by the application adaptation itself and in particular - by the issue of "letting" the application "know" which is the right behavior change to implement upon changing conditions. Finally, we see no other decision "trigger" to this than CONTEXT DATA – we argue that it can only be context data that would "say" to the application that the surrounding context is changing and hence application behavior updates need to be realized accordingly. Said otherwise, we need data concerning the application context in order to "capture" context changes that in turn require application behavior adaptations. This problem is nevertheless not new and just one example featuring this claim points to the period 2005-08 when the AWARENESS framework was dominated by a similar focus; in particular, the AWARENESS framework was covering tele-monitoring services as follows: a health-monitored person is away from hospital but "wearing" a "body area network" (consisting of body vital sign sensors + device(s) performing processing and connectivity) that would allow the AWARENESS platform "know" if something in the situation of the person is changing that requires an update in the AWARENESS support, for example: in case of an upcoming epileptic seizure, it would no longer be enough to just monitor the person and it would be needed to activate emergency help [11]. There are also other similar examples featured in some of the related work sources considered in the introduction.

Still, in our view, a limitation of all those works is that even though they consider the problem of adapting application behavior based on capturing context data, they only address more or less "simple" cases when it is somehow "straightforward" to align the captured data to the need to do a particular thing. For example, the AWARENESS sensor readings are considered in a simple way – some particular value combinations point to the "conclusion" that "an epileptic seizure is coming"; otherwise it is assumed that the person is in normal condition. In this regard, the AWARENESS platform would count on ECA rules [12].

We would not challenge those achievements. However, we claim that in this way it would be difficult to resolve some more complex situations, especially when the context data readings are not a "straightforward basis" for identifying a context change. This we claim for AWARENESS and also for the related work we have studied – see the introduction and the following section.

We hence argue that the system engineering community still misses EXPLICIT and EXHAUSTIVE ways of considering context data, driven by the purpose of updating application behavior (if needed).

We contribute to filling this gap, by analyzing the relevance of OS - Organizational Semiotics [13] and Data Analytics [14]. In particular, we address the OS Norm Analysis Method as well as Statistical Data Analytics [15] and especially the Naïve Bayesian Classification Approach [16], expecting that they have potential to add value in this regard. This will be especially considered further on in the paper, after the related work analysis and the introduction of several essential relevant concepts.

3   Related Work

The current related work analysis section is organized as follows: Firstly, we consider our previous work that we find relevant with regard to the identified problem (see Sect. 2); Secondly, we expand our analysis to cover also other relevant work.

As it concerns our previous work: • In [8], we have considered the specification of context-aware applications, making it explicit that following context changes, the application behavior is to be updated accordingly. Even though we have proposed some solution directions in this regard, we have only implicitly considered context data and the challenge of approaching it. • In [17], we have taken a systemics [18] perspective over context-awareness, addressing in this regard the environment and its changes, to which the system should adapt. Nevertheless, context data has been considered just abstractly. • In [6], we have considered three system adaptation perspectives with regard to context-aware systems, namely: (a) driven by the goal of optimizing the system-internal processes; (b) driven by the goal of maximizing the user-perceived effectiveness; (c) driven by the goal of achieving sensitivity to public values. Further, we have explicitly established that in each of those cases we have a different perspective over the context – as it concerns (a), the context is about what is happening inside the system; as it concerns (b), the context concerns the user, as it concerns (c), the context concerns public values. Nevertheless, we have only implicitly considered in this regard the way context data is used. • In [7], we have considered business process modeling from the perspective of context-awareness, addressing in particular business process variants – different business process variants could be relevant to corresponding context situations. Again, we have only implicitly considered in this regard the way context data is used.

As it concerns other related work: • Anind Dey is among the most recognizable researchers addressing context-awareness [3, 4]. He has serious achievements in considering the notion of context and also the development of context-aware applications. We argue nevertheless that he has not explicitly considered the challenge of properly using context data for sensing a context change, counting instead on a more "intuitive" approach to this challenge. • The same (lack of explicit consideration of context data) holds for most recognizable R&D context-awareness projects, such as AWARENESS [11], as discussed already. • Bosems and Van Sinderen have considered the notion of "context-aware computing" as the combination of sensor, reasoning, and other technology that provides systems with real-time awareness ... [10] but the "reasoning" has not been explicitly considered and is mainly related to ECA rules [12] that in our view have only limited "power" as it concerns complex situations and corresponding context data considerations. Further, those authors are more focused on deriving higher-level context information based on "raw" context data than on the consideration of the context information itself for adequately sensing context changes. • The useful survey of Alegre et al. [9] is mainly focused on the development (featuring implementation concerns) of context-aware applications as well as on the consideration of some public values but not so much on the consideration of context data. • The same holds for the works of Alférez and Pelechano [1, 2] – they consider the dynamic evolution of context-aware systems, the development itself, and the relation to web services. • A service-orientation perspective with no explicit context data consideration is also characterizing the works of Abeywickrama [19, 20].

Even though we do not claim exhaustiveness with regard to the current related work analysis, we are convinced that it covers some of the most representative researchers and works relevant to the problem considered in this paper.

Hence, we argue that it is still a question how to effectively consider context data for the sake of adequately updating the behavior of a context-aware application (if needed).

As mentioned in the previous section, our proposal is featured in the following two sections, with us firstly bringing forward the conceptual background and secondly – our proposed solution directions.

4   Conceptual Background

The current section is organized as follows: Firstly, we present the meta-model "governing" the essential concepts that we consider relevant with regard to context-awareness; Secondly, we address some of them, namely the concepts "system", "environment", and "user" – we argue that those concepts are important as it concerns the context-data-driven adaptation of application behavior; Finally, we summarize our context-awareness views, also touching upon context-aware applications.

4.1   Meta-Model

We refer to our previous work [6] featuring a proposed meta-model that we consider relevant to the problem addressed in the current paper. The meta-model is presented in Fig. 1, using the notations of the UML Class Diagram [21].

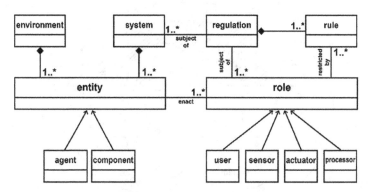

Fig. 1. Considered meta-model (Source: [6], p. 197)

As it is seen in the figure, we consider a *system* and its *environment*. Both are composed of numerous *entities* which in turn can be *components* (non pro-active) or *agents* (pro-active and intelligent). One *entity* (an *agent*, for example) can enact many different *roles* (and in this research, we limit ourselves to four role categories, namely: *user*, *sensor*, *actuator*, and *processor*) that are restricted by corresponding *rules* and are subject of *regulations*. A regulation in turn is composed of many *rules* and is affecting not only the *roles* but the *system* as a whole.

Since we are taking particularly an *agent perspective*, we consider it important *matching roles to their corresponding executing agents* because it is not for sure that *anybody* would have the right capabilities of fulfilling a *role*.

4.2   Essential Concepts - Elaboration

As mentioned already, in the current sub-section we address the concepts: "system", "environment", "user". In this regard, we refer to the *system definition* of Bunge [18]:

> **Definition**: Let T be a nonempty set. Then the ordered triple σ = $<C, E, S>$ is **system** over T if and only if C (standing for *Composition*) and E (standing for *Environment*) are mutually disjoint subsets of T (i.e. $C \cap E = \varnothing$), and S (standing for *Structure*) is a nonempty set of active relations on the union of C and E. The system is *conceptual* if T is a set of conceptual items, and *concrete* (or material) if $T \subseteq \Theta$ is a set of concrete entities, i.e. things.

Hence: • There are "items" belonging to the system under consideration; • There are also items not belonging to the system under consideration (Some of those items would appear to belong to the system environment; Others would therefore appear to belong neither to the system nor to the system environment).

What about the USER? This notion is not explicitly considered above and we need to discuss it – for this, we use Fig. 2.

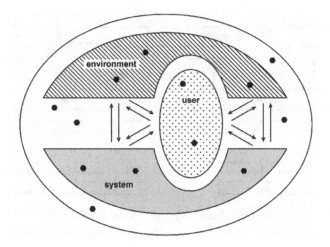

Fig. 2. Considering the notions of *system, environment,* and *user*

As the figure suggests, it is a "delicate" issue whether the *user* belongs to the *system* or to the *environment*. From one point of view, the *system* is driven by the goal of delivering something to the *user* and hence, the user is to be considered part of the *system*; nevertheless, from another point of view, the *user* is not among the entities who are delivering the product/service because the *user* is consuming it and hence the *user* is not to be considered part of the *system* (and is thus part of the *environment*) [17]. It is therefore not surprising that a lack of consensus is observed about how the *user* is to be considered. Hence, we clearly distinguish between: (i) what belongs to the *system*; (ii) what belongs to the *environment*; (iii) what belongs to the *user*.

Further, in line with what was stated above: there are items that neither belong to the *system*, nor to the *environment*, nor to the *user*.

Finally, those "items" (visualized in Fig. 2 as small black hexagons) actually reflect ENTITIES (as according to the meta-model – see Fig. 1) and they in turn fulfill actor-roles (ROLES, for short), for example: if a professor sends a fax, then (s)he is fulfilling the *role* "secretary".

In summary, there is interaction among entities (fulfilling corresponding roles) in several perspectives: • between system and environment; • between system and user; • between environment and user. Other entities are not involved in interactions, at least as it concerns the view over the system under consideration.

For example: John brings his Mitsubishi Colt to a Mitsubishi garage [22] for a motor vehicle service and they establish that one of the exhaust pipes would need to be replaced. Their doing the replacement for John concerns a *system-user* "relation".

Nevertheless, they do not have in stock the particular Mitsubishi part (an exhaust pipe) needed for the car of John and they have to order it from an "external" company – Bosal [23]. Their arranging this with Bosal concerns a *system-environment* relation. Still, since Bosal is outside the Mitsubishi "family", the order can only be paid (and thus guaranteed) by the *user* directly. Hence, in order to allow the garage to fulfill the order, John would have to do a payment to Bosal (this is just for the exhaust pipe itself; apart from this, John would have to pay to the garage for their servicing the car, replacing the exhaust pipe, and so on) and this concerns an *environment-user* relation. In summary, as it can be seen from the above example, often, in delivering a service to the *user*, the "system" needs some interaction with entities belonging to the system *environment*. It is also possible that the *user* himself/herself would need to interact with entities belonging to the system *environment*, in the process of utilizing a service delivered by the *system*. The entities belonging to the system *environment* are only those entities with whom the *system* and/or the *user* would need to interact in the process of the *system-to-user* service delivery. All other system-external entities are "outside" the system *environment*.

As it concerns the perspectives considered in the 2nd paragraph of the introduction, in the remaining of this paper, we only focus on application behavior adaptations driven by the goal of maximizing the user-perceived effectiveness. Further, as mentioned in the introduction, we only consider in the paper situations that can be "foreseen" during the design, such that corresponding behavior variants (specified at design time) are triggered accordingly. This also corresponds to the assumptions made in the introduction.

Thus, considering Fig. 2 could be a good starting point in approaching the problem (see Sect. 2), taking the above into account. In this, we are to focus on the system-to-user service delivery. Further, we are to be "sensitive" to the different situations the user may find himself/herself in. Finally, for each of those situations, the system should offer a corresponding adequate behavior variant.

Those issues are already context-awareness-specific and will be considered in the following sub-section.

4.3   Adopting Context-Awareness

Referring to previous work [8], we consider as a key context-awareness feature the capability of a system to adapt its behavior based on the user situation, as illustrated in Fig. 3. As the figure suggests, each situation of the user "asks for" a corresponding system behavior variant.

This is in line with what was already stated about our particular focus in the current paper, just covering the goal of achieving a user-perceived effectiveness and also abstracting from situations not foreseen at design time.

We also abstract from numerous design-related issues, such as the system behavior specifications, the "switch" between one behavior variant to another, and so on.

We only focus in this paper on CONTEXT DATA and HOW it helps identifying the USER SITUATION. Referring to the example considered in the previous subsection: If John is the only person driving the Mitsubishi Colt and we are able to "sense" if the car is moving or not, then based on sensor data, we would know if John

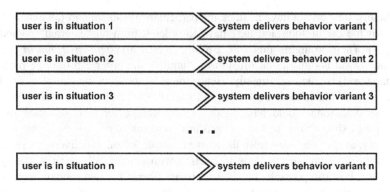

Fig. 3. Visualizing a key feature of context-aware systems

is in his car, driving, or John is outside his car. If John is driving, then particular (vehicle-specific) services would be offered to him; otherwise, standard services would be offered.

This is a simple example featuring a case when it is straightforward to use context data in order to immediately establish the user situation (this in turn gives the possibility of offering the right services accordingly).

Nevertheless, real-life cases may be more complex. For example: The managers of the HKairport Electronics Shop, located at the Hong Kong Airport [24], would look for ways to effectively approach customers, taking into account that all customers are passengers whose time is often severely restricted by pending flights. Still, many passengers have loyalty cards that would immediately provide the shop with much data. Then if Suzan, Dave, and Steve are three customers possessing loyalty cards, how could it be established for each of them whether (s)he is more likely to buy this or that kind of product or not? If in particular, the person under consideration is SUZAN and the product type – TABLET, then the question is: IS IT MORE LIKELY THAT SUZAN PURCHASES A TABLET? This points to exactly two user situations: (i) It is more likely that Suzan purchases a tablet – Situation 1; (ii) It is more likely that Suzan would not purchase a tablet – Situation 2. If it is Situation 1, then the tablets vendor would immediately approach Suzan with focused questions and suggestions. If it is Situation 2, then the tablets vendor would most probably "ignore" Suzan and approach another customer instead. Hence, it is not as easy as in the above example (featuring John and his Colt) to establish (based on the context data) which the "current" user situation is.

Further, we argue that this is not so much an issue of how we derive the context data (one possibility is to use sensors, another possibility is to use reports, and so on) but it is more an issue of WHAT WE DO (and HOW) with the context data, such that we adequately establish the "current" user situation.

How we propose dealing with this challenge is featured in the following section.

5 Proposed Solution Directions

The current section is organized as follows: Firstly, we carry out an analysis featuring the context data consideration challenge with regard to context-aware systems, in general, and context-aware applications – in particular. Secondly, we introduce and discuss semiotic norms and Bayesian modeling as relevant and potentially useful with regard to the mentioned challenge. Finally, we provide partial exemplification, as a first step in justifying and validating the appropriateness of using semiotic norms and Bayesian modeling to establish the user situation.

5.1 Analysis

We argue that a key issue to be discussed when addressing context data is how we get the data. In this regard, our observation is (considering related work – see Sect. 3) that most often context-aware applications count on sensor data. An example for this is the AWARENESS Body Area Network (BAN) that uses sensors attached to a person's body, for getting "vital signs - vs" (vs represent "higher-level" context data featuring blood pressure, pulse, and so on, that is "inferred" based on "lower-level" sensor readings), for the sake of determining the situation of the person [11]. Nevertheless, it is also possible to count on "predictions", referring to Statistics [15] and/or Machine Learning [14]. For instance, in the HKairport Electronics Shop (see the example considered in the previous section), it might be possible to predict the likelihood that a particular customer would purchase a particular kind of product – this in turn would allow for determining his or her situation (if the person would most probably purchase a particular kind of product, then (s)he would be treated in one way; otherwise, the person would be treated in another way). Anyway, the idea of using prediction data instead of sensor data has advantages and drawbacks. It is certainly useful to apply Statistics/Machine Learning for getting a precise prediction concerning the situation of the user, especially in complex cases when the applicability of sensors is limited. At the same time, predictions, as uniquely based on the *training data*, would not evolve in time (as the user needs may); thus, prediction-based applications might get outdated soon. We argue that a solution would be to use Machine Learning also for adapting predictions if the context would change.

Hence, we observe that most current context-aware systems are either SENSOR-based or PREDICTION-based, and, not claiming exhaustiveness, we assume two types of context-aware applications, namely: *sensor-based context-aware applications* and *prediction-based context-aware applications*.

Further, we have no doubt that in simple cases (for example: "user is at home" vs "user is driving" vs "other") developers would lean towards counting on sensors, while in more complex cases (when for example the behavior of the user would need to be "foreseen") developers would lean towards using predictions, as illustrated in Fig. 4(a). That is because in "simple" cases, we usually have some "physical" conditions determining the situation of the user and those conditions would often be easy to capture by means of sensors [25]. We argue that in contrast, most "complex" cases concern the "mental state" of the user (and/or (an)other person(s)) and this would be difficult to "capture" by means of sensors (at least counting on the current advances of sensor technology); nevertheless, prediction techniques could be effective in such cases because they would help "deriving" information about the "mental state" of a person, by considering *training data* that is featuring other persons [14].

Finally, we position such *training-data*-based approaches as mainly relevant to "complex" cases just because a simple case would not "justify" sophisticated analytics activities. In our view, in "simple" cases, it would be more appropriate applying *rules*. This is illustrated in Fig. 4(b).

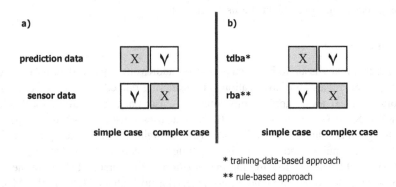

Fig. 4. Sensor-based vs prediction-based context-aware systems; Rule-based approaches vs training-data-based approaches.

We are thus challenged to address: • "simple" cases, counting on SENSOR DATA and RULE-BASED APPROACHES; • "complex" cases, counting on PREDICTION DATA and TRAINING-DATA-BASED APPROACHES.

In this, we are neither claiming that all "simple" cases should assume counting on sensor data and rule-based approaches (and that all "complex" cases should assume counting on prediction data and training-data-based approaches) nor we are claiming that it would always be possible to clearly distinguish between a "simple" and a "complex" case. Actually, we use those labels ("simple" vs "complex") mainly to distinguish between cases driven mostly by physical conditions and cases driven mostly by the "mental state" of persons. It is therefore established that physical conditions are usually easier to tackle by using sensors and rules while "mental states" would require more sophisticated "instrumentarium", possibly assuming prediction data and training-data-based techniques.

Hence, the contribution of the current paper (besides its analytical part) is partitioned in two streams: • RULE-BASED CAPTURING OF THE USER SITUATION; • TRAINING-DATA-BASED CAPTURING OF THE USER SITUATION.

As it concerns the rule-based capturing of the user situation, we consider ECA rules [12] to be currently most popular, applied in many developments, as for example the AWARENESS framework [11]. Even though we would not criticize ECA rules (we actually acknowledge their usefulness in many (mostly simple) cases), we would allow ourselves claiming that often a more solid approach is needed, especially in more complex cases when the rules would need to be aligned among each other and also with other techniques. That's why we would better appreciate a rule technique that not only has solid theoretical roots but also can be effectively combined with other modeling techniques. We argue that such a technique is the Norm Analysis Method that is "within" Organizational Semiotics [13]. In the following sub-section, we will briefly introduce the method and explain its relevant strengths.

As for the training-data-based capturing of the user situation, this concerns *supervised machine learning* [14] - when predictions are made with the help of labelled datasets, as in the case of *classification* (when the output variable is categorical) or in the case of *regression* [15] (that is about the relationship between two or more variables where a change in one variable is associated with a change in another variable). We argue that the *Naïve Bayesian Classification Approach* [14], that is helpful in establishing (based on attributes data and probabilities calculations) which hypothesis (out of two or more) is most likely to "occur", is a useful tool – we will briefly introduce it in the following section and we will also explain its relevant strengths.

5.2   Elaboration

As mentioned already, in this sub-section we will address the Norm Analysis Method and the Naïve Bayesian Classification Approach – they will be briefly introduced and their relevant strengths will be explained (as it concerns the context-data-driven establishment of the user situation, that is to trigger in turn application behavior adaptations).

5.2.1   Norm Analysis Method

With regard to *Organizational Semiotics* (*OS*), in general, and the *Norm Analysis Method*, in particular, we refer to [13, 17].

OS is based on the *Semiotics* theory and is focused on the nature, characteristics, and behavior of *signs*. *OS* adopts a subjectivist philosophical stance and an agent-in-action ontology; this philosophical position states that, for all practical purposes, nothing exists without a perceiving agent and the agent engaging in actions. Another essential *OS* concept is the notion of *affordance*: the affordance of the environment is considered to be "what it offers the animal, what it provides or furnishes, either for good or ill…".

When studying enterprises from the perspective of entities' behavior, it is necessary to specify the *norms* based on which this behavior is realized. Norms (featured by the OS Norm Analysis Method) are the rules and patterns of behavior, either formal or informal, explicit or implicit, existing within a society, an enterprise, or even a group of people working together to achieve a common goal. Norms are determined by Society or collective groups, and serve as a standard for the members to coordinate their actions. Hence, specifying an organization can be done by specifying the norms. Four norm types exist: *evaluative*, *perceptual*, *cognitive*, and *behavioral norms*. Each type of norms governs human behavior from different aspects. In business process modeling, most rules and regulations fall into the category of BEHAVIORAL NORMS - they

prescribe what people *must, may, must not* do, reflecting the *three deontic operators*: •
is obliged; • is permitted; • is prohibited. Hence, the following behavioral norm format
is adopted:

```
whenever <condition>
if <state>
then <agent>
is <deontic operator>
to <action>
```

It is essential to recognize that norms are not as rigid as logical conditions. If a
person does not drink water for certain duration of time, (s)he cannot survive. But an
individual who breaks the working pattern of a group does not have to be punished in
any way. Further, for those actions that are *permitted*, whether the agent will take an
action or not is seldom deterministic.

A *norm analysis* is normally carried out on the basis of the results of a semantic
analysis that would have "delineated" the area of concern. The behavior patterns
specified in the semantic model are part of the fundamental norms that retain the
ontologically determined relationships between agents and actions without imposing
any further constraints.

The Norm Analysis Method can also be successfully related to other modeling
tools.

As it concerns context-aware applications, we argue that in most of the SIMPLE
cases (cases that are mainly driven by behavior patterns in the physical perspective),
applying norms would be useful and effective.

We partially justify this claim by means of an illustrative example, presented in the
following sub-section.

5.2.2 Naïve Bayesian Classification Approach

With regard to the *Naïve Bayesian Classification Approach* (*NBCA*), we refer to [14,
26]. *NBCA* concerns *Machine Learning* (*ML*), in general, and *Supervised ML* (*SML*), in
particular. *ML* is a method of teaching computers to make predictions based on some
data. Further, let's consider the equation: $y=f(x)$ where x is the INPUT VARIABLE
and y is the OUTPUT VARIABLE. *SML* works under SUPERVISION (it's "learning")
– a machine is streamed with data which is LABELLED, such that the machine can
make a prediction (with the help of a labelled data set – data for which we already
know the target "answer"). *SML* is basically of two types (see the previous sub-
section): • CLASSIFICATION – when the output variable is *categorical* (i.e. with two
or more classes), for example: *red* or *blue*, *male* or *female*, and so on; • REGRESSION
– when the output variable is a *real* or *continuous* value (*regression* is about a relationship between two or more variables where a change in one of them is associated
with a change in another one).

The BAYESIAN CLASSIFICATION (BC), in particular, represents a *SML* method
as well as a STATISTICAL method for classification, assuming an underlying probabilistic model. BC allows us to capture uncertainty about the model in a principled

way, by determining the outcomes' probabilities. The BAYESIAN THEOREM is important in this regard - it is featuring the *a-posteriori* probability that a hypothesis holds given observed data; here, the following is to be explained: • *a-priori probability*: a probability that is derived purely by deductive reasoning; • *a-posteriori probability*: the revised probability of an event occurring after taking into consideration new information. The theorem is as follows:

$$P(H|\mathbf{X}) = (P(\mathbf{X}|H)P(H))/P(\mathbf{X})$$

and for grasping "P($\mathbf{X}$ | H)", one should be aware that it is all about HYPOTHESES (for example: *Hypothesis 1* - Person will make a holiday booking; *Hypothesis 2* - Person will not make a holiday booking) and it is also about CLASSIFYING A DATA TUPLE (for example: featuring attributes, such as age, income, and so on). Thus, P($\mathbf{X}$ | H) is about the probability, given a particular hypothesis (for example: *Hypothesis 1*), that the "item" has those "characteristics" (the particular values of the attributes, such as age, income, and so on, as provided for classification). P(H) is just the general (*a-priori*) probability that a hypothesis occurs (for example: the probability that *Hypothesis 1* occurs). Finally, P($\mathbf{X}$) is called "marginal likelihood" and it is the average likelihood over a range of attribute values (for example: if we have provided a particular tuple $\mathbf{X}$ for classification, with its particular attribute values, then the marginal likelihood would be featuring the probability that a data tuple has exactly those attribute values).

The *NBCA* builds on the *Bayesian Theorem* in the sense that the goal is to predict which hypothesis is most likely to occur with regard to a data tuple – this would mean the highest value for P(H | $\mathbf{X}$). This thus also means the highest value for P($\mathbf{X}$ | H)P(H).

Hence, if we MAXIMIZE P($\mathbf{X}$ | H)P(H), then we know which hypothesis will occur most likely, given the particular data tuple to be considered.

As it concerns context-aware applications, we argue that in many COMPLEX cases (cases that would often concern the "mental state" of a person), applying *NBCA* would be useful and effective.

We partially justify this claim by means of an illustrative example, presented in the following sub-section.

5.3 Exemplification

Both examples, considered in the current sub-section, are "imaginary" toy examples aiming at illustrating our motivated claims concerning the potential strengths of the Norm Analysis Method and NBCA. The first example is inspired by the AWARE-NESS case [11] but is directed towards an application scenario that goes beyond the AWARENESS scope, namely Disaster Management [27]. The second example is inspired by the AllElectronics Case (featured in [14]) and adapted to fit the context-awareness focus (to some extent, imaginary details have been added).

5.3.1 Norm-Driven Context-Awareness Featuring Disaster Management

Briefing: Rescue workers are discovering Nick who seems to be injured. Since rescue operations are life-critical, they cannot be dominated by the intuitive judgement of rescue workers. Instead, in what they do, rescue workers are expected to follow rigorous rules (norms). The case situation is illustrated in Fig. 5 and it is to be noted that the considered information is simplified and partial, just supposed to serve as illustration.

As it is seen from the figure, there is an injured person and there are two hypotheses (corresponding to two user situation types), namely: (i) There is an ambulance in close proximity (by this, it is meant: within 30 km); (ii) There is no ambulance available in close proximity. The rescue workers who have discovered the injured person are instructed to WAIT in the event of (i) and try to help – in the event of (ii). The idea is the following: • If there is an ambulance nearby, it would be less risky for the life and the health of the injured person to "wait" just for several minutes and then receive specialized help from the healthcare professionals who would arrive in the ambulance, rather than receiving urgent help immediately but not from healthcare professionals (because the rescue workers are not healthcare professionals even though they are trained to give first aid). • Nevertheless, with no ambulance available nearby, it might be too risky keeping the injured person wait for too long and the help provided by the rescue workers would be appreciated even though they are not healthcare professionals.

Next to that, the considered rescue procedure assumes the "30 km" as "measure" for what is to be considered as "nearby", as mentioned already.

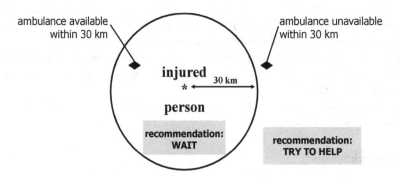

Fig. 5. Helping an injured person – featuring two user situation types

Hence, one would recognize the need for a context-aware system and exactly two user situation types are to be considered: • THE USER IS INJURED AND IT IS POSSIBLE THAT THE USER RECEIVES PROFESSIONAL HELP WITHIN "SEVERAL" MINUTES; • THE USER IS INJURED AND RECEIVING PROFESSIONAL HELP WITHIN "SEVERAL" MINUTES IS IMPOSSIBLE.

Firstly, it is obvious that sensors (+positioning technology [28, 29]) could be used for establishing the user situation. Secondly, we apply semiotic norms (featured in the

Norm Analysis Method) to specify the desired system behavior (we use the abbreviation "rw" for "rescue worker(s)" and the abbreviation "ip" for "injured person"):

```
whenever rw have discovered an ip        whenever rw have discovered an ip
  if there is an ambulance nearby           if there is no ambulance nearby
  then rw                                    then rw
  is obliged                                 is allowed
  to wait                                    to give first aid
```

In this way, norms help in ESTABLISHING THE USER SITUATION. Also, we may consider hierarchies of norms [17], with norms at one "level" governing norms "underneath". Then for the level beneath we bring forward the following norm:

```
whenever ip+rw are waiting for an ambulance
  if ip worsens dramatically
  then rw
  is allowed
  to give first aid
```

And so on… (the rescue worker is ALLOWED, see the second and the third norms, because it is only him or her who could best decide whether (s)he has the capabilities to help and therefore (s)he cannot be "forced" to take action). That is how norms can be used for the benefit of the specification of context-aware applications. Norms are not only more exhaustive than ECA rules (as seen from the example) but they can be organized in hierarchies – something useful as a basis for analysis and design activities.

5.3.2   Prediction-Driven Context-Awareness Featuring Holiday Bookings

Briefing: The managers of an imaginary Travel Agency (TA) are interested to know about the "next" potential customer approaching TA whether it is more likely that (s)he would book a holiday package with them or not. For this they have TRAINING DATA featuring 14 persons who have approached TA in the past. Categorization was applied, concerning the following attributes: AGE (young (y), middle aged (m), senior (s)); INCOME (high (h), medium (m), low (l)); BOOKINGS – previous holiday bookings with TA (yes (y), no (n)); RATING – by this is meant "credit rating" (fair (f), excellent (e)). As mentioned already, we have used and adapted training data from an example considered in [14]. As for the training data itself, it is as follows: • 1-John-y-h-n-f; • 2-Nancy-y-h-n-e; • 3-Arnold-m-h-n-f; • 4-Eva-s-m-n-f; • 5-Richard-s-l-y-f; • 6-Kate-s-l-y-e; • 7-Sam-m-l-y-e; • 8-Dave-y-m-n-f; • 9-Sara-y-l-y-f; • 10-Tom-s-m-y-f; • 11-Boris-y-m-y-e; • 12-Ivan-m-m-n-e; • 13-Pattie-m-h-y-f; • 14-Carlos-s-m-n-e. Further, those who have done booking after approaching TA (Hypothesis 1) are: Arnold, Eva, Richard, Sam, Sara, Tom, Boris, Ivan, and Pattie; the rest have not done booking after approaching TA (Hypothesis 2). Finally, Ben, who is approaching TA is: SENIOR, of HIGH income, with NO previous bookings with TA, and his credit rating is FAIR. The **QUESTION** is whether it is more likely that Ben books a holiday package with TA or that he would not do so. Depending on the answer, TA would establish the USER SITUATION and adapt its "behavior" accordingly: if it is expected that Ben would book a package, TA would address him with a personal promotional offer.

=> We are to classify the data tuple **X** (**senior, high, no, fair**), needing to MAXIMIZE **P(X|H$_i$)X P(H$_i$)**; i = 1, 2, where P(H$_1$) = P(books_holiday = yes), P(H$_2$)= P(books_holiday = no). Hence, P(H$_1$) = 9/14 = 0,643, P(H$_2$) = 5/14 = 0,357.

Further:

```
P(X|H₁)=P(X|books_hol.=yes) =        P(X|H₂)=P(X|books_hol.=no) =
= P(age=s|books_hol.=yes) x          = P(age=s|books_hol.=no) x
x P(inc.=h|books_hol.=yes) x         x P(inc.=h|books_hol.=no) x
x P(book.=n|books_hol.=yes) x        x P(book.=n|books_hol.=no) x
x  P (cr.r.=f|books_hol.=yes) =      x P (cr.r.=f|books_hol.=no) =
= 3/9 x 2/9 x 3/9 x 6/9 = 0,016      = 2/5 x 2/5 x 4/5 x 2/5 = 0,051
```

Since we need to maximize **P(X|H$_i$)X P(H$_i$)**, we should just compare (i) 0,016 x 0,643 = **0,010** and (ii) 0,051 x 0,357 = **0,018**; (ii) is bigger than (i). Thus, we point to **HYPOTHESIS 2 (H$_2$: books_holiday=no)**. Hence, the classifier predicts **books_holiday=no** for tuple **X**. Said otherwise, it is more likely that Ben would NOT book a holiday package with TA.

That is how TA establishes the USER SITUATION, such that it is capable of adapting its behavior accordingly – no need to address Ben with a personal promotional offer.

6 Conclusions

This paper builds on previous research of the authors, touching upon the specification of context-aware ICT applications and inspiring a key assumption, namely: a context-aware application is to adapt its behavior depending on the USER situation (we hence abstract from considering context-aware applications whose bottom-line goal is to optimize INTERNAL processes and/or to respond to PUBLIC values). In this, we find it useful to prepare at DESIGN TIME application behavior VARIANTS for each of the user situation types that are likely to occur. There are achievements in that direction. There are also advances concerning the capturing of context data – by counting on sensors, reports, and so on. Nevertheless, we find "room for improvement" as it concerns what we do with the available context data (and how we do it), such that we effectively and precisely establish the "current" user situation. Hence, a key contribution of the current paper is our exploring the potentials of semiotic norms and Bayesian modeling in this regard. We provide a conceptual overview, an analysis, and partial exemplifications. We need a more solid validation of our findings and this we plan as future work.

References

1. Alférez, G.H., Pelechano, V.: Dynamic evolution of context-aware systems with models at runtime. In: France, R.B., Kazmeier, J., Breu, R., Atkinson, C. (eds.) MODELS 2012. LNCS, vol. 7590, pp. 70–86. Springer, Heidelberg (2012). https://doi.org/10.1007/978-3-642-33666-9_6
2. Alférez, G.H., Pelechano, V.: Context-aware autonomous web services in software product lines. In: Proceedings of the 15th International SPLC Conference on IEEE, CA, USA (2011)
3. Dey, A.K., Abowd, G.D., Salber, D.: A conceptual framework and a toolkit for supporting the rapid prototyping of context-aware applications. Hum. Comput. Interact. **16**, 2 (2001)
4. Dey, A.K., Newberger, A.: Support for context-aware intelligibility and control. In: Proceedings of the SIGCHI Conference on Human Factors in Computer Systems. ACM, USA (2009)
5. Papadimitriou, G.: Future Internet: The Cross-ETP (2009). http://www.future-internet.eu/fileadmin/documents/reports/Cross-ETPs_FI_Vision_Document_v1_0.pdf. Accessed December 2011
6. Shishkov, B., Larsen, J.B., Warnier, M., Janssen, M.: Three categories of context-aware systems. In: Shishkov, B. (ed.) BMSD 2018. LNBIP, vol. 319, pp. 185–202. Springer, Cham (2018). https://doi.org/10.1007/978-3-319-94214-8_12
7. Shishkov, B., Mendling, J.: Business process variability and public values. In: Shishkov, B. (ed.) BMSD 2018. LNBIP, vol. 319, pp. 401–411. Springer, Cham (2018). https://doi.org/10.1007/978-3-319-94214-8_31
8. Shishkov, B., van Sinderen, M.: From user context states to context-aware applications. In: Filipe, J., Cordeiro, J., Cardoso, J. (eds.) ICEIS 2007. LNBIP, vol. 12, pp. 225–239. Springer, Heidelberg (2008). https://doi.org/10.1007/978-3-540-88710-2_18
9. Alegre, U., Augusto, J.C., Clark, T.: Engineering context-aware systems and applications. J. Syst. Softw. 117, C (July) (2016)
10. Bosems, S., van Sinderen, M.: Models in the design of context-aware well-being applications. In: Meersman, R., et al. (eds.) OTM 2014. LNCS, vol. 8842, pp. 37–42. Springer, Heidelberg (2014). https://doi.org/10.1007/978-3-662-45550-0_6
11. AWARENESS: Freeband AWARENESS Project (2008). http://www.freeband.nl
12. Cano, J., Delaval, G., Rutten, E.: Coordination of ECA rules by verification and control. In: Kühn, E., Pugliese, R. (eds.) COORDINATION 2014. LNCS, vol. 8459, pp. 33–48. Springer, Heidelberg (2014). https://doi.org/10.1007/978-3-662-43376-8_3
13. Liu, K.: Semiotics in Information Systems Engineering. Cambridge University Press, New York (2000)
14. Han, J., Kamber, M., Pei, J.: Data Mining: Concepts and Techniques, 3rd edn. Morgan Kaufmann Publ. Inc., San Francisco (2011)
15. Levin, R.I., Rubin, D.S.: Statistics for Management. Prentice Hall, Englewood Cliffs (1997)
16. Hristea, F.T.: The Naïve Bayes Model for Unsupervised Word sense Disambiguation. SpringerBriefs in Statistics. Springer, Heidelberg (2013). https://doi.org/10.1007/978-3-642-33693-5
17. Shishkov, B.: Enterprise Information Systems, A Modeling Approach. IICREST, Sofia (2017)
18. Bunge, M.A.: Treatise on Basic Philosophy. A World of Systems, vol. 4. D. Reidel Publishing Company, Dordrecht (1979)
19. Abeywickrama, D.B.: Context-aware services engineering for service-oriented architectures. In: Bouguettaya, A., Sheng, Q., Daniel, F. (eds.) Web Services Foundations. Springer, New York (2014). https://doi.org/10.1007/978-1-4614-7518-7_12

20. Abeywickrama, D.B., Ramakrishnan, S.: Context-aware services engineering: models, transformations, and verification. ACM Trans. Internet Technol. J. **11**(3) (2012). Article 10. ACM
21. UML: The Unified Modeling Language (2019). http://www.uml.org
22. Mitsubishi Motors: Mitsubishi Motors Corporation (2019). http://www.mitsubishi-motors.com
23. BOSAL: Bosal Group (2019). http://www.bosal.com
24. HKairport Shop: Hong Kong Airport Electronics Shop (2019). https://www.hkairportshop.com/en_hk/electronics.html
25. Shishkov, B., Mitrakos, D.: Towards context-aware border security control. In: BMSD 2016, 6th International Symposium on Business Modeling and Software Design. SCITEPRESS (2016)
26. Witten, I., Frank, E., Hall, M.: Data Mining: Practical Machine Learning Tools and Techniques, 3rd edn. M. Kaufmann Publ. Inc., San Francisco (2011)
27. Wellington J.J., Ramesh P.: Role of Internet of Things in disaster management. In: Proceedings of the International ICIIECS Conference, Coimbatore (2017)
28. Garvanov, I., Kabakchiev, H., Behar, V., Garvanova, M., Iyinbor, R.: On the modeling of innovative navigation systems. In: Shishkov, B. (ed.) BMSD 2019. LNBIP, vol 356. Springer, Cham (2019)
29. Garvanov, I, Kabakchiev, Ch., Behar, V., Rohling, H.: Experimental study of moving man detection by acoustic forward scattering radar system. In: Proceedings of the 6th ICTRS Conference. ACM, New York (2017)

Business Models of Store-Oriented Software Ecosystems: A Variability Modeling Approach

Sebastian Gottschalk[(✉)], Florian Rittmeier, and Gregor Engels

Paderborn University, Paderborn, Germany
{sebastian.gottschalk,florianr,engels}@uni-paderborn.de

Abstract. In the last years, store-oriented software ecosystems are gaining more and more attention from a business perspective. In these ecosystems, third-party developers upload extensions to a store which can be downloaded by end users. While the functional scope of such ecosystems is relatively similar, the underlying business models differ greatly in and between their different product domains (e.g. Mobile Phone, Smart TV). This variability, in turn, makes it challenging for store providers to find a business model that fits their own needs.

To handle this variability, we introduce the Business Variability Model (BVM) for modeling business model decisions. The basis of these decisions is the analysis of 60 store-oriented software ecosystems in eight different product domains. We map their business model decisions to the Business Model Canvas, condense them to a variability model and discuss particular variants and their dependencies. Our work provides store providers a new approach for modeling business model decisions together with insights of existing business models. This, in turn, supports them in creating new and improving existing business models.

Keywords: Software ecosystems · Business models · Variabilities

1 Introduction

In the last years, software ecosystems are gaining more and more attention from a business perspective. What started with Apple's iOS and Google's Android in the area of mobile phones [5] is transferred to an increasing number of product domains. In the literature, many definitions of software ecosystems exist [14]. For the purpose of this paper, we use the definition of Bosch et al. who define software ecosystems as "a software platform, a set of internal and external developers and a community of domain experts in service to a community of users that compose relevant solution elements to satisfy their needs" [1]. Most of these software ecosystems are store-oriented software ecosystems [10].

This work was partially supported by the German Research Foundation (DFG) within the Collaborative Research Center "On-The-Fly Computing" (CRC 901).

© Springer Nature Switzerland AG 2019
B. Shishkov (Ed.): BMSD 2019, LNBIP 356, pp. 153–169, 2019.
https://doi.org/10.1007/978-3-030-24854-3_10

In store-oriented software ecosystems (see Fig. 1), the store provider, third-party developers, and end users are interacting with each other through a store interface. The store provider provides a software platform in form of a store with different features. Examples of these features are a catalog of extensions together with the possibility to rate and review them. Moreover, he can develop extensions to publish them in the store. This development and the publication is also possible for third-party developers who try to reach end users with their extensions. The end users can use the functions of the store and execute extensions of the store provider and third-party developers.

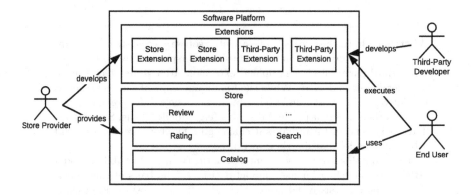

Fig. 1. Overview of a store-oriented software ecosystem

While the functional scope of such ecosystems is relatively similar and the technological decisions are well-understood [10], less research focused on business models of such ecosystems. For the term of the business model, we use the definition of Osterwalder et al. who point out that "a business model describes the rationale of how an organization creates, delivers, and captures value" [19]. Various software ecosystems have different business models, which are used more and more to differentiate in and between product domains [3]. In the area of software ecosystems, the trend of using a store as interface is strengthened by the increasing connectivity of products [4] and the rising amount of platform business models [20]. Examples of these business model decisions are the hardware-bundling of Apple's iOS, the platform-independence of Valve's gaming store STEAM[1] or the subscription model of Sony's PlayStation. A good example of the impact of wrong business model decisions is Nokia's Symbian OS, which failed with business model decisions like high commission fees for third-party developers, incompatibilities between different versions of the ecosystem and poor user experience for end users [2]. This, in turn, leads us to the question of the different business model decisions that exist for the individual product areas and what variabilities and dependencies can be derived from them.

---

[1] https://store.steampowered.com/.

To answer this question, we analyze 60 stores in eight different product domains and identify the most important business model decisions using the taxonomy development method of Nickerson et al. [18]. To structure these decisions, we introduce the Business Variability Model (BVM) based on the Business Model Canvas (BMC) and its nine building blocks (Customer Segments, Value Proposition, Channels, Customer Relationships, Key Activities, Key Resources, Key Partners, Revenue Streams, Cost Structure). The advantage of our Business Variability Model compared to the Business Model Canvas is the possibility to differentiate between mandatory and optional business model decisions and to model dependencies between these decisions. The result of our work is a variability model for these business model decisions as well as a deeper analysis of the variants for revenue streams and their dependencies to the channels. Our work supports store providers in developing new and improving existing business models for store-oriented software ecosystems.

In the following, Sect. 2 considers the related work of the topic. Section 3 describes our used research method and Sect. 4 shows the derived variability model. Based on the variability model, the variants of revenue streams together with their dependencies to the channels are analyzed in a more fine-graded way. In Sect. 5 we show the validity of our variability model by describing the ecosystem of Sony's PlayStation. After that, we discuss our results in Sect. 6. Finally, a conclusion is given in Sect. 7.

2   Related Work

There are already several articles in the literature that deal with individual parts of business models of store-oriented software ecosystems. For example, there are articles on the general strategy of a software ecosystem [5,7,8,17,22], whose individual customer segments are analyzed [5,8,10,13,15,17,22] and the associated value propositions [5,6,8,13,15,17,21,22] are discovered. To reach customers, they need to be acquired [5,6,13,17] and relationships need to be maintained [5,13,17,21,22]. Income [5,6,10,15,17,21,22] is generated by providing services to customers. In order to operate the ecosystem, partnerships need to be formed [5,6,10,17], activities must be carried out [5,15,17] and resources must be created [5,6,8,10,15,17]. This leads to costs [5,6,17] for the store provider. However, while many contributions are limited to individual business areas or the direct comparison of different ecosystems in case studies, only a few contributions [5,8,10,17] attempt to identify the key variabilities in the business models.

Goncalves et al. [5] describe the ongoing platformization process in the mobile network area and how mobile network operators can benefit from that. To do this they analyze different kinds of software ecosystems and group them into four patterns by the variabilities in customers and assets control. These patterns are Enabler Platform, System Integrator Platform, Neutral Platform and Broker Platform. For each pattern they give a small overview of their features, discuss success factors and point out how these patterns can be adapted to mobile operators.

Mueller et al. [17] analyze the competition among different mobile app stores. To do that they are using a literature review to point out the most important business parts of app stores like store features, value propositions, revenue and costs streams together with the main stakeholders of the store. They model the value streams around the customers and partners of the ecosystems and compare the value influence of single partners to the value of the related mobile app store.

Jansen et al. [8] analyze the characteristics, policies, and features of an app store for the store owner, end users and third-party developers based on different case studies. After introducing the core features of app stores, they point out user-focused features (App Findability, App Quality, App Store Usability) and developer-focused features (Feedback Potential, Monetization Potential, App Store Usability, Visibility) as variation points with different variants.

Jazayeri et al. [10] propose a variability model for architectural design decisions of store-oriented software ecosystems. They combine a systematic literature review with the examination of software ecosystems to conduct variabilities in the areas of business, application and infrastructure decisions. By focussing on the technical aspects of these ecosystems, they give, for the business perspective, just an abstract view of the variabilities of complementary partnerships, fees, openness factors, and license agreements. After applying this variability model to a set of store-oriented software ecosystems [11], they derive three patterns for software ecosystems, namely Resale Software Ecosystems, Partner-based Software Ecosystems, and Open Source Software-Based Ecosystems.

3   Research Method

In the paper, we develop a variability model for business model decisions. Therefore, we combine the concept of variability modeling with the structure of the Business Model Canvas. For the underlying decisions, we are using a taxonomy development method which was proposed by Nickerson et al. [18]. The method can be used to classify objects based on their common characteristics. To use the method, we need to define meta-characteristics and ending-conditions together with empirical-to-conceptional and conceptional-to-empirical iteration steps.

The meta-characteristics are the most comprehensive characteristics that can be used as the basis for the choices in the taxonomy. Based on this meta-characteristics we are running combinations of empirical-to-conceptional and conceptual-to-empirical iterations. After each iteration, the taxonomy is checked against objective and subjective ending conditions. While objective ending conditions can be clearly assessed, subjective ending conditions leave space for interpretation. At the time all ending conditions are fulfilled, we are using the taxonomy as the structure for our variability model. After deriving this variability model, we create the dependencies between the individual variation points and variants (see Fig. 3).

To start with the taxonomy development, we need at first to define the meta-characteristic. As we are using the Business Model Canvas as our structure to define the business decisions, we are using the nine building blocks (see Fig. 2)

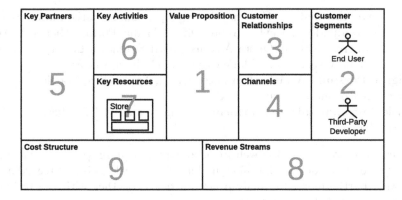

Fig. 2. Business model of the store provider

as start points for our meta-characteristics. To focus on the store as the key element and its dependencies to third-party developers and end users, we design the business model of the store provider as a two-sided market with the store as a key resource. Other stakeholders within the business model are defined as key partners of the store provider. This view of a two-sided market is also used often in the literature of software ecosystems [1,8]. Moreover, we distinguish all variabilities between store provider, third-party developer and end user to separate them by their stakeholder. As an objective condition, we want to examine all selected objectives (Stores, Papers) and as subjective condition, we want to create an appropriate and cross-domain usable model that can be easily extended.

In the empirical-to-conceptional iteration, we analyze a set of 60 store-oriented software ecosystems in eight different product domains with respect to their business model. As product domains, we choose a broad area of domains where the concept of store-oriented software ecosystems is already successfully implemented through different business models. The following list provides an overview of the different product domains and their included software ecosystems:

- **Mobile Phone**: Amazon Appstore, Apple App Store, Aptiode, F-Droid, Get-Jar, Google Play, Samsung Galaxy Store, SlideMe, UpToDown
- **Video Game Console**: Microsoft Store, Nintendo eShop, Ouya Games, PlayStation Store
- **Smart TV**: Amazon Fire OS Store, Google Play, LG AppStore, Panasonic MyHomeScreen, Roku ChannelStore, Samsung Galaxy Store, Tizen Store, VEWD AppStore
- **Personal Computer**: Canonical Snapcraft, Chocolatey, FlatHub, GNOME Shell Extensions, Mac AppStore, Microsoft Store, Npackd, Plasma Discover, Softtonic
- **Gaming Platform**: EA Origin, EPIC Store, Good Old Gaming, Green Man Gaming, Humble Store, Ubisoft Uplay, Valves STEAM

- **Software Extension**: Chrome WebStore, Eclipse Marketplace, Firefox Addons, Kodi Media Center, Libre Office, Media Portal, Microsoft App-Source, Microsoft Store, Opera Addons, Safari Extension Library, Thunderbird Addons, Visual Studio Marketplace, VLC Media Player
- **Digital Personal Assistent**: Amazon Alexa, Apple's Siri, Google Assistent, Microsoft Cortana, Samsung's Bixby
- **Task Automatization Platform**: Automate.io, IFTTT, Microsoft Flow, Slack, Zapier

For each store, we inspect the website as an end user and if possible as a third-party developer to derive the different business model decisions regarding to the BMC. Furthermore, we analyze news articles together with the technical documentations of the ecosystems.

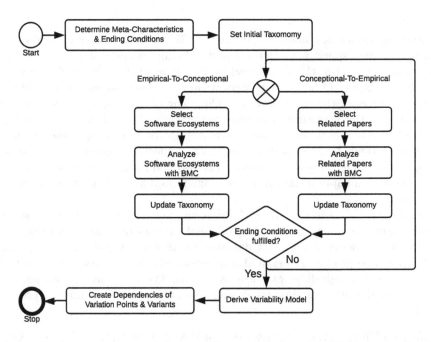

Fig. 3. Development process of the variability model (based on Nickerson et al. [18])

In the conceptual-to-empirical iteration, we analyze related work which based on the systematic literature review of Jazayeri et al. [9] and additional papers provided by our domain knowledge. In the literature review, they analyze the different features of IT Service Markets. One of the extracted features is the business model whose selected papers we are using as our starting papers. We inspect each paper on their business model decisions regarding the BMC and discuss the results in terms of their indirect influence on other parts of the business model decisions.

4 Business Variability Model

In this section, we give an overview of the Business Variability Model (BVM). After we introduce some initial considerations of the variability modeling, we present the variability model for store-oriented software ecosystems. In the following steps, we focus on the revenue streams as a variation group of the business models and discusses the dependencies inside the model regarding the revenue streams and channels.

4.1 Initial Considerations

The modeling of variability in product lines has a long history in the area of software development [23]. A software product line (SPL) comprises several versions of a software system which are based on a shared platform. In some parts of this platform, variabilities are defined, which can be fulfilled with different variants. The approach enables a fast and cost-effective adaptation of software systems. While variability modeling also has a long history in the area of business processes [12], to the best of our knowledge, there was no explicit modeling of variabilities for business model decisions in research.

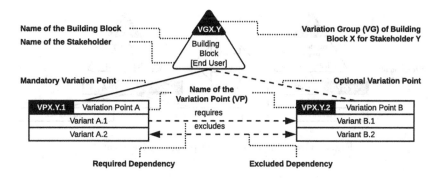

Fig. 4. Legend for Business Variability Model (BVM)

To use the variability modeling in case of business model decisions (see Fig. 4), we create the Business Variability Model (BVM) as a modified version of the Orthogonal Variability Model (OVM) by Metzger et al. [16]. With respect to the work of Zhang et al. [24] we are using a three-level variability model with levels called Variation Group (VG), Variation Point (VP) and Variant.

Overall, the model structure can be divided into the nine building blocks of the Business Model Canvas, whereby there can be variabilities for each stakeholder. The structure was simplified to represent a building block and a stakeholder in a single variation group. The first number X of the variation group represents a building block (1 = Value Proposition, 2 = Customer Segments, ...; see Fig. 2 for specific blocks) and the second number Y represents the stakeholder identifier (1 = Store Provider, 2 = End User, 3 = Third-Party Developer). For example, VP1.2 refers to the value proposition of the end user. For each variation group, required and optional variation points are defined. Moreover, the variation points can have required or excluding dependencies to each other. These variation points can be described by different variants, which can have required or excluding dependencies themselves. If a variation point is used by multiple stakeholders, the structure can be simplified by using a x instead of the stakeholder identifier. In this case, the stakeholder can have different variants of the shared variation point. Moreover, we add two grouping strategies (see Fig. 5) of grouping variation points and variants to simplify the model structure. By grouping variation points and variants of the same type (mandatory, optional) to each other, the structure can be represented in a compressed way.

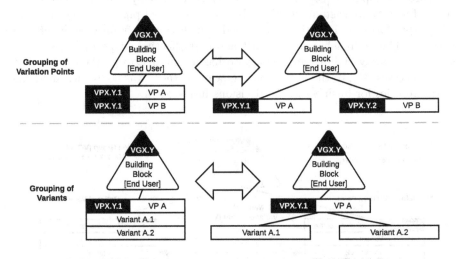

Fig. 5. Grouping of variation points and variants

With the help of this BVM, we are able to create a meta-structure for possible Business Models. Moreover, with the created dependencies we are able to analyze if changes in some parts of the business model lead to changes in or have conflicts with other parts of the business model. Because within this paper we are not able to describe all variation points, variants, and their dependencies, we are focussing on the revenue streams and their dependencies to the channels.

4.2   Modeling of Variation Groups and Variation Points

Within this section, the variability model (see Fig. 6) is presented. In the model for each business model decision, the most important points are picked out and described through different variation points.

In order to improve the structure of the model, we divide it into the perspectives of Product/Service, Customer, Activity, and Financial.

Within the **Product/Service Perspective**, the *Value Propositions* are described for each customer group that is determined by the store provider. For example, the end user can be promised a catalog with mass-market or high-quality extensions (see V1.2.3). A case of existing ecosystems are the quality guidelines of Apple's iOS which are more restrictive than for Google's Android. In contrast, the third-party developer can be offered a large or specialized group of end users (see V1.3.3). For the specialized group a good example are video game consoles with gamers as the target group.

In the **Customer Perspective**, the different customer segments, the sales channels and the relationships to the customer groups are described. Within the *Customer Segments*, the different customer group characterizations are carried out. For example, the store provider can choose a high-price solution for a small target group or reach a larger target group with a low entry price (see V2.2.1). Within the *Customer Relationships*, the store provider needs strategies to reach the respective customer groups. For example, a change of an ecosystem can be made more difficult for end users by so-called lock-in strategy [13] (see V3.2.2). Finally, it must be decided within the *Channels* how the ecosystem will be delivered to the respective customer. For example, it is possible to bundle an ecosystem with hardware or a software product (see V4.2.1). This bundling can be seen on Sony's PlayStation, where hardware and software are bundled together. In contrast, most web browsers bundle their stores with their software products.

Within the **Activity Perspective**, the partnerships concluded, the activities carried out and the used resources are described. Within the *Key Partners*, partners are included that are necessary for the store provider to achieve its value propositions. For example, it may be necessary to have a partner to deliver the hardware or distribute the software [5] (see V5.1.1). Most software ecosystems are using external partners for the payment process and the cloud infrastructure. The *Key Activities* are used to describe the most important tasks of the store provider. For example, it is necessary for the provider to carry out quality control of the submitted extensions (see V6.1.3). For all stakeholders, there may also be *Key Resources* that are crucial for the use of the ecosystem. For example, third-party developers need developer tools to create their extensions [10] (see V7.3.2).

The **Financial Perspective** is about comparing the revenues and costs for the individual stakeholders. Within the *Revenue Streams*, the stakeholders, which are responsible for the respective flows, are modeled. For example, an end user can purchase a hardware bundle or an extension (see V8.2.1). The *Cost Structure* breaks down which stakeholders generate the respective costs. For example, parts of the revenue can be passed to the third-party developer as commission when an extension is sold (see V9.3.2).

4.3 Modeling of Variants

In this section, we focus on the different revenue streams, as on the one hand, they decide on the financial success of store-oriented software ecosystems and on the other hand they show the variety of revenue streams of different product domains.

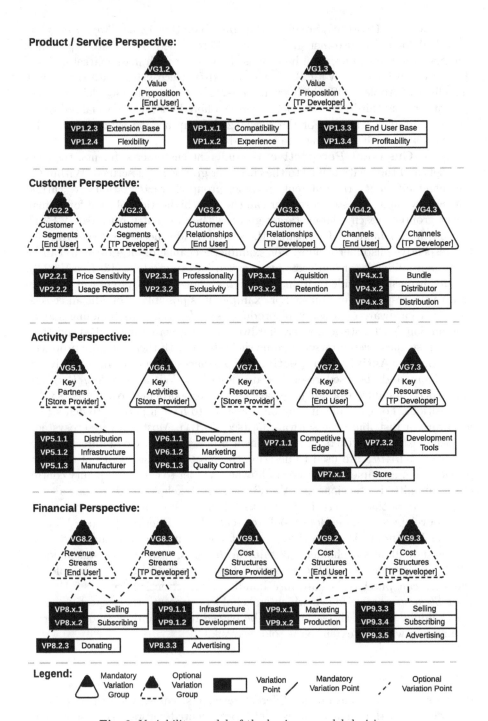

Fig. 6. Variability model of the business model decisions

The variation groups of the revenue streams (see Fig. 7) can be divided into the variation points of selling, subscribing, donating and advertising with respect to the end user and the third-party developer.

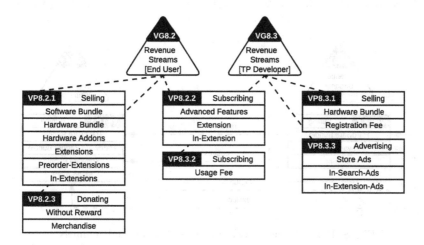

Fig. 7. Variants of revenue streams

The store provider can generate revenue from the **End User** by *Selling* different parts of the software ecosystem. If he has bundled the ecosystem, he can sell the software product itself (e.g. Microsoft AppSource with Microsoft Word) or a complete hardware bundle (e.g. Apple Store with iPhone). Moreover, he can sell hardware addons to the existing ecosystem (e.g. Apple Watch). Inside the store, he is able to sell extensions, providing preordering of extensions (e.g Xbox game preordering) or additional in-extensions. To generate a continuous income stream, he can use *Subscribing* offers. Here, the end user can subscribe to advanced features (e.g. PlayStation Plus) together with extensions and in-extensions. The last part of the revenue streams of the store provider are the *Donating* offers, which are often used by non-profit ecosystem provider. Here, the end user can donate without a reward (e.g. Kodi MediaCenter) or get merchandise articles for their support (e.g. Firefox Add-ons).

The store provider can generate revenue from the **Third-Party Developer** by *Selling* different parts of the software ecosystem. If the development of extensions needs separate hardware he can sell it to the developer (e.g. Oculus Rift). Moreover, he can charge a fee for registering as a developer (e.g. Android Developer). This fee can also be paid by *Subscribing* to the ecosystem on an annual basis (e.g. Apple Developer). Moreover, revenue can be generated by *Advertising*. Here, the developer can pay for Store Ads, In-Search-Ads or In-Extensions-Ads.

4.4 Modeling of Dependencies

In this section, we focus on the dependencies between revenue streams and channels. This is because, for channels, in particular, there are many different bundling approaches which have a direct influence on the respective revenue.

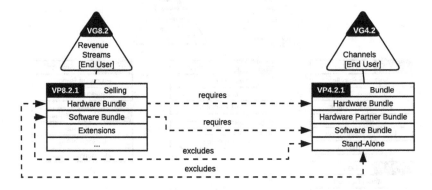

Fig. 8. Dependencies between revenue streams and channels

In the bundling variation point, the store provider is able to choose different bundle options for the **End User** (see Fig. 8). The first option is to bundle the specific ecosystems with an own *Hardware Bundle* (e.g. AppStore for Apple's iPhone). If the hardware bundle is not provided by the store provider itself we call it *Hardware Partner Bundle* (e.g. different hardware manufacturers for Google Android). Moreover, the ecosystem can be provided as a *Software Bundle* (e.g. Microsoft AppSource with Microsoft Word) or as *Stand-Alone* (e.g. Valve's STEAM). If the store provider wants to generate revenue from selling a hardware or software bundle, he needs to use the corresponding option in the bundling of the channel. Conversely, he can not generate revenue from hardware and software bundles when he distributes his ecosystem as Stand-Alone.

5 Describing an Existing Ecosystem

To show the validity of our approach, we provide a concrete instance of Sony's PlayStation Ecosystem using our variability model. In Tables 1 and 2 we point out the Value Propositions (Va), Customer Segments (CS), Customer Relationships (CR), Channels (Ch), Key Partners (KP), Key Resources (KR), Key Activities (KA), Revenue Streams (RS) and Cost Structure (Co) of the ecosystem. To simplify the tables, we remove all variation points, which are not used in the ecosystem.

Table 1. Describing the PlayStation Ecosystem: Part 1

VG	VP	Store provider	End user	TP-Developer
Va	Extension Base	-	High Amount of Games, Specialized for Gaming	-
Va	Compability	-	High Compability though less Fragmentation	
Va	Experience	-	Simple User Interface, High Customization	Easy Development Tools
Va	End User Base	-	-	High Amount of End Users, Specialized Target Group
Va	Profitability	-	-	High Price Points for Games, Sales Events
CS	Price Sensitivity	-	High Price Points for Games	-
CS	Usage Reason	-	Gaming, Streaming	-
CS	Professionality	-	-	Mostly Professional Developer Studios
CS	Exclusivity	-	-	Partly Exclusive Developer Studios
CR	Aquisition	-	High Amount of Games, Exclusive Games, Hardware Subsidies	High End User Base, Exclusive Deals, Low Entry Fee
CR	Retention	-	Lock-In, Exclusive Games, Subscription Model, Gamification	Lock-In, Fair Commission Model
Ch	Bundle	-	Hardware-Bundle	-
Ch	Distributor	-	Partner-Based-Distribution	Self-Distribution
Ch	Distribution	-	Online Shops, Retail Stores, Own Website	Own Website
KP	Distributor	Online Shops, Retail Stores	-	-
KP	Infrastructure	Amazon Web Services, OpenStack	-	-
KP	Manufacturer	Foxconn Tech	-	-
KA	Development	Hardware, Software, SDKs	-	-
KA	Marketing	Ecosystem, Playstation Plus	-	-
KA	Quality Checks	High Quality	-	-

6   Discussion

In this paper, we create a variability model to model the business model decisions of store-oriented software ecosystems. Because the field of business models is highly dynamic and the valuation of the importance of different business model

Table 2. Describing the PlayStation Ecosystem: Part 2

VG	VP	Store provider	End user	TP-Developer
KR	Competitive Edge	Exclusive Brands	-	-
KR	Store	-	Store for Downloading Games	Store for Uploading Games
KR	Development Tools	-	-	Hardware-Kit, SDK
RS	Selling	-	Hardware Bundle, Hardware Addons, Games, Game Addons, Preorder Games	Developer Kit, Developer License
RS	Subscribing	Advanced Features (Playstation Plus)	-	-
Co	Infrastructure	Cost for Infrastructure	-	-
Co	Development	Software, Hardware, Games	-	-
Co	Marketing	-	Acquire End User	Acquire Developer
Co	Production	-	Hardware	Hardware
Co	Selling	-	-	Games, Game Addons, Preorder Games
Co	Subscribing	-	-	Games (Playstation Plus)

decisions directly relates to the background experiences of the researchers, the variability model cannot be seen as a closed result for business modeling. Analysis of other researchers or business model decisions of future ecosystems may require changes to the model. Nevertheless, we are convinced that with the analysis of 60 ecosystems and the usage of the taxonomy development method of Nickerson et al. [18], we developed a good starting point for store providers to create new and to improve existing business models.

With the Business Variability Model (BVM), we provide a model to structure these business model decisions. By using the well-accepted Business Model Canvas (BMC) as a starting point, we create a structure which is generic enough to model additional variabilities of other researchers and adopt changes in the future. Therefore, this extendibility is chosen as a subjective ending condition of the taxonomy development.

7   Conclusion and Future Work

In the last years, software ecosystems in different product domains are gaining an increased amount of attention from the business perspective. Because business models develop dynamically within these product domains, it is challenging for store providers to get a comprehensive overview of the different business models. To help store providers with this overview, we have introduced the Business

Variability Model (BVM) to model business model decisions. Based on a modified version of the Orthogonal Variability Model [16] and the Business Model Canvas [19], we develop a three-level (Variation Group, Variation Point, Variant) variability model that simplifies the handling of business model decisions of different stakeholders. The advantage of our Business Variability Model compared to the Business Model Canvas is the possibility to differentiate between mandatory and optional business model decisions and to model dependencies between these decisions. After providing a summarized view of the different design decisions of store providers, we take a deeper look into the different revenue streams and their dependencies to the channels of such software ecosystems. With the results of this paper, the store providers should get an approach to model different business model decisions and receive insights about current existing business models of store-oriented software ecosystems. Both, in turn, will support them by improving their current business situation.

For the future, we have also identified two interesting research directions with deriving of design patterns and the usage of concepts of dynamic software product lines. For deriving of design patterns, we need to model the business model of each software ecosystem using our variability model. Now, we can use pattern mining to identify common patterns of different product domains. As an example of a pattern, the providers of video game consoles combine a closed platform solution together with a subscription service and exclusive brands for customer acquisition. The second point is the usage of concepts of dynamic software product lines. In this paper, we are using the concepts of static software product lines to model the variabilities of the business model. Because business models are highly dynamic it is worth to look if this dynamic can be modeled with them. As an example of this dynamic in the last years, the providers of mobile phone ecosystems started to generate a new revenue stream with the selling of In-Search-Ads.

References

1. Bosch, J., Bosch-Sijtsema, P.: From integration to composition: on the impact of software product lines, global development and ecosystems. J. Syst. Softw. **83**(1), 67–76 (2010). https://doi.org/10.1016/j.jss.2009.06.051
2. Bouwman, H., Carlsson, C., Carlsson, J., Nikou, S., Sell, A., Walden, P.: How nokia failed to nail the smartphone market. In: 25th European Regional Conference of the International Telecommunications Society (ITS) (2014)
3. Chesbrough, H.: Business model innovation: it's not just about technology anymore. Strategy Leadership. **35**(6), 12–17 (2007). https://doi.org/10.1108/10878570710833714
4. Porter, M.E., Heppelmann, J.E.: How smart, connected products are transforming competition. Harvard Bus. Rev. **92**(11), 64–88 (2014)
5. Gonçalves, V., Walravens, N., Ballon, P.: How about an app store? Enablers and constraints in platform strategies for mobile network operators. In: Ninth International Conference on Mobile Business and Ninth Global Mobility Roundtable (ICMB-GMR), pp. 66–73. IEEE (2010). https://doi.org/10.1109/ICMB-GMR.2010.41

6. Holzer, A., Ondrus, J.: Mobile application market: a developer's perspective. Telematics Inform. **28**(1), 22–31 (2011). https://doi.org/10.1016/j.tele.2010.05.006
7. Jansen, S.: Measuring the health of open source software ecosystems: moving beyond the scope of project health. Inf. Softw. Technol. **56**(11), 1508–1519 (2014). https://doi.org/10.1016/j.infsof.2014.04.006
8. Jansen, S., Bloemendal, E.: Defining app stores: the role of curated marketplaces in software ecosystems. In: Herzwurm, G., Margaria, T. (eds.) ICSOB 2013. LNBIP, vol. 150, pp. 195–206. Springer, Heidelberg (2013). https://doi.org/10.1007/978-3-642-39336-5_19
9. Jazayeri, B., Platenius, M.C., Engels, G., Kundisch, D.: Features of IT service markets: a systematic literature review. In: Sheng, Q.Z., Stroulia, E., Tata, S., Bhiri, S. (eds.) ICSOC 2016. LNCS, vol. 9936, pp. 301–316. Springer, Cham (2016). https://doi.org/10.1007/978-3-319-46295-0_19
10. Jazayeri, B., Zimmermann, O., Engels, G., Kundisch, D.: A variability model for store-oriented software ecosystems: an enterprise perspective. In: Maximilien, M., Vallecillo, A., Wang, J., Oriol, M. (eds.) ICSOC 2017. LNCS, vol. 10601, pp. 573–588. Springer, Cham (2017). https://doi.org/10.1007/978-3-319-69035-3_42
11. Jazayeri, B., Zimmermann, O., Engels, G., Küster, J., Kundisch, D., Szopinski, D.: Design options of store-oriented software ecosystems: an investigation of business decisions. In: Shishkov, B. (ed.) BMSD 2018. LNBIP, vol. 319, pp. 390–400. Springer, Cham (2018). https://doi.org/10.1007/978-3-319-94214-8_30
12. La Rosa, M., van der Aalst, W.M.P., Dumas, M., Milani, F.P.: Business process variability modeling. ACM Comput. Surv. **50**(1), 1–45 (2017). https://doi.org/10.1145/3041957
13. Lee, S.M., Kim, N.R., Hong, S.G.: Key success factors for mobile app platform activation. Serv. Bus. **11**(1), 207–227 (2017). https://doi.org/10.1007/s11628-016-0329-y
14. Manikas, K., Hansen, K.M.: Software ecosystems - a systematic literature review. J. Syst. Softw. **86**(5), 1294–1306 (2013). https://doi.org/10.1016/j.jss.2012.12.026
15. Menychtas, A., et al.: 4CaaSt marketplace: an advanced business environment for trading cloud services. Future Gener. Comput. Syst. **41**, 104–120 (2014). https://doi.org/10.1016/j.future.2014.02.020
16. Metzger, A., Pohl, K., Heymans, P., Schobbens, P.Y., Saval, G.: Disambiguating the documentation of variability in software product lines: a separation of concerns, formalization and automated analysis. In: International Requirements Engineering Conference (RE), pp. 243–253. IEEE (2007). https://doi.org/10.1109/RE.2007.61
17. Müller, R.M., Kijl, B., Martens, J.K.J.: A comparison of inter-organizational business models of mobile app stores: there is more than open vs. closed. J. Theor. Appl. Electron. Commer. Res. **6**(2), 13–14 (2011). https://doi.org/10.4067/S0718-18762011000200007
18. Nickerson, R.C., Varshney, U., Muntermann, J.: A method for taxonomy development and its application in information systems. Eur. J. Inf. Syst. **22**(3), 336–359 (2013). https://doi.org/10.1057/ejis.2012.26
19. Osterwalder, A., Pigneur, Y.: Business Model Generation: A Handbook for Visionaries, Game Changers, and Challengers. Wiley, Hoboken (2010)
20. Parker, G., van Alstyne, M., Choudary, S.P.: Platform revolution: Platform Revolution: How Networked Markets Are Transforming the Economy - and How to Make Them Work for You. W.W. Norton & Company, New York and London (2016)

21. Roma, P., Ragaglia, D.: Revenue models, in-app purchase, and the app performance: evidence from Apple's app store and google play. Electron. Commer. Res. Appl. **17**, 173–190 (2016). https://doi.org/10.1016/j.elerap.2016.04.007

22. Tuunainen, V.K., Tuunanen, T., Piispanen, J.: Mobile service platforms: comparing Nokia OVI and Apple app store with the IISIn model. In: International Conference on Mobile Business (ICMB), pp. 74–83. IEEE (2011). https://doi.org/10.1109/ICMB.2011.42

23. van Gurp, J., Bosch, J., Svahnberg, M.: On the notion of variability in software product lines. In: Conference on Software Architecture (CSA), pp. 45–54. IEEE (2001). https://doi.org/10.1109/WICSA.2001.948406

24. Zhang, B., Becker, M., Patzke, T., Sierszecki, K., Savolainen, J.E.: Variability evolution and erosion in industrial product lines. In: 17th International Software Product Line Conference (SPLC), pp. 168–177. ACM (2013). https://doi.org/10.1145/2491627.2491645

VR-EA: Virtual Reality Visualization of Enterprise Architecture Models with ArchiMate and BPMN

Roy Oberhauser[(✉)] and Camil Pogolski

Computer Science Department, Aalen University, Aalen, Germany
{roy.oberhauser,camil.pogolski}@hs-aalen.de

Abstract. The digital transformation occurring throughout enterprises results in an increasingly dynamic and complex IT landscape. As the structures with which enterprise architecture (EA) deals become more digital, larger, complex, and dynamic, new approaches for modeling, documenting, and conveying EA structural and relational aspects are needed. The potential for virtual reality (VR) to address upcoming EA modeling challenges has as yet been insufficiently explored. This paper contributes a VR hypermodel solution concept for visualizing, navigating, interacting with ArchiMate and Business Process Modeling Notation (BPMN) models in VR. An implementation demonstrates its feasibility and a case study is used to show its potential.

Keywords: Virtual reality · Enterprise architecture · Business process models · BPMN · ArchiMate · Visualization

1 Introduction

Multiple contemporaneous trends and challenges are being faced by enterprises, including the smaller and not so information technology (IT)-centric enterprises: (1) *digital transformation/automation*, (2) *agile business processes*, and (3) *service-networked software with frequent deployments*. First, a major *digital transformation* of industries is underway (Muro et al. 2017). While the digitalization rate (digital score) may vary across industries and economies, it is nevertheless impacting business strategies and necessarily the enterprise architecture (EA) that supports the business. As big data, data analytics, business intelligence, and machine learning make inroads into enterprises, improved decision-making capabilities at all levels and across organizational entities empowers employees with new insights and assistance and bringing further automation that in turn affects business functions and processes, and thus affecting and changing the actual EA. Second, enterprises are facing competitive pressure to implement *agile business processes* that are fast, lean, and more effective, with enterprise management, processes, and projects moving towards continuously flexible, responsive, and efficient business forms to accelerate product and service delivery (e.g., Scrum, DevOps, BizDevOps). The IT infrastructure needed to support these dynamic processes implies a much more dynamic and complex EA to support these both rapidly changing and highly-integrated business processes. Finally, the IT

© Springer Nature Switzerland AG 2019
B. Shishkov (Ed.): BMSD 2019, LNBIP 356, pp. 170–187, 2019.
https://doi.org/10.1007/978-3-030-24854-3_11

infrastructure is rapidly changing from local, siloed, and static deployments to cloud-centric, networked, and containerized micro-functionality with frequent new deployments (Forsgren et al. 2017). Software/data functionality becomes easily reusable and accessible via standard protocols and formats independent of programming language or platform, and thus more connected and integrated. The scale and impact on IT landscapes can be appreciated via various "death star"-like microservice network landscape visualizations (Munns 2015) as exemplified in Fig. 1.

Fig. 1. Visualization of microservices at Amazon (Munns 2015)

Enterprise architecture (EA) comprises the structural and behavioral aspects needed for an enterprise to function and adapt in alignment with some vision. To this end, it involves comprehensive and cohesive modeling and documentation. Considering the trends and challenges mentioned, the reality that EA is attempting to comprehensively model, document, and change has become much more complex than in previous decades. To cope with this new reality, new EA modeling paradigms and EA modeling tool approaches are needed. EA seeks to provide a comprehensive set of cohesive models to describe the enterprise structure and functions, while individual models are logically arranged to provide further detail about an enterprise (Jarvis 2003).

Virtual Reality (VR) could potentially assist with visualizing this growing and complex set of models and their interrelationships. VR is defined as a "real or simulated environment in which the perceiver experiences telepresence" (Steuer 1992), a mediated visual environment which is created and then experienced. VR has made inroads in various domains and become readily accessible as hardware prices have dropped and capabilities improved. As EA models grow in complexity and reflect the deeper integration of both the business and IT reality, an immersive EA environment could provide an additional visualization capability to comprehend the "big picture" for structurally and hierarchically complex and interconnected diagrams, while providing an immersive experience for EA models in a 3D space viewable from different perspectives.

As to modeling EA, ArchiMate (Open Group 2017a) provides a visual EA modeling language for visualizing, describing, and analyzing the various elements involved in EA. This includes business and organizational structures, business processes, information flows, IT applications and systems, and technical infrastructure. While the scope of ArchiMate is used to model high-level enterprise processes and to depict their relations to the enterprise context, it is not intended to be a detailed workflow modeling language. For this, the Business Process Model and Notation (BPMN) (OMG 2011) supports the modeling of detailed subprocesses and tasks from the abstract to an executable specification. However, BPMN does not cope with modeling the wider enterprise context like the goals and requirements the process is intended to fulfill, nor for modeling the supporting application services and infrastructure. Thus, the two notations can be viewed as complementing one another in providing more context for a business process, while providing sufficient detail of a business process to the point of executability. In our view, various parts of the detailed business process could and should be seen within the larger enterprise scope to better understand the business process context and any potential dependencies.

In general, modeling provides an abstracted or simplified representation of a system that can assist with understanding relationships between elements or concepts of interest. Typically, views are used to represent some stakeholder concern and portray the relevant aspects of the model. However, with typical 2D view depictions, one can lose insight into the interrelationships across views and where relevant model elements are to be found. By leveraging the third dimension provided in VR, the overall interrelationships of the models and views can be indicated and considered.

In prior work, we described VR-BPMN (Oberhauser et al. 2018), our VR solution concept for visualizing, navigating, annotating, and interacting with BPMN models that supports teleportation, fly -through navigation, depicting subprocesses via stacked hyperplanes, drawing annotative associations between BPMN elements, coloring model elements, and tagging textual elements using mixed reality keyboard support. That approach and implementation resulted in a BPMN-specific VR solution. For this paper, we have generalized our approach to enable visualization of generic model elements, rather than many specific shapes, we use cubes with a textual label and optionally displaying any assigned visual icon to represent the element type. Relationships between elements can be shown, and related elements can be grouped in layers or views. We applied this generalized approach to leverage an immersive VR capability for EA and BPMN models. This paper contributes a generalized VR-MF and the more specific VR-EA, a VR hypermodel solution concept for EA model visualization, navigation, and interaction. To address the deeper integration, complexity, and interconnectedness of EA with business processes, it facilitates the convergence of Archimate enterprise models and BPMN models in VR, enabling both to be visualized and analyzed in the same field of view. Details on the implementation prototype are provided, and we evaluate our implementation using the ArchiSurance case study.

The remainder of this paper is structured as follows: Sect. 2 discusses related work. In Sect. 3 the VR-EA solution concept is described. Section 4 then provides details on our prototype implementation. The evaluation using a case study is described in Sect. 5, and a conclusion follows in Sect. 6.

2 Related Work

Work related to EA visualization includes (Rehring et al. 2019), who applied 3D visualization in augmented reality in support of EA decision making. (Naranjo et al. 2014) describe PRIMate based on PRIMROSe, a visual graph-based enterprise analysis framework, and show a graph, treemap, and 3D visualization of an the ArchiSurance ArchiMate model. As to harmonizing ArchiMate, BPMN, and UML, (van den Berg 2012) analyzes the various metamodels and shows how one could practically combine the notations across views and diagrams. We are unaware of any VR-specific work with ArchiMate, EA model convergence, or EA hypermodels.

BPMN-related work includes the process visualization and virtualization areas. As to process visualization techniques, (Du et al. 2012) provide a survey, concluding that 3D can improve the layout and can increase the information content of process models. Work related to process visualization includes (Betz et al. 2008), who described an approach for 3D representation of business process models based on Petri nets with organizational models, showing that a 3D process representation can facilitate process-specific information access. (Hipp et al. 2015) described and empirically evaluated various business process visualization alternatives: bubbles, BPMN3D that maps data objects associated to a BPMN element to a "third dimension", network, and thin lines; however, no 3D space nor an implementation is described. With regard to virtual worlds, (Brown et al. 2011) investigated collaborative process modeling and communication, implementing a 3D BPMN modeling environment in the virtual world Second Life, and also used the Open Simulator (Brown 2010). The 3D Flight Navigator (Effinger 2012) was implemented in Java with OpenGL, and projects parts of BPMN collaboration diagrams onto fixed hyperplanes and provides a heads-up display for navigating the process. No major BPMS vendors currently sell VR variants of their products.

In contrast, out VR-MF/VR-EA solution concept enables VR-centric visualization, can be implemented on standard game engine technology (Unity) and uses common VR hardware (HTC Vive). It supports hypermodeling, e.g., combining ArchiMate and BPMN models in the same space, provides automatic layout of views as stacked 3D hyperplanes, and visualizes the reality of inter-view relations of elements.

3 Solution Concept

Our generalized VR modeling solution concept provides a VR-based domain-independent hypermodeling framework (VR-MF shown in Fig. 2) that addresses three primary aspects especially affecting models in VR: visualization, navigation, and interaction. Rather than requiring unique and specific 3D shapes, we use cubes with a textual label and display an optional type icon (if provided) on the cube sides. Relationships between elements can be shown, and related elements can be grouped in layers or views. Our support for EA models in VR is called VR-EA in Fig. 2, and encompasses both BPMN and ArchiMate models.

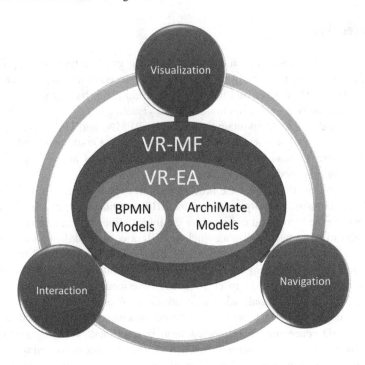

Fig. 2. The VR-MF (general) and VR-EA (EA-specific) solution concept

ArchiMate models use a graphical notation consisting of a collection of concepts (approximately 50) to portray a wide scope of EA elements and relationships. Elements can be behavioral, structural, motivational, or some composite. These concepts can participate in various layers: strategy, business, application, technology, physical, and implementation & migration, the layers having colors associated with them. Cross-cutting aspects involved include: passive structure, active structure, behavior, and motivation. Views are used to convey information addressing concerns of specific stakeholders. On the other hand, BPMN models focus on business processes and consist of Business Process Diagrams (BPDs) composed of graphical elements consisting of flow objects, connecting objects, swim lanes, and artifacts (OMG 2011).

Visualization. The graphical elements involved in ArchiMate and BPMN are specified in 2D. While many visual options and metaphors are possible, our view is that diverging too far from the images in the specification would reduce the recognition and standardization afforded by the respective specification. Thus, to differentiate elements by type, we chose to use generic 3D cubes and project the relevant standard 2D image for the object type onto all sides as a texture, which can thus be perceived from all angles. In contrast to 2D space, one challenge in 3D space element placement is that one can never be sure if an element is not hidden behind another element at any particular vantage point if the element is opaque. However, if one makes the element partially transparent, then it can become confusing as to which element one is actually focusing on. We thus chose to make the elements opaque in order to avoid this visual confusion, and by briefly adjusting one's perspective one can visually check that nothing is hidden behind an element. Moreover, visualizing text is an issue in VR due to the relatively low resolutions currently available and the distance from the virtual camera position to the text. Also, labels for ArchiMate and BPMN elements can differ widely in length, yet should not interfere with understanding the underlying diagram structure. We thus place labels above the elements (analogous to billboards), make them partially transparent in order not to completely hide any elements behind the label, and the labels are made to automatically rotate towards the camera to improve legibility from any given angle. For dealing with longer labels we constrain the maximum billboard width (to reduce over-lapping), raise the billboard height, and reduce the text font size. For visualizing and differentiating the various diagrams, hyperplanes are used to take advantage of the 3D space, with each plane representing one diagram. In BPMN, subprocesses are projected onto a plane beneath its superprocess.

The ArchiMate specification advises "...viewpoints and views...should not be considered in isolation: views are inter-related and, often, it is exactly a combination of views together with their underlying inter-dependency relationships that is the best way to describe and communicate a piece of architecture. It should, however, be noted that viewpoints and views have a limiting character. They are eventually a restriction of the whole system (and architecture) to a partial number of aspects – a view is just a partial incomplete depiction of the system" (Open Group 2017a). Consequently, our VR-EA solution involves a *reality-centric principle* for visualization. What we mean by this is that by default we depict the true complexity and interrelatedness of the model element, permitting the user to hide the views, layers, or elements that are currently not of interest. View-centric portrayals be definition necessarily hide these aspects and thus parts of this reality. Given the growing complexity in EA and IT landscapes, we believe an over-simplification can be detrimental to understanding, e.g. by potentially over-looking a key dependency across views or requiring a user to remember to look at multiple views to see the overall impact of a change. While current ArchiMate tools such as Archi provide an automatic Visualiser or View Generator, they are limited to the single element in focus.

Navigation. The immersion afforded by VR requires addressing how to intuitively navigate the space while reducing the likelihood of potential VR sickness symptoms. Two navigation modes are included in the solution concept: the default uses gliding controls, enabling users to *fly through* the VR space and get an overview of the entire model from any angle they wish. Alternatively, teleporting permits a user to select a destination and be instantly placed there (i.e., by moving the camera to that position); this can be disconcerting but may reduce the likelihood of VR sickness that can occur when moving through a virtual space for those prone to it.

Interaction. Neither ArchiMate nor BPMN specify exactly how users are to interact and interface with graphical visual elements. In our VR concept, user-element inter-action is done primarily via the VR controllers. Views are stacked hyperplanes and can be made visible or invisible by selecting the plane. Inter-view connections can be enabled or disabled. A specific connection can be selected to emphasize it.

4 Realization

Initially, our realization primarily addresses visualization and navigation of existing models. Future work will include support for creating and improving models in VR.

The Unity game engine was chosen for VR visualization due to its multi-platform support, direct VR integration, popularity, and cost, and we utilize the SteamVR plugin and runtime. Blender was used to develop certain visual model elements. For testing with VR hardware, we used the HTC Vive, a room scale VR set with a head-mounted display and two wireless handheld controllers tracked by two base stations.

The implementation architecture for our prototype is shown in Fig. 3. The Unity engine makes use of the various assets such as Models, Scenes, and Scripts, which in turn access external model files. A plugin adapter interface allows various model file formats (e.g., BPMN, ArchiMate) to be parsed and converted to the internal generic object representation.

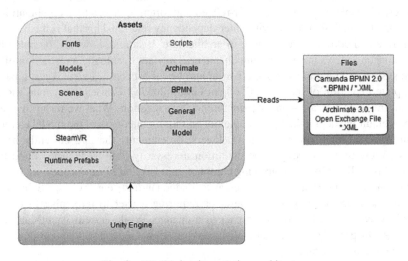

Fig. 3. VR-EA implementation architecture

Generic cubes are used to depict model elements. If an icon is assigned to the type, it is depicted on all 6 sides, otherwise the element type (as text) is shown instead (see Fig. 4 where BusinessService is projected on the Claims Payment Service cube). The positioning of elements within a view or layer is done by reading out the position in the models and applying an adjustable scaling factor (0.05 for BPMN and 0.04 for ArchiMate). Ordering of the views as stacked layers is done relative to each other to avoid collisions and to better portray relations and cluster by known views. The hypermodeling capability is shown in Fig. 5, where two BPMN models (an Invoice Process (left) (ORYX-Editor 2009) and Insurance Claim Process (center) (GitHub 2017)) are shown in the same layer (vertical height) as the Business Process View from the ArchiMate model (based on ArchiSurance (Open Group 2017b)). For comparison, Fig. 6 shows the BPMN Insurance Claim Processing model from Fig. 5 as the typical non-VR BPMN diagram.

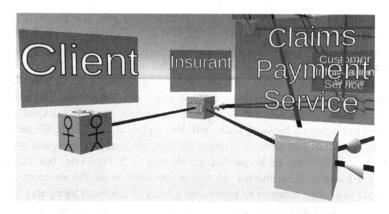

Fig. 4. VR-EA cubes with and without icons (labeled with the element type if unassigned)

Fig. 5. VR-EA hypermodel showing BPMN models (left and center) in the same vertical layer as the Business Process View in the ArchiMate model (ArchiSurance) on the right.

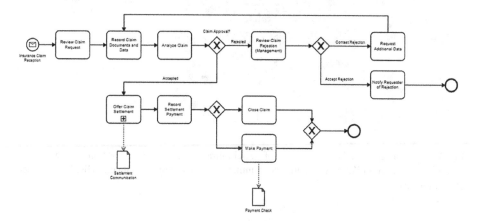

Fig. 6. Example BPMN Insurance Claim Processing model (GitHub 2017).

To implement our *reality-centric visualization principle,* we chose to initially visualize *all* elements and relations of both ArchiMate and BPMN and allow the user to hide those not desired. As with the death-star-like microservice depictions, while it may initially appear overwhelming, the user is presented with everything that exists in the models, rather than not knowing and then attempting to search for or discover these "accidentally". Moreover, they can navigate to those areas of interest, and planes can be turned on or off. To support fly-through navigation, the left trackpad controls altitude and the right one forward, backward, left, and right movement. Element labels orient themselves to the camera position as one navigates. The labels are semi-transparent, to allow one to know that an element is behind one, but this affects readability negatively. Nevertheless, we find it important to see the structure, and one can navigate to another location to better read a label of interest. Orthogonal layout of connectors was used and connector types are place along the connector in order to avoid collision issues with placement. ArchiMate does not provide bend point information, whereas BPMN does. Inter-model connectors (between BPMN and ArchiMate or between BPMN diagrams) can be placed across models to associate corresponding elements of interest.

We ran into issues with the normalized ArchiMate models missing information that can be used for proper element placement, thus we place elements next to each other when lacking proper positioning and bend-point information. We noticed that other ArchiMate tools also exhibit this issue (see Fig. 7) when they import an exported ArchiMate file (which does not contain the additional information retained by the tools in which the modeling was performed in their proprietary format).

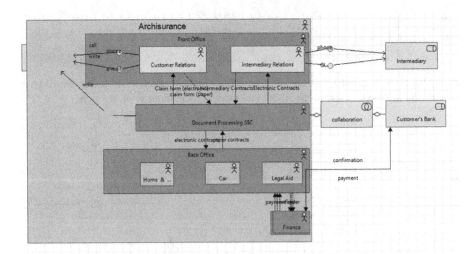

Fig. 7. Unadjusted Modelio import of ArchiSurance Actor Cooperation View (note foreground/background/overlap and containment issues for Finance, HRM, Product Development)

5   Evaluation

To evaluate and compare VR-EA with typical alternative 2D ArchiMate tools such as Archi, we use the well-known ArchiSurance case study (Open Group 2017b) used to illustrate the ArchiMate modeling language (whereby we apply it outside of its TOGAF context). Figure 8 shows the ArchiSurance model loaded in VR-EA.

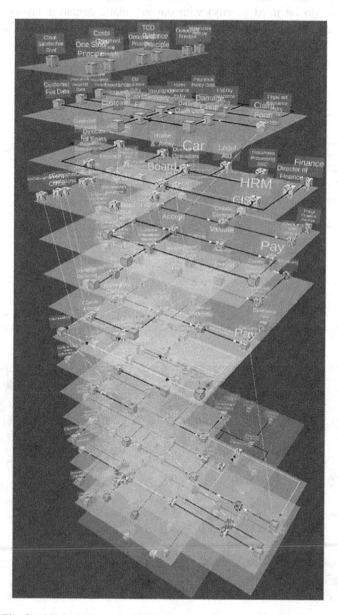

Fig. 8. All ArchiSurance elements and relations visualized in VR-EA

Based on our *reality-centric visualization principle*, we intentionally keep the inter-view connections visible to convey the underlying relations and actual complexity (reality) not readily seen with typical 2D rendering of views. This is analogous to the deathstar-like visualizations for microservices referred to in Sect. 1, which we note could also be simplified if desired.

Figure 9 shows the ArchiSurance Actor Cooperation View in the tool Archi. In contrast, Fig. 10 shows this view in VR-EA with containers shown via blue rectangles. Due to a bug (to be fixed shortly) with our automatic container layout placement implementation, we manually corrected their positioning before taking the screenshots.

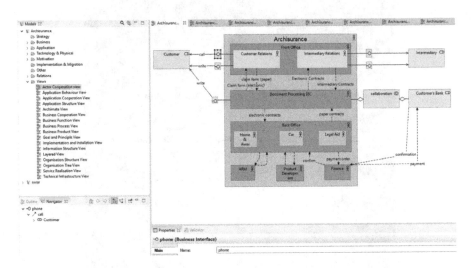

Fig. 9. Screenshot of the ArchiSurance Actor Cooperation View shown in Archi

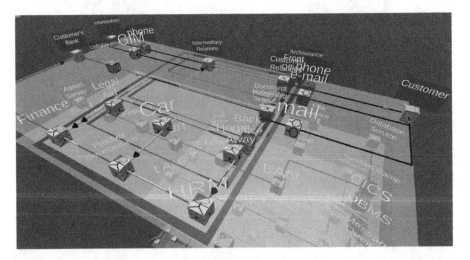

Fig. 10. VR-EA showing the Actor Cooperation View and showing containment as blue boxes

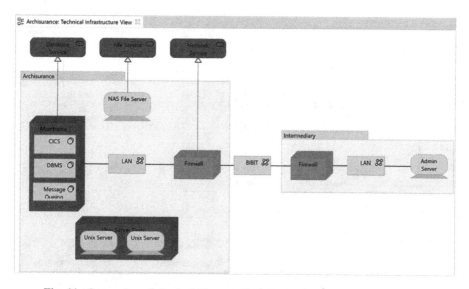

Fig. 11. Screenshot of the ArchiSurance Technical Infrastructure View in Archi

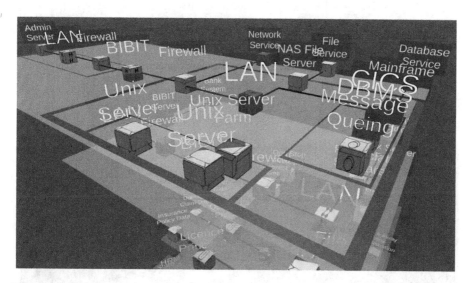

Fig. 12. VR-EA ArchiSurance Technical Infrastructure View (partial) showing containment via blue flat boxes

Figure 11 shows the ArchiSurance Technical Infrastructure View in Archi and in Fig. 12 in VR-EA.

Figure 13 shows the ArchiSurance Business Cooperation View in Archi and in Fig. 14 in VR-EA.

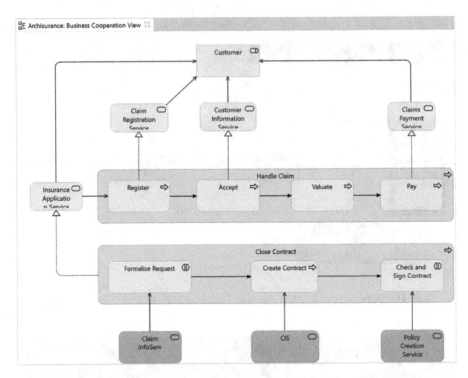

Fig. 13. Screenshot of the ArchiSurance Business Cooperation View in Archi

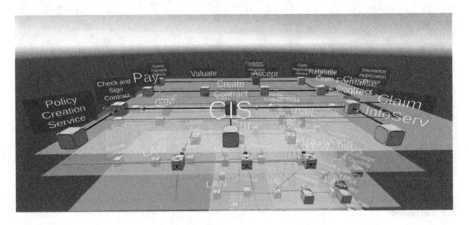

Fig. 14. VR-EA ArchiSurance Business Cooperation View (containers as blue rectangles)

Figure 15 shows the ArchiSurance Implementation and Installation View in Archi and in Fig. 16 in VR-EA.

While white cross-view lines indicate where elements reoccur in other views, if a stakeholder wishes to determine where the Customer is directly involved, in VR-EA

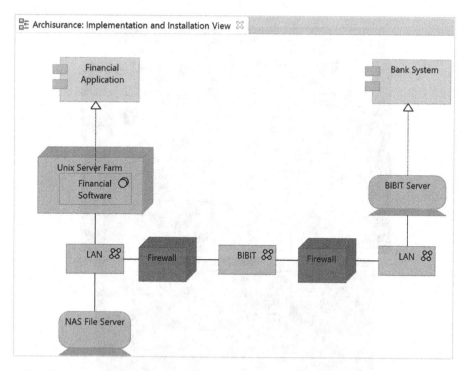

Fig. 15. Screenshot of the ArchiSurance Implementation and Installation View in Archi

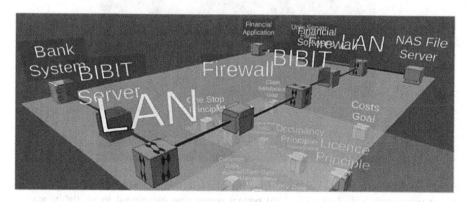

Fig. 16. VR-EA ArchiSurance Implementation and Installation View

these are immediately evident by selecting the Customer inter-view connector (shown in red in Fig. 17), enabling one via emphasis to follow the colored connector (red) to all Customer elements in various views.

In contrast, no ArchiSurance view provides this information directly. As an ArchiMate tool example, Archi offers the ability to generate a view for the Customer as shown in Fig. 18a or by selecting the Customer element and using the Visualizer

Fig. 17. ArchiSurance Customer inter-view connector selection (colored red) spanning 6 views: (a) top perspective with 2 views and (b) bottom perspective spanning 4 views (white arrows added to emphasize the red-colored connector) (Color figure online)

(Fig. 18b), but the associated views and thus context for these elements are still not clear. In essence, this Customer reality and all the rest of the reality remains hidden in such a tool until one explicitly creates views that show it.

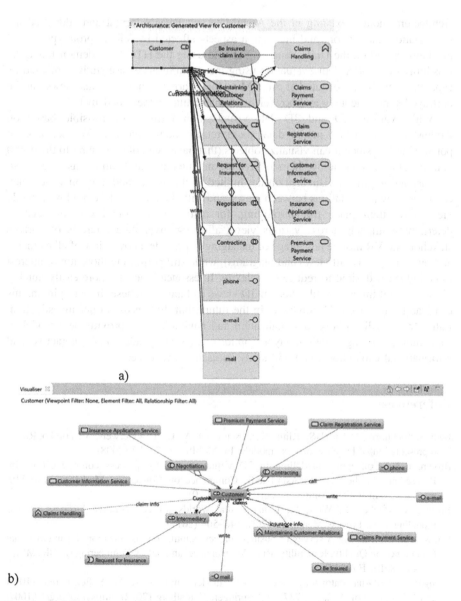

Fig. 18. ArchiSurance screenshots in Archi (a) Generated View for the Customer (top) and (b) Visualiser for the Customer (bottom)

6   Conclusion

With our VR modeling framework VR-MF, we contributed a generalized approach for loading and visualizing different models in VR to create an immersive experience with hypermodels. With VR-EA, we have shown the specific capability to display enterprise architecture models existing in the ArchiMate and BPMN format and addressed the visualization, navigation, and interaction aspects affected by VR. A prototype implementation based on the Unity game engine und using the HTC Vive demonstrated the feasibility of VR-EA. Our evaluation using the ArchiSurance case study compared its capabilities with that of another ArchiMate tool, showing how various views can be portrayed simultaneously and how element interconnectedness is depicted.

While various 2D and 3D data visualization formats are possible based on ArchiMate and BPMN model data, these remain non-immersive. We see a great potential in VR since it can visualize objects (that have symbolic meaning to the users) in a spatial format and allow them to navigate and interact with them in this space. Two dimensional graphical visualization are limited in the ability and area on which they can inter-view interrelations between views, and with the growing IT complexity, while views have their place for simplifying, for certain more complex tasks, such as determining impacts across various views affecting diversified interests of various stakeholders, VR has the advantage of managing to provide an overview of all elements and relations (across all views and diagrams), while still permitting those not of interest to be hidden if desired to reduce complexity. In essence, one can more easily quickly view cross-cutting aspect-like custom 3D views and navigate these. In our opinion, this can lead to improved EA modeling in the future, but this needs further investigation. Future work will go beyond visualization and navigation and provide new modeling capabilities, offering different layout options, integrating additional interactive and informational capabilities, and will study its usage in practice.

References

Betz, S., Eichhorn, D., Hickl, S., Klink, S., Koschmider, A., Li, Y., Oberweis, A., Trunko, R.: 3D representation of business process models. In: MobIS, pp. 73–87 (2008)

Brown, R.A.: Conceptual modelling in 3D virtual worlds for process communication. In: Proceedings of the Seventh Asia-Pacific Conference on Conceptual Modelling, vol. 110, pp. 25–32. Australian Computer Society, Inc. (2010)

Brown, R., Recker, J., West, S.: Using virtual worlds for collaborative business process modeling. Bus. Process Manag. J. 17(3), 546–564 (2011)

Du, X., Gu, C., Zhu, N.: A survey of business process simulation visualization. In: International Conference on Quality, Reliability, Risk, Maintenance, and Safety Engineering (ICQR2MSE), pp. 43–48. IEEE (2012)

Effinger, P.: A 3D-navigator for business process models. In: La Rosa, M., Soffer, P. (eds.) BPM 2012. LNBIP, vol. 132, pp. 737–743. Springer, Heidelberg (2012). https://doi.org/10.1007/978-3-642-36285-9_74

Forsgren, N., Kim, G., Kersten, N., Humble, J., Brown, A.: State of DevOps report. Puppet + DORA (2017). https://puppet.com/resources/whitepaper/2017-state-of-devops-report

GitHub (2017). https://github.com/camunda/camunda-bpm-platform/blob/master/examples/invoice/src/main/resources/invoice.v2.bpmn

Hipp, M., Strauss, A., Michelberger, B., Mutschler, B., Reichert, M.: Enabling a user-friendly visualization of business process models. In: Fournier, F., Mendling, J. (eds.) BPM 2014.

LNBIP, vol. 202, pp. 395–407. Springer, Cham (2015). https://doi.org/10.1007/978-3-319-15895-2_33

Jarvis, B.: Enterprise Architecture: Understanding the Bigger Picture – A Best Practice Guide for Decision Makers in IT. The UK National Computing Centre, Manchester (2003)

Munns, C.: I Love APIs: Microservices at Amazon (2015). https://www.slideshare.net/apigee/i-love-apis-2015-microservices-at-amazon-54487258

Muro, M., Liu, S., Whiton, J., Kulkarni, S.: Digitalization and the American Workforce. Brookings Institution Metropolitan Policy Program (2017). https://www.brookings.edu/wp-content/uploads/2017/11/mpp_2017nov15_digitalization_full_report.pdf

Naranjo, D., Sánchez, M., Villalobos, J.: Towards a unified and modular approach for visual analysis of enterprise models. In: 2014 IEEE 18th International Enterprise Distributed Object Computing Conference Workshops and Demonstrations, pp. 77–86. IEEE (2014)

Oberhauser, R., Pogolski, C., Matic, A.: VR-BPMN: visualizing BPMN models in virtual reality. In: Shishkov, B. (ed.) BMSD 2018. LNBIP, vol. 319, pp. 83–97. Springer, Cham (2018). https://doi.org/10.1007/978-3-319-94214-8_6

OMG: Business Process Model and Notation (BPMN) Version 2.0. OMG (2011)

Open Group: ArchiMate 3.0.1 Specification. The Open Group (2017a)

Open Group: ArchiSurance Case Study, Version 2. The Open Group (2017b)

ORYX-Editor: Insurance Claim Processing. BPI (2009). https://www.businessprocessincubator.com/content/insurance-claim-processing/

Rehring, K., Greulich, M., Bredenfeld, L., Ahlemann, F.: Let's get in touch-decision making about enterprise architecture using 3D visualization in augmented reality. In: Proceedings of the 52nd Hawaii International Conference on System Sciences (HICSS). IEEE (2019)

Steuer, J.: Defining virtual reality: dimensions determining telepresence. J. Commun. **42**(4), 73–93 (1992)

van den Berg, M., Real IRM Solutions: ArchiMate, BPMN and UML: An approach to harmonizing the notations. Orbus, software, white paper (2012)

Towards Integrating Software Development and Multimedia Content Creation

Noriko Hanakawa[1(✉)] and Masaki Obana[2]

[1] Information Management Department, Hannan University,
Matsubara, Osaka, Japan
hanakawa@hannan-u.ac.jp
[2] Department of Information Science and Technolog,
Osaka Institute of Technology, Hirakata, Osaka, Japan
obana@is.oit.ac.jp

Abstract. Recently, computer system and user interfaces have been greatly evolved. Especially, multimedia contents are becoming more important because of the improvement of users' impression and usability. Quality of multimedia contents may determine the application evaluation more than the quality of functions of the software. Although the importance of multimedia contents increases, integration of software development process and multimedia creation process is not discussed in the research field. Therefore, we propose a new integrated approach featuring software development and multimedia content creation. The new approach is implemented through a development process whose model is automatically generated by an algorithm that has already been specified. The algorithm facilitates the generation of phases and stages, based on the relationships among development documents. This results in a new development process. Further, quality control and progress control are easily governed by the process model that is in turn based on the document relations. Similarly to software measurements (supported by particular techniques), the completion rates of each document can be measured. Hence, we also have also metrics for quality and progress. Thus, the integrated process model and the metrics will be useful in controlling quality and progress, as it concerns applications that bring together software and multimedia content.

Keywords: Process model · Software · Multimedia contents · Quality control · Progress control

1 Introduction

Many current software applications ("applications", for short) comprise code and multimedia content. Code means programming source code while multimedia means movies, audios, animations, pictures, and so on. For example: A sightseeing application is not only about the source code but is also about multimedia contents; conventional manners, eating instructions, train riding instructions, and so on, are conveyed to foreigners through multimedia contents - see Fig. 1. Such contents can also be supported by technologies featuring Augmented Reality (AR) and Virtual Reality (VR), for example: the development of inspection systems can be usefully supported by AR

B. Shishkov (Ed.): BMSD 2019, LNBIP 356, pp. 188–200, 2019.
https://doi.org/10.1007/978-3-030-24854-3_12

Fig. 1. Sightseeing application

technologies, as Fig. 2 suggests. As it concerns a building, plumbing and power distribution cables are often "hidden" in the walls. However, a smart building inspection system could provide to building inspectors virtual views of such cables. Hence, the application source code, the multimedia contents, and the supportive AR (or VA) technologies are often much related to each other in current applications.

However, industries of software development and multimedia content production have serious problems. Application software is developed by system development companies, multimedia contents are developed by contents production companies. The two industries separately have original histories, development management ways and business practices. Often, a customer who needs a media-rich application would have to order the "software content" (the program source code) from one vendor and the "multimedia content" from another vendor. This duality assumes considering requirements twice. In addition, the software development itself should undergo a particular development process, such as waterfall development, agile development, and so on. This development process is actually governing (by means of rules) the software quality and progress controls. However, multimedia contents are rarely produced sticking to rigorous processes/rules and hence progress and quality controls are often insufficient. Especially, quantitative progress control and quality control in multimedia production are insufficiently subject of research. For this reason, it is not surprising that sometimes, multimedia production is controlled subjectively. For example, a media creator would say: "Somehow, I feel uncomfortable" or "It is somehow incomplete".

Therefore, we propose a new integrated approach featuring software development and multimedia content creation. The approach allows for establishing "equal" control

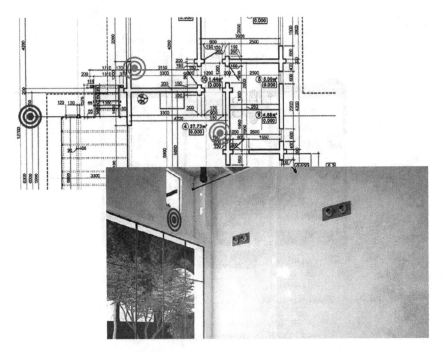

Fig. 2. Building inspection system with AR

mechanisms (as it concerns quality and progress) "between" software contents and multimedia contents. Basically, software techniques (featuring quality control metrics and progress control metrics) are applied to controls that concern the multimedia content. Hence, a process featuring the integration between software development and multimedia creation is proposed.

The remaining of this paper is organized as follows: In Sect. 2, we outline related work. In Sect. 3, we present the proposed process model whose applicability is illustrated in Sect. 4. Finally, in Sect. 5 we conclude the paper, providing also an outline for suture research.

2 Related Works

A research field of multimedia creation process mainly focuses on web site creations. A main target of the web site creation is usually movies and pictures and HTML structures without programs and software. In investigation of the web site creation, quantitative quality control and process control are not sufficient [2]. Moreover, Yviquel proposed an empirical learning course for creating multimedia contents, however, process and control ways were not mentioned [3]. On the other hand, Ikeda proposed an up-stream development process for multimedia creation support method [4]. However, the method did not deal with the integration software development process with multimedia creation process.

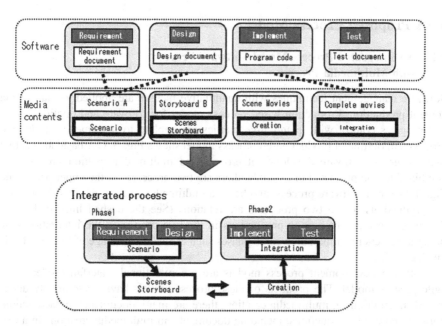

Fig. 3. An outline of generating an integrated process

In addition. There are many research results that integrated multimedia contents and computer system. Especially, e-learning system including multimedia learning contents have been proposed in computer education research field. The research results are mainly reported of education efficiency for the e-learning system [5]. Educational efficiency is main theme of the research field. Therefore, development process and quality control and process control are not discussed. Of course, educational efficiency is an important quality for application system including software and multimedia contents. We will use the techniques of evaluating educational efficiency in order to evaluate final product quality in the new process model.

On the other hand, there are many software metrics research results in software engineering research field. Basically, software development process model is useful to control software quality and progress. Software process models have big potential quality and process control. Especially, software metrics for quality and progress can be often based on software process models [6–8]. The software measurement techniques are sufficiently matures in software development process research field. In this paper, the software measurement techniques based on process models are applied to an integrated process software and multimedia contents. Therefore, the proposed process model integrating software and multimedia will be useful in order to control quality and progress.

3   A Proposed Process Model

3.1   An Integrated Process Model Software Process with Multimedia Process

Software management techniques with quantitative metrics are applied to multimedia content production. Production based process model for software and quality control and progress control with quantitative metrics are applied to multimedia production process. An outline of product based process model shows Fig. 3. Our basic idea is that two processes, software development process and multimedia creation process, are combined to one process. For example, there are two processes in the upper part of the Fig. 3. One is a software process, another is a multimedia creation process. Moreover, the productions of the two processes are relations (See the dashed lines in Fig. 3). Based on the relations among productions in the two processes, the integration new process are generated including some phases such as the lower image of Fig. 3. This is our basic idea.

Software development process models are a conventional waterfall model or an agile process model. The products of these process models have been already determined. In addition, in multimedia creation, there are many documents in each action. Table 1 shows all productions, including documents, in multimedia creations in a real projection team. Basically, relationships between software and multimedia products are the most important key concept. If a document A for software has relationships with multimedia production B, an activity of creating the document A and an activity of

Table 1. All processes and productions in creating multimedia contents

Process	Action	Document	Media production
Analysis1	Analysis of requirement	Requirement documents	
Analysis2	Analysis of story	Scenario	Scenes
Design1	Design scenes	Story boards of scenes	Pictures of scenes
Design2	Design material	Story boards of materials	Pictures of materials
Creation1	Creating materials	Lists of materials with using public materials	Materials
Creation2	Adding movement of materials	Programs for movement	Material with movement
Creation3	Creating background	Lists of images with using public images	Images of background
Creation4	Integrating materials with background images		Movies of scenes
Integration1	Integrating all movies		Whole movies
Integration2	Verifying movies	Checklists of the requirement	Checked movies for requirement
Integration3	Evaluation of movies	Checklists of movies' quality	Checked movies for quality

creation the multimedia production B should be in the same one phase. Such phase generation algorithms has been already proposed in [1].

3.2   Multimedia Creation Process

In this section, multimedia creation process is described because of comparing software development process. Table 1 shows a process of multimedia creation with phases and actions and documents and media production. The documents in the Table 1 are examples in a project of multimedia production including movies and music in a real projection mapping team.

The processes and documents (See Table 1) for multimedia creation are explained in this section. In general, at first, multimedia creators analyze customers' requirements in the analysis phase 1. As same as software development, in the analysis phase, multimedia creators make requirement documents. Then, multimedia creators make a scenario according to customers' requirements. The scenario means a story of multimedia contents. For example, a movie scenario is story and scenes of the movie, a music scenario is music composition such as first movement and second movement of symphony. If music is very short, the scenario means a concept of music.

Next, media creators do design phases. Story boards of scenes are created in the first design phase. Story boards of scenes are visual sketches of each scene in the scenario. Sketches are the scene's rough images drawn by painters. In the second design phase, materials in each scene are designed in the story board of materials. The materials mean persons or things that appear in the scene. Each material is designed in rough image as one of the story board of materials.

Then, next phase is creation including 4 steps. Media creators make materials that were designed in the previous phase. Then, the media creators add the materials to movement. For example, a girl character is a material, the girl character walking. The walking is a kind of material movements. In addition, the scenes need a background image such as blue sky or grassland. The media creators make images of background of the scenes. Finally in the creation phase, the background images of the scenes are integrated with the materials with movements. For example, "a girl character is walking on grassland under the blue sky" is a movie of the scene in the scenario.

After that, media creators do the integration phases. The integration means that all materials and scene movies and audios and music are integrated. Of course, the integration phases include not only integration of movies and music but also verification and evaluation. The verification means that the integration movies meet the customers' requirements, the evaluation is the checking of the integration movies' quality.

3.3   Relations Between Software Products and Multimedia Products

Relationships between software products and multimedia products are clarified in this section. The software products are according to a typical waterfall models, the multimedia products are according to Table 1. Figure 4 shows relationships among software products and multimedia products. In Fig. 4, there are two categories, products and documents. Software products include design diagrams and source codes, software documents include requirement documents and design documents. Multimedia

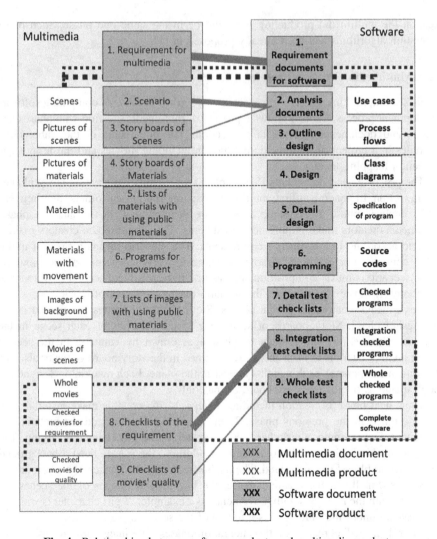

Fig. 4. Relationships between software products and multimedia products

products include scenes and materials and movies, multimedia documents include requirement documents, scenario and lists of materials.

The relationships in the Fig. 4 are determined by real documents and real products in the real projection mapping project that made movies, music and software. The gray solid lines in the Fig. 4 show the relationships among software documents and multimedia documents. The broken lines in the Fig. 4 show the relationships among software products and multimedia products. Bold line in the Fig. 4 means strong relation, thin line means week relation.

As shown in the Fig. 4, the documents and the products in the requirement and analysis phases have strong relations. Also, the documents and products in the integration phase and test phase have strong relations. That is, at the beginning stage of a

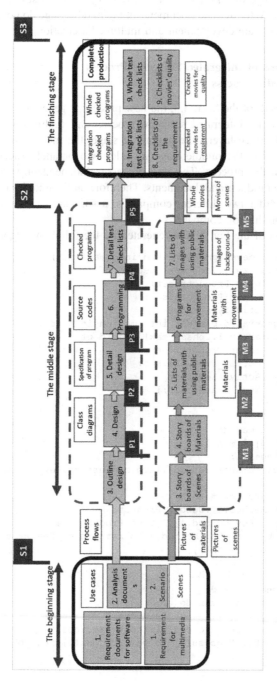

Fig. 5. A new process of integrated software process and multimedia process

project, software development has strong relations with multimedia creation. As same as, at the finishing stage of a project, software development has strong relations with multimedia creation. Activities and documents at the middle stage do not have so much relations between software development and multimedia creation.

3.4   A New Process of Integrated Software Process and Multimedia Process

According to the result of the Sect. 3.3, the new process is generated. Figure 5 shows the new process of the integrated software process and multimedia process. It is roughly divided into three layers, the beginning stage, the middle stage and the finishing stage. Especially, the middle stage includes two parallel processes, software process and multimedia process. The two processes independently can go without relationships among products and documents. Therefore, at the middle stage, customers can independently order two different companies, a software development company and a multimedia production company.

The new process of the Fig. 5 was generated by the following algorithm.

```
Input:(* Software development method information *)
      Dev_Method:array[1..act_max] record of
               {   Input_Products:set;
                   Output_Products:set;
                   Activity:string;    }
Output:(* The generated process information in algorithm 1*)
      Dev_Process:array[1..phase_max] record of
                  {  Input_Products:set;
                     Output_Products:set;
                     Activities:set;
                     Next_phases:set;}
algorithm1:
  index:=0;
  for i:=1 to act_max do
  { if Dev_Method[i] ≠ nil{
      index:= index+1;
      Add members of Dev_Method[i] to members of Dev_Process[index].

      for j:=i+1 to act_max do
      { if (Dev_Method[i].Output_Products ∩
                  Dev_Method[j].Output_Products)≠φ {
        Add members of Dev_Method[j]to members of Dev_Process[index].
        Dev_Method[j]=:nil;}
      }}
  }
  for i:=1 to phase_max do
  { for j:=i+1 to phase_max do
    { if (Dev_Process[i].Output_Priducts ∩
                  Dev_Process[j].Input_Products)≠φ
            Add Dev_Process[j] to Dev_Process[i].Next_phases.
    }
  }
```

The above algorithm had been proposed in [1]. The details of the algorithm are described in [1].

In the Fig. 5, the phase of the beginning stage is integrated software development and multimedia creation because the requirement analysis is common actions between software development and multimedia creation. That is, use cases documents for software development and scenario and scenes documents for multimedia creation have strong relations each other. Software developers and multimedia creators should have deep communications according to these documents and actions.

On the other hand, at the middle stage, there are two independent processes, software development process and multimedia creation process. The actions and documents can be performed without deep communications between software developers and multimedia creators. In each process, quality and progress can be controlled by themselves.

Then, at the finishing stage, the final integrated product is completed. The final product is integrated software products with multimedia products. That is, application software including multimedia contents has been completed in the finishing stage. Therefore, the final product should been evaluated not only a software viewpoint but also a multimedia viewpoint. Even if the software functions are perfect, if the human interface including multimedia contents is not sufficient, the overall evaluation of the system will be low. Even if the software functions are perfect, if the help navigations including multimedia contest are low quality, users' satisfactions will be low. Of course, the software functions' behaviors and the descriptions of the help function using multimedia should exactly match. In addition, some application system includes valuable multimedia contents such as a sigh seeing application with VR and AR, projection mapping show contents. The multimedia contents are more valuable than software functions in such application system. Users' satisfactions strongly depend on quality if multimedia contents. Such final product of the application system should be evaluated with emphasis on quality of multimedia contents.

4 Quality Control and Progress Control of the Integrated Process

4.1 Quality Control of Extra Documents' Relations Among Stages

In the Fig. 5, there are extra documents between the beginning stage and the middle stage, between the middle stage and the finishing stage. The documents are "process flows" for software and "picture of materials" and "picture of scenes" for multimedia. Basically, there should be no documents between phases because phases should be independent from the previous phase and the next phase. However, we set the extra documents between two stages. The meanings of the extra documents are relationships of the two stages. For example, the "process flows" document may be made at the not only the beginning stage but also the muddle stage. Some actions of the beginning stage related with the "process flows" as same as some actions of the middle stage related with the "process flows".

The extra documents are valuable data in order to quality control of the integrated process. Quality control images are shown in Fig. 6. The extra documents are important metrics in order to control quality. The extra documents are modified both the two stages. We focus on the number of modification of the extra documents on each stage. In the normal case, the curve of the number times of the modifications of the extra shows normal distribution. At the first stage, the extra documents are modified frequently. Then, although the number of times of the modifications is large at the beginning of the second stage, the number of times of the modifications steadily decrease.

In the good case, the extra documents are almost modified in the first stage. In the second stage, there is few modifications of the extra documents. The pattern is a good case because the extra documents almost complete in the previous phase. The extra documents do not need any modifications in the second stage because the extra documents are already high quality. The quality of the products in the first stage may be high.

In the bad case, the extra documents are frequently modified not only the first stage but also the second stage. The quality of the extra documents may be low because the extra documents need many modifications in the second stage.

In short, the number of times of modification of extra documents is a good indication of quality of a project. Therefore, the number of times of modification of extra documents may become one of important quality metrics. Measurement of the metrics is useful to understand product quality at each phase and stage.

However, multimedia contents should be evaluated by human subjectivity at the final stage. Of course, quality control in the middle of the project is important, but again, the final human subjective evaluation should be emphasized when the whole application system is completed. One of our future research is how we determine quantitative metrics of human impression for the application system including multimedia contents.

4.2 How to Determine Extra Documents

In the mentioned above quality control, the existence of extra documents is a key point. Of course, we can generate a process model without extra documents. If we do not set up several extra documents, the phases and stages will be very large in the process model because all related documents should be set in one phase. Too big phases and too large stages may prevent not only applicable quality control but also corresponding progress control. We need to set extra documents on purpose. Unfortunately, the way of extracting extra documents is not yet formalized. We pick up some extra documents while trying and erroring, and manually decide while checking the size of the phase and the size of the stage. The trying and erroring decision depend on empirical knowledge and experimental skills. We will make a clear formalized way for determining applicable extra documents.

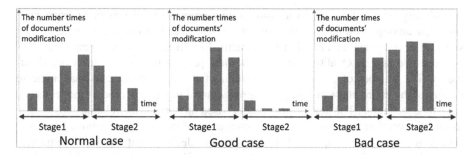

Fig. 6. Quality control of the new integrated process

4.3   Progress Control with the New Integrated Process

The new integrated process model is useful to control progress. The milestones technique matches with the new integrated process model. The milestones in software process management is a definition of product completion date. Milestones should be set up at the end of phases or stages. Because phases and stages include many documents, a milestone should check completions of all documents in a phase. In addition, a milestone has a date when all documents complete. Date of a milestone is a date that all developers and creators must follow. If someone misses the date of a milestone, the whole project may be late in the schedule. Milestones are important to control project progress.

Once you have built a process by documents relations such as the new integrated process model, setting milestones is easy. The Fig. 5 shows several milestones of the new integrated process model. The "S1" to "S3" flags mean the milestones of the three stages of the project. The "P1" to "P5" flags mean the milestones of the software development process in the middle stage, the "M1" to "M5" flags mean the milestones of the multimedia creation process in the middle stage. A manager sets a concrete date of each milestone of the new integrated process. Then, at the date of the milestone, a manager checks completion rates of the documents that belong to the phase and the stage. Progress control with milestones is easy under the new integrated process model including software development and multimedia creation.

5   Conclusion

Recently, current applications comprise code and multimedia content. Although such media-rich applications are popular, there is significant mismatch between software development and multimedia content creation. Especially, a common way for quality control and progress control is insufficient. Therefore, we propose an approach featuring the integration of software development and multimedia content creation. The feature of generating process is to collect relations among software development documents and multimedia creation documents. We collected empirical documents in the real project that made a projection mapping system including software and multimedia contents. An algorithms of generating process based on documents' relations was already proposed in [1] As a result, a new process model was build using relationships among documents. There are three stages and independent processes for software development and multimedia contents. In addition, there are extra documents between two stages. Quality control in the new process model uses the extra documents. The number of times of modification of the extra documents may indicate quality of the entire phase and stage. Progress control in the new process model uses a milestone technique. The new process model based on documents' relationships is easy to set up several milestones. The main contribution of our proposed approach is equal control for progress and quality between software development and multimedia creation. Limitation of our approach is a lack of a general way of identifying relationships among various documents for software and multimedia.

In future, the general way of identifying relationships among various documents for software and multimedia. After that, the new process model will be applied to real projects. Especially, quality control and progress control in the new process model will be evaluated in empirical approaches.

References

1. Hanakawa, N., Iida, H., Matumoto, K.-i., Torii, K.: Generation of object-oriented software process using milestones. Int. J. Softw. Eng. Knowl. Eng. 9(4), 445–466 (1999)
2. Barry, C., Lang, M.: A survey of multimedia and Web development techniques and methodology usage. IEEE Multimedia 8(2), 52–60 (2001)
3. Yviquel, H., et al.: Orcc: multimedia development made easy. The 21st ACM International Conference on Multimedia, pp. 863–866 (2013)
4. Ikeda, T., Hirano, Y., Yuguchi, T., Hoshi, T.: Data model for multimedia applications and its development environment. J. Inf. Process. Soc. Jpn. 40(1), 2–12 (1999)
5. Lau, R.W., Yen, N.Y., Li, F., Wah, B.: Recent development in multimedia e-learning technologies". International Journal of World wide web 17(2), 189–198 (2014)
6. Hanakawa, N., Matsumoto, K., Torii, K.: Knowledge-based software process simulation model. Int. J. Ann. Softw. Eng. 14, 383–406 (2002)
7. Obana, M., Hanakawa, N.: Process evaluation based on meeting quality of requirement analysis phase in software development projects. Int. J. Softw. Eng. Appl. 7(10), 828–843 (2014)
8. Obana, M., Hanakawa, N., Iida, H.: A Process Complexity-Product Quality (PCPQ) model based on process fragment with workflow management tables. In: Caivano, D., Oivo, M., Baldassarre, M.T., Visaggio, G. (eds.) PROFES 2011. LNCS, vol. 6759, pp. 171–185. Springer, Heidelberg (2011). https://doi.org/10.1007/978-3-642-21843-9_15

Short Papers

Business Process Optimization with Reinforcement Learning

Johan Silvander[✉]

Software Engineering Research Lab Sweden, Blekinge Institute of Technology,
Karlskrona, Sweden
Johan.Silvander@bth.se

Abstract. We investigate the use of deep reinforcement learning to optimize business processes in a business support system. The focus of this paper is to investigate how a reinforcement learning algorithm named Q-Learning, using deep learning, can be configured in order to support optimization of business processes in an environment which includes some degree of uncertainty. We make the investigation possible by implementing a software agent with the help of a deep learning tool set. The study shows that reinforcement learning is a useful technique for business process optimization but more guidance regarding parameter setting is needed in this area.

Keywords: Business process optimization · Reinforcement learning · Deep learning

1 Introduction

Software supporting an enterprise's business, also known as a business support system (BSS), needs to support the correlation of activities between actors as well as influence the activities based on knowledge about the compositional systems the enterprise acts in. A compositional system is a system composed of hierarchies of parts, with these parts themselves being meaningful entities, and being reusable in meaningful combinations [4]. The actors in a compositional system may be humans or machines. By using software agents as machine actors, enterprises can support their continued demand for change, inject further intelligence into enterprises, and simplify the environment for both customers and employees [1]. This indicates that a BSS must be able to be part of an environment which includes some degree of uncertainty.

Since we aim to build, and support a BSS which can act in an environment which includes some degrees of uncertainty, we investigate how machine learning can be used to support the optimization of business processes in such environments.

Machine learning can be seen as a sub-set of artificial intelligence and deep learning can be seen as a sub-set of machine learning [5]. Deep learning is achieved with the help deep neural networks (DNN). The main areas of machine

© Springer Nature Switzerland AG 2019
B. Shishkov (Ed.): BMSD 2019, LNBIP 356, pp. 203–212, 2019.
https://doi.org/10.1007/978-3-030-24854-3_13

learning can be divided into supervised learning, unsupervised learning, and reinforcement learning (RL). However, we admit that there are other ways to define the different areas of machine learning.

We have chosen to use RL since it can learn by interacting with an environment where the dynamics and rewards are not known exactly [9]. In the area of RL there exist several algorithms which can act with a model-free configuration. A model-free RL do not require explicit representations of transitions and reward models. We are using a model-free RL algorithm named Q-Learning [17]. Q-Learning is one of the most popular model-free RL algorithms [9].

The use of RL together with deep learning became popular after a demonstration of how a software agent can play Atari^{TM}games at super-human levels [12]. Implementations of RL algorithms with the help of deep learning is named deep reinforcement learning (DRL). We have implemented the Q-Learning algorithm with the help of a deep learning tool set [8]. More information regarding the implementation issue is given in Sect. 3.

Our work is inspired by several different papers. Born et al. [2] presents an auto-completion mechanism for supporting the creation of executable business process models. The mechanism builds on a combination of a context-based analysis, taking pre- and post-conditions into account, and by evaluating the non-functional properties of the functionally and context wise fitting services. We include these mechanisms by creating different process flows based on the different business intents in the system, adding failure states, and using user evaluation as a feedback mechanism. Reinforcement learning works well in games and we decided to use RL for business process optimization since there exists an analogy between games and business processes [15].

Wang et al. [19] use Q-learning to obtain the optimal execution policies of service compositions at run time. They use the feedback of the users to drive the RL. We extend the user feedback mechanism with a stochastic behavior, by introducing randomness to the user feedback. This is inline with how Lin and Pai [11] add feedback to the business process. Instead of talking about the users, they model the business partners with the help of agents. The business partners can be seen as users of the business process. We use two different business processes which mimics the feedback from different business partners. Huang et al. [7] defines a resource as an actor that carries out business process activities, and are considering durable resources, i.e. resources that are claimed and released during the execution, but are neither created nor destroyed. This is in-line with our approach of simulating software agents.

On their work with business process simulators, Borrajo et al. [3] concluded that it is only possible for very small environments to enumerate the state and action space, and to store the Q-function in a single table. We mitigate these problems by using DRL. In the work of Huang et al. [7], the business process resource allocation performance is optimized given a certain process structure and they suggest RL would help to determine a more efficient business process structure when it is initially designed, when it needs to be upgraded, or when it is repaired. Since we are using software agents, the design of the process structure can be changed.

How to configure business process optimization is stated as a topic for future investigations by Lin and Pai [11]. The focus of this paper is to investigate how a Q-Learning algorithm using deep learning, can be configured in order to support optimization of business processes in an environment which includes some degree of uncertainty. We make this investigation possible by implementing a software agent with the help of a deep learning tool set [8].

In Sect. 2 we present the background, the methodology is described in Sect. 3, and the results are presented in Sect. 4. The analysis of the results, and a discussion are presented in Sect. 5, and finally, in Sect. 6, the conclusion and future research are presented.

2   Background

Together with Ericsson AB we are investigating and elaborating the requirements needed to support the planning and monitoring of business intents in their next-generation BSS and its business studio. During the study we are using the design science framework [6] as our research framework.

In our previous work [16] we introduced the ideas of intent-driven systems, and introduced Pask's conversation theory [14] as a model to describe intent-driven systems. We defined a *context frame* as the total domain information for a specific domain an actor has obtained.

We view an enterprise as a hierarchical line-of-command structure in which business rules at the top steer, align, and control the activities and behaviors further down in the structure. Business rules also steer all behavior in a BSS, in pursuit of the goal of creating and maintaining a successful business.

The difference between a business rule and a business intent is a small shift of perspective. A business rule is static and states what to do in a given situation, while a business intent states the desired or optimal outcome of a given situation. An intent can range in complexity from an atom intent to an algorithm of intents that combines a set of sub-intents. An atom intent on one level, is likely to fan out into several intents on a lower level. During the interaction about an intent the actors have to prove their understanding of the intent in order to gain a common understanding and knowledge about the intent. This interaction can evolve over several steps and might re-shape the original intent. This requires an architecture which can support context frame awareness in a compositional way. We define this type of systems as intent-driven systems. The intent-driven system shall be used to realize a BSS and its business studio.

Intents must be formulated for both human actor, and machine actor consumption to facilitate automation in a BSS. The level of automation, of decision and action selection, depends on the involved components' capabilities and rights of taking decisions and performing actions.

Any actor can have intents. When an actor publicly declare an intent in a certain context frame, it becomes a stated intent. A stated intent could be a declaration of what an actor promise to provide, or a requirement an actor try to impose on another actor. A decision about whether an actor has kept its promise or not, can be done by the promising actor as well as any actor which is observing the behavior of the promising actor.

The architecture must support an intent-driven system to optimize itself by continuously compare, and evaluate both business outcomes and its own capabilities. The results may require continuous adaptions of a business intent's definition and execution. This requires components with a high, but adaptable, level of automation. We have chosen to describe the architecture of an intent-driven system as a compositional systems of context frames. To our knowledge no such BSS exists in the industry today.

3   Methodology

In order for a deep learning agent to function, its input must be in the form of numbers. We have created a software environment which normalize the inputs to a value between zero and one, inclusive. The environment exposes an application programming interface (API) which mimics the OpenAI gym API [13]. The responsibility of the software environment is to simulate the behavior of the different business processes, the assessments in the form of exposed preferences of the results from the business processes, the capabilities(business process activities) and their values, and the rules used to select the different capabilities.

The environment is exposing the outcome from two different business processes, assessments for each business process outcome, and three capabilities. Each business process is triggered by a specific type of business event. Each of these business event types are represented with an integer value. Each capability has two actions which can be imposed on the capability. Each action has an expected outcome in the form of an integer value. Since a capability mimics activities performed by human actors or machine actors, we are enforcing a stochastic behavior by introducing a degree of randomness to each possible action on a capability. The result of the stochastic behavior will introduce three different outcomes from an action with a certain probability; the expected outcome, the expected outcome of the other possible action, and no activity is performed. An assessment of a promise exposes its preferences for each terminal state as a value between zero and one (in a terminal state is when it exist values for each capability). Each assessment is related to a specific context. An assessment representing the result of using a n-armed contextual bandit for capturing customer preferences.

In order for an actor to improve the result of the promise, we have introduced a possibility to impose a penalty on certain undesired behaviors. Trying to use a capability which already has provided a value is an example of a behavior which could be desired to penalize.

A promise is a combination of capability values. The aim is to select the promises such as the values of the assessments are maximized. We use a RL algorithm to adapt the promises in order to meet the assessments. We are using a temporal difference RL algorithm called Q-Learning [17]. This algorithm is adopted to be used with deep learning [5]. The need for adaption of the original Q-Learning algorithm is mainly due to how the difference between an agent's proposed value and the actual value in the interacting environment is minimized when using deep learning. In deep learning, stochastic gradient descent is used to minimize this difference. The use of stochastic gradient descent requires some adaptation of the code in the original Q-Learning algorithm. The adapted Q-Learning algorithm is then called Deep Q-Learning Network (DQN) [12]. The DQN is an off-policy value-based RL algorithm. The off-policy feature makes it possible to use knowledge obtained outside the actual learning situation. By using this knowledge during the interaction with the environment, it is possible to improve the learning.

Based on experiences we are using a fully connected DNN with two layers, ReLU as the activation functions, mean square error as the loss function, and Adam as the back propagation algorithm [5]. An important trait of RL is the possibility to exploit learned behavior vs. explore new behaviors which might improve the result. In order to implement the exploit-explore behavior we are using a simple, but yet efficient, algorithm called epsilon decay.

The use of a DQN requires tuning of several parameters. We are tuning two RL specific parameters called gamma and the epsilon decay rate, a parameter shared by RL and deep learning called alpha in RL and learning rate in the deep learning community, and the number of weights in the different layers of the deep network. In addition, we tune two algorithm specific parameters, target network copy rate, and replay sample size.

The metrics we use to evaluate our DQN are the effectiveness of the promise, the value function of the states, and the loss. We are using a callback in Keras [8] which provides us with the best model based on the loss. We compare the effectiveness of the promise between the latest model and the best model. This gives an indication of the stability of the model.

We use Keras [8] with Tensorflow [18] as the backend deep learning framework. Python is the selected implementation language since it have many deep learning contributions. The implementation is done with the help of Jupyter notebook, from the Anaconda distribution for Mac (x86 64-bits), which supports Python 3.6.6.

4   Result

Since a RL agent is learning by interacting with an environment, several interactions are needed in order for the agent to learn how to act in a way that fulfills the intents of the different actors. We start to tune the agent in an environment which includes no randomness. The parameters which we are tuning are described in Sect. 3.

Since our agent shall act in an environment which includes some degrees of uncertainty, we introduce randomness into the environment and use general techniques from the field of deep learning, as well as specific RL techniques, which are used to make the agent more resilient to changes in the environment.

In order to tune the parameters we start with a deterministic environment. In Table 1, the selected values after the tuning are in the third column, and the start values are in *italic*. The rational for selecting these values is based on experience and best practice from solutions of similar complexity.

Table 1. Parameter tuning in a deterministic environment (start values are in *italic*).

Parameter	-	Selected	-	Comments
learning rate (lr)	0.0001	0.001	*0.01*	The low lr is slow and do not find the solution, nor get the value function right. The high lr over-shoots and has a lossy and oscillating behavior.
weights	64–16	*64–32*	64–64	Neither the lower setting nor the higher setting improve the result. Both introduce more loss but the lower setting has a more stable value function but is slower.
weights cont	32–16	-	32–32	None of the settings improve the result. The lower setting is slower to learn but is less lossy than the higher setting.
gamma	0.85	*0.9*	0.95	The low gamma value is not improving the measures. The high gamma value is slower to learn and introduce more loss.
epsilon	0.1	*0.01*	0.001	The low epsilon do not explore enough to find the right solution. The high epsilon introduce an unstable value function

In the our RL algorithm we are only using rewards as the tool to achieve a learning agent. A technique used to improve the rate of learning is to combine rewards and penalties. When we are introducing a small penalty the result is not improving, and the learning is slower.

The selected parameter values in Table 1 are not optimal in a stochastic environment. The result shows a slower learning and more loss. In order to remedy this problems we are trying to use two different kinds of regularization methods which are common to use in DNN, batch normalization and L2-norm [5]. The use of batch normalization gives the worst result of all tests. The loss and the value function are continues increasing during the test. The use of the L2-norm do not improve the result. The value function is never reaching the correct values and the loss is never decreasing.

Instead of using common DNN regularization methods we implement two RL specific methods named target network, and replay [12]. The target network is implemented by adding an extra network which is updated during each iteration. The original network is left unchanged for a number of iterations, which is decided by the copy rate parameter. After this number of iterations the target network is copied to the original network. This prevents the original network to be affected by changes that might create an oscillating behavior. The replay is implemented by adding a buffer from which actions are randomly selected.

This prevents the network from learning from a series of undesired actions. Instead these actions are not appearing as a series of actions and will not affect the networks learning as strong as they would otherwise.

The implementation of target network, and replay significantly improves the result in a stochastic environment, and gives the best result in a deterministic environment. The two parameters we tune are; the number of replay samples, and the target network copy rate. We start with the replay sample and keep the target network copy rate to one. By keeping the target network copy rate to one, the algorithm behaves as there is no target network implemented. This gives us the possibility to tune the replay samples by itself. The result of the tuning is shown in Table 2. In Table 2, the selected values after the tuning are in the third column, and the start values are in *italic*.

Table 2. Additional parameter tuning in a stochastic environment (start values are in *italic*).

Parameter	-	Selected	-	Comments
replay samples	4	*8*	16	Both the low and the higher value do not find the optimal solution, and introduce more loss. For all the values the state values are not stable. Note: tncr = 1
target network copy rate (tncr)	*8*	16	32	The low value and the high value do not find the optimal solution but the high value has a more stable value function of the two settings

When the amount of randomness is increased the solution starts to degrade and a re-tuning of the parameters in Table 2 is needed.

5   Analysis and Discussion

The most critical parameter to tune is the learning rate. The epsilon decay rate is the second most parameter to tune. If the epsilon decay parameter is too low the algorithm might not explore enough to learn the problem. If the parameter is too high it will introduce loss by exploring when the right actions already are known. The optimal values of the weights and the gamma parameter are not obvious. For the weights we decide to use 64-32, but 64-16 can be chosen as well. The selection of the gamma value can be considered as a standard setting but in our case a value of 0.85 can be an alternative. By introducing a small penalty the learning process becomes slower, which is the opposite of what we want to achieve. When we are introducing a high penalty the learning stops before the algorithm finds the optimal result.

The use of regularization, with the help of batch normalization or L2-norm, do not improve the result. The problem of using batch normalization in reinforcement learning is discussed by Lillicrap et al. [10]. Since the L2-norm is used to penalize small weight values and promote high weight values, it might act as a greedy algorithm, which is preventing the algorithm to find new solutions.

The use of replay and target network achieved the best result in both deterministic and stochastic environments. We start to tune the replay buffer size since it is used improve the algorithm when the environment is stochastic. The target network rate stabilize the update of the weights since every change to the weights are not immediately introduced. Both these techniques can be regarded as reinforcement learning regularization techniques. When we introduce more randomness into the capabilities behavior the tuned algorithm will start to degrade. This is another source of problems when tuning the parameters of the DQN algorithm.

When the complexity of the business processes increase, more states might be needed to represent the environment. During this study we represent the states with the help of one-hot encoding. One-hot encoding can be described as an input vector with the size equal to the number of states. During each interaction all the positions are set to zero, except the position of the actual state, which is set to one.

When the number of states groves another type of state representation might be more effective and efficient. One option is to use a matrix to represent the values of the context frames, and the values of the capabilities. The number of states, and their representation in the input layer, will affect the number of weights in the first layer. This might cascade to the output layer and even require additional layers. Best practices exist for the number of weights and the number of layers but they can only be regarded as a starting point for the actual tuning. The same is true for the other parameters.

Since the performance of the solution degraded when the actors behavior became more stochastic, other types of RL algorithms can be used for the problem at hand. One promising type of algorithms is the actor-critic algorithms [17]. By using the off-policy characteristic of the algorithm we can using different techniques [9] to add knowledge into the algorithm. This will introduce other optimization challenges and affect the implementation of the solution.

This study shows that a very important part of an efficient solution is to find a rule of thumb for parameter settings in the area of business process optimization.

6   Conclusion and Future Research

We have investigate how to use a software agent to optimize business processes which are acting in an environment with some degree of uncertainty. We are using machine learning in order to optimize the business processes, and reinforcement learning is a good candidate when the agent's environment exposes some degree of uncertainty. The agent is implemented with the help of a reinforcement learning algorithm named Q-Learning. The Q-Learning algorithm has been adopted to be used as a deep reinforcement learning algorithm. By using deep reinforcement learning we mitigate the problems of only being able to simulate very small environments [3].

Lin and Pai [11] state that the configuration of business process optimization is a topic for future investigations. The focus of this paper is to investigate how a Q-Learning algorithm using deep learning, can be configured in order to support optimization of business processes in an environment which includes some degree of uncertainty. We make the investigation possible by implementing a software agent with the help of a deep learning tool set [8].

We argue that deep reinforcement learning is a useful technique for business process optimization. In order to improve our understanding of the problem, we will continue to investigate how the use of deep reinforcement learning for optimization of business process can be improved by addressing the issues discussed in Sect. 5. However, this study shows that a very important part of an efficient solution, in the area of business process optimization, is to find a rule of thumb for the parameter settings of the reinforcement learning agent.

Acknowledgements. We would like to thank the reviewers for their valuable comments.

References

1. Aspray, W., Keil-Slawik, R., Parnas, D.L.: Position papers for Dagstuhl seminar 9635 on history of software engineering. Hist. Softw. Eng., 61 (1997)
2. Born, M., Brelage, C., Markovic, I., Pfeiffer, D., Weber, I.: Auto-completion for executable business process models. In: Ardagna, D., Mecella, M., Yang, J. (eds.) BPM 2008. LNBIP, vol. 17, pp. 510–515. Springer, Heidelberg (2009). https://doi.org/10.1007/978-3-642-00328-8_51
3. Borrajo, F., Bueno, Y., de Pablo, I., Santos, B., Fernández, F., García, J., Sagredo, I.: SIMBA: a simulator for business education and research. Decis. Support Syst. **48**(3), 498–506 (2010)
4. Geman, S.: Hierarchy in machine and natural vision. In: Proceedings of the 11th Scandinavian Conference on Image Analysis, pp. 1–13 (1999)
5. Goodfellow, I., Bengio, Y., Courville, A.: Deep Learning. MIT Press, Cambridge (2016)
6. Hevner, A.R., March, S.T., Park, J., Ram, S.: Design science in the information systems research. MSI Q. **28**(1), 75–105 (2004)
7. Huang, Z., Van Der Aalst, W.M., Lu, X., Duan, H.: Reinforcement learning based resource allocation in business process management. Data Knowl. Eng. **70**(1), 127–145 (2011)
8. Keras: Keras (2018). https://keras.io/. Accessed 30 Nov 2018
9. Kochenderfer, M.: Decision Making Under Uncertainty. MIT Press, Cambridge (2015)
10. Lillicrap, T.P., et al.: Continuous control with deep reinforcement learning. ArXiv e-prints, September 2015. arXiv:1509.02971
11. Lin, F.R., Pai, Y.H.: Using multi-agent simulation and learning to design new business processes. IEEE Trans. Syst. Man Cybernet. Part A (Syst. Hum.) **30**(3), 380–384 (2000)
12. Mnih, V., et al.: Human-level control through deep reinforcement learning. Nature **518**, 529 (2015)
13. OpenAI: OpenAI Gym (2018). https://gym.openai.com/. Accessed 30 Nov 2018

14. Pask, G.: Conversation Theory. Elsevier, Amsterdam (1976)
15. Silvander, J., Wilson, M., Wnuk, K.: Encouraging business flexibility by improved context descriptions. In: Shishkov, B. (ed.) Proceedings of the Seventh International Symposium on Business Modeling and Software Design, Barcelona, ScitePress, pp. 225–228 (2017)
16. Silvander, J., Wilson, M., Wnuk, K., Svahnberg, M.: Supporting continuous changes to business intents. Int. J. Softw. Eng. Knowl. Eng. **27**(8), 1167–1198 (2017)
17. Sutton, R., Barto, A.: Reinforcement Learning: An Introduction, 2nd edn. A Bradford Book, Hardcover (2018)
18. Tensorflow: Tensorflow (2018). https://www.tensorflow.org/. Accessed 30 Nov 2018
19. Wang, H., Zhou, X., Zhou, X., Liu, W., Li, W., Bouguettaya, A.: Adaptive service composition based on reinforcement learning. In: Maglio, P.P., Weske, M., Yang, J., Fantinato, M. (eds.) ICSOC 2010. LNCS, vol. 6470, pp. 92–107. Springer, Heidelberg (2010). https://doi.org/10.1007/978-3-642-17358-5_7

A Comparative Study of Methods for Deciding to Open Data

Ahmad Luthfi[1,2](✉) and Marijn Janssen[1]

[1] Faculty of Technology, Policy and Management, Delft University
of Technology, Jaffalaan 5, 2628 BX Delft, The Netherlands
{a.luthfi, M.F.W.H.A.Janssen}@tudelft.nl
[2] Universitas Islam Indonesia, Yogyakarta, Indonesia
ahmad.luthfi@uii.ac.id

Abstract. Governments may have their own business processes to decide to open data, which might be supported by decision-making tools. At the same time, analyzing potential benefits, costs, risks, and other effects-adverse of disclosing data are challenging. In the literature, there are various methods to analyze the potential advantages and disadvantages of opening data. Nevertheless, none of them provides discussion into the comparative studies in terms of strengths and weaknesses. In this study, we compare three methods for disclosing data, namely Bayesian-belief networks, Fuzzy multi-criteria decision-making, and Decision tree analysis. The comparative study is a mechanism for further studying the development of a knowledge domain by performing a feature-by-feature at the same level of functionalities. The result of this research shows that the methods have different strengths and weaknesses. The Bayesian-belief Networks has higher accuracy in comparison, and able to construct the causal relationships of the selected variable under uncertainties. Yet, this method is more resource intensive. This study can contribute to the decision-makers and respected researchers to a better comprehend and provide recommendation related to the three methods comparison.

Keywords: Methods · Decision-making · Open data ·
Bayesian-belief networks · Fuzzy multi-criteria decision making ·
Decision tree analysis

1 Introduction

The disclosing of public sector information through open government data initiatives can provide numerous advantages to the public domain at a large scale [1, 2]. Opening the various types of dataset might drive high demand from stakeholders like business enablers, researchers, and non-governmental organizations for specific purposes [3, 4]. At this moment, the governments may have their own business process to avoid human or technological system mistakes from open data decisions [5]. In reality, the way to analyze the risks, costs, and other effects-adverse of disclosing data to the potential stakeholders are cumbersome [6].

© Springer Nature Switzerland AG 2019
B. Shishkov (Ed.): BMSD 2019, LNBIP 356, pp. 213–220, 2019.
https://doi.org/10.1007/978-3-030-24854-3_14

There have been works of literature introduce the methods to analyze the potential advantages and disadvantages of opening data and its consequences [6–8]. Methods like Bayesian-belief networks, Fuzzy multi-criteria decision-making, Decision tree analysis, and privacy risks scoring model were used to analyze the potential risks and benefits of opening data [6, 7, 9]. However, none of them provides insight into the comparative studies in terms of strengths and weaknesses. The comparative method is a mechanism for further studying of a knowledge domain by performing comparison a feature-by-feature of selected parameters at the same level of functionalities [10, 11].

In this study, the comparison method is divided into three main groups. First, input parameters that consist of three variables, namely experimental data, data type, and posterior probability. Second, output parameters are decomposed into four variables, namely efficiency, easiness, effectiveness, and complexity. Third, output parameters structure into three variables, namely understandability, subjectivity, and accuracy. We use systematic literature as the main sources to compare each parameter.

The goal of a comparative study conducted in this paper is to explain a better comprehension of the causal process in terms of an event, feature, and relationships by presenting together their complexities in the explanatory parameters [10, 11]. This research can contribute to the decision-makers and respected researchers to a better understanding and provide recommendation related to the three methods comparison. This paper decomposes of five main sections. In Sect. 1, the current issues and problems definitions are described. Section 2 reviews of related literature are provided. Section 3 the comparison methods and its parameter are defined. Section 4 the comparative studies between three methods are presented. Finally, the paper will be summarized in Sect. 5.

2 Literature Review

In this paper, the comparative studies use three approaches namely Bayesian-belief networks, Fuzzy multi-criteria decision-making, and Decision tree analysis. There are several reasons for using the Bayesian-belief Networks method in open data studies. First, the Bayesian-belief networks are able to capture causal knowledge between selected variables [12]. Second, this theory provides an efficient integration between empirical data and expert's judgment [13]. Third, the Bayesian-belief networks can improve a better understanding of the causal relationships and its consequences [14]. Moreover, the use of Fuzzy set theory in the open data domain is aiming to manage problem complexities of the decision alternatives [15]. The main function of the Fuzzy logic is to capture the expertise of open experts and to express it with computational approach [16, 17]. The properness of the alternative compares to the criteria and the priority weights of each criterion can be analyzed and computed using linguistic matrix values reflected by the fuzzy [17, 18]. The scores for each criterion are summed up to rank the importance of the alternatives decision in open data [28, 29].

The use of decision tree analysis, furthermore, is to construct a feasible decision from the complex problems in the open data domain. A decision-tree is a decision support theory that uses a schematic tree-shaped diagram of decisions and their reasonable consequences of the conditional control arguments [19, 20]. In addition, decision tree analysis can serve a number of purposes when complicated problems in the decision-making process of releasing data are found. There are some advantages in using decision tree analysis to the decision-making problems [21]. First, Decision tree analysis is able to create comprehensible rules and easy to interpret. Second, Decision tree analysis is able to take into account both continuous and categorical decision variables. Third, Decision tree analysis can provide a clear indication of which variable is becoming the most priority in predicting the outcome of the alternative decisions. Fourth, Decision tree analysis can perform a classification without requiring a computational background in depth.

From the systematic literature of the three selected approaches in analyzing the risks and benefits of opening data, we summarize the specific functionalities of each parameter. First, Bayesian-belief Networks present a directed cyclic graph based on the probabilities of event occurrence [22, 23]. Besides, Bayesian belief networks can perform quantitative judgments by considering the probability distribution to the degree of belief an event both top-down and bottom-up reasoning [6, 24]. Second, Fuzzy Multi-criteria decision-making constructs a hierarchical structure to adjust many types of problem definitions easily, but not focus on incentive data and its consequences [17]. Third, Decision tree analysis predicts the rate of return of various investment strategies to handle the multi-factors response [19]. The important interaction between decision nodes can determine the worst, best, and expected values for the different cases and their problem complexities [21].

3 Research Approach

3.1 Comparison Parameters

In this study, the comparison parameters will be divided into three main parts. First, the input parameter consists of three variables, namely experimental data, data types, and posterior probability. Second, the process parameter decomposes into four variables, namely efficiency, easiness, effectiveness, and complexity. Third, the output parameter consists of three variables, namely understandability, subjectivity, and accuracy. The three sub-parameters used can be explained in detail, as follows:

1. **Input**

    First, experimental data refers to data produced in measurable activities by doing an experimental or quasi-experimental design [25]. The experimental data may be quantitative or qualitative platform using different investigation methods. Second, dataset type refers to a specific type of dataset presented in tabular form and each column of the table represents a specific meaning of values [26]. Third, posterior probabilities define as an uncertainty proposition of the conditional probability that is allocated after the relevant evidence is considered [6].

2. **Process**

    It is started from an efficiency parameter refers to the ability to avoid wasting efforts, energy, and time in doing the evaluation process. In a mathematical sense, it is a measurable instrument of the selected variable to ensure the effort to produce and establish a specific outcome with a less or minimum amount of costs and unnecessary endeavor [25]. Second, the easiness of the selected method in analyzing the selected method means the ease of manner and rules of the evaluation process [22]. Third, the effectiveness refers to the capability of generating the desired result, which means it has an expected outcome and a clear impression [10]. Fourth, the complexity of the process refers to the behavior of a system in interacting components into multiple ways and reasonable [25].

3. **Output**

The first sub-parameter considers to the understandability of the process. Understandability means that the process of the evaluation is easy to recognize and being understood. Second, subjectivity refers to a subject's personal insights and judgments influenced by individual feelings, desires, expertise in discovering, and level of beliefs in terms of phenomena [25]. Third, the accuracy of the results in evaluating means the accuracy and precision of measurements [22]. A measurement system in specific could be accurate but not precise and vice versa.

4   Result

The following Table 1 gives a summary of comparative study using three methods in open data domain.

Table 1 describes some different characteristics of the three methods in terms of similar parameters. To classify the different and similarity including its consequences, more explanation can be given as follows:

Bayesian-belief Networks requires maximum allocation time in processing the evaluation instead of the other two methods. This approach is noticeably difficult to under-stand and interpret the proposed model. The subjectivity of this method is potentially found during the process because of the limited resources to quantify the risks and benefits factors. The decision-makers of dataset officer require the capability in mathematics background. However, the advantage of using this method is the expected of the result is more accurate in a range of uncertainties.

Fuzzy Multi-criteria Decision Making consumes time in moderate level in evaluating the dataset. This method is relatively difficult to comprehend and interpret the model. The pairwise comparison tasks may also need an advanced level in mathematics because there are some applied calculus formulations to be used. The expected results show moderate bias in the quantification process. The benefits in using this method are the dataset consistently estimates the selected parameter.

Decision Tree Analysis is summarized based on assign payoffs the number of values of the possible investment. This method has a constraint when decision-makers are changing variables during the analysis process, it might be possible to redraw the existing tree. However, the advantage of using Decision Tree Analysis is relatively easy to understand and interpret the model.

In summary, all models have their pros and cons. Which one is favoured is dependent on the needs.

Table 1. Comparative studies of methods in opening data

Parameter	Bayesian-belief networks	Fuzzy multi-criteria decision making	Decision tree analysis
Input			
Experimental data	Data is summarized based on the likelihood function from the observe dataset [6, 10]	Data is summarized based on the pairwise comparison matrix [7]	Data is summarized based on the assign payoffs process of possible investments [19]
Data type	Numerical and categorical [27]	Numerical and categorical [17]	Numerical and categorical [20]
Probability	Posterior probability distribution [10]	Posterior probability distribution [17]	Posterior and conditional probability distribution [28]
Process			
Efficiency	Time consuming (maximum) [27]	Time consuming (moderate) [18]	Time consuming (minimum) [21]
Easiness	Highly difficult to understand and interpret the model. Advanced in the mathematical background is required [29]	Moderately difficult to understand and interpret the model. Advanced in the mathematical background is required [30]	Relatively easy to understand and interpret the model. Basic in the mathematical background is required [21]
Effectiveness	Constructing a causal relationship between variables and provide decision recommendation [25]	Constructing a hierarchy of decisions including its alternative and ranking them into best options [16]	Constructing a structured decisions estimation and its consequences [28]
Complexity	Require the size of the belief-network to simulate and construct complex conditional probabilities [6]	Require rule base analysis to construct a pairwise comparison matrix [16]	Changing variables during the analysis process might be possible to redraw the existing tree. Irrational expectations can lead to flaws and errors in the decision tree [20]
Output			
Understandability	Require high level to comprehend the process and expected results [22]	Require high level to comprehend the process and expected results [31]	Require a moderate level to comprehend the process and expected results [19]

(continued)

Table 1. (*continued*)

Parameter	Bayesian-belief networks	Fuzzy multi-criteria decision making	Decision tree analysis
Input			
Subjectivity	The elicitation data and information from the experts might possible bias of the quantification process [25]	The elicitation data and information from the experts might somewhat bias of the quantification process [17]	The elicitation data and information from the experts might possible bias of the quantification process [19]
Accuracy	The expected of the value is more accurate when there is less uncertainty in the input parameter. The output is distributed over a range of uncertainties [6, 27]	The estimation result is more consistent compared to reference data approach [31]	The expected result is accurate and able to predict the future outcome [19]

5   Conclusion

Currently, various works of literature have introduced the methods to analyze the potential advantages and disadvantages including its consequences in the open data domain. However, none of them provides insight into their strengths and weaknesses. The comparative study in this paper results in some important findings. First, Bayesian-belief Networks is advance in accuracy because of the very tight steps and rules, but in some cases, this method tends to inefficiency and too complex to be used. Second, Fuzzy Multi-criteria Decision-making is successfully constructing decision-making alternatives and expects to provide the rank of decision options. This method consumes many times to process the entire evaluation because of the many mathematical works at the same time. Third, Decision Tree Analysis is relatively easy to understand and interpret the model. Yet, changing variables during the analysis process might be possible to require redrawing the existing tree. This paper can contribute to the researchers and decision-makers to a better understanding of the method comparison in analyzing the risks and benefits of opening data. In future work, we recommend adding some other approaches like clustering analysis and artificial neural networks to obtain different insights. In addition, to develop a method based on the best parts of each method are not having its disadvantages. Of such an effort is feasible or utopia has to be researched.

References

1. Zuiderwijk, A., Janssen, M.: Open data policies, their implementation and impact: a framework for comparison. Gov. Inf. Q. **31**(1), 17–29 (2013)
2. Zuiderwijk, A., Janssen, M.: Towards decision support for disclosing data: closed or open data? Inf. Policy **20**(2–3), 103–107 (2015)
3. van Veenstra, A.F., van den Broek, T.A.: Opening moves – drivers, enablers and barriers of open data in a semi-public organization. In: Wimmer, M.A., Janssen, M., Scholl, H.J. (eds.) EGOV 2013. LNCS, vol. 8074, pp. 50–61. Springer, Heidelberg (2013). https://doi.org/10.1007/978-3-642-40358-3_5
4. Ubaldi, B.: Open Government Data: Towards Empirical Analysis of Open Government Data Initiatives. OECD Working Papers on Public Governance, 22, 60 (2013)
5. Luthfi, A., Janssen, M., Crompvoets, J.: Framework for analyzing how governments open their data: institution, technology, and process aspects influencing decision-making. In: EGOV-CeDEM-ePart 2018. Edition Donau-Universität Krems, Donau-Universität Krems, Austria (2018)
6. Luthfi, A., Janssen, M., Crompvoets, J.: A causal explanatory model of Bayesian-belief networks for analysing the risks of opening data. In: Shishkov, B. (ed.) BMSD 2018. LNBIP, vol. 319, pp. 289–297. Springer, Cham (2018). https://doi.org/10.1007/978-3-319-94214-8_20
7. Luthfi, A., et al.: A fuzzy multi-criteria decision making approach for analyzing the risks and benefits of opening data. In: 17th IFIP WG 6.11 Conference on e-Business, e-Services, and e-Society, I3E 2018. 2018. Gulf University for Science and Technology (GUST), Kuwait: Springer LNCS 11195 (2018)
8. Luthfi, A., Janssen, M.: A conceptual model of decision-making support for opening data. In: Katsikas, S., Zorkadis, V. (eds.) e-Democracy 2017. CCIS, vol. 792, pp. 95–105. Springer, Cham (2017). https://doi.org/10.1007/978-3-319-71117-1_7
9. Ali-Eldin, A.M.T., Zuiderwijk, A., Janssen, M.: Opening more data: a new privacy scoring model of open data. In: Seventh International Symposium on Business Modelling and Software Design (BMSD2017), SCITEPRESS - Science and Technology Publication, Lda, Barcelona (2017)
10. Nojava, F., Qian, S., Stow, C.: Comparative analysis of discretization methods in Bayesian networks. Environ. Modell. Softw. **87**, 64–71 (2017)
11. Jan, B., et al.: Deep learning in big data analytics: a comparative study. Comput. Electron. Eng. **75**, 275–287 (2019)
12. Preece, A.: Building the right system right - evaluating V&V methods in knowledge engineering. In: The Eleventh Workshop on Knowledge Acquisition, Modelling and Management, Voyager Inn, Banff, Alberta, Canada (1998)
13. Uusitalo, L.: Advantages and challanges of Bayesian networks in environmental modelling. Ecol. Modell. **203**(3–4), 312–318 (2007)
14. Fenton, N., Neil, M.: Risks Assessment and Decision Analysis with Bayesian Networks. CRC Press, Noca Raton (2012)
15. Teicher, M.: Interviewing subject matter experts. In: International Cost Estimating and Analysis Association (ICEAA) (2015)
16. Rezaei, P., et al.: Application of fuzzy multi-criteria decision making analysis for evaluating and selecting the best location for construction of underground dam. Acta Polytech. Hung. **10**(7), 187–205 (2013)
17. Ceballos, B., Lamata, M.T., Pelta, D.: Fuzzy multicriteria decision-making methods: a comparative analysis. Int. J. Intell. Syst. **32**, 722–738 (2017)

18. Kahraman, C., Onar, S.C., Oztaysi, B.: Fuzzy multicriteria decision-making: a literature review. Int. J. Comput. Intell. Syst. **8**(4), 637–666 (2015)
19. Delgado-Gómez, D., Laria, J.C., Ruiz-Hernández, D.: Computerized adaptive test and decision trees: a unifying approach. Expert Syst. Appl. **117**, 358–366 (2019)
20. Yeoa, B., Grant, D.: Predicting service industry performance using decision tree analysis. Int. J. Inf. Manag. **38**(1), 288–300 (2018)
21. Yuanyuan, P., Derek, B.A., Bob, L.: Rockburst prediction in kimberlite using decision tree with incomplete data. J. Sustain. Mining **17**, 158–165 (2018)
22. Chakraborty, S., et al.: A Bayesian network-based customer satisfaction model: a tool for management decisions in railway transport. J. Decis. Anal. **3**(4), 2–24 (2016)
23. Xiong, J., et al.: Personalized visual satisfaction profiles from comparative preferences using Bayesian inference. Energy Procedia **122**, 522–547 (2017)
24. Castillo, E., et al.: Complexity reduction and sensitivity analysis in road probabilistic safety assessment Bayesian network models: complexity reduction and sensitivity analysis. Comput.-Aided Civil Infrastruct. Eng. **32**(6), 546–561 (2017)
25. Beuzen, T.: A comparison of methods for discretizing continuous variables in Bayesian Networks. Environ. Modell. Softw. **108**, 61–66 (2018)
26. Safarov, I., Grimmelikhuijsen, S., Meijer, A.: Utilization of open government data: a systematic literature review of types, conditions, effects and users. Inf. Policy **22**(1), 1–24 (2017)
27. Herland, K., Hämmäinen, H., Kekolahti, P.: Information security risks assessment of smartphones using Bayesian networks. J. Cyber Secur. **4**, 65–85 (2016)
28. Adina Tofan, C.: Decision tree method applied in cost-based decisions in an enterprise. Procedia Econ. Finance **32**, 1088–1092 (2015)
29. Horný, M.: Bayesian Networks, in Technical Report No. 5. 2014, Department of Health Policy & Management: Boston University School of Public Health
30. Mohsen, D., et al.: A combined fuzzy MCDM approach for identifiying the suitable lands for urban development: an example from Bandar ABBS Iran. J. Urban and Environ. Eng. **8**(1), 11–27 (2014)
31. Werro, N.: Fuzzy Classification of Online Customers. Fuzzy Management Methods (2015)

On the Roles of Project, Program and Portfolio Governance

Bruno Fragoso[✉], André Vasconcelos, and José Borbinha

INESC-ID, Instituto Superior Técnico, Universidade de Lisboa, Lisbon, Portugal
{bruno.fragoso,andre.vasconcelos,
jlb}@tecnico.ulisboa.pt

Abstract. This work proposes a new motivation for a literature review on the concepts of roles in project, program and portfolio governance within organizational overall governance. Recent literature has been promoting a paradigm change in the way how the research and practitioner communities should approach project management. Under such change, it mattered to better understand in a first moment which drivers regarding project, program and portfolio governance roles motivated or, in part, enabled such change. In a second moment the focus was placed on the way how project, program and portfolio governance roles (whereas the concept of role demonstrates to need clarifications under the main standards and practitioners books) are addressed from that paradigm shift onwards. As a result, we concluded that current standards and practitioners books do not promote and effective integration with organizational governance, and although initiatives as Research Project Management promote a shift by addressing a required multidisciplinary approach on project management discipline, such governance alignment is yet to be achieved. The conclusion and final remarks on the future work, stresses onto the evidenced gaps in promoting a coherent set of theories, models and tools in project management discipline, and the apparent suitability of Enterprise Engineering discipline to address them.

Keywords: Project · Program · Portfolio · Roles · Organizational governance · Governing body · Competences

1 Introduction

The literature regarding project, program and portfolio is vast and multidisciplinary, being most a result of the need for adding complementary elements, or contextual adequacy requirements, framed by its context. "Projects do not exist in a vacuum and an appreciation of the context within which the project is being performed will assist those involved in project management to deliver a project" [1]. Such permeability of projects towards context was always notorious and several approaches try to cope with the 'correct formula' to promote the most of organizational alignment under such contextual variables, being that the dominant strand is/was "the rational, universal, deterministic model – what has been termed the 'hard' systems model, emphasizing the planning and control dimensions of project management" [2].

© Springer Nature Switzerland AG 2019
B. Shishkov (Ed.): BMSD 2019, LNBIP 356, pp. 221–228, 2019.
https://doi.org/10.1007/978-3-030-24854-3_15

The five directions' framework presented by the Rethinking Project Management research network (RPM) [2], a landmark in the history of project management, promoted a paradigm change in the way how the research and practitioner communities approached project management, having as main aim to "identify and define an interdisciplinary research agenda aimed at enriching and extending the field beyond its current foundations" [2].

Although the widespread trend on project management practitioners remains onto the prevalence of deterministic and mechanics view on the project management discipline, subsequent analysis on research (funded on the findings on the RPM report) noted that "it became more consistently represented with a few yearly contributions". The understanding on project success and its performance on such research goes "far beyond traditional value creation and benefit realization" [3], as highlighted by Svejvig and Andersen in 2015, upon a structured review of the 'RPM literature'. Also in 2016, Dalcher [4] noted that, although already observed by the RPM network in 2006, "the bodies of knowledge were initially formulated, and have been subsequently maintained largely in terms of the certification programmes. Ironically, despite the enormous changes in the development in the discipline, the bodies of knowledge appear to have maintained their basic structure" [4].

As a common ground between the different approaches is the noted and evidenced relation between the effectiveness of a project, program and portfolio governance with the overall organizational governance on the project success (not considering for such if success is either measured in terms of benefit realization or a multidimensional performance assessment). However, although such relevance is clear, the theories, models and tools seem to fail in providing a clear and effective governance between projects, programs and portfolios within the overall organizational structures. Can such theories, models and tools be found in the standards? And if not, how did RPM findings foster the research on governance roles relation on projects, programs and portfolio in the quest for such solution?

Stating so, and in the scope of project, program and portfolio governance roles and organizational governance problem domain, it matters to firstly assess on how do practitioners' books and standards presently address the governance roles on project, program and portfolio link with organizational governance. Such understanding will better help to identify the motivations related with governance roles in RPM's multidimensional approach framework. On top of it, and as a preliminary analysis on the RPM multidisciplinary subsequent studies, tools and frameworks focused on the project, program and portfolio governance and organizational governance, it matters to cope with the production level, in quantitative terms, resulted in 'yearly contributions' in the recent years to better assess on the focus and attention given by research and practitioners community.

For such endeavor, we first developed an assessment on the governance roles, in particular onto the concept of 'role' against the content in the work of ISO Technical Committee 258 (ISO/TC 258) - Sect. 2, which we will consider to be the standard of the book of practitioners. This because the most referenced ones, such as PMBOK [5] or APM BOK [1] follow and contribute for the referential of ISO/TC 258 [6–9]. From there, an analysis on the motivations to the Rethinking Project Management (RPM) research network in aspects related with governance roles in project, program and portfolio (particularly the references on links with organizational governance's roles and structures) - Sect. 3. After such motivational elements, assumed to be a concern on the research community towards the increase of value in governance roles, the same motivations are the drive to enlarge the search onto posterior works by research community with contribute proposal for the RPM direction's proposals [3, 4, 10, 11], and accessing the scholar main finding in the last three years related with project, program and portfolio governance - Sect. 3.1. Followed by conclusion - Sect. 4.

2 Governance Roles in Present Approach to Project

Before exploring how the concept of governance role in the reference standards in project, program and portfolio manager, we need to define it in order to have a clear understanding along this work on what the concepts comprises. Surprisingly, not one of the standards identified [1, 6–9, 12, 13] in this work presents a definition on the concept of role. Looking at the definition for role and actor presented by the notation in Archimate modeling language, whereas role is "the responsibility for performing specific behavior, to which an actor can be assigned, or the part an actor plays in a particular action or event" [14], and actor while a "a business entity that is capable of performing behavior" [14]; concepts such as 'performance', 'behavior' or 'responsibility' seems adequate to understand what a role, and actor, is under an organization domain.

The concept of actor-role under this work can then understood as 'an entity that is capable of performing behavior, and has the responsibility to perform specific behaviors according to a status'. It is under this concept definition of "actor-role", which seems suitable to be instantiated in any given domain, and for project, program and portfolio in particular. Having the concept defined, is clearly understood from now that the standards deal and indicate with actor-roles, but not define them outside the project, program and portfolio domain being therefore in coherence with the deterministic system in place by the standards.

Considering the actor-role of stakeholder in project, program or portfolio, is usually the concept used in the practitioners books to assume the link in the role definition aspects, with the organization. "The roles and responsibilities of stakeholders should be defined and communicated based on the organization and project goals" [6]. Such link is at a different abstraction level of the roles it specializes within what in ISO 21500:2012 introduced as "Project organization" [6], comprising from the project manager to special interest groups with some level of interest in the project outcome or scope of intervention. ISO TC/258 guidance centers therefore in the project instruments, such as the Project Plan, the formalization and state, among others, of the roles expected from the different project, program or portfolio development phases. "Typically the project management plan defines the roles, responsibilities, organization and procedures for the management of risk, issues, change control, schedule, cost, communication, configuration management, quality, health, environment, safety and other subjects as needed" [6].

In PMBOK [5] two definitions can be found. One under a section of Resource management; "The function assumed by, or assigned to, a person in the project. Examples of project roles are civil engineer, business analyst, and testing coordinator" [5]; and the other on the glossary: "A defined function to be performed by a project team member, such as testing, filing, inspecting, or coding" [5]. Both concepts define a role while a function, both instantiated in the context of the project. However, when the same reference practitioner book uses the concept of governance roles [5], the concept coherence can be questioned.

Also, other practitioner book, APM BoK [1] does not define what a role is, being in line with the other references to roles in the quoted referential. An innovative aspect on the concept approach by this standard is that, although the concept of role remains undefined, the concept of organizational roles are entitled to a concept definition: "Organisational roles are the roles performed by individuals or groups in a project" [1] adding that "Roles have to be defined for the unique circumstances of a project. These roles may differ from those that the individuals hold within the organisation. For example, a project manager's boss in the functional organisation may be a member of the project team and report to the project manager on all matters relating to the project" [1].

Whether it is a project, program or portfolio governance role, while a set of expected behaviors from the project governance activity, or an organizational governance role, while a set of expected behaviors of organizational governance system, the concept formulated in the beginning of this section comprises the required semantics to address it, when promoting a review on research literature, where the concepts and the context they are used vary in terms of significance. Being also evidenced under the standards and practitioners books on project, program and portfolio as deterministic systems, supported on processes and normative nature, being all process oriented and highlighting in this sense the project as a tool (from strategy execution into operation's benefits realization).

3   Revisiting Project Management

RPM results from a crescent set of voices, including [15–18], towards the need for the project management, while a discipline, to evolve and denote a different approach on the project while an organization within an organization. RPM appears in 2004 motivated by a growing concern in research community towards the theoretical foundations of the project management discipline, such as Koskela and Howell [17] when state: "It is no exaggeration to claim that project management as a discipline is in crisis, and that a paradigm change, long overdue, has to be realized" [17], anticipating "a paradigmatic transformation of the discipline of project management is needed" [17]. The RPM network findings report noted that the classical project approach fails "to deal adequately with the emergent nature of front-end[1] work, for tending to treat all

---

[1] "the front-end (encompassing issues such as governance, project leadership, project sponsorship, strategy, value management and benefits management)" [2].

projects as if they were the same, and for not accounting sufficiently for human issue, which are often the most significant" [2].

On top of that in 1995, Packendorff [15] noted that, "When projects are regarded as tools, the various motives of the individuals in the project organization for participating (and, of course, for individuals outside the project not participating) are also neglected" [15]. This factor, among others, lead the extensive research and theories regarding project management to support the metaphorically shift conceptualization of a project as a tool, which as seen in previous section is still followed by the referenced standards, for a project while "a temporary organization:

- is an organized (collective) course of action aimed at evoking a non-routine process and/or completing a non-routine product;
- has a predetermined point in time or time-related conditional state when the organization and/or its mission is collectively expected to cease to exist;
- has some kind of performance evaluation criteria;
- is so complex in terms of roles and number of roles that it requires conscious organizing efforts (i.e. not spontaneous self-organizing)" [15].

In the proposal of RPM research network to Engineering and Physical Sciences Research Council (EPSRC) [19] we can find evidences on a larger focus on the human behaviors and its impact on the relations within the organization. One of the motivations was that "Conventional project management theory is too narrowly-focused" where as seen in the previous section, the reviewed references focused on the internal aspect of the functioning of the project, even in [9], with the concepts on project, program and portfolios governing bodies as autonomous and disconnected of the organization (or not expressing potential ways to address such concerns).

In the motivations expressed in the RPM proposal were also identified that "in recent years [written in 2004] it has become clear that the techniques in the bodies of knowledge do not explain the behaviour of complex projects" [19] and the "growing criticisms of the field's intellectual and philosophical foundations. (...). In essence, conventional project management theory remains wedded to the epistemological/ontological foundations of the 1950s/1960s, with its emphasis on machine-like conceptions of organisations and projects, and realist assumptions about 'organisations' and 'projects' as entities existing 'out there' independently of the people involved [19].

All these motivations, under a focused perspective on project, program and portfolio governance roles, led "the current conceptual base of project management continues to attract criticism for its lack of relevance to practice" [2], although "the main argument was not that to what extent project management body of knowledge with its concepts, methodologies and tools is worthless and should be abandoned, but rather that a new research network was needed to enrich and extend the field beyond its current intellectual foundations, and connect it more closely to the challenges of contemporary project management practice" [2].

Becomes clearer at this point, and focusing on the recent quoted literature reviews and RPM research directions, that is still missing under project, program and portfolio discipline a coherent set of theories to better support actor-role definition in practice, but with RPM fostering the research field for a more coherent set of multidisciplinary approaches on the overall project management in general, but also for the organizational governance alignment with project, program and portfolio roles. Although not explicit along the RPM report, it is visible the clear link in the importance of governance mechanism for the overall organization efficiency, being project, programs and portfolio included in such. As more recent analysis would come to confirm, as shown in the next section.

3.1 Follow Up on Governance Roles Finding and Considerations

In 2016, ten years after the RPM final report, a special issue in International Journal of Managing Projects in Business (IJMPB) on "Reflections of 10 years of rethinking project management – legacy and future" [20], Söderlund and Geraldi [21] evidenced that since RPM findings, "social practices and project actors have received increased attention. Extant research explored areas including but is not limited to the role of relationships in the making of projects, for example, through research on contracts and relational contracts" [21], the appliance of agent network theory, among other concerns oriented to project actor.

However, as the authors highlight: "studies on project governance have limited focus on the actual practices of governance, such as political processes, sense making and decisions", alerting for "a potentially dismissive attitude towards technologies, including project methods and tools" [21], that needs to be avoided in the future. Almost as highlighting the wrong idea on the engineering and technology limited contribution towards something else than outside the project standards.

More recently, 2019, in a literature review on project governance and stakeholders, was also highlighted the fact that still, "project management literature lacks from an inclusive framework which defines the roles, relationships and positions of internal and external stakeholders inside and outside of the organization's governance structure" [22].

4   Conclusion and Future Work

Confirmed the assumption that the theories, models and tools in project management discipline seem to fail in providing a clear and effective governance between projects, programs and portfolios within the overall organizational structures, we can now say that theories, models and tools as in standards fail to provide a coherent guidance on promoting such efficiency in practice (answering in this way to: 'Can such theories, models and tools be found in the standards?'. As such, at present time, and 13 years after the RPM final report, such set of theories and models are yet to be found in an integrative and efficient way towards organizational governance, even on the different directions which RPM set as guidance in its framework. However, the boost in the research production with particular focus on projects, programs and portfolios governance roles have been empirically getting greater focus and actuality to be addressed (answering in this way to: 'and if not, how did RPM findings foster the research on governance roles relation on projects, programs and portfolio in the quest for such solution?').

As future work, a closer analysis on addressing the efficiency promoted by project, program and portfolio governance roles within organizational governance, but through the organization perspective under the theories, models and tools that, although young, Enterprise Engineering discipline have demonstrated to cope with some of the problems identified in this work, stating for instance the concept of actor-role. An updated ontology for project, program and portfolio governance in organizations, a semantic framing on the associated behaviors by individuals in organizations dealing with projects, programs or portfolios, just to name a few challenges which Enterprise Engineering extensive body of knowledge, such as [23–26] just to reference a few, denote a clear relevance when addressing the theme of organizational governance.

Acknowledgements. This work was supported by national funds through Fundação para a Ciência e a Tecnologia (FCT) with reference UID/CEC/50021/2019.

References

1. APM: APM Body of Knowelge. APM, High Wycombe, Buckinghamshire (2006)
2. Winter, M., Smith, C., Morris, P., Cicmil, S.: Directions for future research in project management: the main findings of a UK government-funded research network. Int. J. Proj. Manag. **24**, 638–649 (2006). https://doi.org/10.1016/j.ijproman.2006.08.009
3. Svejvig, P., Andersen, P.: Rethinking project management: a structured literature review with a critical look at the brave new world. Int. J. Proj. Manag. **33**, 278–290 (2015). https://doi.org/10.1016/j.ijproman.2014.06.004
4. Dalcher, D.: Rethinking project practice: emerging insights from a series of books for practitioners. Int. J. Manag. Proj. Bus. **9**, 798–821 (2016). https://doi.org/10.1108/ijmpb-03-2016-0027
5. PMI: A Guide to the project management body of knowledge (PMBOK Guide). Project Management Institute, Inc. (2017)
6. ISO: ISO 21500:2012 - Guidance on project management (2012)
7. ISO: ISO 21503:2017 - Project, programme and portfolio management — Guidance on programme management. Presented at the (2017)
8. ISO: ISO 21504:2015 - Project, programme and portfolio management — Guidance on portfolio management (2015)
9. ISO: ISO 21505:2017 - Project, programme and portfolio management — Guidance on Governance (2017)
10. Söderholm, A., Lundin, R.A., Jacobsson, M.: Towards a multi-perspective research program on projects and temporary organizations: analyzing the Scandinavian turn and the rethinking effort. Int. J. Manag. Proj. Bus. **9**, 752–766 (2016). https://doi.org/10.1108/ijmpb-10-2015-0100
11. Svejvig, P., Grex, S.: The Danish agenda for rethinking project management. Int. J. Manag. Proj. Bus. **9**, 822–844 (2016). https://doi.org/10.1108/ijmpb-11-2015-0107
12. PMI: A Guide to the project management body of knowledge. Choice Rev. Online **34**, 34-1636-34-1636 (1996). https://doi.org/10.5860/choice.34-1636
13. PMI: ANSI/PMI 08-004-2008 - Organizational Project Management Maturity Model (OPM3) (2008)
14. The Open Group: ArchiMate 3.0.1 Specification. The Open Group (2017)

15. Packendorff, J.: Inquiring into the temporary organization: new directions for project management research. Scand. J. Manag. **11**, 319–333 (1995)
16. Jugdev, K., Thomas, J., Delisle, C.: Rethinking project management - Old truths and new insights (2001)
17. Koskela, L., Howell, G.: The underlying theory of project management is obsolete. In: Frontiers of Project Management Research and Applications, pp. 22–34. Project Management Institute, Seattle, Washington (2002)
18. Sahlin-Andersson, K., Söderholm, A.: Beyond project management temporary - permanent dilemma, Malmo (2002)
19. Winter, M., Smith, C.: Rethinking Project Management - Final Report - EPSRC Network 2004–2006, pp. 1–7 (2006)
20. Walker, D.: Editorial - Reflections of 10 years of thinking project management – legacy and future. Int. J. Manag. Proj. Bus. **9**, 710–715 (2016). https://doi.org/10.1108/ijmpb-07-2016-0060
21. Söderlund, J., Geraldi, J.: Project studies and engaged scholarship: directions towards contextualized and reflexive research on projects. Int. J. Manag. Proj. Bus. **9**, 767–797 (2016). https://doi.org/10.1108/ijmpb-02-2016-0016
22. Derakhshan, R., Turner, R., Mancini, M.: Project governance and stakeholders: a literature review. Int. J. Proj. Manag. **37**, 98–116 (2019). https://doi.org/10.1016/j.ijproman.2018.10.007
23. Tribolet, J., Sousa, P., Caetano, A.: The role of enterprise governance and cartography enterprise engineering. Enterp. Model. Inf. Syst. Archit. J. **9**(1), 38–49 (2014)
24. Hoogervorst, J.A.P.: Enterprise Governance and Enterprise Engineering (2009)
25. Proper, E., Op't Land, M., Cloo, J., Waage, M., Steghuis, C.: Enterprise Architecture - Creating Value by Informed Governance. Springer, Heidelberg (2009). https://doi.org/10.1007/978-3-540-85232-2
26. Dietz, J.L.G., et al.: The discipline of enterprise engineering. Int. J. Organ. Des. Eng. **3**, 86 (2013). https://doi.org/10.1504/ijode.2013.053669

Governance as a Condition for Creating Business Value from Enterprise Architecture

Marijn Janssen[(⊠)]

Faculty of Technology, Policy and Management,
Delft University of Technology, Jaffalaan 5, Delft, The Netherlands
M.F.W.H.A.Janssen@tudelft.nl

Abstract. IT Governance is often viewed as an important factor for creating business value for firms. However, there is limited work investigating the relationship between architectural governance and the contributions of enterprise architecture (EA) to firm performance. Based on a study of more than 15 cases the analyzes shows that architectural governance is a condition for the ability to create business value from the EA function. The cases also show that architectural governance depends on the context and there is no best way of EA governance that fits very situation. Architectural governance complements enterprise architecture and should ensure that EA efforts are coordinated and used by the business to improve firm performance. In many cases EA and architectural governance were found to be strongly connected, making it difficult to separate them. This strong dependence suggests that a change in EA influences the governance and vice versa. Architectural governance introduces more bureaucracy and administrative work, but paradoxically can result in the creation of more business flexibility and agility.

Keywords: IT governance · Architectural governance business value ·
Architecture · Enterprise architecture · Contingency approach

1 Introduction

Enterprise architecture (EA) has been heralded as an instrument to create business value for organizations [1, 2]. Architecture is about abstraction of the enterprise and its environment and acts as a means of communication and decision making regarding that environment [3]. Enterprise architectures define and interrelate data, hardware, software, and communication resources, as well as the supporting organization required to maintain the overall physical structure required by the architecture [4]. EA uses frameworks, enterprise models, architectural principles and standards to direct the IT function. Although EA is considered as a silver bullet by organizations [5], there is discussion about the value creation of EA, and this is even considered as a myth [6]. One reason for this myth is that EA does not create value by itself, but only support opportunities for value creation or the ability to realize them [6]. Governance should ensure that the EA models, principles and standards are actually used and are translated into firm value. In this paper we investigate the role of governance to create value form EA. We label this type of governance as 'architectural governance'. Architectural

© Springer Nature Switzerland AG 2019
B. Shishkov (Ed.): BMSD 2019, LNBIP 356, pp. 229–235, 2019.
https://doi.org/10.1007/978-3-030-24854-3_16

governance is needed for both the *development* of the EA models, principles and standards and the *use* of EA by organizations to create business value.

Governance has been linked to increased organizational performance [7, 8]. IT governance mechanisms, or governance mechanisms for short, focus on decision making authorities and processes for aligning business and IT. IT-governance has various definitions, including "framework for decision rights and accountabilities to encourage desirable" ([9], p. 261) and "all the mechanisms for preparing, making, implementing and executing decisions" ([10], p. 8). Architectural governance can be viewed as a type of IT-governance which is focusses on ensuring the proper working of the EA function. The EA function can be defined as the *"organizational functions, roles and bodies involved with creating, maintaining, ratifying, enforcing, and observing Enterprise Architecture decision-making – established in the enterprise architecture and EA policy"* ([11], p. 105). The EA functions develops models, principles and standards for use by IT development and maintenance.

There has been limited research about EA governance. In other domains, like organizational networks, governance has been recognized as a critical variable that influences strongly their performance and effectiveness [12]. In this research the relationship between the EA function and EA governance and its influence on the creation of business value is investigated.

2 Background

IT governance systematically determines who makes each type of decision (a decision right), who has input to a decision (an input right) and how these people (or groups) are held accountable for their role [13]. There are two separate streams of governance that have followed parallel paths of advancement [14]. One streams deals with IT Governance forms and the other stream focusses with IT governance contingencies [14].

The first stream is based on the notion of centralized and decentralized decision-making. Allocating decision-making authorities to central or decentral organizational parts changes over time and can be viewed as a 'pendulum swing' [15]. The first stream deals with how to create best of both centralization and decentralization [14]. This streams classifies governance into forms like business monarchy, IT monarchy, feudal, IT duopoly, Federal and Anarchy [16].

The other stream investigates on the governance fit with the environment. In this stream it is investigated how multiple, interacting contingency factors influence the modes of governance and identifies factors like economies of scope and absorptive capacity, and IT knowledge of line managers [9] but also firm size, industry and organizational structure [14]. Contingency approaches stresses the context awareness of the development of applications [17].

The combination of streams result in a contingency approach and looking at governance structures. Brown and Grant [14] found that the merging of these streams resulted in the contemporary view on IT-governance as represented by Weill and Ross [7]. IT-governance should reflect the realities of complex organizations and therefore at governance mechanisms should be looked. Types of governance mechanisms include processes, structures and relational mechanisms [15] and decision, communication and alignment processes [13, 16]. We will use these types of mechanisms to investigate the architectural governance.

3 Research Approach

In this explorative research more than 15 cases were analyzed having various architectural functions and governance arrangements. The architectural functions investigated could be limited or comprehensive, whereas the type of arrangements varied from decentral to central architectural governance. The EA functions of the companies surveyed could cover only a few persons or more than 20 persons. Sometimes there was one single EA department, whereas in other cases enterprise architects were found in multiple departments. Some of the arrangements had hardly any architectural governance, whereas others had very tight governance. Architectural governance could be focused on the use of the EA by other IT departments but also on the relationship between EA function and the business.

To analyses each of the cases at least one interview was conducted. The interviewee could be an enterprise architect, information manager or somebody else in charge of the architecture function in the organizations. Sometimes people from the line management (business side) were interviewed, but not in all cases. In addition, reports and other documentation were studied when available. Over half of the organizations were public sector organizations, whereas the private sector organizations were mainly large companies.

4 Conceptualizing EA and Governance

The cases show that EA governance can be diverse. EA governance is a complicated endeavor, as it involves both IT and business departments as shown in Fig. 1. The governance mechanisms used for interacting with the IT department can be different from the governance mechanisms for dealing with the businesses. The organization and the needs are different for these type of governance mechanisms. Furthermore, these departments having different resources, capabilities, processes and levels of IT-readiness and knowledge. We recommend to make a difference in the interaction with the business and IT-organization.

EA governance is dependent on the EA function and the purpose and can be dependent on all kinds of factors, like, role of ICT for business performance, trust, leadership, culture, firm size, IT-maturity and readiness and so on. Therefore we view EA and EA governance as being mutual dependent and having a recursive relationship as shown in the Fig. 2. Both are needed to contribute to firm performance. Architectural governance without having an EA does not make any sense. If there is only an EA and no architectural governance, then the EA will not be used.

EA Governance does not per se result in firm performance. Therefore we take a *contingency approach* in this research [9, 14]. A contingency approach assumes that most appropriate style of governance is dependent on the situational context. In such a

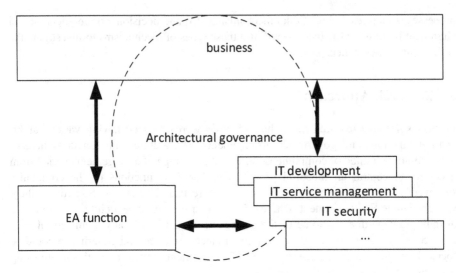

Fig. 1. The scope of architectural governance

view there is no single approach that results in the best performance. The contingency factors are shown at the top of Fig. 2.

Both the architecture function and the governance are influenced by all kinds of contingency factors. Both the architecture function and the architectural governance influence business performance. The architecture functions is influenced by the action and decisions of humans in the organizations and architectural governance can enable or constraint the development and use of EA.

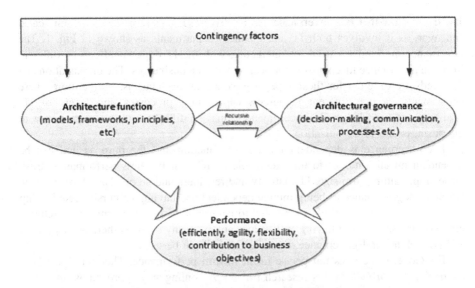

Fig. 2. Conceptual framework for investigating the cases

5 Findings: Governance as a Condition for Creating Value

The findings in the case study confirm the strong interrelationship between the architecture functions and architectural governance. Sometimes a comprehensive architecture functions was found, whereas the governance was limited and the other way around. Both central and decentral governance can result in the creation of business value according to the interviewees.

The creation of value from EA and governance is a complex process which plays at various levels for different problems. A variety of approaches are possible which seems to be dependent on contingency factors such as the sector (industry), size of the firm, leadership, complexity of the IT landscape, organizational culture, IT-readiness and organizational structure. An important factor seems to be the maturity if the EA function. The longer ago the function was introduced the more contribution to firm performance was made. Also if ICT was viewed as one of the core businesses of the organization under study seems to be an important factors.

Surprisingly, more centralized organizations did not always have central architectural governance. It could be that the architectural governance was decentral within the departments, whereas the organizational decision-making was central. This could indicate a less developed architectural function. However, this can also suggest that organizational structure and architectural governance are not related.

EA and governance was found to be dependent on the organizational intentions of having an architecture. Facilitating innovating can be a role of architecture, whereas architecture can also be used to standardize and avoid variety. Hence, the architecture use is strongly related to the organizational strategy, which is found to be an important contingency factor. In the past the focus on creating flexible operating models based on modular architectures [18], whereas nowadays the focus is much more on contributing to innovation. This requires a change in focus of the architectural function, as the focus shifts from IT-departments to the business. As the goals of EA are shifting, so should the governance mechanisms. In innovating the capabilities and potential of new technology is explored and architects should support the creation of new innovations and not on the reuse of existing technology and building blocks. This requires a change in governance and in mindset. In one organizations even a different architect was hired to solely focus on business development and innovation.

In addition the life-cycle of the EA function seems to influence the governance. Immature or starting EA efforts have less strict governance, whereas more mature EA functions have more governance mechanism in place. This suggests that the EA function and EA governance influence each other and co-evolve with each other. The level of maturity seems to be explanatory variables for both the EA function and governance.

In our cases the level of governance varies from hardly any governance to detailed and profound governance mechanism. The following variations were found:

- *Over control*; Adding too much governance is counter effective and will only add to the administrative burden. There are too many people involved in decision-making, too many decision-making authorities and too many formalized processes. This results in long-lasting decision-making processes and slow down of the speed of decision-making.

- *Embedded:* the EA is embedded in the organization and all employees know the architecture and understand why making use of them is needed. There are decision-making boards and processes for ensuing that EA is used, but these do not result in large delay or undermine projects. EA is used purposes full.
- *Comply or explain*: Use the architecture, its models, principles and standards, or explain why you use these not This model has the risk of flimsy excuses for not having to use the EA. As such, being firms about the use of EA is important.
- *Known architecture*: everybody in the organization is aware of the architecture and is communicated to all persons.
- *Voluntary use*: Some use the architecture if appropriate. This might be the case when EA is developed form some aspects, but for other parts the EA is not suitable (yet). This model has the risk of neglecting and no further development of EA as the business benefit remains limited.
- *No governance*: architecture is now known by the organizations. EA is a function which is not taken serious. Often architectures might be avoided.

The interviewees indicated that both extremes (no governance and over control) did not result in higher firm performance. Hence, governance mechanisms should be designed and introduced with care. Architectural governance introduces more bureaucracy and administrative work as all kinds of decision-making authorities, governance processes and procedures are introduced. Paradoxically the introduction of more governance can result in more flexibility and agility, but too many mechanism will be counterproductive.

6   Conclusions

The findings shows that EA governance can result into improved firm performance and that sound architectural governance is a condition for success. Governance should ensure that architecture is known and the architecture models, principles and standards are followed and translated into firm value. Governance mechanism used were found to be different. As a consequence, the cases were difficult to compare with each other. We recommend to develop a classification of types of architectural governance. Such a classicisation can help to compare governance mechanism and its effect on firm performance.

Our findings suggests that architectural governance researchers should adapt a *contingency approach*, as what is effective governance is dependent on the context. Factors that were identified include ICT as core business, leadership, organizational culture, industry, firm size, readiness, IT maturity, complexity of the IT landscape, organizational structure, and the maturity of the EA function. In future research the effects of these factors can be investigated.

Governance was not always found to be problem-driven and updated over time. This can easily result in too much governance which in turn can decrease firm performance. As business and IT problems change, so does the governance. In the current climate the governance needs to be focussed on contributing to innovation, whereas in the past governance was aimed at creating a flexible operating model. The risks is that more and more governance mechanisms are added without replacing or removing previous governance mechanisms. Although new governance mechanisms are needed, remaining the previous one might be counterproductive.

References

1. Tamm, T., Seddon, P.B., Shanks, G., Reynolds, P.: How does enterprise architecture add value to organisations? Commun. Assoc. Inf. Syst. **28**, Article 10 (2011)
2. Niemi, E.I., Pekkola, S.: Enterprise architecture benefit realization: review of the models and a case study of a public organization. Data Base Adv. Inf. Syst. **47**(3), 55–80 (2016)
3. Van der Raadt, B., Soetendal, J., Perdeck, M., Van Vliet, H.: Polyphony in architecture. Presented at the Proceedings 26th International Conference on Software Engineering (ICSE 2004) (2004)
4. Richardson, L., Jackson, B.M., Dickson, G.: A principle-based enterprise architecture: lessons from Texaco and Star Enterprise. MIS Q. **14**(4), 385–403 (1990)
5. Hjort-Madsen, K.: Enterprise architecture implementation and management: a case study on interoperability. In: 39th Annual Hawaii International Conference on System Sciences (HICSS 2006), Kauai, Hawaii. IEEE (2006)
6. Gong, Y., Janssen, M.: The value of and myths about enterprise architecture. Int. J. Inf. Manag. **46**, 1–9 (2019)
7. Weill, P., Ross, J.W.: IT Governance: How Top Performers Manage IT Decision Rights for Superior Results. Harvard Business School, Watertown, MA (2004)
8. Provan, K.G., Kenis, P.: Modes of network governance: structure, management, and effectiveness. J. Public Adm. Res. Theory **18**(2), 229–252 (2008)
9. Sambamurthy, V., Zmud, R.W.: Arrangements for information technology governance: a theory of multiple contingencies. Manag. Inf. Syst. Q. (MISQ) **23**(2), 261–290 (1999)
10. Loukis, E., Janssen, M., Dawes, S., Zheng, L.: Evolving ICT and governance in organizational networks. conceptual and theoretical foundations. Electron. Mark. **26**(1), 7–14 (2016)
11. Van Der Raadt, B., Van Vliet, H.: Designing the enterprise architecture function. Presented at the International Conference on the Quality of Software Architectures (2008)
12. Provan, K.G., Milward, H.B.: A preliminary theory of interorganizational network effectiveness: a comparative study of four community mental health systems. Adm. Sci. Q. **40**, 1–33 (1995)
13. Weill, P.: Don't just lead, govern: how best performing organisations govern IT. MIS Q. Exec. **3**(1), 1–17 (2004)
14. Brown, A.E., Grant, G.G.: Framing the frameworks: a review of IT governance research. Commun. AIS **25**(1), 696–712 (2005)
15. Peterson, R.: Crafting information technology governance. Inf. Syst. Manag. **21**(4), 7–22 (2004)
16. Weill, P., Ross, J.W.: A matrixed approach to designing IT governance. MIT Sloan Manag. Rev. **46**(2), 26–34 (2005)
17. Shishkov, B., van Sinderen, M.: From user context states to context-aware applications. In: Filipe, J., Cordeiro, J., Cardoso, J. (eds.) ICEIS 2007. LNBIP, vol. 12, pp. 225–239. Springer, Heidelberg (2008). https://doi.org/10.1007/978-3-540-88710-2_18
18. Ross, J.W.: Creating a strategic IT architecture competency: learning in stages. MISQ Q. Exec. **2**(1), 31–43 (2003)

Microservice Architecture from Enterprise Architecture Management Perspective

Carlos Pinheiro[1]([✉]), André Vasconcelos[2,3], and Sergio Guerreiro[2,3]

[1] Universidade Aberta, Lisbon, Portugal
1701005@estudante.uab.pt
[2] Instituto Superior Técnico, University of Lisbon,
Av. Rovisco Pais 1, 1049-001 Lisbon, Portugal
{andre.vasconcelos,
sergio.guerreiro}@tecnico.ulisboa.pt
[3] INESC-ID, Rua Alves Redol 9, 1000-029 Lisbon, Portugal

Abstract. Microservice Architecture (MSA) is an architectural style to build distributed applications as a collection of independently deployable services. When adopting MSA, companies must drive some aspects that impact the organizational efficiency in order to guarantee *(i)* the strategic benefits of services; *(ii)* promote the best resources usage and *(iii)* separate the scopes of enterprise architecture (EA) decisions and microservice teams' decisions. This paper assesses the relevant factors about MSA from the enterprise architecture management (EAM) perspective and proposes an ArchiMate metamodel which serve as an architectural reference. Two methods with different approaches were selected to compose the model proposed, Extreme Enterprise Architecture Planning (XEAP) a top-down approach used here to plan microservices products and EA-Mini-Descriptions a bottom-up approach used to keep the EA up to date. In the end, *(i)* a model defining principles and governance guidelines, *(ii)* a generic model defining architectural responsibilities, and *(iii)* an architectural reference for technology standards which enable the enterprise governance of MSA, are engineered.

Keywords: Enterprise architecture management ·
Adaptive enterprise architecture · Adaptable enterprise architecture ·
Microservice architecture · SOA

1 Introduction

Microservice Architecture has aroused a great interest recently [1–4]. It aims to build distributed systems based on small and independent services. In contrast to SOA, which commonly is built under a strong and centralized governance, most of MSA references advocate for decentralized governance, however this decentralization can hinder communication at the enterprise level [4]. Traditional Enterprise Architecture Management (EAM) approaches seem to have difficulties to deal with these micro-granular systems [5]. Therefore, are no able to guarantee the fulfillment of enterprise needs. Nonetheless, it is important to manage the alignment and integration between the modeling of these systems and the enterprise architecture needs by several factors,

© Springer Nature Switzerland AG 2019
B. Shishkov (Ed.): BMSD 2019, LNBIP 356, pp. 236–245, 2019.
https://doi.org/10.1007/978-3-030-24854-3_17

such as planning business capacity, guaranteeing right investment levels, controlling costs, ensuring compliance with enterprise policies and principles, among others [3]. This paper assesses the relevant aspects about microservice architecture (MSA) regarding the EAM concerns and models them based on ArchiMate [6] and TOGAF 9.2 [7], in order to serve as a template for EA modeling pursuing to ensure the alignment between EAM needs and MSA implementation. Thus, this paper contributes to the enterprise architecture (EA) body of knowledge.

2 Background

Enterprise Architecture (EA) is a coherent set of principles, methods, and models used to design the organizational structure, containing business processes, information systems, and IT infrastructure to govern business and IT initiative over time, and keep the alignment with strategic objectives and drivers of an organization [7]. TOGAF [7] presents relevant EA building blocks, however, it does not define neither a language nor a notation for architectural description. This purpose is accomplished by ArchiMate [6].

Microservice can be defined as a strongly encapsulated and loosely coupled application service with a well-defined scope, which can be deployed independently, run in an individual process and communicates through light technologies, built to provide a business's capability with high availability and scalability [8]. MSA is a style of architecture for distributed systems based on microservices that target scalability and applies Service-Oriented Architecture (SOA), but extends SOA principles adding new constraints to ensure the independence of service [9, 10]. Microservices must be product-oriented [8, 11], this perspective expands the impact of decentralized governance, implying that the organizational structure to support the business process, development, operation, and architecture governance should be planned with vision focusing on products.

While adopting MSA, it is important to embrace an adaptable governance in a simple and fast way that enables to track the components modeled in the EA. In this sense the XEAP applies characteristics of software development agile methods to the domain of EA [12] used here for fast planning of microservice architecture initiative.

3 Related Work

The growth of interest in micro-services in the industry and in the scientific universe is demonstrated by Soldani et al. [3] and Di Francesco et al. [2]. Soldani explores pains and gains of microservices and shows that at design time the principal pain is related to the difficulty in determine the right microservice's scope and granularity.

Yale et al. [10] reinforce that microservices are part of an enterprise landscape and affirm that the duplication of functions and microservices is favored by the lack of clarity in microservice scope and ownership definitions, which implies multiplying costs for all business areas of the organization. They indicate that the autonomous choice of the technology, even though beneficial from the developer's perspective, can be problematic from the corporate view, exemplifying that tracking and managing licensing arrangements throughout this set may become impossible at the corporate level and if managed only by the team, it will not be economically efficient.

Salah et al. [13], demonstrated that the main reason to migrate to the MSA is to obtain elastic scaling. They pointed out that keeping each individual team well trained and able to evolve the microservices can be time and cost consuming. Also, the flexibility that MSA offers can raise the complexity of coordination between different teams.

Lenarduzzi and Korte [4] surveyed pros and cons of possible team structures and indicate some negative impacts on enterprise communication regarding the adoption of microservices due to the nature of decentralized governance, and argue that this creates a problem in strategies synchronization of the corporation as a whole.

Drews [14] describes the new role of EAM in the Bimodal Enterprise Architecture to deliver services to consumers faster and faster where an agile team structure is created to develop and operate new products usually built using microservices (Fast IT). He pointed out that despite the high autonomy of the teams, EAM still needs to support teams on cross issues of services/microservices, but playing a more consultative role, focus on making recommendations instead of restricting architectural decisions, keeping track of permanent changes in IT architecture and enabling cost transparency.

Zimmermann [15] advocates that microservice complexity is moved from inner to outer architecture, demanding advanced EA methodologies to integrate the structures with micro-granular architectures within an adaptive EA. In this way, Bogner and Zimmermann [16] proposed the EA-Mini-Descriptions model, which are architectural descriptions for each microservice that can be combined into a larger model, unifying microservices into a holistic dynamically-adjustable reference architecture.

Balakrushnan et al. [9] demonstrated the scopes of enterprise architecture governance concerns by describing the microservice governance contexts in a federalized EA, pointing out EA Governance scope aspects such as legal and security policies, architecture criterion, flexible technology standards and knowledge management.

4   Proposal

In the EA context, information systems are already covered by TOGAF and ArchiMate, and The Open Group has already published a Microservice Reference Architecture [17], nevertheless, not presented in ArchiMate and considering only a green field scenario where all microservice aspects can be managed without concerns about legacies. However, this paper focuses on presenting MSA Reference Architecture for companies that are usually highly regulated and will probably adopt this architecture in a brown field scenario, where the context is likely to have a strong corporate culture, legacy structures and corporate standards. This paper aims to complement The Open Group Microservice Reference Architecture by aggregating three key elements: an agile approach to plan and model the MSA at the EA level [12]; a reference architecture modeled in ArchiMate [6]; and a deep MSA view composed by micro-granular descriptions as a way to keep the EA up-to-date [18].

The XEAP [12] provides a holistic reasonable method which details the architectures through an interactive cycle of design. Thus, we use the XEAP just as an agile guideline process to identify the boundary of microservices based on the organizational business process structure and to define the right team to own the microservices.

On the other hand, to encourage decentralized governance the EAM should provide corporate options to support the decisions of microservice teams, maintaining strategic alignment, optimizing investments, and controlling IT costs.

The impacts of MSA on the EAM were grouped in the contexts described below (Table 1).

Table 1. Consequences of MSA on the EAM

Business Process Context	Microservices development must be closely aligned with the design of organization's business process, which must be decomposed to a business function that defines the microservice's responsibility [9]. Thus, it should be interesting to keep the logical dependence relationship of these microservices with others architectural components in the EA model
Organizational Structure	The product's orientation, advocated by MSA [3, 8, 11], implies a strong view of the organizational structure around business products. Thus, this structure should be planned in EA model
Technology Context	Microservices can be implemented across multiple platforms, languages and technologies, allowing the best choice to support microservice requirements [9]. However, from the enterprise's viewpoint, it is important to manage risks over business continuity and control costs. For knowledge management it may be beneficial to use shared technologies, which permits the company to efficiently keep the teams well-trained [13]. Of course, a new technology can be used, but it seems to make sense to maintain a centralized catalog of the technology for each need in a pool of recommended technologies in the EA Model
Infrastructure Context	Usually a microservice is published in a cloud, which has a cost which must be monitored. On the other hand, sometimes, companies have a corporate contract that monetizes licenses and the use of clouds, making it relevant for EAM [10]. The main information of the cloud used should be mapped in EA model in order to allow the company to implement some global mechanism of monitoring the health and cost of this cloud
Integration Context	Consumers from outside of the system communicate with microservice through an API with a public contract [9]. It is usually exposed in a centralized API gateway. As a key integration element of the microservice with other services, it seems natural to represent these APIs in the EA model
Governance Context	A single team should owner the whole microservices lifecycle, which autonomously governs every aspect of its microservices. However sometimes overarching guidance is needed [8]

4.1 Values and Principles

The first step in XEAP is defining values and principles to determine the scope and the objective of EA planning [12]. Here, we propose an initial set of architectural principles to define the governance scopes of EAM in cases of use of MSA. The proposed principles shown in Fig. 1 are based on the MSA Governance Framework by The Open Group [9, 17]. It sheds a light upon the concerns of EAM and Microservice governance scopes. Any governance principle that emerges should update this figure.

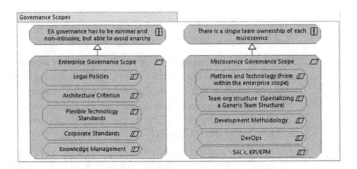

Fig. 1. Principles and governance scopes

4.2 Business Processes and Product Model

Defining the microservices ownership is not an easy task, since the boundaries between the different business features of a system application may be unclear [3]. Also, considering that microservices do not share anything, including data [11], we adapted the CRUD Matrix from the XEAP proposal [12] in order to identify information clusters and the products, to distribute the microservices ownership based on these products, and to determine the proper scope and granularity to microservices.

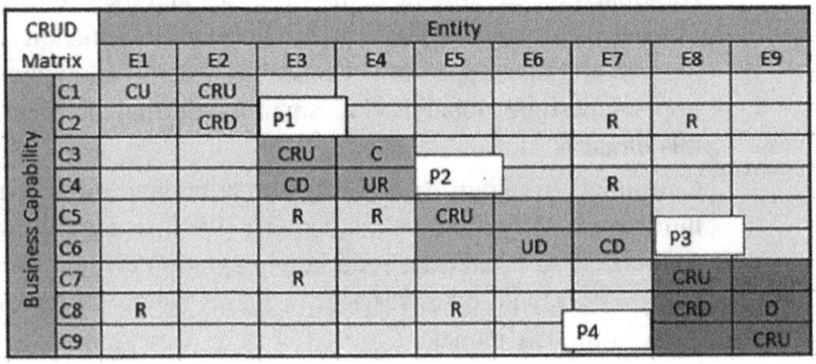

CRUD Matrix	Entity								
	E1	E2	E3	E4	E5	E6	E7	E8	E9
C1	CU	CRU							
C2		CRD	P1				R	R	
C3			CRU	C					
C4			CD	UR	P2		R		
C5			R	R	CRU				
C6						UD	CD	P3	
C7			R					CRU	
C8	R				R			CRD	D
C9							P4		CRU

(Left vertical label: Business Capability)

Fig. 2. CRUD matrix to determine the products (Adapted from [12])

4.3   Technology Architecture (Flexible Technology Standards)

To describe the microservice architecture, it is important to perceive the separation between inner and outer architectures [5]. For example, the API gateway is an important cross and centralized tool used to communicate with every microservices, thus it is part of outer architecture, while the language used to develop the microservice is part of inner architectures. For each layer the model in Fig. 3 provides a catalog of important technologies, EA requirements, and suggestions for microservices extracted from Balakrushnan [9] and Yale [10], allowing the microservice team to choose the best technology to implement their needs, but controlling technology diversity.

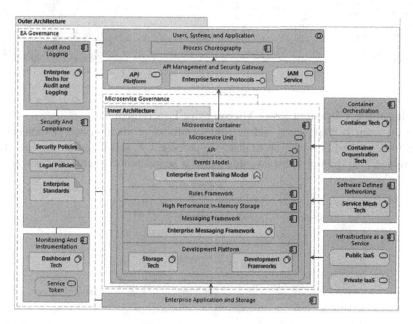

Fig. 3. Microservice enterprise reference architecture restrictions and recommendations

The Responsibilities for Architectural Components

Keeping in mind that it is desirable to delegate as many decisions as possible to the microservice team and that new technologies or business changes may give opportunities to review these responsibilities, we propose the matrix in Table 2, which defines the responsibilities of governance roles over each architectural point. In this matrix the lines represent the governance concerns shown in Fig. 1, and the columns, architectural components shown in Fig. 3. The cells indicate if the main responsibility resides in Enterprise IT Team Governance (ET), autonomously in the Microservice Team (MT), or in the Microservice team within enterprise Restrictions (MR).

Table 2. Governance scope matrix

Governance Scope Matrix	Outer Architecture									Inner Architecture							
	Users, Systems, and Application	API Management and Security Gateway	Monitoring And Instrumentation	Container Orchestration	Audit And Logging	Security And Compliance	Software Defined Networking	Enterprise Applications and Storage	Infrastructure as a Service	Microservice Container	Microservice Unit	Microservice API	Events Model	Rules Framework	High Performance In-Memory Storage	Messaging Framework	Development Platform
Legal and Security Policies	ET	ET	ET		ET	ET		ET									
Architecture Criterion	ET	ET	ET	ET	ET	ET	ET	ET	ET	MT	MT	MT	MT	MT	MT	MT	MR
Technology Standards		ET	ET	ET	ET	ET	ET	ET	ET	MT	MT	MT	MT	MT	MT	MT	MT
Enterprise Standards	ET	ET	ET	ET	ET	ET	ET	ET	ET				MR			MR	MR
Knowledge Management										MT	MT	MT	MT	MT	MT	MT	MT
Platform and Technology										MR	MT	MT	MR	MT	MT	MR	MR
Team org structure											MR						
Development Methodology										MT	MT	MT	MT	MT	MT	MT	MT
DevOps										MT	MT	MT	MT	MT	MT	MT	MT
SLA´s, KPI/KPM										MT	MT	MT	MT	MT	MT	MT	MT

Keeping the EA Updated From Microservice Evolvement

Once the team is empowered and gets the control over microservice governance, in order to keep the EA model up to date, we propose a model based on the EA-Mini-Description [16]. Figure 4 displays this model's adaptation to ArchiMate views.

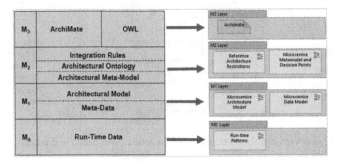

Fig. 4. EA-Mini-Description (Adapted from [16])

The model and logic of EA-Mini-Description here is used to allow the microservice architecture evolvement to automatically update the EA Model. In layer M3 was described that ArchiMate was used for modelling all views about the microservice architecture. In layer M2 the Reference Architecture Restrictions is represented, it describes the main technologies and patterns that the microservice architecture is supposed to follow and links to the same diagram defined in Fig. 3 (Flexible technology standards). On the other hand, a guide should be provided to indicate the architectural decision points. The M1 layer presents an architecture view of a single microservice, which details the microservice enriched with information resulted from the microservice team choices over the options available in the EA and a metadata model view, containing properties such as API endpoint, usage costs or purpose. In the M0 is prescribed a standard to define what runtime data should collected and provided by the microservice to support an operational and business analysis at EAM level.

5   Evaluation of Feasibility

We created an argumentative map, shown in Table 3, to correlate the models proposed with The Open Group Microservice Architecture and with the EA-Mini-Description to validate the perspective of its coherence and feasibility of use it by enterprise architects to govern corporate aspects of MSA.

Table 3. Evaluation map of baseline architectures reference and propose

The Open Group Microservice Architecture	
Key Governing Principles of MSA	The proposal is aligned, but we extend the key principles adding two others: *(i)* EA governance has to be minimal and non-intrusive, but able to avoid anarchy, and *(ii)* there is a single team ownership of each microservice as suggested by The Open Group [17]
Microservices Reference Architecture	The components present in Flexible Technology Standards are aligned with the Microservices Reference Architecture presented by The Open Group [17], however we relate the respective EA governance artifacts in the same diagram for each component and discuss non-intrusive drivers to support some architectural decisions
EA-Mini-Descriptions	
M3 Layer	The use of ArchiMate is addressed to accommodate the model proposed and establish a standard notation which facilitates communication among the teams and enterprise stakeholders [16]
M2 Layer	The Microservice Enterprise Reference Architecture Restrictions (Fig. 3) is incorporated in this level enabling to keep it up to date. Also, we suggested a view correlating the microservice metamodel with decision points to help choose the options available. It should follow some reference such as the one proposed by Haselböck [19], however these elements are not deeply analyzed in this paper
M1 Layer	We proposed to create a specific data model and architecture model in this layer for each microservice, which is not described in this paper, due to its specificity. The interest of EA in this layer is to ensure that it is documented and easily found
Not based on pre-existing microservice reference architectures	
CRUD Matrix to Determine Products	This address the definition of microservices scope
The Governance Scope Matrix	Define the responsibility for each architectural artifact identified

The four TOGAF's architectural domains are contemplated. Business Architecture drives principles and governance scopes, definitions of products. The Applications and Data Architectures drive the Product Application Model through the CRUD Matrix to Determine the Products Fig. 2. The Technology Architecture is covered by Microservice Enterprise Reference Architecture Restrictions describing Flexible Technology Standards (Fig. 3). Therefore, this evaluation proves the feasibility and utility of these models to describe EAM concerns in the context of MSA adoption.

6 Conclusions and Future Work

The initial research indicated that it appears to exist difficulties for companies to maintain alignment between IT governance needs and the use of microservices architecture in order to control costs and to manage technology knowledge. Some related works provided a set of perspectives and models which when integrated, contributed for the development of this paper. Thus, this research resulted in an ArchiMate model defining governance principles, MSA product scopes, microservices governance responsibilities and an enterprise technology architecture standard view for MSA, which enables to easily maintain relevant requirements and recommendations from EAM needs for the microservices team, as well as keeping relevant information about microservices and their evolvement up-to-date, providing cost transparency and balancing the benefits of decentralized governance of microservices.

This proposal has not been deepened in the criteria analysis of EA decisions for governance at enterprise or microservice levels. It certainly opens a point of discussion about the actual benefits in keeping each aspect under EA governance or simply leaving it to the microservice team. The existence of the difficulty for companies to maintain the alignment between MSA and EAM in IT governance, as well as the aspects discussed and addressed in this paper, needs confirmation. The model proposed in the paper still must be validated. Methods to automate model updating from the bottom up perspective can be investigated. Also, other theoretical strategies can enrich the model proposed. Lastly, the model proposed should be evaluated in a real case.

Acknowledgments. This work was supported by national funds through Fundação para a Ciência e a Tecnologia (FCT) with reference UID/CEC/50021/2019 and by the European Commission program H2020 under the grant agreement 822404 (project QualiChain).

References

1. Thomas, A.: Hype Cycle for Application Architecture, 2018. Gartner, Inc. (2018)
2. Di Francesco, P., Malavolta, I., Lago, P.: Research on architecting microservices: trends, focus, and potential for industrial adoption. In: 2017 IEEE International Conference on Software Architecture (ICSA), pp. 21–30 (2017). https://doi.org/10.1109/icsa.2017.24
3. Soldani, J., Tamburri, D.A., Van Den Heuvel, W.-J.: The pains and gains of microservices: a systematic grey literature review. J. Syst. Softw. **146**, 215–232 (2018). https://doi.org/10.1016/j.jss.2018.09.082

4. Lenarduzzi, V., Sievi-Korte, O.: On the negative impact of team independence in microservices software development. In: 2th International Workshop on Microservices: Agile and DevOps Experience (MADE18) (2018)

5. Bogner, J., Zimmermann, A.: Adaptable digital enterprise architecture with microservices. In: 10th Advanced Summer School on Service Oriented Computing, pp. 59–61 (2016)

6. The Open Group: ArchiMate® 3.0.1 Specification. Open Gr. Stand. (2017)

7. The Open Group: The TOGAF® Standard, Version 9.2 (2018). https://publications.opengroup.org/standards/togaf/c182

8. Newman, S.: Building Microservices. O'Reilly Media, Sebastopol (2015)

9. Balakrushnan, S., Mamnoon, O., Bell, J., Currier, B., Harrington, Ed., Helstrom, B., Maloney, P., Martins, M.: Microservices Architecture. The Open Group, San Francisco (2016)

10. Yu, Y., Silveira, H., Sundaram, M.: A microservice based reference architecture model in the context of enterprise architecture. In: 2016 IEEE Advanced Information Management, Communicates, Electronic and Automation Control Conference (IMCEC), pp. 1856–1860 (2016). https://doi.org/10.1109/imcec.2016.7867539

11. Fowler, M., Lewis, J.: Microservices - a definition of this new architectural term. In: ThoughtWorks (2014). https://martinfowler.com/articles/microservices.html

12. Ramos, H., Vasconcelos, A.: eXtreme enterprise architecture planning. In: Proceedings of the 29th Annual ACM Symposium on Applied Computing - SAC 2014, pp. 1417–1419 (2014). https://doi.org/10.1145/2554850.2555130

13. Salah, T., Zemerly, M.J., Yeun, C.Y., Al-Qutayri, M., Al-Hammadi, Y.: The evolution of distributed systems towards microservices architecture. In: 2016 11th International Conference for Internet Technology and Secured Transactions (ICITST), pp. 318–325 (2016). https://doi.org/10.1109/icitst.2016.7856721

14. Drews, P., Schirmer, I., Horlach, B., Tekaat, C.: Bimodal enterprise architecture management: the emergence of a new EAM function for a BizDevOps-based fast IT. In: IEEE 21st International Enterprise Distributed Object Computing Workshop (EDOCW), pp. 57–64 (2017). https://doi.org/10.1109/edocw.2017.18

15. Zimmermann, A., Schmidt, R., Sandkuhl, K., Jugel, D., Bogner, J., Mohring, M.: Decision management for micro-granular digital architecture. In: Proceedings - IEEE International Enterprise Distributed Object Computing Workshop, EDOCW, pp. 29–38, October 2017. https://doi.org/10.1109/edocw.2017.14

16. Bogner, J., Zimmermann, A.: towards integrating microservices with adaptable enterprise architecture. In: Proceedings - IEEE International Enterprise Distributed Object Computing Workshop, EDOCW, pp. 158–163, September 2016. https://doi.org/10.1109/edocw.2016.7584392

17. The SOA Source Book - Microservices Architecture. The Open Group (2016). http://www.opengroup.org/soa/source-book/msawp/index.htm

18. Zimmermann, A., Bogner, J., Schmidt, R., Jugel, D., Schweda, C., Möhring, M.: Digital enterprise architecture with micro-granular systems and services. In: BIR Workshops (2016)

19. Haselböck, S., Weinreich, R., Buchgeher, G.: Decision models for microservices: design areas, stakeholders, use cases, and requirements. In: Lopes, A., de Lemos, R. (eds.) ECSA 2017. LNCS, vol. 10475, pp. 155–170. Springer, Cham (2017). https://doi.org/10.1007/978-3-319-65831-5_11

A Case Management Approach
to Risk Management

Tiago Ferreira, Diogo Gonçalves, Ricardo Vieira[(✉)],
Diogo Proença, and José Borbinha

INESC-ID, Instituto Superior Técnico, Universidade de Lisboa, Lisbon, Portugal
{tiago.barros.ferreira,diogo.p.goncalves,
rjcv,diogo.proenca,jlb}@tecnico.ulisboa.pt

Abstract. Risk management is a development activity and increasingly plays a crucial role in organization's management. Organizations develop and implement enterprise risk management strategies intending to improve their business model and bring them better results. Enterprise risk management strategies are based on the implementation of a risk management process and supporting structure. Together, this process and structure make a system. The ISO ISO 31000:2018 standard is currently the main global reference framework for risk management systems, proposing the general principles and guidelines, regardless of context. This standard depicts the process of risk management as a case rather than a sequential process flow. To that end, we explored the potential and limitations of the conceptual modeling language "Case Management Model and Notation" (CMMN) for the elaboration of the related conceptual conceptual diagrams, and the "Decision Model and Notation" (DMN) notation to model risk decisions. The application of the model is also demonstrated for a real case.

Keywords: Risk management · CMMN · DMN · Risk management process

1 Introduction

As described in [1], risk is the "effect of uncertainty on objectives", an effect being "a deviation from the expected". The effect can be positive, negative or both, and thus it can address, create or result in opportunities or threats. Still according to [1], risk can be expressed in terms of: (i) **Risk sources:** An element that, alone or in combination with others, has the potential to cause the risk; (ii) **Potential events:** Occurrence or change of a particular set of circumstances; (iii) **Consequences:** Outcome of an event that affects the objectives; and (iv) **Likelihood:** Chance of something happening.

In an organization, every process, from the simplest to the most complex, is subject to risks and its consequences can have positive or negative effects on the organizations' goals. Enterprise Risk Management (ERM) is thus a very important activity to support the achievement of the organizations' goals.

Risk management is defined as "coordinated activities to direct and control an organization with regard to risk" [1]. ERM, as a risk management activity, comprises the identification of the potential events in the whole organization that can affect the

B. Shishkov (Ed.): BMSD 2019, LNBIP 356, pp. 246–256, 2019.
https://doi.org/10.1007/978-3-030-24854-3_18

objectives, the respective risk appetite, and thus, with reasonable assurance, the fulfillment of the organization's goals [2].

Many organizations nowadays have their risk management framework, including activities to identify their risks, and their prevention measures, documented. To this end, ISO 31000 standard is at this moment the main reference for risk management frameworks, proposing the general principles and guidelines for risk management, regardless of their context.

The guidelines for risk management processes described in ISO 31000 suggest a process in which the flow is not always deterministic since each activity involves great collaboration between various types of actors and where deciding what to do next can depend on many factors. Moreover, different techniques, such as those described in [3], may be applied in risk identification and should consider several factors such as causes, events, consequences and risk sources. These facts make the problem potentially relevant to be modeled with CMMN, a modeling language that has been recently affirmed for this type of processes.

This paper is structured in five more sections. Section two presents the concept of case management and the CMMN language. In section three we propose a CMMN modelling of risk management as a case, for both the ISO 31000 standard and in section four for the application case of a real organization that has a defined ERM framework. Section five presents a comparative analysis on of those two models. Section six presents conclusions.

2   Case Management Model and Notation

Automating processes increases their efficiency. But not all processes can be automated, and as such, for situations where they require more flexibility, a proper approach is required in building the process where flow control is not used to describe the process. Case management empowers workers by providing them with access to all information about the process and giving them autonomy and control over how a process evolves, [4].

In this type of process, the main concepts are: (i) A set of unordered activities that can be performed completely to solve a business problem; (ii) Activities occur in an unpredictable order; (iii) Events determine the process; therefore, the resulting case may vary depending on the current event; (iv) External documents are a fundamental part of the process.

The Object Management Group (OMG) introduced CMMN [5], a notation to model and graphically express these knowledge-intensive and weakly-structured processes.

CMMN can be used in addition to BPMN. CMMN uses an event-centric and case file concept approach, bringing new flexibility to business process. CMMN can specify what can happen in a process, but not how it should happen. From this perspective, a case has two distinct phases, the design-time phase and the run-time phase. During the design-time phase the business analysts model the plan items that are always part of the case model and the discretionary items, that are modeled but are not immediately added to the execution plan. During the run-time phase case workers execute the plan executing the planned items and optionally add, in current time, discretionary items to the execution plan of the case instance. The flow control of the case is thus exercised by the case workers assigning them greater responsibility in the case.

The complete case behavior is modeled using the elements illustrated in Fig. 1[1], and is captured by the case plan model:

- **Stage:** It is an "episode" of the case. It groups various language elements including tasks, milestones, case file items, and events.
- **Task:** It is a unit of work. They can be divided into human blocking tasks, non-blocking human tasks, process-tasks, case-tasks, and decision-tasks.
- **Discretionary element (only for tasks and stages):** An element that can be added, to the execution plan of the case instance by the case worker.
- **Event listener:** Represents an event that may occur during a case instance. They distinguish themselves in timer event listener and user event listener.
- **Case file item:** All data and data structures stored in the case file. It can represent all kinds of data, including a data value in a database, a row in a database, a document, a spreadsheet, a picture, a video, a voice recording, a directory, a folder, etc.
- **Milestone:** Represents an achievable target, defined to enable evaluation of progress of the case. The completion of a set of tasks or the availability of key deliverables (information in the case file) typically leads to achieving a milestone.

Fig. 1. Graphical representation of the main elements of CMMN notation.

3   Modeling Risk Management as a Case

The Enterprise Architect modeling tool[2] was used to model the risk management processes of the two contexts under analysis (ISO 31000 and INCM).

The final diagram results from a careful analysis of the generic risk management process as described in [1]. Each requirement of the process was analyzed to extract the key factors to be covered. The result is represented in Fig. 2.

The S01 stage contains four blocking human tasks as they all must wait until the case worker associated with them completes the task. According to [1], the risk criteria "are dynamic and should be continually reviewed and amended, if necessary" which

---

[1] Adapted from Denis Gagné, BPMN-CMMN-DMN: An intro to the triple crown of process improvement standards, https://pt.slideshare.net/dgagne/bpmncmmndmn-an-intro-to-the-triple-crown-of-process-improvement-standards-denis-gagne (accessed April 5th, 2019).

[2] https://sparxsystems.com/.

means that T04 is not a mandatory task (discretionary task), and as a result the stage must contain a planning table. All the information created and used during this stage is kept in the F01 case file item, and each time it is modified the milestone M01 is achieved (milestone with repetition decorator). As top management oversees this stage, it is triggered by an IfPart entry criteria, which is a condition defined by top management. It is also triggered by the result of T13 (the OnPart entry criteria linked by T13). It has the repetition decorator, so it can be repeated multiple times (each time one of the entry criteria activates it), and the manual activation decorator, so it gives top

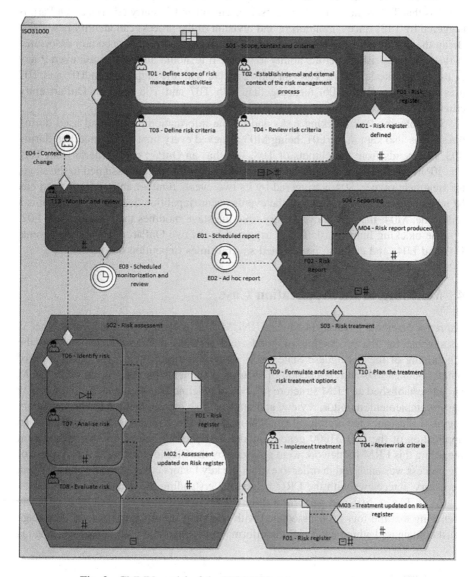

Fig. 2. CMMN model of the ISO31000 risk management process.

management the ability to decide if it should initiate the stage even if any of the entry criteria is true.

S02 contains three blocking human tasks, each one with the repetition decorator, so they can also be repeated each time their entry criteria are satisfied. All the information created and used during this stage is also kept in the F01, and each time it is modified M02 is achieved. S02 case worker is the risk owner, so the stage contains an IfPart entry criteria that is defined by the risk owner.

Since T08 uses the outputs from T07 and T07 uses the outputs from T06, the task T06 has an IfPart entry criteria defined by the risk owner (possibly defining the condition is that T06 is the first task of the stage. The other T06 entry criteria, an OnPart, is triggered by T13, since a monitoring and revision of the process can identify new risks. Being the risk owner in charge of this tasks, the manual activation decorator associated to the task gives risk owner the ability to decide if it should initiate the task even if any of the entry criteria is true. T08 can only execute with the outputs from T07 and T07 uses the outputs from T06, meaning that both T07 and T08 have an OnPart entry criteria associated with T06 and T07 respectively.

S03 contains four blocking tasks and all the information created and used during the stage is also kept in the F01, being M03 achieved every time F01 is modified during S03. It depends from the outputs of T08, so it has an OnPart entry criteria from T08. The IfPart entry criteria is a condition defined by the case worker assigned to the stage, the treatment owner. S04 is triggered by its two events (OnPart entry criteria) and can be repeated every time that any of the events occur (repetition decorator). It contains a milestone, M04, that is achieved every time the stage modifies the case file item F02.

The blocking human task T13 is triggered by its two OnPart entry criteria (events E03 and E04) and can also be repeated several times (repetition decorator).

4   Modeling of the Application Case

Imprensa Nacional – Casa da Moeda (INCM)[3] is a Portuguese organization that is responsible for the production of goods and services that are fundamental to the functioning of the Portuguese State, such as the minting of coins, the publication of official publications and production of security documents like the citizen card. INCM already established an ERM structure [6], where it defined the elements to continuously design, implement, monitor, review, and improve risk management in the organization. Figure 3 illustrates the high level CMMN model of the application case, defined as an application of the ISO 31000 generic model described in Sect. 3. All documentation regarding this ERM framework were provided by the CRO of the INCM. Each phase of the process was analyzed in order to extract the key factors covered by the phase. When necessary, interviews with the CRO helped understanding the details.

As in Fig. 4, S01 can perform a different set of activities for each case instance, menacing that the four tasks associated with this stage are discretionary, and the stage must contain a planning table. All the information created and used during this stage is

---

[3] https://www.incm.pt/.

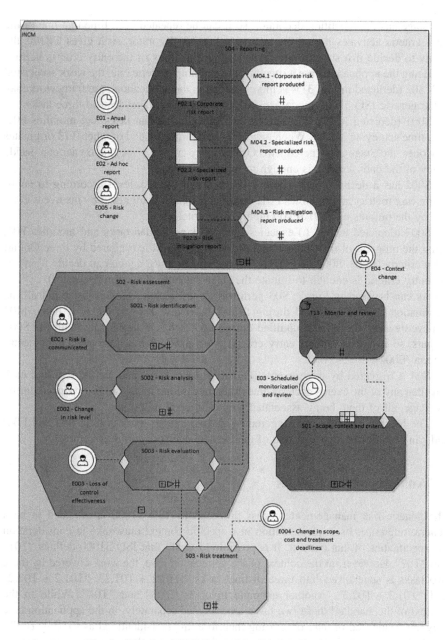

Fig. 3. High level CMMN model of the application case.

kept in the F01, and each time it is modified, M01 is achieved (milestone with the repetition decorator). Being the Corporate risk management committee (CRMC) in charge of this stage, it is triggered by an IfPart entry criteria, which is a condition defined by CRMC. It is also triggered by T13 (the OnPart entry criteria linked by T13).

The stage has the repetition decorator, so it can be repeated each time that one of the entry criteria activates it, and the manual activation decorator, so it gives CRMC the ability to decide if it should initiate the stage even if any of the entry criteria is true.

Being the application case a specific case and not a generic one, the work associated with S02 (depicted in Fig. 3) was more detailed in the application case framework than in the generic ISO 31000 model, so S02 contains three stages instead three tasks.

S001 (depicted in Fig. 5) executes two blocking human tasks and modifies F01, each time achieving M02.1. When new risks are communicated or when T13 originates new ones, the Stage is triggered (two OnPart entry criteria). The risk owner can decide if any of the entry criteria is enough to initiate the stage.

S002 has a decision task where it is calculated the risk level according to application case metrics and modifies F01, reaching M02.2 It is triggered by the event E002 and by the outputs of S001 (two OnPart entry criteria).

S003 (depicted in Fig. 6) executes four blocking human tasks and modifies F01, being the progress of this stage associated with M02.3. It is triggered by three OnPart entry criteria (E003, S002 and S03). The risk owner, once again, can decide if any of the entry criteria is enough to initiate the stage (manual activation decorator).

As can be seen in Fig. 7, S03 performs three blocking human tasks and all the information created and used during this stage is also kept in the F01, being M03 achieved every time F01 is modified during S03. It has a dependency with the S003 outputs, so it has an OnPart entry criteria from S003. It has a second OnPart entry criteria (E004).

S04 is triggered by three events (OnPart entry criteria) and can be repeated each time that any of the events occur. Three different case file items can be produced during the stage, all of them being associated with a different milestone.

The blocking task T13 is triggered by its two OnPart entry criteria E03 and E04) and can be repeated any time one of the events occur (repetition decorator).

5 Analysis of the Results

The generic risk management process proposed by ISO 31000 is intended to be a generic reference. Its implementation in a specific context must take in consideration the specificities of that context. It is possible to verify that ISO 31000 defines "T01" and "T02". However, in the context of the application case, the work covered by these two tasks is specialized into three distinct tasks: "T01.1 + T01.2", "T01.2 + T02.2" and "T01.3 + T02.3". Another example involves "T03" and "T04". While in the context of the standard these two tasks are modeled separately, in the application case they are condensed in only one, being therefore this task identified as "T03 + T04".

A final example is the fact that the standard foresees the creation of one generic report, being identified as "F02" while the application case foresees the creation of three different types of risk reports, which are therefore identified as "F02.1", "F02.2" and "F02.3".

Also, in the application case are new specific elements not detailed in ISO 31000:

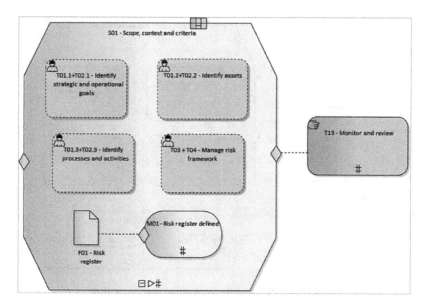

Fig. 4. Stage S01 of the application case expanded.

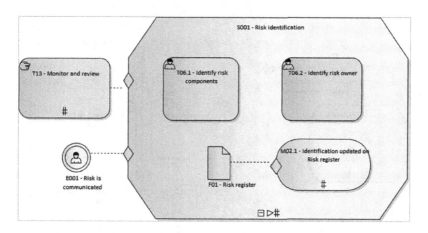

Fig. 5. Stage S001 of the application case expanded.

- **"E001", "E002", "E003" and "E004":** This results from the fact that the application case is a specific case and so it defines in his process a set of specific events that fit their context;
- **"T001":** This is relevant because INCM has its specific risks categorized, which does not exist in a generic reference as the ISO 31000 standard;

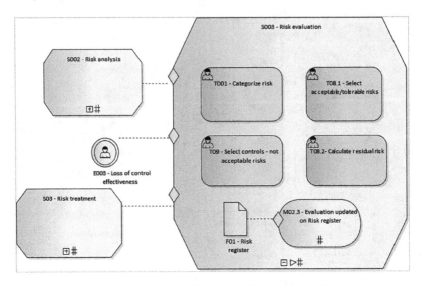

Fig. 6. Stage S003 of the application case expanded.

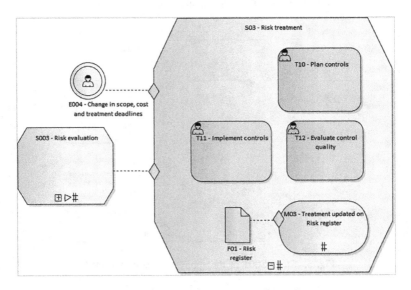

Fig. 7. Stage S03 of the application case expanded.

- **"S001", "S002" and "S003":** These are derived from the CMMN language modeling syntax. Wanting to decompose a task into multiple tasks it is necessary to include them in a stage. Taking as an example the risk identification phase: while the standard identifies that phase as a task ("T06"), in the application case context the risk identification phase includes "T06.1", "T06.2", "F01" and "M02.1". Thus, all these elements are grouped within the stage "S001- Risk Identification".

A final example of the specialization of the application case relates to an extra entry criterion in stage "S003". As in Fig. 2, "T08" only contains the entry criteria activated by "T07", while in Fig. 3, "S003" contains the entry criteria activated by "S002" and "S003" (the entry criteria related to "E003", as explained above, is due to the fact that INCM defines in its process specific events that fit its context). This derives from the process stage where each one performs "T09" and "T12". While in the context of the standard "T09" and "T12" are executed in "S03", in the context of application case "T09" is executed in "S003" and "T12" in "S03". Since "T12" can initiate a new execution of "T09", the latter being modeled in different steps as in the application case process, it is necessary that the stage where "T12" is inserted re-activates the stage where "T09" is inserted, thus forcing a new entry criteria associated with "S003".

6   Conclusion

The implementation of an efficient ERM presents itself as a competitive advantage in the business world. Although not mandatory, the organizations, including the application case detailed in this paper, have been developing ERM structures following the good practices described in [1] and [2].

Although organizations try to automate their processes in order to optimize their work pace and maximize profit, many of these processes involve collaboration between various types of stakeholders and are event dependent. The growth of case management techniques, namely the CMMN, has been playing an important role in supporting this kind of processes that are unpredictable, knowledge intensive and weakly structured.

In this paper an intensive analysis was performed on both the process described in the ISO31000 standard and the application case framework and it was concluded that they were both capable of being modeled through the CMMN language. From the resulting of the case model it was possible to establish a comparison between the two processes and to conclude that the process described in the application case follows the model proposed in the standard.

CMMN, as a recent modeling language, still lacks references to help in its practical application. We expect to have contributed to that by publishing this work.

Acknowledgements. This work was supported by national funds through Fundação para a Ciência e a Tecnologia (FCT) with reference UID/CEC/50021/2019.

References

1. International Organization for Standardization: ISO 31000:2018(E), Risk management - guidelines (2018)
2. Committee of Sponsoring Organizations of the Treadway Commission: ERM - Integrating with Strategy and Performance (2017)
3. International Organization for Standardization: ISO/IEC 31010:2009, risk management – risk assessment techniques, Geneva, Switzerland (2009)
4. Object Management Group: Case Management Model and Notation (CMMN), 01 December 2016. http://www.omg.org/spec/CMMN/1.1

5. Marin, M.: Introduction to the Case Management Model and Notation (CMMN), 18 August 2016. https://arxiv.org/pdf/1608.05011.pdf%20-%20conceitos%20cmmn22.pdf. Accessed 26 Apr 2018
6. Vieira, R.: PA18 - Descrição do processo. Framework de gestão de riscos corporativos. INCM (2018)

Analysing Enterprise Ontology
and Its Suitability for Model-Based
Software Development

José Cordeiro[1,2(✉)]

[1] INCITE – Centre for Innovation in Science and Technology,
IPS, Setúbal, Portugal
jose.cordeiro@estsetubal.ips.pt
[2] Setúbal School of Technology, Polytechnic Institute of Setúbal,
Campus do IPS, Setúbal, Portugal

Abstract. Enterprise Ontology (EO) is a well-known theory that captures the essence of an organisation. It is rooted in the Language Action Perspective that acknowledges language as the primary dimension of human cooperative activity. This theory, proposed by Jan Dietz, provides the foundations for designing and engineering of enterprises seen as social information systems. In this paper, we analyse some fundamental aspects of EO using an adapted framework for comparing methodologies. We present also a systematic review of the literature to find how EO and its modelling methodology are used to develop enterprise software applications.

Keywords: Enterprise Ontology · Enterprise engineering · DEMO ·
Language action perspective · Information systems ·
Information systems development · Model-Based software development

1 Introduction

Enterprise Ontology (EO) is a well-known theory that captures the essence of any organisation. This theory, proposed by Jan Dietz [1], provides the foundations for designing and engineering of enterprises seen as social information systems. It is rooted in the Language Action Perspective [see 2] that acknowledges language as the primary dimension of human cooperative activity. Jan Dietz introduces the Ψ-theory defined by four axioms and one theorem that gives its theoretical basis. For designing and engineering organizations, EO is supported by the DEMO[1] methodology that defines a modelling method composed by four distinct aspect models. These models are represented by diagrams and/or auxiliary tables and lists and they express the essential of an Enterprise – its *construction,* independent of its implementation – its *function* [1].

In this paper, we present an analysis of EO, using a simple framework for comparing methodologies, proposed in [3] and adapted for our analysis. Also, a systematic review of the literature on Enterprise Ontology is conducted to understand how EO, in

---

[1] DEMO stands for Design & Engineering Methodology for Organizations.

© Springer Nature Switzerland AG 2019
B. Shishkov (Ed.): BMSD 2019, LNBIP 356, pp. 257–269, 2019.
https://doi.org/10.1007/978-3-030-24854-3_19

particular the DEMO models, is used to produce real computer applications for enterprises.

This paper is organized as follows: Sect. 2 gives a brief overview of EO, Sect. 3 presents our analysis of this theory, Sect. 4 is dedicated to the systematic literature review, Sect. 5 concludes and points some future research directions.

2 Enterprise Ontology

Enterprise Ontology (EO) is focused on the ontological level of organizations. At this level, it looks at people, the way they interact, commit themselves and produce results. The fundamental elements are *language acts* produced by people that generate commitments to act, and triggers the real actions that support the functioning of organizations. The central modelling element is the Business Transaction, depicted in Fig. 1, that defines a pattern of *language acts*. EO is about the construction and operation of an organization. The Ψ-theory establishes the theoretical support for EO.

2.1 The Ψ-Theory

The Ψ-theory [1] is defined in four axioms and one theorem. The first axiom – **the Operation Axiom** – presents an organization as a group of actors performing two types of acts: coordination acts (C-acts) and production acts (P-acts). C-acts are *language acts* used by actors to engage themselves in commitments and to ultimately originate the P-acts that produce the effective work. The result of performing a C-act is a coordination fact (C-fact), whereas the result of performing a P-act is a production fact (P-fact) which convey the information about *world changes* resulting from these actions. The second axiom – **the Transaction Axiom** – comes from the observation that P-acts and C-acts occur within a universal pattern so called a *business transaction*. This transaction is a key concept of the Ψ-theory and EO. The complete transaction pattern is seen as a *socionomic* law that underlies the conducting of any business always and everywhere. This transaction has its roots in the notions of conversation for action [2] and the Workflow Loop [5] both from the Language Action Perspective (LAP). In Fig. 1 we depict the basic transaction pattern that has three phases: an *order phase*, where the negotiation about the P-act to be executed takes place. In this phase two types of C-acts are performed: a request by the initiator actor and a promise to accomplish it by the executor actor. The next phase is the *execution phase* where the P-act is performed. Finally, the *result phase* ends the transaction with a C-act stating the execution completion and a C-act accepting its result. The third axiom – **the Composition Axiom** – is concerned with the interrelation between P-facts in a *production world* (P-world). Finally, the fourth axiom – **the Distinction Axiom** – is about the human abilities that have a significant role in performing C-acts namely the *performa*, *informa* and *forma* abilities. The performa ability is considered the essential human ability for doing business and is part of the ontological level of EO. **The Organization Theorem** completes the Ψ-theory by stating that "the organization of an enterprise is a heterogeneous system that is constituted as the layered integration of

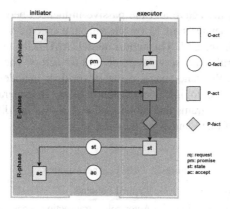

Fig. 1. The basic transaction pattern (adapted from [4])

three homogeneous systems: the B-organization (from business), the I-organization (from intellect), and the D-organization (from Document)" [111, p. 115].

2.2 The DEMO Methodology

The DEMO methodology defines the steps for designing and engineering organizations and uses a modelling representation composed by four distinct aspect models: the construction model, the process model, the action model and the state model that together constitutes the complete ontological knowledge of an organization (Fig. 2). **The construction model (CM)** specifies transactions types, associated actors' roles and information banks (conceptual stores of C-facts or P-facts). The CM is divided in two similar models: the interaction model (IAM) and the interpretive model (ISM) that

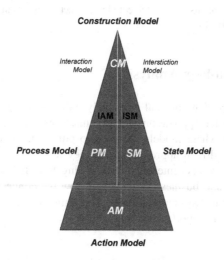

Fig. 2. The four DEMO aspect models (adapted from [1])

shows us respectively the active and the passive influences between actor roles. **The process model (PM)** details the CM by showing the specific transaction patterns for each transaction type in the CM. **The action model (AM)** is the most detailed level and it specifies the action rules that serve as guidelines for actors. The last model, **the state model (SM)** specifies the state space of the P-world. It includes object classes, fact types, result types and ontological coexistence rules. In general, these models are expressed by different diagrams and tables. Table 1 shows the different diagrams and tables used by each of them and what they depict.

Table 1. DEMO aspect models

Model	Expressed by	Typical contents
Interaction	Actor Transaction Diagram (ATD)	Actor roles, transaction types and their connecting links
	Transactions Result Table (TRT)	Transaction and result types
Process	Process Structure Diagram (PSD)	C-act/C-result, P-act/P-result, causal and conditional links and responsibility areas of actor roles
	Information Use Table (IUT)	Process steps and object class, fact types or result types
Action	Action Rule Specifications (ARS)	Action rules
State	Object Fact Diagram (OFD)	Object classes, fact types, result types and existential laws
	Object Property List (OPL)	Property types, object classes, scales
Interstriction	Actor Bank Diagram (ABD)	Information banks, actor roles and information links
	Bank Contents Table (BCT)	Object classes, fact types, result types and production banks

3 Enterprise Ontology Analysis

It should be emphasised that our goal is to analyse the use of EO models for effective development of computer applications for organisations. This can be achieved by a model-based approach where models are used to guide the development process, or otherwise, by a model-driven approach where they are used to generate part of the application code. We are also interested in knowing how EO sees, understands and models organisational and business systems and how the connection between models and technical or computer systems is made. The philosophical stance and its related view is, in this sense, an important aspect.

3.1   The Analysis Framework

Establishing a proper analysis scope and focus is not an easy task (e.g. 3), therefore we adapted and used a framework for comparing methodologies proposed in [3]. Also, given the different possible meanings of methodology, method or approach, it is important to understand what Avison and Fitzgerald in [3] mean by "a methodology":

"A systems development methodology is a recommended means to achieve the development, or part of the development, of information systems based on a set of rationales and an underlying philosophy that supports, justifies and makes coherent such a recommendation for a particular context. The recommended means usually includes the identification of phases, procedures, tasks, rules, techniques, guidelines, documentation and tools. They might also include recommendations concerning the management and organisation of the approach and the identification and training of the participants" [3].

According to this description, a methodology also includes its underlying principles that contain the philosophy or paradigm and partially the view correspondent to the followed approach.

The framework proposed by Avison and Fitzgerald is composed of 7 steps as follows:

1. **Philosophy** – regards the principle, or set of principles, that underlie the methodology composed by the following factors:
   (i)   Paradigm – the world view, simplistically differentiated by the science versus the system paradigms. It can also be analysed according to the ontological and epistemological stance adopted.
   (ii)   Objectives – focus in understanding if the target system would be a purely technical, computerised system or, otherwise will cover the organisational and business aspects as well.
   (iii) Domain – the scope of its application regarding the problems it addresses such as narrow problems or larger organisational problems.
   (iv)   Target – regards its applicability as specifically target for a problem or general purpose.
2. **Model** – concerns the modelling representational aspects of the methodology. They capture the problem essence and the way the methodology sees the world. Models can be (a) verbal, (b) analytical or mathematical, (c) iconic, pictorial, or schematic or (d) use simulation.
3. **Techniques and tools** – refer to, in the case of techniques, document aids such as models and diagrams used to analyse and/or represent the methodology or, in the case of tools, to computer applications that help carrying the methodology.
4. **Scope** – the different covered stages of the systems development life cycle.
5. **Output** – the deliverables produced in the different phases of the development process.
6. **Practice** – relates to the practical aspects such as methodology background, user base or participants.
7. **Product** – the methodology as a commercial product, what it delivers.

This framework includes some steps not important for our analysis such as the product step and, some too broad to be considered in just one step such as the philosophy step. Therefore, an adapted version of this framework was created that is shown in Table 2. In this adapted framework steps 5, 6 and 7 of the original frameworks were removed because they address practical aspects of the information development process that are not directly related to the substantive development of information systems. Steps 3 and 4 were kept, step 2 was slightly changed and, step 1 was split in two separate steps. In this last case, the paradigm adopted by EO is an important aspect of its approach that needs to be highlighted, the added step of application domain combines the remaining factors of the original philosophy step.

Table 2. A Framework for analysing EO

Step	Name	Description
1	Philosophy	The paradigm or philosophical stance adopted by the methodology such as its ontology and epistemology
2	Application Domain	Type of problems and environments addressed
3	Representation	Representational aspects such as visual models, formal languages, simulation, and the emphasis of its specific view of the world
4	Techniques and Tools	Applications and representational aids to the information system development process
5	Scope	Covered stages of the information system life cycle development process

3.2   EO/DEMO Analysis

Philosophy. EO claims to follow a social constructivist philosophical stance as Jan Dietz asserts [1, pg. 8]. To these stances he adds the functionalist and the interpretive paradigm explaining that EO follows a functionalist approach. However, this functionalist approach is built upon the interpretative perspective of LAP resulting in the complementary use of both paradigms. Effectively, although based on social constructivism and interpretivism, EO has an objectivist basis. This is reinforced by its ontological model that defines formally and precisely its world view.

Application Domain. Regarding the application domain EO is directed towards the organisational and business environment. Although it is applied to any kind of business activity system, it is used mainly to model systems where interaction and communication between humans play a fundamental role. In this sense, it can be used to model information systems where there is no associated information technology.

Representation. For representation purposes, EO relies in a group of four distinct aspect models namely the construction model, the process model, the action model and the state model, which captures the essence of an organisation. These models are used to show the essential business structure and business processes based on the business transaction pattern. Given this basis, the view focus is language-action acts performed by individuals delegating to a secondary role the details of originated production-acts. EO aspect models, besides providing diagrammatically the structural and process view uses a pseudo-algorithmic language to express action rules.

Techniques and Tools. EO has a complete modelling method for creating the aspect models of a system. This method covers rigorously all details of the modelling process and, it is the key technique used by EO. Concerning tools, EO has several tools available to support it. In this case, there are at least, seven commercial applications for helping to write aspect models diagrams [6].

Scope. EO covers mainly the problem analysis and requirements phases; however, the produced diagrams are sufficiently objective to help deriving the implementation. They include all the design details to create supporting databases and workflow systems. There is only a limitation in the type of systems that can be built that is restricted to systems where human communication plays the major role.

EO is based in the LAP soft ideas, but its definition and application reveals a formal approach with all modelling details carefully developed, and without presenting objective problems. We think the main issue in this theory relies in its excessive focus on the business transaction pattern for modelling organisations. This pattern, based in the workflow loop and the basic conversation for action mentioned before, is built from a group of communicative acts, mainly assertive and commissive, missing other kinds of language acts and other possible patterns. In fact, in many situations the business transaction pattern is not fully matched, there are cases where parts of the pattern may not be present. Also, in many situations several human actions are not considered because they do not participate in a business transaction pattern. An additional issue in the business transaction pattern and in EO models in general, is the relatively small importance given to production acts. These acts are not seen as belonging to the essential or ontological level of an organisation and so, they are sent to a secondary level. Many times, these acts constitute the major human action performed and their analysis and detailing would be of utmost importance for the organisation model.

Due to the focus on communication, also resources or physical elements are not completely addressed and modelled as they are seen as not belonging to the ontological level.

Besides the problems faced due to the exclusive use of the business pattern also the overall representation in EO has a relatively narrow scope as it only addresses a particular type of business processes although they are understood as the essential business processes of an organisation.

3.3   EO/DEMO Discussion

The view proposed by EO based on LAP is much different from other approaches. This view emphasises *intentional human communication* with the purpose of *change the world*. From this perspective, any human form of organisation, no matter how primitive it is, can be effectively modelled. A drawback of this view is that by basing a system in the way things get done, EO misses how they are really done. Much work is produced under the so-called 'production-acts' that is underestimated. From a technical perspective a lot of support may be given in computer applications to production acts that don't have any modelling support.

In a general view of EO/DEMO, we think there are many benefits in adopting this approach such as:

- EO is supported by strong philosophical roots originated in LAP and further developed and enhanced in a powerful ontological model. The social and human aspects are omnipresent because it is based on human communication. Social and business aspects like commitment and responsibility can be directly derived from EO models.
- The focus on language acts is also a focus on human aspects and particularly in human acts that should be an advantage when modelling organisational reality.
- EO is a very well elaborated theory leading to the engineering of a system according to a well-defined and rigorous methodology and modelling formalism. This allows for a precise and objective system creation.

As expected, there is also a list of some identified drawbacks:

- The strength about considering and model human communications can also be a weakness because it misses other human actions thrown to a secondary role.
- Underlying EO there is a business process modelling orientation plus an interaction structural view missing other organisational aspects and views.
- The excessive formalisation provided by the ontological model and its expression in WOSL leads to a rigid structure that may have problems to cope with change. The meaning of terms related to nouns and relationships is understood as universal within a world ontology and this may lead to adaptation and change issues.
- Practical applications are limited in scope because they are restricted by a necessary relationship with language acts. Other types of organisational applications are not easily derived from EO models.
- There is not a direct relationship between EO models and their software applications besides the definition of actor role agendas related to task management systems. EO models reflect a view of an organisation and not a view to be used as part of an application design.

4   Systematic Review of the EO Literature

To understand how EO is used in computer applications, the IT part of an information system, we conducted a systematic review of the literature that is presented in the next sections.

4.1   Systematic Review Process and Preliminary Results

To find EO relevant papers, we searched first for the terms "Enterprise Ontology" and "Dietz" using the B-on Search Engine [7] and second for all citations to the Enterprise Ontology book of Dietz [1] using the Google Scholar [8]. We think that a reference to this book is almost mandatory in any paper related to EO. As a result we received about

2820 results from the first search and 1100 from the second one. From both searches we retrieved all full texts available. After removing all duplicates, we end up with a total of 635 documents. A simple analysis allowed us to exclude 15 incomplete papers, 26 papers that didn't refer EO, 81 thesis and 11 documents that weren't EO articles. From the remaining 502 documents, 331 just made a reference to EO without any relevant relationship to EO. Therefore, our analysis is based on 171 papers.

4.2 Intermediate Results with Paper Clusters Found

From the analysis of the 171 papers in this step, we found 4 clusters of papers with more than 5 papers that are based in the same ideas that we think it is worth mentioning. These clusters are presented in Table 3, with the total papers found and just one selected reference for space reasons. Follows their descriptions:

1. The first cluster, is based in a theory that extends EO with Engestrom's Activity Theory [10]. In this case, a set of rules are defined for integrating EO business transactions with notions from Activity Theory.
2. The second cluster, is supported by the idea of integrating of DEMO and Value Modelling [11]. By including Function, Value and Purpose concepts in EO, the authors seek to improve system model quality.
3. The third cluster, introduces a new system modelling approach – NOMIS [13] – that incorporate the concepts of EO in one of its views, the interaction view. It is based on human *observable* actions, where the "human" language acts from the business transactions are incorporated.
4. The last cluster, relates to the SDBC approach [15] that considers the static, dynamic and information viewpoints both in the business modelling and software design of business systems. DEMO, in this approach, is used as an extension of the business modelling dynamic viewpoint.

Table 3. Clusters of related papers using EO

Cluster	#Papers	Description	Refs.
1	12	Extends EO with Activity Theory	[9]
2	11	Adds Value Modelling to EO	[12]
3	8	Focus in human actions, using EO concepts in its interaction view	[14]
4	5	Incorporate EO in its dynamic business modelling view	[16]

All papers in these clusters are related to information or business systems modelling, where the models can be used for an analysis phase of an information system development (ISD). However, none of them presented a real application derived from their models.

We also found a set of 17 theoretical papers, 12 of them authored by Jan Dietz.

In the remaining papers, 33 presented and used aspect models of different case studies to analyze enterprises from different perspectives, such as quality, auditing, governance, etc. Another 17 are dedicated to comparisons between EO/DEMO with other approaches, 18 are about reengineering enterprises with EO/DEMO, 20 propose an integration of EO/DEMO with other theories and 10 are purely technical, 7 of them related to how to derive aspect models from other modelling methods. From the remaining 20 papers, only 13 presented computer applications.

4.3 Final Results

We identified just 13 papers referring computer applications, the complete list is depicted in Table 4. In this list, the work of Liu and Iijima, P6 [22] and P5 [21] is the most relevant. They developed DEMO++ [22], an ontology-based conceptual model for simulation that combines ontology with implementation, allowing for the simulation of DEMO models. DEMO++ is also used in P1 [17] in the simulation of an healthcare system. Simulation was also addressed earlier by Joseph Barjis, P9 [25] and P12 [28], where a simulation application based on Petri nets is used. Still related to simulation, Ribeiro et al., P3 [19], uses multiagent systems to study the effects of cooperation in business organizational settings modelled with DEMO. Another approach is followed by Marques and Santos, P4 [20], that created a prototype that implements a database for organizational transactions based on EO. Their intent is to monitor these transactions in real time. Heng and Liu, P2 [18], integrate language-action into blogs to control collaborative processes, although its application doesn't use DEMO as it is, instead they extend DEMO' language acts by using more types of language acts. Dvorak et al., P7 [23], designed a confirmation engine based on the transaction axiom of the PSI theory. Ran and Nayak, P8 [24], developed a Web application that validate its EO model that integrates different aspects of knowledge externalization. Papagiannis et al., P10 [26], introduced a measurable value-added

Table 4. EO papers presenting computer applications

Paper	Title	Refs.
1	A Design and Engineering Methodology for Organization-based simulation model for operating room scheduling problems	[17]
2	A new standard of on-line customer service process: Integrating language-action into blogs	[18]
3	Agent-Based Simulation and Cooperation in Business Organizational Settings	[19]
4	An Enterprise Ontology-Based Database for Continuous Monitoring Application	[20]
5	Automatic Model Transformation for Enterprise Simulation	[21]
6	Business process simulation in the context of enterprise engineering	[22]
7	Confirmation Engine Design Based on PSI Theory	[23]
8	ENTERPRISE ONTOLOGY MODEL FOR TACIT KNOWLEDGE EXTERNALIZATION IN SOCIO-TECHNICAL ENTERPRISES	[24]
9	Executable Ontological Business Process Model	[25]
10	National Patient Flow Framework: An Ontological Patient-Oriented Redesign	[26]
11	NEXT: Generating Tailored ERP Applications from Ontological Enterprise Models	[27]
12	The importance of business process modeling in software systems design	[28]
13	UNIVERSAL ENTERPRISE ADAPTIVE OBJECT MODEL: A SEMANTIC WEB-BASED IMPLEMENTATION OF ORGANIZATIONAL SELF-AWARENESS	[29]

patient flow in a healthcare system. The ontological rules which govern this flow are designed in Xemod and encompassed in a CLIPS knowledge base. Van der Schuur et al., P11 [27], introduce NEXT, a novel model-driven software generation approach with the goal of generating ERP software tailored to the needs of the modelled enterprise. Although, this application is still in the "design phase". The last paper of Aveiro and Pinto, P13 [29], also proposed a model-driven approach that aims providing modelling constructs and a method for continuous update of its models as reality changes. However is still under development.

4.4 Discussion

From this systematic review of literature, it is evident a lack of proper computer applications within the EO/DEMO approach. Also, most application developed are related to model the organization, being for organizational analysis, or simulation. As mentioned before the aspect models of DEMO, have a business process nature embedded in its Business Transaction Pattern, although we didn't find any application using this perspective. A possible application, in this case, would be a task management system to manage all C-acts and P-acts. Another possibility, would be an implementation of a fact base for all C-facts and P-facts, and a rule database to store the action model rules.

5 Conclusions

This paper analysed Enterprise Ontology, its modelling artefacts, as the basis for developing computer applications. A first empirical analysis is done using an adaptation of the framework proposed in [3] for methodologies comparison. Different strengths and weakness were identified. To complete this analysis with facts, a systematic review of EO/DEMO literature was undertaken, with a primary goal to identify computer applications obtained using this approach. Results shown that there is shortage in this type of deliverables when applying the EO/DEMO approach.

References

1. Dietz, J.: Enterprise Ontology, Theory and Methodology. Springer, Heidelberg (2006). https://doi.org/10.1007/3-540-33149-2
2. Winograd, T., Flores, F.: Understanding Computers and Cognition. Ablex Publishing Corporation, Norwood (1986)
3. Avison, D., Fitzgerald, G.: Information Systems Development: Methodologies, Techniques and Tools, 3rd edn. McGraw-Hill Education, Maidenhead (2003)
4. Dietz, J.L.: The deep structure of business processes. Commun. ACM **49**(5), 58–64 (2006)
5. Medina-Mora, R., Winograd, T., Flores, R., Flores, F.: The action workflow approach to workflow management technology. In: Turner, J., Kraut, R. (eds.) Proceedings of the 4th Conference on Computer Supported Cooperative Work. ACM, New York (1992)
6. DEMO Tools – Enterprise engineering website. http://www.ee-institute.org/en/demo/tools. Accessed Mar 2019

7. B-on: Online Knowledge Library. https://www.b-on.pt/en/. Accessed Mar 2019
8. Google Scholar. https://scholar.google.com/. Accessed Mar 2019
9. Gonçalves, A.: Capturing activity diagrams from ontological model. Int. J. Res. Bus. Technol. **2**(3), 33–44 (2013). https://doi.org/10.17722/ijrbt.v2i3.57
10. Engestrom, Y.: Learning by Expanding: An Activity Theoretical Approach to Developmental Research. Orienta-Konsultit, Helsinki (1987)
11. Gordijn, J., Akkermans, J.M.: Value-based requirements engineering: exploring innovative e-commerce ideas. Requirements Eng. **8**(2), 114–134 (2003). https://doi.org/10.1007/s00766-003-0169-x
12. Pombinho, J., Aveiro, D., Tribolet, J.: A matching ontology for e3Value and DEMO – a sound bridging of business modelling and enterprise engineering. In: 2014 IEEE 16th Conference on Business Informatics, vol. 2, pp. 17–24 (2014). https://doi.org/10.1109/CBI.2014.48
13. Cordeiro, J.: Normative Approach to Information Systems Modelling. Ph.D. thesis. The University of Reading, UK (2011)
14. Cordeiro, J.: A new way of modelling information systems and business processes – the NOMIS approach. In: Shishkov, B. (ed.) Business Modeling and Software Design. BMSD 2014. Lecture Notes in Business Information Processing, vol. 220, pp. 102–118. Springer, Cham (2015)
15. Shishkov, B.: Software specification based on re-usable business components. Ph.D. thesis, Delft University of Technology. Sieca Repro, Delft, The Netherlands (2005)
16. Shishkov, B., Quartel, D.: Combining SDBC and ISDL in the Modeling and Refinement of Business Processes BT - Enterprise Information Systems. Springer, Heidelberg (2008). Manolopoulos, Y., Filipe, J., Constantopoulos, P., Cordeiro, J. (eds.)
17. Yahia, Z., Iijima, J., Harraz, N.A., Eltawil, A.B.: A design and engineering methodology for organization-based simulation model for operating room scheduling problems. SIMULATION Trans. Soc. Model. Simul. **93**(5), 363–378 (2017). https://doi.org/10.1177/0037549716687376
18. Yang, H.-L., Liu, C.-L.: A new standard of on-line customer service process: integrating language-action into blogs. Comput. Stan. Interfaces **31**(1), 227–245 (2009). https://doi.org/10.1016/j.csi.2007.12.003
19. Ribeiro, C., Borbinha, J., Tribolet, J., Pereira, J.: Agent-based simulation and cooperation in business organizational settings. In: The Fourth International Conference on Advances in System Simulation, SIMUL 2012, pp. 58–63 (2012)
20. Marques, R.P., Santos, H., Santos, C.: An enterprise ontology-based database for continuous monitoring application. In: 2013 IEEE 15th Conference on Business Informatics (CBI), pp. 7–12 (2013). https://doi.org/10.1109/CBI.2013.10
21. Liu, Y., Iijima, J.: Automatic model transformation for enterprise simulation. In: Aveiro, D., Tribolet, J., Gouveia, D. (eds.) EEWC 2014. LNBIP, vol. 174, pp. 136–150. Springer, Cham (2014). https://doi.org/10.1007/978-3-319-06505-2_10
22. Liu, Y., Iijima, J.: Business process simulation in the context of enterprise engineering. J. Simul. **9**(3), 206–222 (2015). https://doi.org/10.1057/jos.2014.35
23. Dvorák, O., Pergl, R., Kroha, P.: Confirmation engine design based on PSI theory. In: 17th IEEE Conference on Business Informatics, Workshop on Cross-Organizational and Crosscompany BPM (XOC-BPM), Lisbon (2015)
24. Rao, S.S., Nayak, A.: Enterprise ontology model for tacit knowledge externalization in socio-technical enterprises. Interdisc. J. Inf. Knowl. Manag. **12** (2017)
25. Barjis, J.: Executable ontological business process model. In: ECIS, pp. 2086–2097 (2007)

26. Papagiannis, F., Roudsari, A., Danas, K.: National patient flow framework: an ontological patient-oriented redesign. In: International Perspectives in Health Informatics, vol. 164 (2011). https://doi.org/10.3233/978-1-60750-709-3-305

27. van der Schuur, H., et al.: NEXT: generating tailored ERP applications from ontological enterprise models. In: Poels, G., Gailly, F., Serral Asensio, E., Snoeck, M. (eds.) PoEM 2017. LNBIP, vol. 305, pp. 283–298. Springer, Cham (2017). https://doi.org/10.1007/978-3-319-70241-4_19

28. Barjis, J.: The importance of business process modeling in software systems design. Sci. Comput. Program. **71**(1), 73–87 (2008)

29. Aveiro, D., Pinto, D.: Universal enterprise adaptive object model: a semantic web-based implementation of organizational self-awareness. Intell. Syst. Acc. Financ. Manag. **22**(1), 3–28 (2015)

Business Process Model Driven Automatic Software Requirements Generation

Salam Turkman⬡ and Adel Taweel$^{(✉)}$ ⬡

Computer Science, Birzeit University, Birzeit, Palestine
salma.turk@gmail.com, ataweel@birzeit.edu

Abstract. Requirement engineering is a critical stage in software engineering, it enables requirement engineers extract correct system needs, both functional and non-functional constraints from stakeholders. The majority of the errors found in software functionality are directly linked to the mistakes made during the requirement elicitation phases. Therefore, several approaches have been proposed to enhance existing requirements engineering techniques to both reduce such mistakes and to speed up the requirements engineering process. One type of promising approaches is based on utilizing business process modelling to take benefit from business process models to derive requirements. This paper argues that it is possible to generate requirements from business process models. It proposes an approach to derive system requirements; it employs business process models and then transforms them into requirement models. Evaluation shows the proposed approach was able to generate additional valid use case model features compared to other competing approaches.

Keywords: Requirement engineering · Business process modelling · Use case model

1 Introduction

Requirement engineering is a critical stage in software development [11]. Employing effective requirements engineering techniques and methods are essential to the success of software development projects, not only for achieving them on time and within budget but also for delivering the desired business value [12]. Research has shown that many large projects fail because of inadequate requirements, showing that errors made in the requirements engineering stage "are among the most difficult to detect and the most expensive to correct" [5]. These errors are caused by problems that mostly appear in the requirement elicitation phase [15, 16].

Many approaches have been proposed to enhance the existing requirements engineering techniques; some of these approaches recognized that "understanding a business process is the key to identify the user needs of the software that supports it" [13, 19, 20, 22]. Many organizations have their existing business process models in the form of working instructions and often include enough valid details for specifying software systems, which thus may provide a basis for understanding and modelling software requirements. In recent years, requirements of business applications have changed from command-based applications to workflow-based applications, "at least

© Springer Nature Switzerland AG 2019
B. Shishkov (Ed.): BMSD 2019, LNBIP 356, pp. 270–278, 2019.
https://doi.org/10.1007/978-3-030-24854-3_20

half of industrial software development is connected to business application development" [21]. Thus business process models may provide a promising approach to help produce accurate requirement specifications [10, 14, 24].

Several approaches have proposed methods to automatically generate requirements specifications from business models but these approaches fail to achieve transformation without significant manual intervention or correction [1–4, 13]. This paper argues that not only business process models can be used to derive more accurate software requirements but also these requirements can in majority be generated automatically. It proposes a new business model-driven approach for deriving UML-based requirement specifications. The proposed approach employs a set of systematic steps that start by improving the existing business process model to result into a well-defined business model, which includes the effect of the prospective information system should have on the business processes (named "To-Be" model). It then automatically transforms the "To-Be" business process model to a Use Case diagram. The proposed automatic generation of valid requirement specifications overcomes the often-used tedious and time-consuming manual process. Initial evaluation shows accurate results when compared with other manual approaches; it also shows the generation efficiency is directly proportional to the level of richness of the input business process model.

2 Related Work

Several researchers have proposed approaches to derive use cases diagram from business process models [1–4, 13, 22]. [1] Proposed an algorithm to automatically transform business model in to functional requirements in terms of use case model. The main objective for this approach is to draw up functional requirement more quickly from existing business model instead of building a use case diagram depending on interviews. The algorithm works by first creating meta-models for both the use case diagram and business process model then compares definitions in the two meta-models, to find "which concepts or relations in business process meta-model map to which concepts or relations in the use case meta-model". This approach was evaluated by comparing their results with use cases constructed by performing interviews, although promising however the total error percentage in the generated use case diagram was relatively high at 40%. Another similar study [2] proposed a method to explore associations between the use case model and the business model, but they used "Role Activity Diagrams" or RADs to model business processes. However, they faced several issues in deriving use cases from process models, including the notion of an actor, which is not clear enough in RADs. They found no simple mapping of Roles, in process models, on to Actors in use case diagrams [2]. Their results show, however, the transformation cannot achieve a well-formed use case model because the RAD notation is incompatible with UML-they found that UML actor is often not clearly defined in a RAD.

This work is further developed by [3], however they proposed a method for deriving system models based on business process models. They suggested that the correspondence between the central notion of 'automated activity' in an improved RAD model and that of "action or function" in the use case diagram facilitates the derivation of system models based on business process models. Their method consists of four steps: 1-develop a business process model using RAD model; 2-identify automated activities; 3-link each business objective with automated activities, and 4-develop use case model based on objectives and automated activities. However, this approach have shown several limitations, including lack of process visibility, and focus on use cases only with no notation of associations between them.

Another approach [13] proposed a manual transformation to obtain use case model based on business process models. This approach is the first approach that attempted to generate use case description from business process models. However, it focused on generating the use case description more than the use case diagram noting the value that may be obtained from the description. The use case diagram was generated manually depending on a set of rules, the resultant use case diagram however was not detailed enough. Generated use case diagrams, by this approach, did not cover the association between use cases such as extend, include, invoke and precede. The use case descriptions were specified from a set of predefined natural language sentences mapped manually from BPMN model elements. [4] Proposed a similar manual approach for deriving system requirements from business process models. This approach integrates requirements engineering and business process engineering. It defined BORE: a Business-Oriented approach to Requirements Elicitation. The authors argue that BORE is especially effective when system requirements are not fully knowable up front and must be discovered. [22] studied the use of DEMO (dynamic essential modelling of organisations) for deriving use cases from business models, and investigated most suitable methods or ways for identifying suitable use cases. The suggested methods can be used in combination of the automatic generation approaches to enhance use case derivation.

3   Proposed Approach: BMSpec

Generating valid and useable requirements from business models requires having valid business models. To achieve, BMSepc developed two original methods to enable consistent derivation of use cases from business models. It developed a structured and systematic "to-be" business model preparation and a set of heuristic rules that define the derivation and transformation of uses cases. The structured and systematic method ensures validity of the business model through the consistency of constraints to the correctness of its representation. As mentioned above, BMSpec employed requirement engineering and business model engineering integration from [4] for the "As-Is" business model part. BMSpec consists of two systematic steps as shown in Fig. 1: first, preparation of a well-defined business model. This step requires manual processing and its required effort depends on the status of the existing business process model. Second, automated transformation of business process model to a UML use case model. This step uses a BMSpec developed algorithm to map XML objects in both models. The developed algorithm employs a defined set of heuristic rules that define transformation of objects and relations from business process model to a use case diagram. These steps are described in further details in the following subsections.

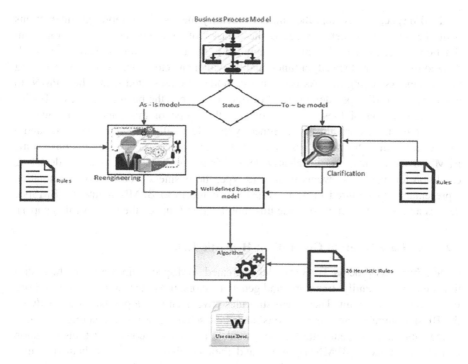

Fig. 1. BMSpec - overall structured approach

3.1   Preparation of a Well-Defined Business Process Model

A manual transformation of the existing business process model is undertaken to ensure model validity and consistency. The level and required effort of transformation depends on the status of the business process model. In cases where the business model is just a manual "As_Is" business process model and does not cover the user interaction with the system, the model needs reengineering in order to build a (To_Be) business process model. The transformation, in this case, includes analysing the purpose of the system and determining the effect of the information system should have on the business processes (To-Be). The key output of this step is to determine the automated tasks that represent user interactions with the system. However, simply automating processes for the sole purpose of automation often does not result into significant improvements [6]. Thus, in business process reengineering, it is recommended that instead of blindly automating manual processes, processes need to be reengineered while taking advantages of the possibilities for automation [7]. Business process reengineering may require "reshaping the way business is done" [8]. This further requires taking an integrated business look at both process and information flows, including looking at how processes use information and how people interact with systems [8].

In order to reengineer the business process model effectively, this reengineering step should focus on both system perspective, i.e. asking "what will make up a well-defined use case?"; and business process perspective, i.e. asking "what is needed from the information system?" [9].

In BMSpec, in this step, the aim is to identify the tasks that represent interactions with the software system. Because these tasks often represent the key important functions, or use cases, that must be included in the use case model. Thus, each well-defined use case must specify a functionality, which an actor wants to achieve by using the system. Assuming the (As-Is) business model is represented using the BPMN, to guide this step, BMSpec defines a set of rules to achieve the business process (To-Be) model (discussion of these rules is outside the scope of this paper). For business process models that are already designed with a clear software system purpose, and a clear effect of the information system on the business processes (To-Be), but have some BPMN notations that are not clearly defined, e.g. specifying task type, or declaring condition for gateways, events name and type, the business process model's notation representation is required to be modified. To conform to BPMN notations, BMSpec defines another set of rules to guide this modification (outside the scope of this paper).

3.2   Use Case Diagram Generation: Heuristic Rules

Once a business process To-Be model is created, BMSpec defines a set of heuristics that are used to identify, transform and generate actors, use cases, and their associations into a use case diagram. These heuristic rules have been developed based on studying the BPMN language and its notations, and their semantic use and meaning, and analysing more than 70 real-time business models to arrive at consistent transformation and interruptions of BPMN notations and their combinations. These heuristic rules have developed into computational algorithms to automate the business process To-Be models transformation and use-case generation into a UML use-case diagram. Description and listing of defined heuristic rules are outside the scope of the paper.

3.3   Automatic Use Case Generation: Algorithm

To automate the process of use case generation from the modified business process models, an algorithm has been developed that automatically reads the business process model, provided as BMPN notation, generates use case diagram as output. It performs three main steps:

1. identifies the business process models activities and nodes
2. identifies processes, workflows, gateways and conditions to ensure consistency and connections between its nodes.
3. applies its defined heuristic rules, on each of the identified activities and maps them to respective use cases. Connectors and actors are also consequently generated.

Table 1.

Case study name	Brief description
Nobel Prize example	It is a real case in which a paper work [13] used manual transformation from business process model for Nobel prize to a use case model. In the manual transformation authors used a set of rules

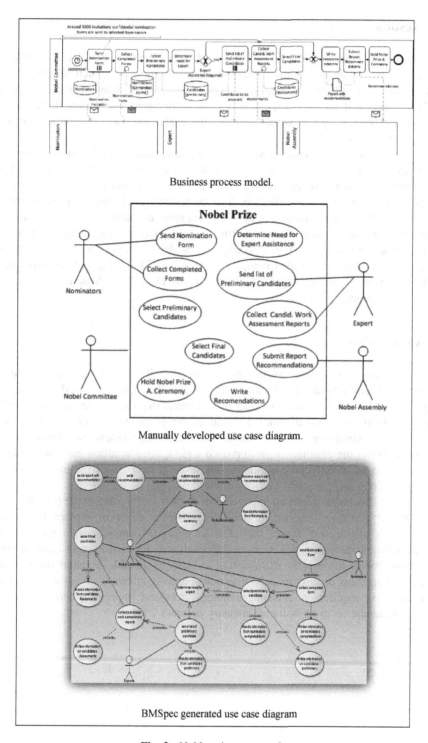

Business process model.

Manually developed use case diagram.

BMSpec generated use case diagram

Fig. 2. Noble prize case study

4 Results

The traditional gold standard testing or model evaluation is used [18]. This is conducted by evaluating the output of traditional requirement elicitation techniques, in which software engineers are employed to build use case diagrams manually, against BMSpec generated use case diagrams, for the same scenarios. Although this is an expensive procedure, yet to ensure validity, the evaluation was done on several different case studies.

As an example of the conducted evaluation and results, Table 1 lists one example of an evaluated case study. Figure 2 shows an example of this case study [13], including its business process model, manually developed use case diagram and its BMSpec generated use case diagram. The case study used traditional requirement engineering elicitation techniques to develop their requirement specification or use case diagram, and manual transformation from business process model to requirement specifications. As shown in Fig. 2, BMSpec was able to identify and extra features, which are not supported in other competing approaches [1–4, 13], such as association between use cases (precede, invoke, include, extend). Detailed evaluation is outside the scope of the paper.

5 Conclusion

The paper argues that business models can be usefully used to generate accurate requirements and software specifications. To achieve, the paper developed a systematic approach (BMSpec) that takes a number of systematic steps using standardized BPMN notations. Evaluation and illustrative results of the proposed BMSpec approach are described and compared against manual traditional requirement engineering techniques. It shows the promise of the approach and higher generation efficiency, which was found to be directly proportional to the level of richness of the input business process model.

While the proposed approach improves the efficiency of the automatic generation of UML-Based use case diagram, it does not however cover or replace the entire requirements engineering stage, nor aims to generate comprehensive requirement specifications. It provides, however, an important step forward to semi-automate the elicitation process through the extraction of as many as possible of requirements from underlying business process models, thus potentially significantly saving development time, reducing requirement misunderstanding errors and improving correct requirements representation using software industry de facto UML.

References

1. Dijkman, R.M., Joosten, S., Ordina, F.: An algorithm to derive use case diagrams from business process models. In: Proceedings of the 6th International Conference on Software Engineering and Applications (SEA), Anaheim, US (2002)
2. Odeh, M., Richard, K.: Bridging the gap between business models and system models. Inf. Softw. Technol. **45**(15), 1053–1060 (2003)
3. Aburub, F.: Activity-based approach to derive system models from business process models. In: 2012 International Conference on Information Society (i-Society). IEEE (2012)
4. Przybylek, A.: A business-oriented approach to requirements elicitation. In: 2014 International Conference on Evaluation of Novel Approaches to Software Engineering (ENASE). IEEE (2014)
5. Boehm, B.W.: Software Engineering Economics, vol. 197. Prentice-Hall, Englewood Cliffs (1981)
6. Weerakkody, V., Currie, W.: (2003) Integrating Business Process Reengineering with Information Systems Development: Issues & Implications. In: van der Aalst, W.M.P., Weske, M. (eds.) Business Process Management. BPM 2003. Lecture Notes in Computer Science, vol. 2678, pp. 302–320. Springer, Heidelberg (2003). https://doi.org/10.1007/3-540-44895-0_21
7. Hammer, M.: Reengineering work: don't automate, obliterate. Harvard Bus. Rev. **68**(4), 104–112 (1990)
8. Kaplan, R.B., Murdock, L.: Rethinking The Corporation: Core Process Redesign, The Mckinsey Quarterly, 2 November 1991
9. Eriksson, E., Magnus, P.: Business Modeling with UML. Business Patterns at Work. Wiley, New York (2000)
10. Dijkman, R., Hofstetter, J., Koehler, J. (eds.): BPMN 2011. LNBIP, vol. 95. Springer, Heidelberg (2011). https://doi.org/10.1007/978-3-642-25160-3
11. Pressman, R.S.: Software Engineering: A Practitioner's Approach. Palgrave Macmillan, New York (2005)
12. Bloch, M., Sven, B., Jürgen, L.: Delivering large-scale IT projects on time, on budget, and on value. McKinsey Q. (2012)
13. Cruz, E.F., Machado, R.J., Santos, M.Y.: From business process models to use case models: a systematic approach. In: Aveiro, D., Tribolet, J., Gouveia, D. (eds.) EEWC 2014. LNBIP, vol. 174, pp. 167–181. Springer, Cham (2014). https://doi.org/10.1007/978-3-319-06505-2_12
14. Indulska, M., Recker, J., Rosemann, M., Green, P.: Business process modeling: current issues and future challenges. In: van Eck, P., Gordijn, J., Wieringa, R. (eds.) CAiSE 2009. LNCS, vol. 5565, pp. 501–514. Springer, Heidelberg (2009). https://doi.org/10.1007/978-3-642-02144-2_39
15. Rajagopal, P., Lee, R., Ahlswede, T., Chiang, C.C., Karolak, D.: A new approach for software requirements elicitation. In: 6th International Conference on Software Engineering, Artificial Intelligence, Networking and Parallel/Distributed Computing and ACIS International Workshop on Self-Assembling Wireless Network, pp. 32–42. IEEE (2005)
16. Brooks Jr., F.P.: No silver bullet: essence and accidents of software engineering. IEEE Comput. (1987)
17. Eriksson, H.-E., Penker, M.: Business Modeling with UML: Business Patterns at Work. Wiley (2000)
18. Kitchenham, B.A., Pickard, L., Linkman, S., Jones, P.: A framework for evaluating a software bidding model. Inf. Softw. Technol. **47**(11), 747–760 (2005)

19. Jalote, P.A.: A Concise Introduction to Software Engineering. Springer Science & Business Media, London (2008). https://doi.org/10.1007/978-1-84800-302-6

20. Mili, H., Tremblay, G., Jaoude, G.B., Lefebvre, É., Elabed, L., Boussaidi, G.E.: Business process modeling languages: sorting through the alphabet soup. ACM Comput. Surv. (CSUR) **43**(1), 4 (2010)

21. Bider, I.: State-oriented business process modeling: principles, theory and practice (2002)

22. Shishkov, B., Dietz, J.L.: Deriving use cases from business processes, the advantages of demo. In: ICEIS, vol. 3, pp. 138–146 (2003)

An Experimental Study
on Decomposition: Process First
or Structure First?

Anil Cetinkaya[1,2(✉)], Selma Suloglu[3], M. Cagri Kaya[1], Alper Karamanlioglu[1],
Gul Tokdemir[4], and Ali H. Dogru[1]

[1] Department of Computer Engineering, Middle East Technical University,
Ankara, Turkey
{cetinkaya,mckaya,alperk,dogru}@ceng.metu.edu.tr
[2] Iskenderun Technical University, Hatay, Turkey
[3] Department of Software Engineering, Rochester Institute of Technology,
Rochester, NY, USA
selma@se.rit.edu
[4] Department of Computer Engineering, Cankaya University, Ankara, Turkey
gtokdemir@cankaya.edu.tr

Abstract. This article explores the answer to the question of considering the process or the structure dimensions earlier, in software development where decomposition is a preferred technique for top-down model
construction. In this research, an experimental study was conducted to
observe which software modeling practice is more convenient: process or
structural modeling, for the beginning. The study was conducted in different courses that include software modeling where students work within
groups to model a system with predefined requirements. The students
used Business Process Modeling Notation and Component-Oriented
Software Engineering Modeling Language modeling tools. Observations
based on the results are analyzed and discussed. The results seem to
prioritize the process dimension.

Keywords: Software modeling · Process modeling ·
Structural modeling · Experimental study

1 Introduction

Modeling is continuously becoming a more critical part of software development. Models are used for specification, and sometimes as the executable media,
replacing code. Different dimensions of modeling have been emphasized during
the infancy of software engineering, and today a re-evaluation is required for the
"no-code development" alternatives. Model Driven Architecture demonstrated
the usage of models for executability and executable process models utilized
in Service-Oriented Architecture (SOA) promoted process models in this direction. Process and structure modeling can be weaved towards methodological

© Springer Nature Switzerland AG 2019
B. Shishkov (Ed.): BMSD 2019, LNBIP 356, pp. 279–289, 2019.
https://doi.org/10.1007/978-3-030-24854-3_21

support for no-code development. Also, variability emerged in Software Product Line approaches as an important specification tool, that has lately been incorporated into Component-Oriented Software Engineering Modeling Language (COSEML), as a reason for its selection for the structure dimension, that is otherwise a slightly more recent tool than Unified Modeling Language (UML).

In this research, to seek for an answer to this question of how to start for a required methodology, an experimental study was conducted in one senior and two graduate classes as project assignments. The students were expected to model process and structural models of provided scenarios in the Department of Computer Engineering at Middle East Technical University (METU).

More specifically, we came up with a set of research questions (RQ) that support our motivation of the study. Design concepts are used to analyze the results to answer RQs which create a foundation to guide engineers in design by a set of processes and notions:

RQ1: Does the order of using a model affect the design or understanding of the system?
Process (sub-process), its functions, and interactions via ordering the function calls are the main concepts in the process model. A set of those functions are accommodated in the structure model. We are searching for a better order between the two modeling activities.

RQ2: Does keeping both process and structural views in mind affect the design or understanding of the system?
Instead of starting with a single model, having two models in our mind with their powerful expressive capabilities may lead to distill valuable information from the system specification. With this question, we want to observe if two concurrent views have beneficial effects on system design and understanding.

RQ3: Which modeling option; process or structural or both, contribute to designing concepts more?
As design concepts provide ways to model the system in different ways, we investigate the perceived benefits of different settings in designing the system.

2   Related Work

Model decomposition is investigated as a significant modeling activity. It supports the purpose to reduce cognitive load. Cognitive Load Theory states that the capacity of the working memory is limited [10]; hence if the amount of information to be processed goes beyond this capacity, comprehension is declined abruptly.

Process modeling, besides being used for representing business related views, provides an executable software model today. It allows for the ordered invocation of functions and storing and retrieving data elements.

The structure of a system pinpoints the major modules of that system and the connections between them [16]. Class and component diagrams of the object orientation are examples of structural models.

Existing studies vary in the usage or configuration order of two models: process and structural. Becker and Klingner propose a component model [2] that allows for configuration of business processes. To represent the processes hierarchically a declarative approach is used. Business Process Modeling Notation (BPMN) is utilized to transform a configuration into a process model. Atiptamvaree and Senivongse present a way [1] to design component-based business process models. An application domain is modeled as a business process model, and then the model is decomposed into process components.

Crnkovic et al. examine the impact of the component-based approach on the development process and lifecycle models within the framework of a specific process model [4]. One of the main objectives of this study is to determine an ideal lifecycle process model for component-based systems. Another aim is to adopt and integrate different types of component-based development processes and component lifecycle models.

In an earlier work of Kaya et al., BPMN and COSEML were used for the hierarchical system decomposition together [9]. A variability guided decomposition was adopted: When a new feature is added to the system starting from the root of the feature model, a corresponding process and a component are added to the BPMN model and the component model, respectively.

There are some studies in the literature on process or structural modeling, which are conducted by applying a questionnaire and interpreting the results. Koschmider et al. present the results of results of an in-depth analysis of the reuse of the business process model from different perspectives in a survey study [11]. Melcher et al. discuss the reliability and validity issues of the measurement instruments to determine how much the respondent understands a process model structurally [13]. Ham et al. introduce MaRMI-III methodology for component-based development [8]. According to the questionnaire, its process model appears to be the best element of MARMI-III. MaRMI-III is also compared with other component-based development methodologies.

Part of the related work consists of experimental studies of software modeling. Chaudron et al. conduct empirical analysis about the effectiveness of software modeling using UML [3]. The paper focuses on the cost and benefits of modeling: It is stated that UML modeling contributes to shared understanding and communication efficiency. Application of UML based on design process model developed for hardware design is demonstrated by Damasevicius and Stuikys [5]. With the help of this process model, object-oriented design concepts in the hardware design domain are adopted and processes are implemented.

An interesting work reported by Shishkov et al. also investigates different modeling dimensions especially in the perspective of enterprise engineering, that provides the structure as the beginning point [17].

3   Experimental Study

A total of 42 groups were assigned to model the same software system using structural and process modeling. BPMN and COSEML were employed to model for process and structural models, respectively. Three settings for the assignments were prepared, each of which dictates using a different order of using process and structural models: While Setting 1 starts modeling by a process model (Phase 1) and then uses structural model (Phase 2), Setting 2 does vice versa. Setting 3 starts the project by using two types of modeling simultaneously and refines the models in the second phase. Each group answered a questionnaire after finishing each phase to reveal how easy or appropriate has been the modeling. Then, all results of the questionnaires were examined by the authors of this paper and the results were discussed.

In our experiment, students are expected to create a process and a structural model for a software application. They are supposed to cover all functionality of the application given as a set of specifications. The detailed description of the two projects is provided in [7].

3.1   Modeling Tools

A web-based process modeling tool, Signavio [12], is used for process modeling. While developing the process model, students are instructed to consider the 7 ± 2 rule [14] for a better understanding of their models. Concerning structural modeling, the COSEML tool [6] is employed which is a graphical tool that can be used for hierarchical development with software components.

3.2   Experiment Setting and Participants

The experiment was conducted at the Department of Computer Engineering METU in two consecutive fall semesters. Two graduate classes (*CENG551 System Development with Abstract Design*, and *SE550 Software Engineering*) in years 2017 and 2018 were included in this experiment. Also, one undergraduate class (*CENG451 Information System Analysis and Design*) in 2018 has been included. Groups were presented with scenarios that explain the system specifications and they were expected to create their process and structural designs based on the given specifications. Different projects have been assigned to the groups in each year in order to minimize the effects of application dependency: Translation Agency System for the first year and Disaster Management System for the second year (can be accessed through [7]). Students formed 42 groups where 17 of them were from *CENG551*, 12 of them from *SE550*, and 13 of them from *CENG451* classes. Each group was allowed to include 2 or 3 students. To observe the order of usage or simultaneous usage of process and structural models, three settings were introduced and each group was assigned to one of those settings:

– **Setting 1:** First process model, then structural model.
– **Setting 2:** First structural model, then process model.
– **Setting 3:** Process and structural models together.

The distribution of groups over these three settings are as described in Table 1.

Table 1. Number of groups assigned to different settings

	Setting 1	Setting 2	Setting 3	Total
CENG551	6	6	5	17
SE550	4	4	4	12
CENG451	4	4	5	13
TOTAL	14	14	14	42

All groups modeled their projects accordingly in two phases. In Phase 1; Setting 1 groups developed the process model of the project, Setting 2 groups developed the structural model of the system, and Setting 3 groups developed the initial versions of the process and structural models simultaneously.

After Phase 1 was completed, all groups were assigned a questionnaire. A similar process was applied to Phase 2. This time, Setting 1 groups developed the structural model, Setting 2 groups developed the process model, and Setting 3 groups finished their initial design for both of the models. In the end, all groups answered the second questionnaire. Finally, all project groups were graded by the teaching assistants and instructors.

In each questionnaire, all participants were asked if they have any previous experience on assigned modeling. either process or structural. Then, each group was asked to rate easiness of the tool usage and learning curve from 1 (hardest) to 10 (easiest) based on their experience with the used approach. Groups were asked if they found the approach appropriate to start with and why. Groups were also asked about how many hours they have spent on learning the process/structural-oriented approach and modeling the system. Additionally, all groups were asked to give their opinions on what functions they think are essential for the project and what they think about the fidelity of their process models.

3.3 Results

We analyzed two sources of information: (i) modeling artifacts, process and structural models, and (ii) student statements and observations from questionnaires.

Modeling artifacts tell us qualitatively how well the models represent the system against project specifications. This effort was undertaken by the teaching assistants and instructors where first teaching assistants graded the models and then passed the assessments to the instructors. Our observations based on the qualitative assessments are given as follows:

Model Updates in Subsequent Phases: We observed the reluctance of the groups to review their models unless feedback was provided to them.

Modeling in Different Settings: The groups assigned to Setting 2 outperformed those in Setting 1 in identifying essential components. However, they were not so successful in defining interactions among such components.

Based on the statements and observations from questionnaires, the results were detailed in a categorized fashion:

Tool Usage and Time Spent on Modeling: Groups think developing a process model with Signavio is comfortable than developing a structural model with COSEML. Besides, the time spent on structural modeling reported more than that on process modeling.

Previous Knowledge: Although there is not enough data to make accurate comments, our experiment indicates groups who have previous modeling experience spent more hours to learn both Signavio and COSEML. This may be because the experienced groups are trying to match their prior knowledge to the new tool they are learning.

Modeling Order: All groups were asked if the model which they have been assigned is suitable to start the design. When they were asked in the first phase, all (100%) of the process modeling groups and 93% of structural modeling groups found their assignments appropriate to start modeling. However, when they were asked the same question in the second phase of the projects, the groups that think process model is proper has declined to 86% and the groups that think structural modeling is appropriate has fallen dramatically to 57%.

Usage of Models to Understand the System: Additionally, all groups were questioned about if the models they created help to understand the system and speed up the modeling of the system. 96% of the process and all of the structural modeling groups have responded positively.

Perceived Design Concepts in Process and Structural models: All of the groups as shown in Table 1 were asked to rate design concepts based on how the applied approach satisfies design concepts between 1 (does not satisfy) to 10 (fully satisfies). The evaluated design concepts as described to the groups are as follows: abstraction, refinement, modularity, software architecture, control hierarchy, structural partitioning, data structure, and software procedure [15].

Table 2. Design concept ratings with respect to different models

Design element	Process model	Structural model	PM & SM	Weighted average
Abstraction	**7.96**	7.71	7.21	7.63
Refinement	**7.04**	6.93	6.93	6.96
Modularity	7	**8.46**	6.5	7.32
Software architecture	6.32	**7.07**	6.46	6.62
Control hierarchy	7.43	**7.57**	6.79	7.26
Structural partitioning	6.39	**7.93**	5.5	6.6
Data structure	5.39	**5.86**	4.86	5.37
Software procedure	**6.96**	5.68	6.92	6.52
Average grade	78.91	**81.98**	77.06	79.31

According to the results, irrespective of usage of the model either first or later, Table 2 shows that structural model has a clear advantage on the satisfaction of modularity (8.46), software architecture (7.07) and structural partitioning (7.93) in the design phase. On the other hand, the process model offers better abstraction (7.96), refinement (7.04) and software procedure (6.96) compared to the other approaches. It is interesting to see that simultaneous usage of the process and the structural models do not seem to have significant satisfaction in any of the design concepts.

As can be seen in Table 3, we see an overall decrease in the satisfaction of design concepts in the second phases of both process and structural models. We can see a reflection of this situation on the average grades as they are also decreasing along with the fallen satisfaction levels which are reasonable since the ratings of design concepts constitute a base for the overall design quality as well as the average grades. The general decrease in second phases can also be interpreted as a phenomenon such that students having a hard time grasping a different perspective when they already have experienced with a different approach.

Table 3. Design concept ratings based on Phases

Design element	PM first	PM later	SM first	SM later
Abstraction	**8.36**	7.57	7.57	7.86
Refinement	**7.71**	6.36	6.93	6.93
Modularity	7.57	6.43	**8.79**	8.14
Software architecture	6.93	5.71	**7.14**	7
Control hierarchy	**8.21**	6.64	7.71	7.43
Structural partitioning	6.86	5.93	**8.07**	7.77
Data structure	5.29	5.5	4.93	**6.79**
Software procedure	**7.21**	6.71	5.14	6.21
Average grade	83.6	74.22	**84.92**	79.03

Since the overall design quality can be measured by scores given by the groups, if we look at the results given in Table 4, we can observe that the best overall design quality was achieved by Setting 1 groups when the design is started with process modeling. The worst overall design quality has acquired by the groups that are assigned to Setting 3. When we consider the ratings of design elements for the groups assigned to different types, we can say that Setting 3 groups had problems especially on representing the structural partitioning (5.5), data structures (4.86) and modularity (6.5) of the system. Setting 3 groups also have lower ratings for most of the design elements in general compared to the other settings. The best ratings for almost all of the design elements are scored by Setting 1 groups.

4 Discussion

Based on the results, answers found to the research questions and observations about collaboration effort are provided in the following subsections.

4.1 Answers to Research Questions

RQ1: Does the order of using a model affect the design or understanding of the system?
Observations from quantitative assessments of modeling artifacts show us that mostly the groups starting the design with structural model find hard to define interaction semantics between components. Interaction specification is of importance to construct the system architecture which is prominent in the process model. On the other hand, the groups starting with process model were less effective in defining components of the system but were successful in revealing component interactions. This points out starting with process modeling is better when it comes to choosing a model. We can also interpret these results as process and structural views are complementing each other in the development of a complete system model.

Table 4. Design concept ratings based on Settings

Design element	Setting 1	Setting 2	Setting 3	Combined
Abstraction	**8.11**	7.57	7.21	7.63
Refinement	**7.32**	6.64	6.93	6.96
Modularity	**7.86**	7.61	6.5	7.32
Software architecture	**6.96**	6.43	6.46	6.62
Control hierarchy	**7.82**	7.18	6.79	7.26
Structural partitioning	**7.3**	7	5.5	6.6
Data structure	**6.04**	5.21	4.86	5.37
Software procedure	6.71	5.93	**6.92**	6.52
Average grade	**81.31**	79.57	77.06	79.31

Based on the answers from the questionnaire, groups mostly preferred process model to the structural model. When groups start experiencing a different model than a previous model, the ones starting with process changed their preference (a drop from 100% to 86%). However, the groups that used the structural model first dramatically changed their preference (a drop from 93% to 57%).

RQ2: Does keeping both process and structural views in mind affect the design or understanding of the system?
The groups subject to simultaneous usage of process and structural models have the worst overall design quality. These groups are the ones who have almost no

previous knowledge about the models and tools, and had to learn both models at the same time. These facts may have a huge effect on understanding and modeling the system. We can interpret this outcome as follows: The developers without sufficient previous knowledge about different models and were expected to work with them simultaneously, the information load was huge enough that may hinder the effectiveness of the modeling capabilities. In these cases, starting from process model may be the best approach.

RQ3: Starting with which model, process or structural or both, contribute to design concepts more?

It is clearly seen that starting with process model outperforms the other two settings: starting with structural modeling and using structural and process modeling simultaneously. The best scores for almost all of the design concepts are attributed to process first and structural second. That means groups tend to start with thinking of the system as a set of interactions, as a storyboard and then clarify the main constituents accordingly. This way they think that they understand the system better.

4.2   Collaboration Effort in Groups and Its Reflection on Design Models

Irrespective of our research questions, we observed that some groups provided process models with inconsistent sub-processes. This made us think about their collaboration behavior; we found that these group members were working separately without a common vocabulary or working environment. This behavior manifests itself in the created models which are easily observable. Besides, we found that most of the time students in a group get together and create system models at once, not in an incremental way that we were expecting to see.

5   Threats to Validity

A concise discussion about our concerns is provided here that can be grouped into two topics. First of all, the experimentation was conducted in academic settings rather than industrial. Also, the number of experiments were not big enough for a convincing statistical analysis. These factors may have hindered the capability to draw generalized conclusions. However, despite those constraints, the findings are convergent. The second specific concern is about the third setting where students faced two views simultaneously: they might have conducted those views in a serial manner rather than simultaneously. However, the consistent outcome with a decreased quality in this setting points to a deterring cognitive load suggesting their simultaneous exposure.

6   Conclusion

This research yields some important results for interpretation. Except for specific structure dimension considerations, 'process first' approach generally outperformed the 'structure first' counterpart. This advantage presents itself in better designs and model understanding. One motivation behind this research was to support our future work in developing environments for no-code software development. The outcome of this experimentation also is in agreement with the common paradigm behind SOA and UML centric development. SOA and UML both propose to start with function or process dimensions rather than structure.

References

1. Atiptamvaree, E., Senivongse, T.: A quantitative approach to strategic design of component-based business process model. Int. J. Inf. Technol. **3**(2), 123–130 (2006)
2. Becker, M., Klingner, S.: Towards customer-individual configurations of business process models. In: Bider, I., et al. (eds.) BPMDS/EMMSAD -2012. LNBIP, vol. 113, pp. 121–135. Springer, Heidelberg (2012). https://doi.org/10.1007/978-3-642-31072-0_9
3. Chaudron, M.R., Heijstek, W., Nugroho, A.: How effective is uml modeling? Softw. Syst. Model. **11**(4), 571–580 (2012)
4. Crnkovic, I., Chaudron, M., Larsson, S.: Component-based development process and component lifecycle. In: 2006 International Conference on Software Engineering Advances (ICSEA 2006), p. 44. IEEE (2006)
5. Damasevicius, R., Stuikys, V.: Application of uml for hardware design based on design process model. In: Proceedings of the 2004 Asia and South Pacific Design Automation Conference, pp. 244–249. IEEE Press (2004)
6. Dogru, A.H.: Component oriented software engineering modeling language: COSEML. Computer Engineering Department, Middle East Technical University, Turkey, TR-99-3 (1999)
7. Dogru, A.H.: Example problems for BMSD 2019. https://user.ceng.metu.edu.tr/~dogru/PublicationSupport/ExampleProblemsBMSD2019.pdf. Accessed 09 May 2019
8. Ham, D.H., Kim, J.S., Cho, J.H., Ha, S.J.: MaRMI-III: a methodology for component-based development. ETRI J. **26**(2), 167–180 (2004)
9. Kaya, M.C., Suloglu, S., Tokdemir, G., Tekinerdogan, B., Dogru, A.H.: Variability incorporated simultaneous decomposition of models under structural and procedural views. In: Software Engineering for Variability Intensive Systems : Foundations and Applications, pp. 95–116. CRC Press (2019)
10. Kirschner, P.A.: Cognitive load theory: implications of cognitive load theory on the design of learning (2002)
11. Koschmider, A., Fellmann, M., Schoknecht, A., Oberweis, A.: Analysis of process model reuse: where are we now, where should we go from here? Decis. Support Syst. **66**, 9–19 (2014)
12. Kunze, M., Weske, M.: Signavio-oryx academic initiative. BPM 2010 Demonstration Track, p. 6 (2010)
13. Melcher, J., Mendling, J., Reijers, H.A., Seese, D.: On measuring the understandability of process models. In: Rinderle-Ma, S., Sadiq, S., Leymann, F. (eds.) BPM 2009. LNBIP, vol. 43, pp. 465–476. Springer, Heidelberg (2010). https://doi.org/10.1007/978-3-642-12186-9_44
14. Miller, G.A.: The magical number seven, plus or minus two: some limits on our capacity for processing information. Psychol. Rev. **63**(2), 81 (1956)
15. Pressman, R.S.: Software Engineering: A Practitioner's Approach. Palgrave Macmillan (2005)

16. Selic, B.: Using uml for modeling complex real-time systems. In: Languages, compilers, and tools for embedded systems. pp. 250–260. Springer (1998)
17. Shishkov, B., Larsen, J.B., Warnier, M., Janssen, M.: Three categories of context-aware systems. In: Shishkov, B. (ed.) BMSD 2018. LNBIP, vol. 319, pp. 185–202. Springer, Cham (2018). https://doi.org/10.1007/978-3-319-94214-8_12

Capturing Human Authority
and Responsibility by Considering
Composite Public Values

Magdalena Garvanova[1(✉)] and Boris Shishkov[1,2,3]

[1] Faculty of Information Sciences, University of Library Studies and Information
Technologies, Sofia, Bulgaria
m.garvanova@unibit.bg
[2] Institute of Mathematics and Informatics, Bulgarian Academy of Sciences,
Sofia, Bulgaria
[3] Institute IICREST, Sofia, Bulgaria
b.b.shishkov@iicrest.org

Abstract. Accountability is a key requirement as it concerns current enterprise information systems. In this context, no matter if an action is realized by a human or by a "machine", it is always important to know who is responsible for what was done. This essentially relates to human authority. We argue that it is not always trivial identifying the human authority "behind" (complex) enterprise actions, especially when the actual authority is "blurred" by references to enterprise structures that may have supported a decision "on paper" but have not had the chance of actually opposing that decision, for example. The contribution of this paper concerns a proposal featuring the identification of human authority (mainly in an enterprise context) based on analyzing universal value categories (such as hierarchy and egalitarianism) that are easy to "check" (possibly by means of surveys).

Keywords: Human authority · Public values · System requirements

1 Introduction

Some experts warn that someday artificial intelligence [1] may become smarter than human intelligence – they are inspired by examples, such as ones concerning artificial chess players [2]. Further, neural networks [3] are considered as massively parallel distributed processors that have a natural propensity for storing experimental knowledge and making it available for use. This is claimed to resemble the human brain.

Nevertheless, we argue that currently this "dream" is far from realistic at least for several reasons: (i) Some complex (intuition-driven) mental processes are not easy to reflect in terms of just training-driven knowledge acquisition + "synaptic" weights' consideration. (ii) Human behavior motivation is often driven by commitments, beliefs, love, anger, etc., that go beyond the capacity of modeling. (iii) Any artificial behavior would be severely challenged by exceptional situations, not foreseen at design time [4] – exceptional human actions are often "burdened" by family overlays, cultural overlays, religious overlays, etc. that concern the unique person(s) involved [5].

© Springer Nature Switzerland AG 2019
B. Shishkov (Ed.): BMSD 2019, LNBIP 356, pp. 290–298, 2019.
https://doi.org/10.1007/978-3-030-24854-3_22

Thus, we claim that artificial intelligence is (and will be) SUPPORTIVE (rather than REPLACING) with regard to *enterprise processes* that are essentially **human-centric**. Hence, we argue that allowing artificial intelligence to "act on its own" can be dangerous.

This is the problem addressed in the current paper in general. In particular, we consider **HUMAN AUTHORITY**, inspired by the theme of the ninth edition of the international symposium on **Business Modeling and Software Design** – **BMSD** [6], and also by our observation that *human authority* is where the "limits of the machine" are reached, for example: a drone cannot "decide" to shoot a person (a human in the "background" should have decided so, such that the drone would implement what has been decided). Further, *human authority* is straightforwardly related to *responsibility* and *responsibility* in turn - to *accountability* [7–9], for example: in order to claim who is responsible for a casualty, we need to know who has the *authority* to order what was done.

Hence, the contribution of this paper concerns a proposal (inspired by previous work of the authors) featuring the identification of *human authority* (mainly in an enterprise context) based on analyzing *universal value categories*, such as *hierarchy* and *egalitarianism* [10], because they are easy to "check" (possibly by means of surveys). Especially at enterprises, where most employees "depend" on a corresponding boss, one should not expect unbiased feedback about who is responsible for what. *Authority* and *responsibility* are often HIDDEN within the enterprise structure and culture, and it is often challenging to identify who is DE FACTO guilty for something. For example, in a hierarchical and conservative enterprise, much authority would *de facto* be "in the hands" of one person but in case of an investigation, this fact may be blurred by references to enterprise structures that may have supported a decision "on paper" but have not had the chance of actually opposing that decision.

By addressing *universal value categories* nevertheless, we expect to be able to precisely identify *human authority* concerning a particular situation. This would be useful in adequately analyzing the behavior of an enterprise system.

In previous work [10], we have addressed such *universal value categories*, relating them to the value concept. **Public values** ("values", for short) are *desires of the general public*, that are about *properties considered societally valuable*, such as respecting the privacy of citizens or prohibiting polluting activities [11]. In this, we have considered *atomic values* (encapsulating only one particular behavioral goal) vs *composite values* (reflecting particular human attitudes) [10]; actually, the *composite values* point to the so called *universal value categories*. In our studies, we have established that *atomic values* are easier to operationalize (in the sense that they can be methodologically reflected in technical (software) functional solutions) while *composite values* are difficult to operationalize but are easier to capture and measure. We have partially justified this claim, by means of *self-administrated surveys* – the experimental results have shown that it is not difficult to get public feedback on *composite values*. This has inspired our goal to analyze the potential relations between the concept of *human authority* (that is difficult to capture and measure) and *composite values*.

The remaining of the current paper is organized as follows: In Sect. 2, we analyze further the concepts of "human authority" and "composite value", and we also make a general proposal for relating them. In Sect. 3, we elaborate our proposal, by considering particular *composite values*. In Sect. 4, we discuss previous experience concerning the "measurability" of *composite values*. Finally, in Sect. 5 we conclude the paper.

2 Human Authority and Composite Values

In the following sub-sections, we will firstly consider the concept of *human authority*, then we will consider *composite values*, and in the end, we present our general view on how to relate those concepts.

2.1 Human Authority

Artificial Intelligence and Machine Learning [1] are changing our lives – machines are powerful in processing but often also in decision-making. It is therefore of paramount importance to "guarantee" the human control over this whole thing.

"Who is responsible if a machine does this?" In our view, this question is penetrating Society to date. The more technology advances, the more this question will be dominating. We identify several challenges here: (i) It is insufficiently clear what the concepts of *authority* and *responsibility* are – are they similar to *values* or are they just manifestation of "power"? (ii) How can we identify *authority* and *responsibility* in the Social World and effectively find their "reflections" in the Technical World? (iii) What do those reflections mean? (iv) How can we establish *traceability* between real-life *authority* and *responsibility*, on the one hand, and the corresponding technical realizations, on the other hand? It is to be clarified that by "authority" we mean "human authority".

Consider the following example: A drone used in support of land border police officers [12]. It is possible that (by mistake) the drone shoots a person, photographs somebody's face and against the regulations transmits the image, frightens a citizen who passes by (which is not allowed), and so on. All this concerns *undesired results* with regard to the operation of the drone. Some of them assume just disturbance while others may have significant negative effects (injuring or killing a person, for example). For this reason, *accountability* + *traceability* are crucial in such cases: we need to know who is **RESPONSIBLE** for what the drone has "done". Are the guys at the base station (who are supporting the navigation of the drone in real time) responsible or are the drone software developers responsible or the guys who have produced the drone algorithms? Even though it is not easy to answer those questions, it is for sure that one cannot "blame" the drone simply because never any non-human entity has been blamed for anything. We refer to previous work addressing *accountability* in the drone technology context [8]. Another example: a person uses an ATM, ordering withdrawal of 20 EURO but the machine "gives" him or her 40 EURO while accounting 20 EURO. Then who is responsible for this mechanical mistake resulting in "robbing" the bank? Is this the person maintaining the particular ATM if the maintenance checks are not enough but it is up to somebody else to decide when a check should be realized?

Hence, we argue that just looking at *immediate responsibilities* is not enough and what is needed is to consider the underlying **HUMAN AUTHORITY** – there is somebody who has the authority to launch a drone mission, there is somebody who has the authority to enforce equipment maintenance policies, and so on. Further, this is not necessarily the immediate "boss" at the particular level – as it is well known, often orders are given from "behind the scenes" (for example: it may be that the owner of a company influences the decisions of responsible employees). Then it would be unjustified to claim *responsibility* from somebody who has not got actual power to oppose the decision that (s)he had formally approved.

In summary, understanding and capturing *human authority* is crucial with regard to utilizing (enterprise) information systems.

2.2   Value-Sensitive Design and Composite Values

As mentioned already, values are desires of the general public, that are about properties (concerning the (software) system-to-be) considered societally valuable. "Translating" *values* into *functional solutions* is thus an actual challenge. Even though *Value-Sensitive Design* (*VSD*) is about *weaving values in the design* of (technical) systems [13], we argue that it stays insufficiently concrete as it concerns the *alignment between abstract values and technical (software) solutions*. Still, VSD indirectly inspires ideas in that direction as for example the idea of Shishkov & Mendling to consider *business process variants* as a "bridge" in achieving such an alignment [7], as it concerns *atomic values*.

Still, one would often face *composite values* (reflecting a particular human attitude), for example: the desire to achieve *egalitarianism* [14].

As studied by Garvanova et al., most *atomic values* (such as *privacy*, *transparency*, *accountability*, and so on) are to be considered in a particular context [10] since people consider them differently depending on the context. For example: USUALLY, *privacy* is desired but when HUNTING TERRORISTS, it might be acceptable by many people that authorities compromise their *privacy*. Therefore, studying in general what somebody's attitude is towards *privacy* (for example), could be of limited use. For this reason, we argue that *atomic values could only be adequately operationalized if this concerns context-aware systems* [11]. *Composite values*, in contrast, are not so easy to weave in the design (because they are even more abstract than *atomic values*) but it is easier to capture public opinion concerning them through surveys (or other analyses), as it is claimed by Veenhoven and Kalmijn [15] – they argue that many issues that concern *composite public values* (such as *egalitarianism*, *utilitarianism*, *autonomy*, *embeddedness*, and so on) *can be measured using surveys*.

2.3   Proposal

Inspired by the analysis, provided in the previous sub-sections, we propose capturing *human authority* "through" measuring corresponding *composite values* and an important question is which particular *composite values* to consider.

To find the answer, we consider the concept of *power* that is obviously close to the concept of *human authority*. Then we ask the question: WHAT gives power? In our view, it is more or less three things: (i) the <u>organizational structure</u>; (ii) the <u>broader attitudes</u>; (iii) the <u>behavior models of surrounding persons</u>.

Hence, not claiming exhaustiveness, we have reflected (i), (ii), and (iii) in corresponding *bipolar dimensions*, as follows:

- the *hierarchy* vs. *egalitarianism* dimension, featuring (i);
- the *autonomy* vs. *conservatism* dimension, featuring (ii);
- the *harmony* vs. *mastery* dimension, featuring (iii).

We thus position the *human authority* (AUTHORITY for short, as already stated) concept as related to those dimensions – this is visualized in Fig. 1:

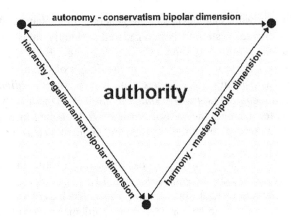

Fig. 1. Relating the authority concept to composite values

As suggested by the figure, by analyzing *composite values* along those dimensions, is expected to be helpful in getting unbiased perception as it concerns *authority*, especially in an enterprise context.

In the following section, we will provide elaboration regarding those three dimensions as well as their relevance to the *authority* concept.

3   Elaboration

In the below sub-sections, we will discuss the *bipolar dimensions* introduced in the previous section as well as their relevance with regard to the *authority* concept.

3.1   Hierarchy vs Egalitarianism

According to Schwartz [16], the *hierarchy* vs *egalitarianism* dimension refers to ensuring *socially responsible behavior* – how to motivate people to coordinate their actions and to respect the rights of others. HIERARCHICAL cultures and organizations use a strict set of regulations, social roles and obligations. The adoption of such a social order in the process of socialization would not only provide obedience to rules (norms) but would also delimit the norms themselves from issues attributed to unequal power (concerning resources, influence, and so on). On the opposite side stand cultures, emphasizing on COMMON INTERESTS AND GOALS, and the need for cooperation of individuals to achieve that. The leading idea is that: "other people are fundamentally equal to myself". This solution is based on the values of *egalitarianism*, as considered by Schwartz. Hence, as it concerns *authority*, it appears that:

- in highly hierarchical structures, decision making, control and *responsibility* are in the "hands" of the "authorities";
- in structures dominated by equal social relations, *responsibility* is "shared".

3.2 Autonomy vs Conservatism

Also referring to Schwartz, the *autonomy* vs. *conservatism* dimension refers to the relationship between the individual and the group – the extent to which people are autonomous or integrated in corresponding groups. In cultures and organizations that are dominated by CONSERVATISM, the *individual* is just considered as a PART OF THE GROUP to which (s)he belongs, not as a "distinct entity". Hence, (s)he identifies himself/herself with the group and shares the community's rules and laws. Dominant values in such societies are those focusing on the status quo and driven by the goal of "preventing" actions or inclinations that might disrupt the group solidarity and/or the traditional order. On the "opposite side" are the cultures in which the individual is regarded as AUTONOMOUS, though connected with a whole group that finds "meaning" in his or her own uniqueness, seeking to express his or her internal characteristics (goals, emotions, motives). Such societies are dominated by values that concern autonomy. They refer to ideas and thoughts (*intellectual autonomy*) or feelings and emotions (*affective autonomy*). Hence, as it concerns *authority*, it appears that:

- in structures dominated by *autonomy*, an individual would often be *responsible* for possible social deviations;
- in structures dominated by *conservatism*, usually the whole community or social group would be considered *responsible* for possible social deviations.

3.3 Harmony vs Mastery

Again referring to Schwartz, the *harmony* vs *mastery* dimension refers to the role of humans in natural and social environments – whether it is more important to adapt to the outside world and to accept it as it is, or constantly seek to change and operate it. Many cultures and organizations solve the relationship between a human being and his or her natural/social environments, by focusing on the *need for adaptation and acceptance of the world as it is, and preservation of the existing order in it*. This response is reflected in the values of HARMONY. The opposite alternative emphasizes on the *need to actively change the world, bringing it in line with the human will and continuous control over environmental parameters*. In such cultures, the world is perceived as an *object of exploitation*, depending on personal or group interests, where the values of MASTERY dominate. Hence, as it concerns *authority*, it appears that:

- when *harmony* with the environment prevails, interests and *responsibilities* are "in favor" of Society;
- when there are "pushes" for *operation* and *control* of the environment, private interests are in the fore-front.

4   Discussion

As mentioned in the introduction, the discussion conducted in the current section aims at partially justifying our claim that COMPOSITE VALUES ARE "EASY-TO-MEASURE". This claim is considered important, with regard to this paper's goal (to propose ways of IDENTIFYING/CAPTURING *authority* – see Sect. 1) mainly because we have convincingly "established" a "link" between *authority* and *composite values* (we made it clear that *authority* would NOT remain vague, with this often leading to "hidden" *responsibility*, if an analysis is put in the perspective of the three considered *bipolar dimensions* (see Fig. 1) corresponding to *composite values*), which brings us to the conclusion that if we can "capture" (measure) *composite values*, we would be effectively able to adequately identify *authority*. Nevertheless, for the sake of brevity, we would not go in much detail about HOW we are "measuring" *composite values*. Instead, we will mention and briefly discuss our previous work featuring concrete achievements in that direction.

In [10], we have presented the results of an online questionnaire survey (carried out in 2017) featuring CULTURAL VALUES and touching upon "items", such as *social power*, *success*, *freedom*, and so on. Addressed with a 9-point scale, each respondent was given the opportunity to assess the "importance" of each *value*. Further, what makes this exploration relevant to the work reported in the current paper is that the surveyed *values* were grouped in exactly the same *bipolar dimensions* as we consider in the paper (see Fig. 1). The empirical data was processed using *IBM SPSS Statistics* [17]. To test the hypotheses of the study, a series of paired-samples T-Tests were considered. We argue that this work has clearly demonstrated that it is possible to effectively "measure" *values* along the direction of the above-mentioned *bipolar dimensions*.

In [18], mean values featuring "measurements" over the above-mentioned *bipolar dimensions*, were generated in Bulgaria and superimposed with regard to corresponding data concerning other countries.

Finally, in [19] the notion of *egalitarianism* was considered both conceptually and empirically, bringing further "evidence" that it is possible to effectively and precisely "measure" *composite values*.

5 Conclusions

This paper builds on previous research of the authors, touching upon public values in general, and in particular – six composite public values, namely: hierarchy, egalitarianism, autonomy, conservatism, harmony, and mastery. We have not only studied their relationship with "atomic" values (such as privacy, transparency, accountability, and so on) but we have also considered the potential for effectively "measuring" composite values (for example: by means of surveys). Hence, we argue that it is possible to effectively "measure" composite values. This has opened the way for us to consider another challenge, namely the challenge of capturing HUMAN AUTHORITY, noting that often human authority remains HIDDEN/BLURRED "behind" organizational structures, regulations, and so on. In this paper, we have contributed to resolving this problem, by explicitly considering the relationship between the notion of "authority" and the above-mentioned six composite values. We have identified relationship "points" and we have discussed them in the current paper, this bringing us to the conclusion that IF we could "measure" composite values (especially the above-mentioned ones), we should be able to effectively "capture" authority, resolving in this way the above-mentioned ambiguity. Nevertheless, as a position paper, this work does not offer actual validation. As future work, we plan carrying out explorative case studies [20] for that purpose.

Acknowledgement. This work is supported by: (i) National Science Fund at the Bulgarian Ministry of Education and Science Project: DN 15/2/11.12.2017; (ii) NIP-2019-09 Project of the University of Library Studies and Information Technologies under the Ordinance of the Bulgarian Ministry of Education and Science.

References

1. Han, J., Kamber, M., Pei, J.: Data Mining: Concepts and Techniques, 3rd edn. Morgan Kaufmann Publ. Inc., San Francisco (2011)
2. Wu, J., Lv, F., Cao, Y., Zhao, Z.: Design and Implementation of Chess Roles Guess Probability in Military Chess Computer Game. In: Proceedings of 27th Chinese Control and Decision Conference - CCDC, Qingdao, China (2015)
3. Haykin, S.: Neural Networks. A Comprehensive Foundation. Prentice Hall, Upper Saddle River (1994)
4. Shishkov, B., van Sinderen, M.: From user context states to context-aware applications. In: Filipe, J., Cordeiro, J., Cardoso, J. (eds.) ICEIS 2007. LNBIP, vol. 12, pp. 225–239. Springer, Heidelberg (2008). https://doi.org/10.1007/978-3-540-88710-2_18
5. Maiese, M.: Embodiment, Emotion, and Cognition. Palgrave Macmillan, Basingstoke (2011)
6. BMSD: The International Symposium on Business Modeling and Software Design (2019). http://www.is-bmsd.org
7. Shishkov, B., Mendling, J.: Business Process Variability and Public Values. In: Shishkov, B. (ed.) BMSD 2018. LNBIP, vol. 319, pp. 401–411. Springer, Cham (2018). https://doi.org/10.1007/978-3-319-94214-8_31

8. Shishkov, B., Hristozov, S., Janssen, M., Van den Hoven, J.: Drones in land border missions: benefits and accountability concerns. In: Proceedings of the 6th International Conference on Telecommunications and Remote Sensing (ICTRS 2017). ACM, New York (2017)

9. Janssen, M.: Governance as a condition for creating business value from enterprise architecture. In: Shishkov, B. (ed.) BMSD 2019. LNBIP, vol. 356, pp. 229–235. Springer, Heidelberg (2019)

10. Garvanova, M., Shishkov, B., Janssen, M.: Composite public values and software specifications. In: Shishkov, B. (ed.) BMSD 2018. LNBIP, vol. 319, pp. 412–420. Springer, Cham (2018). https://doi.org/10.1007/978-3-319-94214-8_32

11. Shishkov, B., Larsen, J.B., Warnier, M., Janssen, M.: Three categories of context-aware systems. In: Shishkov, B. (ed.) BMSD 2018. LNBIP, vol. 319, pp. 185–202. Springer, Cham (2018). https://doi.org/10.1007/978-3-319-94214-8_12

12. Shishkov, B., Mitrakos, D.: Towards context-aware border security control. In: BMSD 2016, 6th International Symposium on Business Modeling and Software Design. SCITEPRESS (2016)

13. Friedman, B., Hendry, D.G., Borning A.: A survey of value sensitive design methods. In: A Survey of Value Sensitive Design Methods, Now Foundations and Trends, vol. 1, p. 76 (2017)

14. Branzei, R., Dimitrov, D., Tijs, S.: Egalitarianism-based Solution Concepts. In: Models in Cooperative Game Theory, pp. 37–42. Springer, Heidelberg (2008). https://doi.org/10.1007/978-3-540-77954-4_4

15. Veenhoven, R., Kalmijn, W.J.: Inequality-adjusted happiness in nations egalitarianism and utilitarianism married in a new index of societal performance. J. Happiness Stud. 6(4), 421–455 (2005)

16. Schwartz, S.H.: The refined theory of basic values. In: Roccas, S., Sagiv, L. (eds.) Values and Behavior, pp. 51–72. Springer, Cham (2017). https://doi.org/10.1007/978-3-319-56352-7_3

17. Pradhananga, Y., Karande, S., Karande, C.: CBA: cloud-based bigdata analytics. In: Proceedings: International Conference on Computing Communication Control and Automation, Pune, 2015, pp. 47–51 (2015)

18. Garvanova, M., Nikolova, B.: Bulgaria on the global cultural value map. In: National Conference "Хармония в различията". University of Library Studies and Information Technologies, Sofia, Bulgaria (2017). (in Bulgarian)

19. Moss, J.: Reassessing Egalitarianism. Palgrave Macmillan, UK (2014)

20. Yin, R.: Case Study Research: Design and Methods. Sage Publications (1994)

On the Modeling of Innovative Navigation Systems

Ivan Garvanov[1(✉)], Hristo Kabakchiev[2], Vera Behar[3],
Magdalena Garvanova[1], and Ruska Iyinbor[4]

[1] University of Library Studies and Information Technologies, Sofia, Bulgaria
{i.garvanov, m.garvanova}@unibit.bg
[2] Sofia University, Sofia, Bulgaria
ckabakchiev@yahoo.com
[3] Institute of Information and Communication Technologies, Sofia, Bulgaria
vera.behar@yahoo.com
[4] Hallmark University, San Antonio, TX, USA
ruskadi@yahoo.com

Abstract. The paper studies an extremely important and promising scientific issue, namely the question of determining the coordinates of moving objects and their navigation in space. For this purpose, we propose a conceptual model of a multi-sensor navigation system, based on a navigation system using pulsar signals. An approximate model of pulsar navigation system is presented as well.

Keywords: Conceptual model · Pulsar navigation system · Pulsar signal

1 Introduction

A current challenge is establishing the coordinates of moving and motionless objects as well as their navigation in space. In the past, people have mainly counted on compasses and measuring devices capturing the angle with regard to a star (for example: the Sun or the Polar Star), and also on maps (terrestrial and nautical). Nevertheless, in recent years, following technical and technological advances, people mainly count on satellite navigation systems, such as GPS, GLONSS, Galileo, BeiDou, and so on. These systems not only allow for precision (in establishing the coordinates of an object) but they provide navigation signal around the Globe. Those developments and their further maturation have led to a wider applicability of navigation technologies, going beyond the facilitation of ships and planes, to reach very many people through the GSM phones and car navigation systems. Moreover, it is already not only the GPS satellites transmitting signals - we should take into account also the signals coming from the GSM base stations, WiFi and other multi-sensor radio systems. Also, there are blending data technologies, spanning over GPS, GSM, WiFi, and other radio sources as well as digital (spatial) maps, spanning over, and shadows - this all contributing to a better precision in determining the coordinates of an object [1].

We hence observe increasing interest towards improvements that relate to the current navigation systems, especially as it concerns precision, and this is also a basis for developing new autonomous navigation systems - this is especially relevant for

B. Shishkov (Ed.): BMSD 2019, LNBIP 356, pp. 299–306, 2019.
https://doi.org/10.1007/978-3-030-24854-3_23

latest technological developments, such as drone technologies and man-less vehicle technologies; they are all about complex context-aware systems where what the system does depend on the surrounding context, and establishing the context is often a matter of positioning [2–4].

The contribution of the current paper is two-fold:

* Firstly, we propose a conceptual model (featuring navigation) that captures new characteristics of several currently popular navigation systems, such of GPS and GSM.

* Secondly, we study the appropriateness of the proposed model with regard to an innovative navigate system, namely a system based on pulsar signals; we hence also propose an autonomous model of radio-pulsar navigation system.

The remaining of the current paper is organized as follows: In Sect. 2, we propose the conceptual navigation model. In Sect. 3, we discuss characteristics of pulsar signals. In Sect. 4, we study a model of radio-pulsar autonomous navigation system. Finally, in Sect. 5, we present the conclusions.

2 Conceptual Model of Navigation System

The triangulation method is used to determine the coordinates in multi-sensor systems such as GPS, GSM, radars, etc., where the coordinates of the sensors need to be known and the distance between the sensors and the object on which coordinates are sought. A conceptual model of a navigation system using electromagnetic waves is shown in Fig. 1. Electromagnetic waves fall into the radio front-end and after filtration, amplification and analog to digital converter are fed into the digital signal processing unit. Signal processing is specific to each radio system, but after sensing and detecting signals from different sensors, signal parameters are estimated. The primary parameter involved in coordinate determination is the time of arrival of the signal from the sensor to the object. The accuracy of measurement of this parameter is essential for the accuracy of the calculation of the coordinates [5, 6].

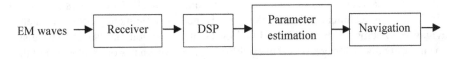

Fig. 1. Conceptual model of navigation system

Knowing the rate of propagation of radio signals in space that is equal to the speed of light, it is possible to calculate the distances from the radio transmitters to the radio receiver. The navigation algorithm consists in solving the triangulation task, resulting in the co-ordinates of the object.

The proposed conceptual model for a navigation system is at the heart of the GPS positioning system. Similarly, the multi-sensor radar systems used to determine the coordinates of flying objects, but use refreshed radar signals from the object and the information from the multi-sensor system is processed in a single management center.

The conceptual model under consideration can be applied to the creation of new navigation systems using natural space signals, such as pulsars.

The idea of using pulsars, rapidly rotating neutron stars, for orientation in space is not new [7–9]. The idea of space navigation is based on the principle used by GPS. Measuring the time of arrival of pulses coming from at least three different pulsars and comparing them with calculated values can be determined spatial coordinates of the receiver. To travel in space, the spacecraft must have the board ("autonomous") navigation system. In the paper, we propose an autonomous model of radio-pulsar navigation system.

3   Pulsar Properties

Pulsars are rotating neutron stars that emit broadband electromagnetic signals Fig. 2 [6]. The period of repetition of pulse signals is the same as the pulsar rotation period. The periodic repetition of the pulse signals is stable over time and is comparable to the accuracy of atomic clocks. The signals from the pulsars differ from each other by the type of their profiles.

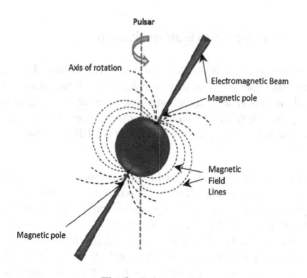

Fig. 2. Pulsar model

The main constraints towards signal detection in the pulsar-based navigation system are the following:

- Very poor SNR of pulsar signals at the receiver input (from −40 dB to −90 dB). The signals from pulsars are very weak because pulsars are located many light years away from Earth. Besides, the signals received from pulsars are corrupted by the addition of noise and distorted due to the propagation channel.

- Pulsar data are often corrupted by the presence of impulsive interference, broadband interference and sometimes periodic terrestrial radiation [10]. Such as radio frequency interference (RFI) originates in unshielded electrical equipment which produces discharges, such as automobile ignition systems, electric motors, and fluorescent lighting, as well as discharge from high-voltage power transmission lines. It may also arise naturally from the radio emission generated in lightning discharges. Such RFI can often be very strong and can even enter receiver systems through the far-out sidelobes of the telescope reception pattern.
- The time-consuming signal processing of pulsar signals. As shown in [7] and [11], in order to detect and extract the pulsar pulse profile about 1–2 h are needed for pulsar observation.

The unknown receiver velocity with respect to the pulsar. As shown in [12] and [13], complications due to Doppler shift arise in the case of an unknown velocity of the receiver when estimating coordinates. This leads to the resulting observed information of the pulsar signal to be an unknown different from that which is observed with respect to a known inertial frame of reference. Thereby, the Doppler shift demands techniques that compensate for the effect. To detect the unknown velocity, one requires a lot of computation power in hardware, as is analysed in [13].

4 Autonomous Pulsar Navigation System

A pulsar navigation system, the structure of which is shown in Fig. 3, consists of a radio-frequency front-end (Antenna, amplifier, band-pass filter, quadrature detector and analog to digital converter), an acquisition block to process the signal from RF front-end and extract pulsar signals and a navigation block to perform navigation algorithms and provide feedback to the acquisition block and the RF front-end.

RF front end
According to [11–13], the signals received by the antenna are amplified using an LNA whose frequency response is centred at the pulsar carrier frequency f_0. The amplified signal is bandpass filtered to remove the harmonics and interferences from the received signal. Then the filtered signal is down converted to the baseband (BW) by a mixer, which operates using a local oscillator at frequency $f_{LO} = f_0$. The output of the mixer is a signal with frequency components $(f_0 + f_{LO})$ and $(f_0 - f_{LO})$, from which the signal with the difference frequency component $f_0 - f_{LO} = 0$ is considered for further processing [14]. After down conversion the signal is sampled and quantized using an analog to digital converter. The sampling process should be performed satisfying retirements of the Nyquist sampling criterion.

The digital beamformer increases the gain in the direction of arrival of the desired signal, and decreases the gain in all other undesired directions (interference).

DSP Front end
Following these would be signal processing steps such as polyphase filtering (to split the input broadband signal into frequency sub-bands) and "de-dispersion".

Dispersion has the effect of delaying a pulse from a pulsar as a function of frequency. Counteracting dispersion (using so-called de-dispersion techniques) is a key task in pulsar observations [5]. The instrumentation used to perform pulsar observations should be designed to assist with this, and much of the data analysis work following an observation involves de-dispersion.

De-dispersion is a procedure to correct for the effects due to the interstellar channel. The method involves correction for the channel effects using either of the techniques: Incoherent or Coherent de-dispersion. Once the pulsar signal has been de-dispersed, we would have as proposed in [15], the "Folding algorithm" [16] implementation. The significance of folding is to generate a pulsar profile which can be compared to known pulsar profiles by the process of correlation. In the process of folding, a real time de-dispersed pulsar signal acts as an input to the folding subsystem. The input would comprise of a discrete time series of data.

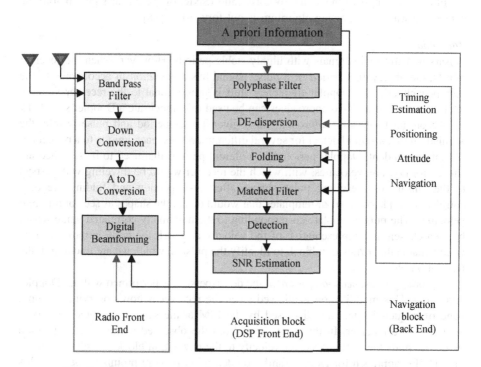

Fig. 3. Block-scheme of the signal processing in pulsar navigation system

As the period is very stable [17], the phase of the pulsar signal would be the same in subsequent periods. The inherent principle of folding is that the received signal corresponding to a single period of the radio wave is added to the already accumulated signal periods (in an accumulator). In this process, it is imperative to realize that we are in time adding the pulsar signal values to the previously received pulsar signals. Thereby, one keeps on adding pulsar signals and attains a signal that has a larger amplitude. Therefore, we obtain a better SNR.

One way to increase SNR of the pulsar signal is proposed in [16]. The authors propose to use the matched filter at the output of the folding procedure in order to improve the SNR of a pulsar signal before automotive detection. In [16] is investigated the improvement in SNR at the output of the matched filter as a function of two parameters: the number of integrated periods (K) and the sampling frequency (f_S) of a pulsar signal.

A new algorithm based on time–frequency distribution and Shannon entropy in S transform domain is proposed for accurate and fast detecting pulsar signals in [17]. The bounds on the expected value of Shannon entropy of white Gaussian noise are derived. Based on these constant signatures, the optimum threshold detection algorithm based on the ROC curve is employed to detect pulsar signals. Finally, the experimental results show that the proposed method has a high detection rate, fast processing speed and low requirements for temporal resolution.

In order to improve the signal-to-noise ratio (SNR) of the pulsar signal before the detector, a wavelet denoising algorithm is put forward in [18].

Back end
Pulsars transmit radio signals with highly stable periods. However, when the receiver moves, the observation period of a pulsar signal has a deviation in accordance to the 'Doppler effect'. The Doppler frequency shift is proportional to the receiver velocity relative to the pulsar. Two approaches can be used to compensate a Doppler shift [11].

According to the *first approach*, for a given pulsar period and pulse profile, the acquisition block should detect for several different profiles, each unique to a particular, velocity dependent, Doppler period. The different periods that need to be searched are chosen for possible velocities, with which the receiver would be traveling with respect to the pulsar. The resulting pulse shapes after de-dispersion and folding are then correlated with known pulsar templates that would depict the shapes as seen at different velocities. The pulsar template corresponding to the maximally correlated value would be then chosen as a representative of the velocity at which the body is moving. This would enable the acquisition block to identify the pulsars, which we are tracking in the navigation block.

According to the *second approach*, the de-dispersion is performed without Doppler correction. This modification is allowed since the receiver is now observing an input band of frequencies that are dispersed by the ISM at the same frequencies observed relative to the receiver. In this case, apart from the observed period, the acquisition block transmits the current receiver velocity to the navigation block as well. As shown in [11], this approach for Doppler shift compensation is more promising because this will enable a simple navigation block that makes use of velocity integrated to estimate the coordinates of the body.

The pulsar navigation can give the continuous position in deep space, that means we can freedom fly successfully in the solar system use celestial navigation that include pulsar and traditional star sensor. It also can less or abolish the dependence of Global Navigation Satellite System (GNSS) which include GPS, GLONSS, Galileo and BeiDou et al.

5 Conclusion

The construction of navigational space systems operating independently over long distances from the Earth is an extremely challenging scientific task. Determining the coordinates of spaceships in space will be essential for conquering space in the future. This article proposed possibility model of the autonomous pulsar navigation system. Given the vast distances from the Earth, the pulsars provide a good coverage of the continuously transmitted pulsar signals in future missions to the Moon and Mars. Now, there are many difficulties in using pulsar signals, but with the development of technology, this idea will become a reality. The potential of pulsars to create positioning systems is enormous and will increase vehicle autonomy.

Acknowledgement. This work is supported by Project DN 07/1/14.12.2016, title: "Investigation of parameters, properties and phenomena of radio signals from pulsars and their interaction with objects".

References

1. Garvanov, I., Kabakchiev, C., Shishkov, B., Garvanova, M.: Towards context-aware vehicle navigation in urban environments: modeling challenges. In: Shishkov, B. (ed.) BMSD 2018. LNBIP, vol. 319, pp. 382–389. Springer, Cham (2018). https://doi.org/10.1007/978-3-319-94214-8_29
2. Shishkov, B., Hristozov, S., Janssen, M., Van den Hoven, J.: Drones in land border missions: benefits and accountability concerns. In: Proceedings of the 6th International Conference on Telecommunications and Remote Sensing (ICTRS 2017). ACM, New York, NY, USA (2017)
3. Shishkov, B., Larsen, J.B., Warnier, M., Janssen, M.: Three categories of context-aware systems. In: Shishkov, B. (ed.) BMSD 2018. LNBIP, vol. 319, pp. 185–202. Springer, Cham (2018). https://doi.org/10.1007/978-3-319-94214-8_12
4. Shishkov, B., Janssen, M.: Enforcing context-awareness and privacy-by-design in the specification of information systems. In: Shishkov, B. (ed.) BMSD 2017. LNBIP, vol. 309, pp. 87–111. Springer, Cham (2018). https://doi.org/10.1007/978-3-319-78428-1_5
5. Bernhardt, M., Beckery, W., Prinz, T., Breithuth, F.M., Walter, U.: Autonomous spacecraft navigation based on pulsar timing information. In: IEEE Proceedings of the 2nd International Conference on Space Technology, Athens, Greece (2011)
6. Dong, J.: Pulsar navigation in the solar system. J. Latex Class Files, 1–8 (2008). arXiv:0812.2635
7. Buist, P., Engelen, S., Noroozi, A., Sundaramoorthy, P., Verhagen, S., Verhoeven, C.: Principles and potential of pulsar navigation. In: 24 International ION Conference, Portland, USA (2011)
8. Buist, P., Engelen, S., Noroozi, A., Sundaramoorthy, P., Verhagen, S., Verhoeven, C.: Overview of pulsar navigation: past, present and future trends. J. Inst. Navig. **58**(2), 153–164 (2011)
9. Sala, J., et al.: Feasibility study for a spacecraft navigation system relying on pulsar timing information. Technical report 03/4202, ARIADNA Study (2004)
10. Chaudhri, V.: Fundamentals, specifications, architecture and hardware towards navigation system based on radio pulsars. M.Sc. thesis, TU Delft (2011)

11. van Straten, W., Bailes, M.: DSPSR: digital signal processing software for pulsar astronomy. Publ. Astron. Soc. Aust. **28**, 1–14 (2011)
12. Engelen, S.: Deep space navigation system using radio pulsars: front-end. M.Sc. thesis, TU Delft (2009)
13. Hankins, H., Rickett, B.: Pulsar signal processing. In: Alder, B., Fernbach, S., Rotenberg, M. (eds.) Methods in Computational Physics. Radio astronomy, vol. 14, pp. 55–129. Academic Press, New York (1975)
14. Garvanov, I., Kabakchiev, C., Behar, V., Garvanova, M.: The experimental study of possibility for pulsar signal detection. In: International Conference "Engineering & Telecommunications – En&T 2016", Moscow-Dolgoprudny, Russia, pp. 68–71 (2016)
15. Kabakchiev, C., Behar, V., Garvanov, I., Kabakchieva, D., Garvanova, M., Rohling, H.: Air target detection in pulsar FSR system. In: International Conference "Engineering & Telecommunications – En&T 2018", Moscow-Dolgoprudny, Russia (2018)
16. Karunanithi, V.: A framework for designing and testing the digital signal processing unit of a pulsar based navigation system. M.Sc. thesis, TU Delft (2012)
17. Heusdens, R., et al.: Match filtering approach for signal acquisition in radio-pulsar navigation. In: Proceedings of the 63rd International Astronautical Congress, Naples, Italy (2012)
18. Garvanov, I., Iyinbor, R., Garvanova, M., Geshev, N.: Denoising of pulsar signal using wavelet transform. In: XVI-th International Conference on Electrical Machines, Drives and Power Systems, Varna, Bulgaria, 6–8 June 2019

Author Index

Printed in the United States
By Bookmasters